Al

M000314736

*To understand where we are in n.
Winter's thought processes—brilliant, maddening, barreling down rabbit trails,
crashing through to magnificent discoveries. He had a call, he believed, to "the
studied application of modest ingenuity to the Christian cause in general," or, in
other words, "the inventor's role." Yet it takes a community to make a missiology,
and we see this throughout the book in the comments and critiques of his peers. I
found myself, chuckling, smiling, and shaking my head as I read. It's almost like
having Ralph back again.*

Miriam Adeney, PhD
Associate Professor of World Christian Studies, Seattle Pacific University
Teaching Fellow, Regent College
Author, *Kingdom without Borders: The Untold Story of Global Christianity*

*Inquisitive, eclectically oriented minds, relentless commitment, indefatigable
energy, far-reaching vision, and absolute spiritual commitment have been the
stuff that has combined so often to produce great Kingdom breakthroughs. Greg
Parsons' Ralph D. Winter: Early Life and Core Missiology gives us a rare inside
look at the making of the man who represented that truly rare combination of
gifts. The book lets us look with fresh perspective on Ralph Winter's life journey
up through his watershed contribution at the 1974 Lausanne Congress on World
Evangelization. If you want to know how the stage was set for the rapid change
from a previously Western dominated to the truly global church of today this book
will provide both fascinating detail and provocative insights.*

Phill Butler
visionSynergy

*I have been reading your thesis for the last 40 minutes or so, and could read it all
night. It is a fascinating history, and so well researched, documented and
written. Thank you for your vision and perseverance in this study. It inspires
me to press on in my research on the Lausanne Movement.*

S. Douglas Birdsall, PhD
Former Executive Chair—Lausanne Committee for World Evangelization

*"...Having known him for 40+ years and having recently read Parsons'
dissertation I thought I knew my friend quite well. But here I found the
pilgrimage of the inner Ralph and found I hardly knew him! ...Now that I have
read it, I'll put it in the CIU library for others to be amazed."*

Robertson McQuilkin
Columbia International University

I appreciated your work immensely. I learned much that I did not know and was confirmed in much that I did know....You have done our friend and mentor a great service and our Lord as well.
I thank you and salute you.

David J. Hesselgrave
Professor of Missions Emeritus
Trinity Evangelical Divinity School

I enjoyed reading your thesis and learning about Dr. Winter's background, especially his life struggles, criticisms, successes, and breakthroughs. The way you tied Dr. Winter's early family and faith life, missionary experiences, theological education by extension initiatives, and teaching experiences to his landmark 1974 paper and presentation at Lausanne, helped me to see new connections between his ideas and background. You certainly were able to do it with a good balance of a perspective from someone close to Dr. Winter, while maintaining objectivity needed in a thesis.

Walker Tzeng
COO - Olivet University

For those who have been curious about how a world-class innovator's mind works, Parsons details the development of each of Winter's three ground-breaking contributions to missiology.
He clearly demonstrates that Winter's genius lay not only at his ability to produce paradigm-shifting insights, but in how he focused on the promotion of those insights and did the grinding work of building global coalitions that would spread, and ultimately implement, each of them.
Parsons also shows how Winter's fertile mind has been responsible for contributions and innovations across a wide range of subjects from mission agency bookkeeping and accounting to publishing. Countless thousand of readers of mission literature have benefited from his founding of the William Carey Library publishing house...

David Dougherty
Mission Mobilization & Leader Development
OMF International

Ralph D. Winter:

Early Life And Core Missiology

Note About the Format

The next page begins the complete dissertation approved by the University of Wales: Trinity Saint David on May 22, 2012, with edits for spelling and clarity. It has been reformatted from the University's standard thesis requirements to normal book size. Thus, page numbers will differ from the original bound thesis. Many changes are related to formatting, intended to assist in readability—such as single spacing and making the author names bold in the Bibliography. Almost all changes are typographical, but in two places I found where I made an error. One was a minor point, the other (top of page 277) stated the reverse of Winter's opinion so I added "not" to the first full sentence on that page and clarified what he was concerned about at the end of that sentence.

Because this is a PhD dissertation, you may wish to skim part of Chapter 1, The Research Design. It includes the overall approach and goals of the study. Either way, do not let the more technical approach of that chapter keep you from the rest of the book!

I have attempted to make the writing interesting while doing the necessary documentation for doctoral work. You will likely find that most of the longer footnotes are as helpful and interesting as the main body of the text. The Appendices also include some very interesting details.

You can find out more about Ralph D. Winter—with additional material being posted—at: www.ralphdwinter.org. Feel free to email me questions, share your story of interaction with Dr. Winter, or interact over the content you are about to read.

Greg H. Parsons, PhD
greg.parsons@frontierventures.org

Cover Design: Amanda Valloza
Cover Photos: Obtained from the Ralph D. Winter Research and Innovation Center, Pasadena, CA. Used with Permission. Most photos, audio interviews and other documents used for this thesis are or will be obtainable online at: www.ralphdwinter.org

William Carey International University Press
1539 E. Howard St. Pasadena, California 91104
Email: wciupress@wciu.edu
© Copyright 2012 by Greg Howard Parsons

Greg Howard Parsons, Author
Ralph D. Winter: Early Life and Core Missiology
ISBN: 9780 86585 0750
Library of Congress Identification Number: 2012944230

Ralph D. Winter:

Early Life And Core Missiology

By

Greg H. Parsons, BA, ThM

A thesis submitted to
the Religious Studies Department
University of Wales: Trinity Saint David
in partial fulfillment of the requirements for
the degree of
Doctor of Philosophy
DP Davies Director of Supervision

This research was undertaken under the auspices of the
University of Wales: Trinity Saint David and was submitted in
partial fulfillment for the award of a Degree of the
University of Wales

May 2012

Abstract

Parsons, Greg H. 2011. "Ralph D. Winter: Early Life and Core Missiology" University of Wales Trinity Saint David, Religious Studies Department. PhD.

Ralph D. Winter (1924–2009) is a well-known figure in evangelical missions strategy and mobilization. His core missiological contributions up to 1976 were: Theological Education by Extension (TEE), Sodalities and Modalities, and his Lausanne 1974 presentation on the priority of cross-cultural evangelism.

Raised in the US by intelligent, industrious and committed Christian parents and mentored by respected leaders and education experiences, Winter became a man who purposed to impact the world positively through a counter-cultural approach to identifying problems needing to be solved.

Beginning in 1958, he spent ten years in the remote mountains of Guatemala with the Mam Native Americans. He interacted with missionaries from various organizations and church backgrounds. He and co-worker James Emery sought to serve and empower rural elders/lay-pastors (functional leaders) by bringing training to them rather than traditional residential training away from their ministry. This began TEE in the region. They and others developed and promoted TEE around the world where it expanded to more than 40 countries and 200 organizations by 1973.

The TEE movement propelled Winter into broader ministry. From 1967–1976 he taught TEE and the global expansion of Christianity at a new school at Fuller Theological Seminary called the School of World Mission. With non-denominational mission agencies growing in record numbers after World War Two, he argued for a clear distinction between the nurturing role of churches (modalities), the pioneering role of sodalities (mission structures) and their value to missionary work.

At Fuller, he observed that half of the world's population was without effective gospel witness. That need, and a call for special cross-cultural evangelism depicted in the E-Scale, became the core of his presentation at The Congress on World Evangelism at Lausanne Switzerland in 1974. That presentation became a turning point for him, his family and the evangelical mission movement.

Abstract Word Count: 300
Final thesis word count Chapters 1-8, exclusive of footnotes: 104,734

Declaration/Copyright Statement

This work has not been accepted in substance for any degree and is not being concurrently submitted in candidature for any degree.

Signed _____ (Candidate)

Date   28 June 2012

STATEMENT 1

This thesis is the result of my own investigation, except where otherwise stated. Where correction services have been used, the extent and nature of the correction is clearly marked in footnote(s). Other sources are acknowledged in the body of the thesis or by footnotes, both with explicit references. A bibliography is appended.

Signed _____ (Candidate)

Date   28 June 2012

STATEMENT 2

I hereby give consent for my thesis, if accepted, to be available for photocopying and for inter-library loan, and for the title and abstract to be made available to outside organizations.

Signed _____ (Candidate)

Date   28 June 2012

Dedication

My wife, Kathleen, continues to amaze me with her love of God and of me. She has been with me throughout this study, agreeing from the start that it needed to be done and that I should do it. That meant she carried a heavier load over the years of the study. She kept me going, in part, by helping me to get study time and, especially toward the end, pressuring me to finish this task. Thank you!

My parents, Charles and Alice Parsons gave me an amazing foundation for life and faith. Dad modeled flexibility and a different way of seeing and enjoying life that contributed to my own creativity and a desire to serve. Mom came to Christ later in life, just before I was born, and has been a spiritual guide through a foundation of prayer ever since. At 87, as I write, she continues to pray for me and probably prayed more for the production of this document than anyone else.

Acknowledgements

A special thanks to a few of those who helped on this project:

As you would expect, my supervisors/mentors with the University of Wales have been valuable to this process. DP Davies' wise guidance and experience were both crucial and an encouragement. Michael Elliot's comments and reflections during the first few years, both on ideas I included and those I missed, were a great help in guiding this process.

Betsy Glanville, PhD, former Director of Doctoral Programs and currently Assistant Professor of Leadership, School of Intercultural Studies, Fuller Theological Seminary, for her helpful advice at the beginning of the process.

Early in the process, Melissa (Bartlotti) Fowler attended to many and varied tasks with amazing speed and "got it" very quickly just as I was getting started in this research.

Kathy Jebbia typed many of Winter's early type-written writings into digital format.

My son, Andrew, helped transcribe interviews and enjoyed getting to know more about Ralph Winter (and others) in the process.

Molly Wall gave wise questions and insights into the design process.

Suzanne Bailey gave her clear, wise council helping to make sure that what I meant is what I said, or, what I said was what I meant.

David C Bundy, Associate Provost for Library Services and Associate Professor of History, School of Intercultural Studies, Fuller Theological Seminary, for allowing me visiting scholar status and for his wise counsel. Others also assisted at Fuller including Nancy Gower, who directs Fuller's Archives, and many others whose names are unknown to me.

Bob Shuster, Billy Graham Center Archives at Wheaton College, went beyond the call of duty to assist me in any way possible.

The staff at the Presbyterian Historical Society, National Archive of the PC (USA) in Philadelphia, Pennsylvania also provided exceptional assistance.

Pete Meyer demonstrated that it always helps to have a Google Senior Ads Quality Statistician who has done his own dissertation to look over your work and tell you if it is clear.

Rob Stone for following various rabbit trails, scanning, copying, checking, and otherwise offering to help.

Brian Lowther, who would jump at the chance to help with graphics/scanning issues related to this project. He now directs the Roberta Winter Institute, which Ralph Winter founded before his death.

Many others, whom I am forgetting.

Thank you all.

Contents

Abstract ii

Declaration/Copyright Statement iii

Dedication iv

Acknowledgements v

Contents vi

List Of Figures xii

List Of Abbreviations xiv
    Explanatory Notes xvi

Chapter 1 The Research Design 1
    Background...1
    Purpose of the Study..2
        Central Research Issue 3
        Assumptions and Limitations 3
    Precedent Research and Literature Review 6
        General Biographical Writings 6
        General Writings 9
        Theological Education by Extension.................................9
        Modality and Sodality 11
        Unreached People Groups..12
        Winter's Interaction with Others 15
    Methodology of the Study...16
        Approach to the Historical Biography Dimensions 17
        Sources and Approach to the Material............................18
            Introduction..18
            Cultural Setting: History, Theology and Missiology............... 18
            Winter's Writings..19
            Interviews 21
            The Writing of Others About Winter or His Ideas 22
            Archives 23
            Analysis 24
        Validity, Reliability and Verification 24
    Summary..26

Chapter 2 Upbringing and Historical Setting 27
Introduction...27
   The Protestant Religious Setting of Early 20th Century America 27
   Historically Shaping Concepts: Evangelism versus Social Action 31
   The Social Setting in the Mid-1900s in the Western U.S. 32
Winter's Family Background 33
   Father: Hugo Winter 33
   Mother: Hazel Patterson Winter 34
   The Boys 35
      Paul..35
      Ralph 36
      David 38
Additional Major Influences Before College 40
   Early Church Experience 40
   Christian Endeavor 40
   Lake Avenue Congregational Church.....................................42
   The Navigators..43
   Ali Asghar 46
   Summary 47
Education: Formal, Non-Formal and Informal............................48
   Formal Education Begins...48
      Caltech – Fall 1942–1944...48
   World War Two...49
      U.S. Navy – January 1945–August 1945..............................49
   Formal and Non-Formal Education Continued 50
      Westmont College – Fall 1945–Spring 1946..........................50
      Princeton Theological Seminary – Fall 1946–Spring 1947.........53
      Fuller Theological Seminary – Fall 1947–Spring 1948..............57
      Summer Institute of Linguistics – Summer 1948.....................58
      Fuller Theological Seminary – Fall 1948–Spring 1949..............59
      Linguistic Society of America at the University of Michigan –
      Summer 1949..60
      Prairie Bible Institute – Fall 1949.......................................60
      Columbia University-Teachers College – Fall 1950–Spring
      1951 62
      An Eventful Summer at home – 1951 62
      Cornell University – Fall 1951–Summer 1953 66
      Back to Princeton – Fall 1953–Spring 1956..........................70
   Additional Influences: Books 71
Analysis...72
   Heredity and Family Influence..73
   Environment 74
      Socialization...76

Education – Informal and Formal 77
Marriage 79

Chapter 3 To the field: Guatemala – 1956–1966 80
Introduction.. 80
Pre-Field Orientation and Training – 1956–57 81
Language School: Costa Rica – 1957 82
Guatemala in the 1950s... 85
Presbyterian Mission Work in Guatemala to the Mid-1900s 88
    National Church Leadership.. 89
    Native Population Mission Work 90
Arrival on the Field – 1958.. 94
    Focus of Ministry 95
    Language Learning: Different Approaches.. 96
    A Different Approach to Everything?... 99
    Mam Christian Center... 102
    Field Relational Issues... 103
    Serving Pastors 105
        Portable Businesses... 105
        Pastors as Shamans 108
    Other Responsibilities.. 111
    Economic Issues and the Outside World.. 112
    Mobilizing for the Task 114
    Educational Work.. 116
    Pastoral Training.. 117
    Extending Education 118
Summary and Analysis 118

Chapter 4 Extending Theological Education 128
Introduction.. 128
The Beginnings of Theological Education by Extension 128
    The Guatemala Program.. 130
    The Program Expands 133
    Ross Kinsler joins Winter and Emery.. 135
Preparation for Growth 137
A TEE Movement?... 141
TEE Defined and Refined 143
TEE Expands 145
    Early Factors Debated Within TEE 150
    Improving TEE Effectiveness.. 151
Evaluating TEE 162
Multiplying Connections.. 171
Transitions.. 172

Analysis...175
Assessment and Contribution.....................................180

Chapter 5 Training Field-Experienced Missionaries: Fuller Theological Seminary — 1967–1976....................... **184**
Introduction..184
Birth of an Idea: A School of Evangelism 186
   Donald A McGavran...187
   Training Others in Church Growth..........................191
   Institute of Church Growth 192
   Moving ICG to Fuller Theological Seminary 193
The School of World Mission and Institute for Church Growth 195
   Church Growth Basics 197
   Homogeneous Unit Principle.................................199
   The Church Growth Concept and Select Perspectives 201
   McGavran's Influence on Missiological Awareness.......................208
   Winter's Arrival to Teach–1967 209
   Winter's Focus at the SWM from 1967–1976 212
      The Growing TEE Movement............................212
   Defending Church Growth Issues............................213
   Select Students' Reaction to Winter's Teaching...........216
   Select Additional Initiatives During the Fuller Years...............216
      Presbyterian Structures 216
      William Carey Library......................................218
      American Society of Missiology and Missiology: An International Review......................................220
      A Follow up Course for the Urbana Student Convention 224
   Select Additional Writings During the Fuller Years 225
Applying The Missiology: Leaving Fuller 226
Analysis...228

Chapter 6 Sodalities and Modalities **231**
Introduction..231
Vertical and Horizontal Structures: The Anatomy of the Christian Mission - 1969...234
Warp and Woof - 1970 236
Churches Instead of Missions? - 1971..........................241
The Planting of Younger Missions - 1972 245
The Two Structures of God's Redemptive Mission - 1973 247
Ghana: Preparation for Marriage Experience - 1978................251
Protestant Mission Societies: The American Experience - 1979255

Select Issues in the Sodalities and Modalities Debate 263
   Biblical Debate 263
   Definition of Church and Mission.................................... 265
      Issues in Modalities and Sodalities 267
Summary and Analysis 274
Assessment and Contribution.. 278
A Growing Concern 282

**Chapter 7 Lausanne 1974 Congress and Cross-Cultural
Evangelism** 283
   Background in Winter's Writing.. 283
      Key 73 285
   The Broader Evangelical Scene in the 1960s.................... 286
      Winter's Focus in 1973 288
         Seeing the Task Graphically.. 289
   Pre-Lausanne Congress Preparations 290
   Major Presentations During the Lausanne Congress 291
      Winter's Pre-Congress paper "The Highest Priority: Cross-
      Cultural Evangelism" 293
         General Questions/Responses from Delegates prior to the
         Congress 296
         Responses to Winter's Pre-Congress Paper............................. 300
      Winter's Paper as Delivered at the Congress 305
         Response to the Responders 305
         Questions About the Statistical Scope of the Task.................... 307
         Questions About the Theological Nature of the Task.............. 316
      Reactions to Winter's Congress Presentation 322
   Some Reactions and Outcomes from Lausanne '74.................... 325
   Summary and Analysis 329
   Assessment and Contribution.. 335
      Next Step: A Mission Sodality for Frontier Mission—1976.......... 338

Chapter 8 Findings and Conclusion 343
   Findings.. 343
   Conclusion.. 349

Appendices.. 351
   Appendix A Sample Lesson Example of Winter's Ideas for
   Learning Languages 352
   Appendix B Sample Lesson Patterns................................. 353
   Appendix C Field Relational Issue Details........................ 355
   Appendix D Winter's Work Responsibilities and Side Projects362

Appendix E 2006 Guatemala Update...................................367
Appendix F Select Pre-TEE on Mission Fields in the 1900s...368
Appendix G Extension Newsletter Example...........................373
Appendix H Mission Agencies and Denominations
Sponsoring or Involved in TEE from *The World Directory of
Theological Education by Extension* by Wayne C. Weld, 1973....374
Appendix I "What Happened to TEE?" By Ted W. Ward....377
Appendix J HUP Consultation, Pasadena, California 1977.....382
Appendix K Select Early Faculty for the School of World
Mission, Fuller Theological Seminary Fall 1965-1968.............383
Appendix L Select Course Descriptions Taught by Ralph D.
Winter at Fuller Theological Seminary School of World
Mission 1966-1976..384
Appendix M Student Experiences with Ralph D. Winter as a
Teacher...386
Appendix N William Carey Library Publishers Book Titles in
Chronological Order – 1969-1976.................................391
Appendix O E-Scale...394
Appendix P *Christianity Today* and Key 73 396
Appendix Q Lausanne 1974 Select Plenary Summaries...........398
Appendix R The Decade Past and the Decade to Come:
Seeing the Task Graphically.....................................399
Appendix S McGavran's Paper....................................409
Appendix T Lausanne Covenant Section Five 412
Appendix U Winter's List of 24 Problems to be Solved..........413

Correspondence and Reports......................................415
    Field, Annual and Other Reports.............................415
    Letters...416
    Emails..419
    Interviews..420

Bibliography 423

List Of Figures

Figure 1 – Guatemala in the 1950s as Armas Returned to Overthrow Arbenz (TIME Magazine, June 28, 1954, 38) 86

Figure 2 – Cultural Gradations in Guatemala Communities 93

Figure 3 – TEE "Events" as listed in Theological Education by Extension, (1969d, 6) 142

Figure 4 – Education Extremes Illustration by Winter 1967 152

Figure 5 – Ted Ward's Split Rail Fence Analogy 155

Figure 6 – Programmed Instruction Example from Principles of Church Growth by Weld and McGavran, 5-14 158

Figure 7 – Programmed Instruction Example #2 from Principles of Church Growth by Weld and McGavran, 5-15 159

Figure 8 – Kinsler's Intertext Book on Jeremiah, 326 160

Figure 9 – Kinsler's Intertext Book on Jeremiah, 327 161

Figure 10 – North American Missions Founded During Two 45-year Periods 185

Figure 11 – Luther to Carey, plus 30 Remarkable Years, 1792-1822 233

Figure 12 – Warp and Weft or Woof 236

Figure 13 – Modality and Sodality 239

Figure 14 – Third-Generation Church Planting 246

Figure 15 – Relationship Between Church and Para-Church Organizations (Winter, 1979b, 150) 258

Figure 16 – Proportion of American Missionaries Under Voluntary Societies and Under Denominational Boards (Winter, 1979b, 151) 259

Figure 17 – Growth of Different Types and Categories of Mission Societies (Winter, 1979b, 153) 260

Figure 18 – The Overall Size of Church-related versus Independent Societies (Winter, 1979b, 153) 260

Figure 19 – Christian Populations Needing Mobilization (1972, 202) 284

Figure 20 – Scope of the Task - Christians and Non-Christians 308

Figure 21 – World Population Clock at Lausanne 74 309

Figure 22 – The World 311

Figure 23 – E-Scale Illustration 312

Figure 24 – E-Scale in Different Societies 313

Figure 25 – Western World 313

Figure 26 – Non-Western World...314

Figure 27 – Pakistan...315

Figure 28 – World Population Growth During the "Christian
Century"...400

Figure 29 – Population Increase Each Year for Every Hundred
People 401

Figure 30 – The Number of Non-Christians Per Christian 402

Figure 31 – Growth of Non-Christians in Africa and Asia.....................403

Figure 32 – Disparity of Missionaries Serving to Major Non-
Christian Religions 404

Figure 33 – Cultural Distinction Illustrations 405

Figure 34 – Cultural Distance from Evangelist to the Culture...............406

Figure 35 – Types of Growth 406

Figure 36 – Types of Mission-Illustration A...407

Figure 37 – Types of Mission-Illustration B 408

List Of Abbreviations

AEPM	Association of Evangelical Professors of Missions
AIT	Afghanistan Institute of Technology
ALET	Associacion Latinoamericana de Escuelas Teologicas (Latin American Association of Theological Schools)
APM	Association of Professors of Missions
ASM	The American Society of Missiology
Caltech	California Institute of Technology
CAM	Central American Mission, now called CAM International
CAMEO	Committee to Assist Ministry Education Overseas, a joint committee of IFMA/EFMA
CE	Christian Endeavor
CLATT	Latin American Committee on Theological Texts
COEMAR	Commission on Ecumenical Mission and Relations of the United Presbyterian Church in the USA
CT	*Christianity Today* magazine
EFMA	Evangelical Foreign Missions Association. Later the Evangelical Fellowship of Mission Agencies, then the Mission Exchange. Merged with CrossGlobal Link (formerly IFMA) in 2012. The new network is Missio Nexus.
EMQ	*Evangelical Missions Quarterly* journal
FTS or Fuller	Fuller Theological Seminary
GL 71	A mission leaders conference held at Green Lake, Wisconsin in 1971
IBS	Inductive Bible Study
ICAA	International Council of Accrediting Agencies
ICG	Institute of Church Growth
IFMA	Interdenominational Foreign Mission Association. Later named CrossGlobal Link. Merged with The Mission Exchange (formerly EFMA) in 2012. The new network is Missio Nexus.
IJFM	*International Journal for Frontier Missions* recently changed from *International Journal for Frontier Missiology*
IMC	International Missionary Council
IRM	*International Review of Mission*
IVCF	InterVarsity Christian Fellowship
LA	Los Angeles
LACC	Lake Avenue Congregational Church
MARC	Mission Advanced Research and Communications Center
MCC	Mam Christian Center
Navs	Navigators

NCC	National Council of Churches
NGO	Non-Government Organization
NT	New Testament
OT	Old Testament
OU	The Open University
PA	*Practical Anthropology* Journal
PCMS	Presbyterian Center for Mission Studies
PFF	Presbyterian Frontier Fellowship
PFMB	Presbyterian Foreign Mission Board
POWE	Presbyterians for World Evangelization
PTS	Princeton Theological Seminary
SBC	Southern Baptist Convention
SIL	Summer Institute of Linguistics
SWM	School of World Mission at Fuller Theological Seminary, originally the name was: School of World Mission and Institute of Church Growth, currently, School of Intercultural Studies
TAFTEE	The Association for Theological Education by Extension (based in India)
TEE	Theological Education by Extension
TEF	Theological Education Fund, which became a part of the World Council of Churches
UCMS	United Christian Missionary Society
UNISA	University of South Africa
USAID	United States Agency International Development
USCWM	U.S. Center for World Mission
WCC	World Council of Churches
WCF	World Christian Foundations
WMC	World Missionary Conferences
WCIU	William Carey International University
WCL	William Carey Library
WWII	World War Two
Wycliffe or WBT	Wycliffe Bible Translators

Explanatory Notes

1. In the text, Bibliographic references include the author or editor's last name and the date, such as: (Winter, 1969). When a specific page is referenced, it is recorded directly after the year: (Winter, 1969, 34). If the year and the author of the work are included in the text, I will only put the page reference, such as: (34). If a reference does not have a page number at the end of the quote, there is another quote in the same paragraph from the same page, and the reference is at the end of the paragraph or after the last quote.

If an author of a work is referenced multiple times in the same paragraph or in continuous paragraphs, without other references intervening, the reference will only include the year: (1969) or the year and page: (1969, 37).

In a few cases, I have summarized or quoted extensively from one book. In these cases, I have only put the usual reference, such as: (Costas, 1974), and then, subsequently, page references only are listed: (137), until the source changes.

If there is no page listed for emails or personal letters, then it was only one page long.

2. I refer to Ralph Winter as "Ralph" up to the point he is finished with all training and begins his missionary service. After that point, I normally use "Winter" but for clarity, on occasion, I use "Ralph" when discussing something related to both Ralph and Roberta, when "Winter" would be unclear.

3. I have obtained charts and graphs from Ralph Winter's files, books and other sources as noted. In some Figures that include Winter's work, I have chosen to use charts that Winter produced and included in his files, instead of the "final version" seen in published books or articles. While the books generally typeset the charts improving their quality for the reader, scanning from the printed book pages often produced poor result. In no case have I modified the data and in each case the book I reference for any Figure has the identical information in the Figure.

4. When referring to source materials, I include original formatting unless otherwise noted. This would include italics, underlining, and capitalization. Because many of the source materials were typewritten or handwritten, computer-formatting standards were not used in the originals. When it is necessary to clarify a quote, term or referent, I do so in brackets, such as [he said]. In no case does this change the meaning. What is within the brackets was not in the original text.

Chapter 1

The Research Design

Background

Ralph D. Winter (1924–2009) ranks among the most influential
missiologists of the 20th Century. Missiologists and Christian leaders
around the world have recognized his many significant contributions to the
evangelical approach to the Great Commission task.[1]

After receiving a BS from Caltech, an MA from Columbia University
Teachers College, a PhD from Cornell, and a BD from Princeton, Winter
served as a missionary in the tribal highland region of Guatemala for ten
years, sustaining and establishing various ministries and businesses. Over
the next 10 years he taught missiology to nearly 1,000 experienced
missionaries at the graduate level at a respected seminary. He founded or
assisted in founding a number of organizations, provided direct leadership
to two of those he founded, and continued to serve them until the end of
his life in 2009 at age of 84. Winter's strategic insights and endeavors have
helped transform the evangelical mission movement of the last half-
century. He was included as one of the twenty-five most influential
evangelicals in America in 2005. (Van Biema, 2005, 42)

To date, there is no complete or even popular biographical work on
Winter, although a number of short articles have been written about him.
This study seeks to provide a thorough account, tying together the threads
of Winter's life and work. That process should shed light on issues within
the history and development of missiological thinking in the West in the
late twentieth century. My hope is that this research will assist others
studying either this period in evangelical outreach, or the life of Winter
and those with whom he interacted.[2]

---

[1] This phrase "great commission" was coined from the command of Jesus to make
disciples of all nations in Matthew 28:19-20. This phrase reflects a 19th and 20th Century
view of the commission Jesus left with his disciples.

[2] It is also my hope that this work will provide ideas, methods, and models for emerging
mission leaders, because Winter's life provides examples that leaders today can follow as
they address the global issues of our day within their church, ministry or business.

My own engagement with Winter has been deep and personal. His life and work have been foundational in the maturation of my own perspectives on missiology and ministry, and my own involvement in global Christian missions. I began following his writings and activities in 1976. Since 1982, I have been on staff with the major organization he and his wife Roberta founded, the U.S. Center for World Mission, and have been a director at that organization since 1990.[3] Through this relationship, I have been privileged to interact on many of the same issues with the same missiologists and leaders as Winter did in the last 30 years of his life. These experiences impacted my own worldview, led me to this study, and compel me to complete it.

Purpose of the Study

The purpose of this study is to uncover factors which contributed to the development of Ralph D. Winter's significant insights and which provided motivation for his endeavors, by chronicling the stages and influences in Winter's life and by analyzing his core missiology.

I will trace the development of Winter's spirituality, missiology, and intellectual pursuits, as available materials allow. I further aim to present an overview of his broad interest in any issue related to what he believed he should engage, within God's purposes, and to explore in-depth his response to select issues, belonging, in a restricted sense, to his early missiological ideas. In doing so, I hope to help connect the ideas and organizations with which Winter was engaged, to give a greater understanding of Ralph Winter as a person and as a man seeking to understand and obey God and His Word.[4]

Finally, I expect this work will assist those who have labored alongside Ralph Winter in the organizations he founded and in the networks with which he interacted, providing them with a greater understanding of him, his approach to leadership and the history of the organizations they have

---

[3] Since 1990, I have also served on the Board of Directors of the William Carey International University, another organization the Winters founded. The USCWM is now under the legal entity called the Frontier Mission Fellowship. Until 2009, Ralph Winter was the General Director.

[4] By providing a base of Winter's life and early missiology, this study should aid others who wish to study further any particular missiological issues Winter addressed, or further explore his life and work as a missiologist, an organizational leader, a broad thinker or a tinkerer.

served. Perhaps it will also provide renewed inspiration for the tasks they face and the identification and solving of global problems before us all.

As with any biography, Winter's life is worth studying and learning from the perspective of personal enrichment alone. By adding elements such as the breadth of his influence, ideas, endeavors and analysis, this particular study is elevated beyond biography alone. Naturally, the details of any life requires that I be highly selective in my approach, especially with one who wrote extensively and so deeply engaged with life.[5]

Central Research Issue

The central research issue at hand is to explain how the influences in Ralph Winter's life came together to produce a missiologist whose endeavors shaped a global movement.

To accomplish this I will endeavor to answer the following questions:

1. How were Winter's personal experiences formative in his development?
2. How did historical events, trends, and key individuals shape Winter's development?
3. What are some of the significant insights Winter embraced and promoted, and how did these insights lead him to take action?
4. What are the primary endeavors undertaken by Winter up to 1976, what was he able to accomplish through them, and how did the success or failure of these endeavors influence him?
5. Where do the ideas and endeavors selected for this study intersect the mission movement and the broader evangelical movement, in relation to both theory and practice?

Assumptions and Limitations

I assume a 20th Century evangelical theological foundation as the basis for views of the Bible and theology in this study.[6] This is the tradition

---

[5] When Winter died, there were 800 boxes of all kinds of raw materials. These included writing files, trip files, and inbound and outbound correspondence files to mention a few.

[6] The basic tenets of recent evangelicalism are: biblical fidelity, apostolic doctrine (including the centrality of the cross), the experience of salvation (conversion internally), the imperative of discipleship or activism (external action because of salvation), the urgency of mission, and the eschatological hope. This is based upon Bebbington, who ends his list with activism (Bebbington, 2005, 21-40), and Bloesch (Bloesch, 1988, 17).

within which Winter was raised, though increasingly throughout his life Winter challenged and re-examined many standard evangelical theological assumptions, interpretations, and practices, especially with regard to how these were communicated in cross-cultural situations.

This is not a quantitative study, but I will seek to qualitatively assess the impact of Winter's life. Because his work has inspired many evangelical Christians to engage more seriously in global issues and ministry, interactions between Winter and other respected evangelical missiologists, professors, and leaders will provide a measure of indication of the breadth of his influence.

This study will not attempt to evaluate the theories of history and criticism. Furthermore, it is not the purpose of the study to deal with the issue of truth and how we can know what is real and what is not. A basic premise of this work is that we can know truth adequately to carry out research and provide interpretation of it.[7]

A study of Winter's life and work will guide this research and, hopefully, speak to the reader. I will not deal with all missiological (or other) ideas Winter discussed. I will limit myself to select, central insights and his core missiology from his early life up to 1976, and especially to those ideas that were an important part of his development and life direction. By "core missiology" or "early missiology" I mean up to the founding of the U.S. Center for World Mission in 1976. This is about 20 years into his ministry, which spanned 53 years from his acceptance as a missionary. I use the word "core" because I believe, as I will argue, that these early areas of ministry and discovery became foundational to his later thinking.

While it would have been ideal to consider all of Winter's missiology, space limitations would not allow more issues to be dealt with effectively. The missiological issues detailed in this thesis are considered by many to be the foundation of Winter's contribution. When brief biographies are written of Winter, these three issues are noted as his significant contributions. His contributions, research, writing and actions after 1976 built upon these three issues. Thus, I will end this thesis in 1976, two years

---

W. Reginald Ward traces early evangelicalism to Central Europe from c. 1670. (2006, 1) It is beyond the scope of this study to include details of that early history; rather our aim is to describe the major characteristics of Evangelicalism as Winter experienced it in the mid-20th Century.

[7] This includes both interviews and source documents relating to a subject's life, which, where possible, must be triangulated with other sources to give validity.

after Winter presented at the Lausanne 1974 Congress, just after he and Roberta founded a sodality, and just before founding a university.

Winter held an interest in a wide variety of subjects, including issues that others might consider outside his field of missiology.[8] This was a natural extension of his perspective of the importance of being a lifelong learner, and of observing connections between diverse subjects and their interrelationship with missiology and theology and practice.[9]

Until late 2008, at 84 years old, Winter continued to write and speak. In 2009, he was no longer traveling but continued to write or dictate and interact with those around him. The time and space constraints of this study do not allow the impact of these later ideas to be assessed. By seeking to provide a foundational study covering Winter's most significant contributions, I will necessarily leave the research and analysis of his later thinking for some future study.

This research is both informed and limited by my own perspectives and vantage point. My personal relationship with Ralph Winter and the fact that he was alive during the first five years of this study provides an added level of perspective. Opinions may differ on whether that enriches or distorts. The intent is to leverage the advantages of my personal relationship both as a trusted "insider," accepted by him and his family, and as one who has engaged actively with his ideas and endeavors for nearly three decades. Winter's influence on my own perspective of missions and ministry should help to extend the depth and breadth with which I am able to examine his ideas. His own availability, and that of some of his family and colleagues, are additional assets, which should help me in this task.

Over the last fifteen years in particular, I had been around Winter enough so that when I heard him discussing something he had been thinking about for many years, I was usually able to accurately anticipate how he would approach and illustrate the subject. Of course, he continued to present new ideas and illustrations, many of which I had never heard. He often connected older ideas, with which I was familiar, with new ones. Rarely did he share a story from his fieldwork or teaching years that I had not heard before. Naturally, many historical materials should provide details Winter never mentioned in my hearing. Ultimately, others will

---

[8] This included his perspective on issues within North American culture and within Western Evangelical sub-culture on topics such as marriage and family issues, the use of alcohol in social settings, science and its impact on religion, etc.

[9] Winter would "ransack" several books a week on a wide range of topics. From February 2006 until November 2007, a period of 16 months, Winter purchased and "ransacked" about 304 books. Naturally, some got more attention than others.

judge whether my long-term close relationship with Winter has influenced this work for good or ill and whether it has led me to inject inaccuracies, misinterpretations, or ignore pertinent facts or personal foibles. While being sensitive to the danger of being too close to my subject to see it in focus, the comments of others both written and from interviews will play an important role in ensuring balance in this study.

Precedent Research and Literature Review

To my knowledge, no one to date has written a comprehensive study of Ralph Winter's life and missiology. Much of what has been written is narrow in focus, reflects either a particular area of interest to or research of the writer, or it is introductory or anecdotal in nature. Other than the general biographical writings, the works mentioned below do not specifically assess Winter's life and contribution, yet they do provide insight into themes in his work which gained attention from others. They also validate the significance of his life, as I have outlined above.

Theses or dissertations written about some of Winter's major ideas are listed below under the appropriate sections. Where there are major works that argued against Winter, I mention them in this section. Fuller details of their debate with Winter are discussed as appropriate in the relevant chapter of the thesis.

General Biographical Writings

A few brief biographical sketches of Winter exist, such as dictionary entries and the personal and popular 48-page booklet *Five Months and a Week* by Roberta H. Winter (written with Ralph's input), describing the period from their meeting until they were married.[10] (Winter, 2001) She also wrote a 43-page unpublished chronicle of Winter's characteristic of being an initiator and thus not always understood by others. (Winter, 2000) It gives a good chronology of events as well as her perspective on his life. I will use this as a chronological guide where helpful and to fill in details of Roberta's interpretation of Ralph, other people and events.

The *Evangelical Dictionary of World Missions* (Moreau et al., 2000) includes an entry on Winter that highlights his life and work, including educational background, missionary service in Guatemala, the beginnings

---

[10] Roberta was Ralph Winter's first wife, who died of cancer in 2001. He married Barbara Scotchmer in 2002.

of Theological Education by Extension (TEE), and his teaching at the School of World Mission (SWM) at Fuller Theological Seminary (FTS).[11] The entry also includes some of the ministries begun during his time at SWM, including William Carey Library (WCL), American Society of Missiology (ASM), and what became a watershed presentation at the Lausanne Committee on World Evangelism (LCWE) Congress in 1974. The entry recounts his founding of the U.S. Center for World Mission (1976) and the William Carey International University (WCIU in 1977) as well.

The *Dictionary* also includes thirteen additional, specific references to Winter and his work as listed under various subjects (page number follows):

1. *Anthropology/Missiological Anthropology* (67) mentions his involvement in the journal *Practical Anthropology* (which became *Missiology*, in part because of Winter's involvement).

2. *Church/Mission Relations* (205) describes his involvement in the discussion about who sends the missionary — the church, or the agency? This issue and the next were central topics in Winter's thinking from the late 1960s onward.

3. *Parachurch Agencies and Missions* (722) relates to the same issue.

4. *Cross-Cultural Evangelism* (244) mentions Winter's 1974 Lausanne presentation as well as the E-Scale he developed.[12]

5. *Fads in Missions* (351) Robertson McQuilkin wrote this article and specifically mentioned that Winter's presentation at Lausanne was not a fad.[13]

6. *Global Consultation on World Evangelization '97* (394) Stan Guthrie notes that Winter spoke at this event and asked "that a more contextualized, de-Westernized gospel be presented to the huge and largely unreached blocs of Hindus, Muslims, and Buddhists." This is an area of Winter's thinking that developed throughout his career and was increasingly emphasized as his understanding of contextualization grew.

---

[11] SWM is the original name of one of three schools at FTS along with the School of Theology and the School of Psychology. SWM has been renamed "School of Intercultural Studies." I will use the names of organizations at the time of the event under discussion. In this case, School of World Mission or SWM.

[12] Which is a scale depicting cultural or linguistic distance from an evangelist to the cultural or people group with which he is seeking to communicate.

[13] McQuilkin was a former missionary and president for many years of Columbia Bible College, now known as Columbia International University.

7. *Great Commission* (563) Under the entry by missiologist David Hesselgrave, Winter is mentioned, with others, as seeing the concept of people groups as the best way to accomplish the discipling of all nations commanded in Matthew 28:19-20.
8. He is also mentioned in this regard under *Peoples, People Groups* (745). These concepts are central to his Lausanne 1974 presentation.
9. *1974 Lausanne meeting* (563) Winter's 1974 Lausanne presentation is mentioned.
10. *10/40 Window* (938) Winter's 1974 Lausanne presentation is mentioned.[14]
11. *Mission Theory* (642) A. Christopher Smith mentions Winter as being one who made "Important contributions to the development of missions theorizing...."
12. *Theological Education by Extension* (944) includes Winter and others who were deeply involved in this movement.
13. *Unevangelized* (981) mentions Winter's Lausanne presentation and chronicles how he applied it in ongoing activities.

In the book, *A History of Presbyterian Mission, 1944–2007*, (Sunquist and Long, 2008, 2, 110-111, 118-122) Winter is mentioned in the second page referring to his book, *Twenty-Five Unbelievable Years*. (Winter and Latourette, 1970) An article called, "Missions with in the Mission" details both Winter's ideas, such as Sodality-Modality, and the organizations or "missions" he helped to found within the Presbyterian denominational structure, such as the Presbyterian Frontier Fellowship and The Presbyterian Order for World Evangelization. (Sunquist and Long, 2008, 2, 110-111, 118-122)

Beyond these dictionary entries, Charles Kraft wrote *SWM/SIS at 40: A Participant/Observer's View of our History*, (Kraft, 2005) which chronicles the history of the SWM from its founding in 1965 until 2005. In it, he included eight pages on Winter's time at SWM and brief references to Winter in other sections of the book.[15] (Kraft, 2005, 89-97) Kraft covers the role Winter played on the faculty, including his local and global

---

[14] The dictionary describes the mobilization idea, "'10/40 Window,' as a rectangular-shaped window 10 degrees by 40 degrees north of the equator spanning the globe from West Africa to Asia, including over 60 countries and more than 2 billion people." (Moreau et al., 2000, 938) The majority of the unreached peoples of the world—those who have never heard the gospel and who are not within reach of churches of their own people—live within this window.

[15] Winter was the first full-time faculty member appointed after Donald McGavran and Alan Tippett.

experiences with TEE and his teaching on the expansion of Christianity. Winter and all the faculty and students interacted on many issues, and no issues were considered "off limits" for discussion and evaluation. Kraft suggests that Donald McGavran found motivation and inspiration in Winter's creative thinking.

General Writings

Several articles or book sections were written to counter some of the views which Winter had espoused. For example, James E. Goff[16] wrote a review of a book on Latin American church growth, which the SWM had helped produce and Winter promoted. Goff pointed out errors in the book and expressed concern about the North American mentality of the church growth model. Goff also wrote an article in the WCC magazine RISK critiquing TEE, expressing similar concerns. Some of the details of these issues will be discussed later.

Theological Education by Extension

The TEE that emanated from the highlands of Guatemala was taken up by other missionaries, Winter began to travel to present the idea of TEE in other parts of Latin America and, later, in other areas of the world. His ideas and those of others who responded to them began to appear more often in print. Many books or articles include references to Winter's ideas on TEE.

The debate in relation to TEE often raised issues surrounding quality. How can you be sure the students are learning what they should? How do you mentor them at a distance? Those who argued for TEE asked questions about the viability of the cost of residential programs, the ability to reach enough students, and why it is assumed that "education" was best accomplished by classroom teaching.

Some theses produced with Winter's involvement address TEE regionally in specific situations. For example, David L Hill wrote *Designing a Theological Education by Extension Program* for the Philippine Baptist

---

[16] Goff, like the Winters, was a missionary with the United Presbyterian Church. He served in several Latin and South American countries. He and his wife Margaret were considered "interpreters of Liberation Theology to Protestant Anglophone audiences." According to: Yale University Library, Divinity School Library Guide to the James and Margaret Goff Papers, Record Group No. 170.

Mission as an MA Thesis at Fuller SWM.[17] (Hill, 1973) He discusses the history of theological training, and proposes a system, which would allow training to spread out to more remote regions such as Luzon and Mindanao.

Some scholarly works discuss TEE concepts more broadly, and offer a study of the whole movement at a certain time. Winter himself edited the first major book on the subject, which was a compilation from a 617-page TEE consultation called *Theological Education by Extension*. (Winter, 1969d) In a PhD dissertation, Fred L. Holland wrote *Theological Education in Context and Change: the Influence of Leadership Training and Anthropology on Ministry for Church Growth.* (Holland, 1978) In it Holland covers the history of TEE, leadership development, anthropology, and church growth. These were all central topics of discussion and research at the SWM.[18]

The *Evangelical Mission Quarterly* (*EMQ*) published a considerable number of articles on TEE during the early years of the movement. The *EMQ* was a joint publication of two major mission associations in the U.S. (IFMA and EFMA[19]). These articles range from describing the concept to evaluating the effectiveness of TEE. Some of the many articles, theses and books produced about TEE discussed specific successes or failures of the movement.

In 1971, Ross Kinsler[20] produced a book for use in TEE programs called *Inductive Study of the Book of Jeremiah: The Word of the Lord in a Time of Crisis*. (Kinsler, 1971)[21]

---

[17] Winter was one of the supervisors or readers for this thesis.

[18] Holland's thesis notes that the church growth movement was not looking for numbers, but, rather, the development of leaders in the context of their ministry. The issue of church growth theory and practice remains a point of discussion in many manuscripts.

[19] I am using organizational names as they were at the time of the reference.

[20] Kinsler served with Winter and James Emery in Guatemala during the early days of TEE and continued promoting TEE throughout his career. His first contribution came in 1978, when he wrote *The Extension Movement in Theological Education: A Call to the Renewal of the Ministry*. (Kinsler, 1978) In 1983 he also contributed *Ministry By the People: Theological Education by Extension* (Kinsler, 1983) published by the WCC. In 1991, Kinsler and Emery, who was a former Guatemala co-worker and the co-founder of TEE, wrote *Opting for Change: A Handbook on Evaluation and Planning for Theological Education by Extension*. (Kinsler and Emery, 1991) It is a workbook-style approach to developing and evaluating a TEE program, and gives self-evaluation tools to those involved directly in TEE, enabling them to set goals and assess results. Recently, Kinsler also published *Diversified Theological Education: Equipping All God's People*, (Kinsler, 2008), which seeks to demonstrate that a major focus of TEE is access to training for all by including case studies from programs then current around the world.

Twenty years after TEE started in Guatemala, a consultation was held in Cyprus. A book was produced from the conference proceedings called *Cyprus: TEE Come of Age*. (Youngblood, 1986) It included an assessment of TEE and a path forward for the movement. Contributors referenced positive contributions, misunderstandings, and weaknesses of the TEE movement.

People in other fields of work around the world who were also considering ways to educate those missed by traditional methods were further recognized at Cyprus. For example, Paulo Freire's work in Brazil, expressed in his books *Pedagogy of the Oppressed* (Freire, 1970) and *Education for Critical Consciousness* (1973), was discussed. One Cyprus presentation pointed to Freire's idea of "problem posing" as an example of a life training method that could be used by theological educators working with established church leaders to improve TEE. Other articles in the book covered the history of the movement to that point, how to cooperate internationally in TEE, and how to evaluate TEE at the Bible College level.[22]

Modality and Sodality

Winter used the terms "modalities" and "sodalities" to describe two distinct structural approaches to accomplishing the work of God in the world. He drew his ideas from his understanding of church history and his interpretation of Acts 13, when Barnabas and Paul leave the Antioch church to begin their mission work. These he saw as two distinct structures. He argued that this distinction is derived, in part, from the different ways individuals participate in each organization. The church is a "modality" which would normally accept anyone regardless of age, sex or marital status. In contrast, Paul's team is a "sodality" or mission organization. A sodality requires what Winter called a "second decision" and so is more selective than a modality. It is made up of those who are allied with its direction and called by God. Membership in a sodality is restricted to those invited to join by the sodality leadership.

---

[21] It is the kind of text the early TEE movement was calling for. It walks the participants, in a "programmed text" fashion, through an inductive study of a book of the Bible, including its background, historical setting, and application for today.

[22] While the conference proceedings provide insight into the development of the TEE movement to that point, it may only be a reflection of Winter's initial work on TEE, as he had, by this time, focused his attention on other issues.

Bruce Camp[23] wrote a DMiss thesis (1992) arguing that the local church should take the lead in missions. He suggests that the concept of "modalities and sodalities" originally proposed by Winter in 1973 is one that can be justified historically but not Biblically. This will be considered further in the Sodality and Modality chapter.

Bob Blincoe wrote a dissertation on the role of sodalities within Protestantism. (Blincoe, 2012) He argued that Luther and Calvin envisioned a "classic shape in the generation of Reformers that followed them, assumed that ecclesiastical hierarchies should retain for themselves the sole authority to initiate God's mission to all the world." (Blincoe, 2012, 9) Blincoe argues that a different paradigm would be shown more effective beginning with the publication of William Carey's Enquiry in 1792.[24] (1891)

History, where Blincoe spends most of his writing, demonstrates both the threat and suspicion that ecclesiastical structures have expressed towards sodalities. He argues that, "in order for the people of God to achieve the greatest good, by which I mean creating durable and effective solutions to many of humanity's greatest problems, it will be necessary for them to negotiate new social contracts with the voluntary associations that their members are starting or joining." (Blincoe, 2012, 9)

Certainly, a number of authors expressed concern in this area, both out of a fear of losing "church" in mission work or of losing "mission" in the midst of maintaining church. Some of the many points made in these works will be discussed, but will not be taken up in this study in any systematic way.

Unreached People Groups

This concept is probably the one for which Winter is best known. He presented the central premise of "unreached people groups" in a Lausanne 1974 meeting. The basic idea is that a people group or culture is "unreached" if it does not have a viable church within its culture.

Ten years after Winter explored the concept of "unreached people groups" and eight years after he founded the U.S. Center for World Mission to focus on the issue, Tim Stafford[25] wrote a cover article for *Christianity Today* (*CT*) on Winter's contribution to the concept of the

---

[23] Camp worked as a local church mission pastor and later as a consultant to local churches in missions.

[24] Several later editions are more readily available.

[25] Stafford is currently a Senior Writer for *CT*.

Unreached People Groups (UPG).[26] It was entitled "Ralph Winter: Looking for the Hidden Peoples" (Stafford, 1984) and demonstrated how broadly the concept of the unreached peoples was growing.

Gerald Haynes wrote a PhD dissertation in 1994 entitled *Meanings of the Term "Unreached People Group": Consequences for Mission Purpose* on the subject of the unreached people groups concept that Winter popularized. (Haynes, 1994) Haynes sought to define the term UPG and determine its strengths and weaknesses in practice. He recognized that Winter's presentation at Lausanne in 1974 helped popularize the concept of UPG, while noting that the idea of UPG came out of McGavran's work on the field before the '74 meeting. Haynes also surveyed one long-standing mission agency seeking to apply the UPG concept within their mission as the unreached peoples idea became popular in the 1980s.[27]

Haynes' findings on meanings of the term UPG are only partially valid. He does not fully explain nor seem to understand the concept of UPG or its history. He adheres to the idea that McGavran's church growth ideas are a sociological construct only and not the result of a serious attempt at Biblical study. Thus, he holds the one-sided position that the church growth movement focuses on evangelism but not discipleship or mentoring.[28]

Additionally, Haynes' sources are very limited. His 1994 work does not reference Winter after 1981, although by 1994 there were several major clarifications of UPG in articles by Winter and others. He references positively the critiques of UPG ideas at that date by Gary Corwin in his article in the *EMQ*. However, he does not reference the original journal in which it was produced, the *International Journal for Frontier Missions* (Jan. 1992, Vol. 9:1), which published the longer proceedings of the annual meeting of the International Society of Frontier Missiology in the fall 1991 where Corwin presented his original paper. At that meeting several authors, including Winter, interacted with Corwin's ideas and concerns. Also included in the January 1992 issue of the *IJFM* are clearer definitions of UPG, the viability of the church, and the need to re-evangelize populations tending away from the faith—all issues of which Haynes

---

[26] These are cultures or people groups globally without viable fellowships or churches in their midst. They were also called "hidden peoples" for a brief period.

[27] The fact that he could interview missionaries and mission leaders about this subject is an example of the impact of Winter's focus on unreached peoples.

[28] These were fairly standard reactions to the Church Growth Movement, although by the time this dissertation was written, much had been written about the centrality of quality in church growth.

seems to be unaware.[29] These omissions color what would otherwise be helpful quantitative research. As a consequence, the questions Haynes asked of the mission leaders and missionaries were innocently ambiguous or misleading, and the idea of UPG in his work is confused.[30]

Hyungjo Kim wrote an MA Thesis entitled *Missiological Study for Reaching the Unreached People Groups: Special Reference to the Korean Mission*. (Kim, 1997) Kim's motivation is strategic: what are effective strategies for Korean Missionaries working with UPG? He examines concepts in the lives of Donald McGavran ('people movements', 'panta ta ethne', and 'the bridges of God'), Alan Tippett (anthropological understanding of mission, power encounter, and 'people movement'), and Ralph Winter (UPG, 'modality and sodality', mission history and UPG in the 10/40 window).[31] All of this is in the context of increasing the creativity of the Korean mission movement. Kim fails to consider available material in his work. He does not define UPG (or other important concepts), and covers other matters at a superficial level. He attributes to Winter areas of focus which Winter did not emphasize (such as the 10/40 window).

Much of the debate on this issue surrounded the Lausanne 1974 Congress, or events that followed it. For example, one follow up event to that Congress was a consultation on the Homogenous Unit Principle (HUP). Winter debated with Victor E.W. Hayward[32] on the historical background to the concept. Klas Lundström also offered a helpful study on Gospel and Culture as it related to history of the WCC and Lausanne Movement (2006).

---

[29] Apparently he did not discuss with or interview Winter directly, and he did not include McGavran's sources dealing with discipleship.

[30] In deference to Haynes, the *IJFM* January issue did not appear until later in 1992.

[31] While the concept of the "10/40 Window" was detailed in *Mission Frontiers* magazine and Winter was the editor, he felt it was misleading because there were major unreached groups outside "the window," not to mention minor ones that should not be forgotten.

[32] Hayward was a missionary to China beginning in 1934. In 1951 he became the General Foreign Secretary of his mission, the Baptist Missionary Society of Great Britain. Then, in 1959, he served as the executive secretary of the WCC department of missionary studies, later working as associate general secretary of the WCC, relating to national and regional Christian councils. (Anderson, 1998, 285)

Winter's Interaction with Others

Winter interacted with others on these issues and in the field of missiology, as well as other disciplines that feed into it, such as culture, statistics (an emphasis in his PhD studies), theology, history, and science. At times, his interaction was indirect. His writings demonstrate his engagement with an issue, but often without direct, specific mention of other(s) who hold a different perspective. Some of his interactions will be covered in more depth than others depending on the uniqueness of the issue, the level of Winter's engagement with a particular argument or person, and that person's significance in global mission. Winter included and was aware of many of the works produced, especially since he was teaching full time. The bibliography for one of his courses at Fuller SWM included a "Tentative Bibliography" of 132 books with a supplement of another 37.[33] These lists included Max Warren, Stephen Neill, Kenneth Scott Latourette, Roland Allen, Lesslie Newbigin, Reinhold Niebuhr, and others. Yet Winter does not directly refer to most of these in his writing except Kenneth Scott Latourette.

One example of Winter's engagement with a significant missiological author was when he responded to the release of David Bosch's book *Transforming Mission.* (Bosch, 1991) He noted that the book "is a *tour de force* of the whole field. It has a lengthy section on the meaning of the word *evangelization.* Bosch dispassionately and objectively traces the different ways the word is used. He does not have the time or space, apparently, to go into the dynamics behind it which, historically considered, would display a downhill erosion." (Winter, 1992, 11)

Winter continued this discussion in his presentation to the International Society for Frontier Missiology in 1991, noting some of the issues Bosch did not or could not include. He discusses the need for Bosch to redefine terms to fit the needs of mainline denominations, who can more easily fund evangelism than pioneering work. He continues with comments about Bosch's book, noting that it:

> ... unfortunately must have gone to press a few minutes too late to take into account the Papal Encyclical which was promulgated December 5, 1990, *Mission of the Redeemer: on*

---

[33] The course title was: "The Training of the Ministry: Lay and Ordained," according to a course syllabus from the FTS, SWM archive Box 1, Folder "Dr. Winter Course Outlines" and "Training of the Ministry Course" 642 (unprocessed as of March, 2009). It is not clear if this supplement was added later in the course, or in a subsequent year, or was an update to a previous list.

the *Permanent Validity of the Church's Missionary Mandate.*[34]
(Winter, 1992, 11)

Winter disagreed with some of Bosch's terms and definitions, just as others would react to Winter's various ideas. Bosch seems to be minimizing an area on which Winter placed great emphasis: the frontiers.[35]

While Winter may have been impacted by authors he does not mention, it is difficult to determine these with any level of certainty. For example, some have compared select ideas of Winter to those of Leslie Newbigin. Winter met Newbigin once, but they had no interaction directly nor indirectly concerning missiology.

Methodology of the Study

Biography, like life, is a process. This study will contribute by telling the story of the life lived by Ralph Winter. My interpretation of his life, from my vantage point, will give rise to a set of observations. Another's vantage point might give rise to a different set of observations. While my choices and claims will reflect my particular perspective, the views of others gathered through the qualitative research process will help fill out the picture and verify the data. (Denzin, 1989, 21) The reader will have to judge how well the information has been integrated into the final result. (Denzin, 1989, 19-20)

> No single method can grasp all the subtle variations in ongoing human experience. Consequently, qualitative researchers deploy a wide range of interconnected interpretive methods, always seeking better ways to make more understandable the worlds of experience they have studied. (Denzin, 2008, 29)

---

[34] Winter continued: "There in that document, more clearly and more effectively than anywhere else I know, the writer of that document determinedly defended the narrow, classical meaning of the word *mission*, and boldly distinguished 'specific missionary work' from either, 1) the assistance of believing, growing, evangelizing Christian communities, or 2) the 're-evangelization' that is necessary where 'entire groups of the baptized have lost a living sense of the faith.'" (Winter, 1992, 11)

[35] Bosch had a section in his book which criticized Fuller's SWM in ways that demonstrated to Winter that Bosch did not understand what was happening there. A resolution of these differences was cut short by Bosch's untimely death in 1992. Later, Winter had the opportunity to meet Bosch's widow, who expressed her husband's apology for that section of the book.

Ultimately, "Unlike quantitative work that can carry its meaning in its tables and summaries, qualitative work carries its meaning in its entire text." (Richardson, 2008, 474) It is my desire that a clear picture of Winter's life and work will be seen, and I will seek to faithfully represent him, his works, and other independent sources.

Approach to the Historical Biography Dimensions

At the basic level, this work will be, as Titon describes it, "the life history," a "written account of a person's life based on spoken conversations and interviews." (Titon, 1980, 283) Naturally, this story will be set in the context of the socio-cultural setting of the time Ralph Winter lived. I will trace the various aspects upon Winter's life and upbringing to find patterns in various life stages as a means of understanding how his life was shaped. I will focus on his life and the interaction with experiences and people, following the pattern of many qualitative researchers and historians who believe that a biography or life story is worth researching and retelling as scholarly doctoral level work.[36] (Creswell, 1998, 17-19)

The subject of a biography has an outer world and an inner life, both of which can only be seen or appreciated to a certain depth. Even a close family member may only see part of the deep, sacred, inner self. (Denzin, 1989, 29) Bruner speaks about a "correspondence between a life as lived, a life as experienced and a life as told" and says that the "anthropologist" or outsider (the one studying the life) needs to distinguish between them. (Bruner, 1984, 7)

"A life lived is what actually happens. A life experienced consists of the images, feelings, sentiments, desires, thoughts, and meanings known to the person whose life it is. ... A life as told, a life history, is a narrative, influenced by the cultural conventions of telling, by the audience, and by the social context." (Bruner, 1984, 7) Also, Denzin suggests that a biographer "writes himself or herself into the life of the subject about whom the individual is writing; likewise the reader reads through her or his perspective." (Creswell, 1998, 206)

This research focuses on a selection of facts about Winter's life and work, and develops interpretations that tie these together. History can be considered a recounting of facts, but each historian sees only a subset of all

---

[36] Two respected historians agreed with this, as noted in email dated Oct. 25, 2005, from Mark Noll to me, and an Oct. 21,2005, email from Wilbur Shenk to me, which also mentioned his dissertation on Henry Venn as an example of a biographical/missiological approach. (Shenk, 1983)

pertinent facts. The constructions and interpretations placed upon them is colored by the historian's own vantage point.

Sources and Approach to the Material

Introduction

This dissertation is written mostly from primary source material in the form of interviews and archival research. Secondary sources were referenced and used for study of the historical and social context surrounding Winter at each stage of his life.

The bulk of the study will be based on Winter's writing (published and unpublished) and interviews. All other sources provide depth, breadth, significance and reflection back to Winter's own accounts, and verification of these accounts. Specific information about data sources is listed below.[37] The study of each will vary in depth depending on the source and the information contained and its significance to Winter's life the best I understand it at this time.

Cultural Setting: History, Theology and Missiology

This research will build upon the historical and cultural setting of the early 1900s to the degree that it is the backdrop for Winter's life and family. Sources that evaluate the general culture and, more importantly, the Christian culture or subculture of the early twentieth century may be helpful. Sources that consider pertinent issues within Christianity, evangelicalism (including fundamentalism), and global mission in that period will provide foundational information.[38] Each of these will provide background to the history of global movements such as Lausanne Committee for World Evangelization (LCWE) and the World Council of

---

[37] In some cases with more information in an Appendix, which will be noted in the text or footnote.

[38] Winter would consider himself a fundamentalist in certain core Biblical areas, but he did not follow the fundamentalist pattern of disengagement with the culture. Nor did he ever pursue any political programme characteristic of certain recent fundamentalist groups.

Churches (WCC), or chronicle debates within Christian circles that may have influenced Winter.[39]

Sources which outline specifics of Winter's experience will also be considered, such as Presbyterian field records from Guatemala and Chuck Kraft's book on the history of SWM. Selections from the work of McGavran and Tippett will also offer a particular perspective on the discussions that fed into the founding of the SWM and its early years. Other themes (such as church growth) will be considered in a general way.

Winter does mention, in writing or in interviews, a few books that, and individuals who, influenced him, and specific attention will be given to these. For example, Yale historian Kenneth Scott Latourette's perspective on the expansion of Christianity had a deep impact on Winter, so a discussion of that perspective is pertinent to understanding Winter's own development.[40]

Resources produced by others who interacted with Winter or who produced works because of him and his ideas will also be consulted as they intersect with the early missiology considered in this thesis. This will include journal articles as well as magazine articles from the popular press.

Winter's Writings

Winter wrote extensively and these writings will be a central source for this thesis. He published only a few books but produced many articles, book forewords and chapters. He is perhaps best known for the presentation he delivered at the LCWE Congress in 1974 entitled "The Highest Priority: Cross Cultural Evangelism" and published in a compendium on the Congress. (Douglas, 1975)

Winter also produced hundreds of additional unpublished documents, some of which were presented verbally, and some which were circulated to a select group. Some of his writings were never brought to a publishable form and include reports, hundreds of letters to family, mission and church leaders, newsletters to churches, articles, and material for presentation to staff or conferences. Some of his work is published as internal documents for the organizations he founded. These will be helpful as they contribute to the purpose of this particular study and help to address the central research issues. Not all documents will be consulted. Winter's email files,

---

[39] One example is *The Gospel and Culture in the World Council of Churches and the Lausanne Movement with particular focus on the period 1973-1996.* (Lundström, 2006)

[40] Winter first met and was taught by Latourette as a missionary candidate.

for example, must be left for others to study, as they cover his later life and thought.

Starting with his service in Guatemala and continuing for about 40 years, Winter recorded thoughts in a journal. These journals are often personal and are under the control of the Winter family, but publishable reflections therein provide further understanding about his reflections and the impact of others around him. When available, these will provide added insight into Winter's perspective on various issues. His personal letters to his parents also provide additional insights, especially for his time in Guatemala.

After he began to use a computer, Winter kept an extensive record of most personal correspondence and files of many of these written exchanges. Naturally, the focus here is not on the minutiae of Winter's personal life. The selection of material from the huge number of both public and personal sources is dictated by the focus of the research design.

Winter often reflected and responded to cultural or theological issues he perceived as significant and in need of challenge, counterbalance, correction, or enrichment by an alternate perspective. He often challenged the cultural and missiological status quo, especially with regard to Western evangelicalism and culture or Western culture in general. These reflections and responses will be reviewed as they relate to the major topics of Winter's writings.

Throughout Winter's adult life he established organizations or structures to accomplish a goal. Some of these failed; others succeeded. Winter's files, parts of his journals, letters, hand-written memos, and legal records provide a record of many of those he started or helped to start, as well as information about organizations he dreamed about starting, or suggested or helped others to start. Where available and helpful to the study, I will chronicle these, noting the appropriate information about the organization, people involved, and any substantial results it accomplished if relevant.

Winter "tinkered" with ideas as he wrote. He would "float" an idea to someone or a small group, and then process it further. Winter was known to return to work on an idea over a period of time, edit it substantially adding concepts until he moved on to another subject.[41] Thus, his writing files include numerous drafts and early versions of papers or presentations, often containing hand-written notes from Winter and his now-deceased

---

[41] He often began engaging with a new issue because he was asked to present something to a group of denominational or other church mission leaders, yet built on the older thinking.

first wife, Roberta, who worked very closely with him. Not all of these can be taken into account, yet they should provide insight into his manner of processing and developing new ideas.

I will use the appropriate materials Winter produced to address the central research issues and to determine which issues are the core of his missiological work.

Interviews

Interviews will play a major role in this study. In part, this is because Winter was alive when this study began and his input offered a crucial reflection on his life and work. In addition, the reflections of his living peers, students, and family members also provide insight. These interviewees include his two brothers and other relatives; former colleagues and supervisors such as Arthur Glasser[42] and Charles Kraft; former students such as Glenn Schwartz; and fellow missionaries such as Ross Kinsler. Close friends and peers, and other mission leaders who co-founded organizations together with Winter or worked closely alongside him also reflect on his life and work. Some of my interviews engaged those who differed from Winter on important issues or approach, as well as those who served under him in the organizations he led. These include people such as Ted Ward, who was involved with TEE, and James Reapsome, who was the first editor of *EMQ* and who interacted with Winter with respect to many of his published articles during his years at Fuller.[43]

Various details from the interviews will be quoted or summarized and included where this supports or illuminates the central research issue. Where appropriate, I will include information that the interviewees felt relevant to their relationship with Winter, information that may be of interest to a current reader or future researcher, and information that provides context for Winter's life. My use of the interviews will be to clarify issues, history, and interpretations of events and relationships in order to determine which insights are significant and merit more attention in this work.

---

[42] Glasser was interviewed in February of 2005. He died December 8, 2009 at 94 years of age.

[43] Some of these "interviews" or clarifying questions may be done via email, and will be noted as such where appropriate.

The Writing of Others About Winter or His Ideas

While not all materials written about Winter or his endeavors can be included, materials will be consulted where possible and included where pertinent. Information in this category includes, for example, records or reports from field supervisors during Winter's time in Guatemala and journals or anecdotal reports from colleagues and fellow missionaries. This provides useful information about the Winters' field work, and successes or struggles with co-workers who approached the work differently. It may also help to verify other sources.

As noted, Winter's first wife, Roberta, wrote several biographical pieces about her husband or their work together. Others wrote responses to his documents or presentations, either in private correspondence or in published journals and periodicals.

David Bosch explored one of Winter's ideas in his book, *Witness to the World*. (Bosch, 1980) Bosch's concerns in the book relate to the theology of mission and, more specifically, what is mission, how does the church understand mission, and what is the relationship between mission and evangelism? (Bosch, 1980, ix-x) Bosch quoted from both Winter and Max Warren[44] in relation to the WCC meeting in Ghana. Both Winter and Warren were concerned about the WCC absorbing the International Missionary Council. Bosch wrote:

> Both Warren and Winter argue that structural anomalies—such as the fact that the IMC was made up of Western *missionary* organizations and the non-Western councils of *churches*—cannot simply be solved by means of yet another structural magic formula. In addition, the integration of the IMC into the WCC (Winter jokingly asks: 'Why did the WCC not integrate into the IMC?') in some respects produced the very thing against which Hoekendijk fought so passionately: the institutionalization of everything, the looking for solutions in structures, the imprisoning of the Holy Spirit. (Bosch, 1980, 180)

Later in the book, Bosch's writing resonates with a concern both he and Winter had for the mission of the church to reach out beyond its cultural borders.

---

[44] Max Warren (1904-1977) was the General Secretary of the Church Missionary Society from 1942-1963.

The (correct) observation that the Church is always in a missionary situation, may in specific circumstances lead to myopia, so that the Church remains busy only with her immediate neighbourhood and, as Ralph Winter puts it, forgets 'that 84 percent of all non-Christians are beyond the normal evangelistic range because (they are) outside of the cultural traditions of any national church anywhere in the world'...[45] (Bosch, 1980, 189)

Yet, from Bosch's perspective in South Africa, the idea of Church Growth seemed Western based, and the concept of the Homogeneous Unit Principle[46] to have extended racism and division in the church. Issues such as these will be considered in this study to the degree they influenced or were influenced by Winter.

Archives

In addition to considerable files Winter maintained throughout his life, primary source information in the following archives was utilized:

1. Lake Avenue Congregational Church, 393 North Lake Avenue, Pasadena, CA 91101, USA. This large and active church contains archives from the period under study, including Winter's time there as a teenager with his family, local/regional Christian Endeavor activities, and his time of service in Guatemala.
2. The Presbyterian Church USA (previously and at the time Winter served in Guatemala called the United Presbyterian Church in the USA), 425 Lombard Street, Philadelphia, PA 19147, USA.
3. The Billy Graham Center at Wheaton College, Wheaton, IL, 60187 USA.
4. The U.S. Center for World Mission, 1605 E. Elizabeth Street, Pasadena, California 91104 USA. Since the vast majority of

---

[45] He continued, "...and that the Mexico City slogan helps little to 'cut through the massive cocoon within which the churches of the world ... now live.'" It is not clear from Winter's paper *Ghana: Preparation for Marriage* what the "Mexico City slogan" is. The full sentence in Winter's paper is: "Only a renewed, contextualizing Pauline mission can possibly cut through the massive cocoon within which the churches of the world and almost all missionaries everywhere now live and move and have their being." (Winter, 1978)

[46] According to McGavran, a Homogeneous Unit is a section of society in which all members have some characteristics in common. McGavran strongly promoted the idea that people like to become Christians with other people who are like them.

his work was not published formally, this will include archival work in his library and personal files at the same location.

5. The William Carey International University, 1539 E Howard Street, Pasadena, CA 91104 USA. Currently, the Latourette Library archive contains the vast majority of Ralph and Roberta's books, files, and documents.

6. Fuller Theological Seminary, 135 N Oakland Avenue, Pasadena, California, 91182, USA.

Analysis

I will examine each item for its contribution to the central research issue and possible contribution to the research questions. I will give consideration to the major themes and arguments as they relate to Winter and his primary contributions, and will analyze his materials inductively to see the development of his thought as well as any recurring substantial themes. Then I will evaluate and interpret the meaning and significance of those themes to determine which were central to what Winter was engaged in. Hopefully, I will also be able to determine the importance to leaders today.

I will consider interviews for their insights into events and endeavors of Winter and those who knew him. These may be personal or professional observations. I will analyze various articles related to major issues of Winter's contribution with regard to intended audiences, (which journal and what audience, for example) theme(s), topics, reaction or responses, and, in turn, any further reply from Winter (or others).

I will consider Winter's endeavors (e.g. establishing William Carey Library) from the perspective of the problem Winter was attempting to solve (publishing students' theses at Fuller SWM) and his proposed solution (start a publishing house). I will examine how his solutions were implemented, who was involved, to what degree they were involved, assuming it is pertinent to the Central Research Issue and space allows.

Validity, Reliability and Verification

This form of biographical study relies on the experiences of the subject as told and interpreted by Winter himself, as well as on the experiences or impressions of Winter shared by others, including myself, both prior to and through the course of this study. As Creswell notes:

The meanings of these experiences are best given by the persons who experience them; thus, a preoccupation with method, validity, reliability, generalizability, and theoretical relevance of the biographical method must be set aside in favor of a concern for meaning and interpretation. (Creswell, 1998, 205)

Meaning and interpretation of events and experiences come from the subject and those with whom he interacts, as well as the biographer and the reader. I will use every effort to ensure that the findings are both reliable and valid by the use of multiple sources and, where possible, triangulation of data in order to improve the reliability and interpretation.

Theoretical triangulation involves the use of several different perspectives in the analysis of the same set of data. Denzin identifies it as that which involves analyzing the same data from different perspectives. (Denzin, 1970, 472) For example, where possible, I will compare claims from Winter about a specific situation in Guatemala with documents such as field reports written by supervisors. Adding a point from an interview with a third party might bring another angle from which to interpret the data. This should help to verify and validate the claims asserted initially by a single source.

To the degree possible, facts will be verified using published independent sources. For example, Winter presented a paper at the All-Asian Congress in 1973. There is a thesis written about that event, which should provide corroboration of or disputation of Winter's perspective on that event. Another source will be materials contained in the Presbyterian Archives, some of which are not written or seen by Winter but are about his experiences and relationships in Guatemala.

I will attempt to use original sources whenever possible.[47] In areas of general knowledge, I have sought acknowledged leaders in their respective fields. For example, related to evangelicalism and fundamentalism in the early- to mid-1900s, I have included Marsden, Carpenter, Noll and Bebbington. Related to the history of Guatemala, I have included the Oxford published scholar, Woodward, other scholarly materials, materials from the Presbyterian archives from that field, and popular sources such as *Time* magazine for the popular U.S. perspective on Guatemala at the time.

I will try to use multiple sources for individual topics whenever possible. For example, when Winter mentioned that Frank Laubach had a major impact on his life, I researched Laubach to verify who he was, where

---

[47] The majority of documents, Winter's writing, photographs, as well as digital recordings of interviews will be posted on: www.ralphdwinter.org

he worked, the issues that he wrote about, the things he accomplished, and how these may have had an impact on Winter. Since most if not all of those who influenced Winter when he was young are no longer alive, it will not be possible to corroborate all information from others who influenced him directly. Where a source is in question, it will be noted in the text or footnotes.

I will seek to quote or summarize from interviews in context, both to minimize misinterpretation and to bring diversity of communication styles to the work.

Working with and for Winter over 26 years may have both positive and negative impact on my study and writing. His way of approaching missiology was very familiar to me. I will work carefully to explain many of these concepts to those less familiar with them. I will attempt to provide detailed support for interpretations and conclusions, citing specific facts to support each where available. I will allow others to see my work and to identify perceived misunderstandings or misinterpretations, but I will not remove elements merely because someone found them unpleasant, (assuming they were well documented by reliable sources).

The data collection methods and sources will be clearly identified, and their value should be clear in the context. Others can verify the sources that are written or recorded. If other researchers arrive at other interpretations of the facts, these can give rise to a fruitful discussion which can further our understanding of Winter's life and contribution.

Summary

The purpose of this study is to uncover factors which contributed to the development of Ralph D. Winter's significant insights and which provided motivation for his endeavors, by chronicling the stages and influences in Winter's life and by analyzing his core missiology. I hope to show the relationships between the life, the writings, the work and the historical context of a substantial figure in twentieth century evangelical missions. I will seek to demonstrate in what follows the factors in his life that led to his significant contributions. I also analyze his core or early missiology. The written page, personal interviews, and archive materials will be the main sources of information. These will enable me to trace the development of Winter through his personal experiences in light of the times in which he lived. I have given an overview of the activities of his life and how they shaped him, or were shaped by him. Through his activities and writings the significance of his life becomes evident.

Chapter 2

Upbringing and Historical Setting

Introduction

The Protestant Religious Setting of Early 20th Century America

Prior to 1900, Protestant Christianity flourished in the U.S.A. "In the nineteenth century, before the modernist-fundamentalist battles split the Protestant house in two, conservative Protestantism enjoyed a remarkable public respectability, influence, and relevance."[1] (Smith and Emerson, 1998, 2) During much of the 1800s, broadly speaking, "evangelical Protestantism controlled almost all of the major denominations, along with their seminaries, divinity schools, missions boards, and other agencies." (Smith and Emerson, 1998, 3)

But that began to change because a "series of profound social, demographic and intellectual transformations began to challenge evangelical Protestantism's security, influence and relevance." (Smith and Emerson, 1998, 5) Towards the end of the 19th century it came under increasing pressure, both from internal conflict and external attack.[2] In general, evangelicals,[3] with sub-groups such as the fundamentalists,[4] were long past their "heyday" by the 1920s. Marsden notes that fundamentalists:

---

[1] Smith and Emerson continue: "Especially during the Victorian era, broadly evangelical Protestants were confident and engaged socially, culturally, politically, and intellectually. Indeed, they were *the* establishment." (Smith and Emerson, 1998,2)

[2] One major example is the Scopes Monkey Trial, which many saw as an attack on Christianity and the Bible as much if not more than on evolution. (Smith and Emerson, 1998, 6-7)

[3] Mark Noll (2003) argues that the core definition of evangelicalism during this particular time, which he calls the "rising" period of Edwards, Whitefield, and the Wesleys, included:
• Justification by faith instead of human works. • Defending the sole sufficiency of Christ for salvation and not human mediation. • Seeing Christ's death on the cross as a once-for-all act, not something that needed to be repeated (as in the Catholic mass). • Believing final authority is the Bible, which every believer should read rather than the Bible

...underwent a remarkable transformation in their relationship to the culture. Respectable "evangelicals" in the 1870s, by the 1920s they had become a laughingstock, ideological strangers in their own land. Their traditions, and the ways they maintained them, and the ways they modified them are all understood better in the context of this collective uprooting. (Marsden, 2006, x)

Marsden contends that this came because of a "profound ambivalence toward the surrounding culture." (Marsden, 2006, x) In many evangelical Christian circles, that reaction was due to the encroachment of modernism. An editorial in *The Atlantic Monthly* summarized the distinction between fundamental evangelicalism and modernism:

Contemporary American evangelicals trace their roots back to the fundamentalist-versus-modernist controversy of the early 20th century, still the key event in American Protestant history. The "modernists" incorporated the ideas of thinkers like Darwin into their theology, and revised their understanding of biblical authority to reflect new scholarly findings on how, by whom, and when the books of the Bible were written. Their beliefs became the foundation of the liberal or mainline Protestantism common today among many Methodists, Episcopalians, Congregationalists, and Presbyterians.

In the 1920s, marginalized fundamentalists (so called because they defended the "fundamental" tenets of classic Christian theology against modernist deviations) formed networks of believers and organizations committed to such doctrines as the literal inerrancy of the Bible. Over time, the fundamentalists split again. One group chose to remain "pure"—and as a result, it remained relatively small in size, and largely powerless. Another group—led by Billy Graham

---

as a means, which the priest interprets. • The priesthood of all believers, rather than inappropriate reliance on a class of priests ordained by the church.

[4] This paper uses the definition of Fundamentalism by Marsden: "Briefly, it was militantly antimodernist Protestant evangelicalism." He continued that they were "close to the traditions of the dominant American revivalist establishment of the nineteenth century, who in the twentieth century militantly opposed both modernism in theology and the cultural changes that modernism endorsed." (Marsden, 2006, 4). Also, "From the 1920s to the 1940s, to be a fundamentalist meant only to be theologically traditional, a believer in the fundamentals of evangelical Christianity and willing to take a militant stand against modernism." (Marsden, 1987, 10)

and known today as evangelicals—sought to preserve its orthodoxy while engaging with modern American life; it wanted an orthodoxy that could reach the masses.[5] (Mead, 2008, 24)

One example of the fundamentalist/modernist clash is the famous split at Princeton Theological Seminary[6] in 1929. Seminary president J. Ross Stevenson, who served from 1914 to 1936, felt the school should represent the breadth of the whole Presbyterian Church. As a result, four important faculty members left Princeton in a public division and started Westminster Theological Seminary.[7]

Some traditions, such as revivalism, pietism, the holiness movements, millenialism, Baptist traditionalism, and Reformed confessionalism were intertwined with fundamentalism.[8] (Marsden, 2006, 4)

In these early days, fundamentalists and less strident evangelicals were united in their opposition to modernism. This became coupled with a "retreat" from not only modernism within the church, but from society as well. This separation contributed to the development of a "Christian" subculture, which accelerated even more the divergence between these Christians and the rest of society.

Without a doubt, the Bible school was the dominant fundamentalist educational institution. Fundamentalists' tendency to reduce the church's mission to evangelism and

---

[5] Smith wrote, "Harold Ockenga, J. Elwin Wright, Wilbur Smith, Edward Carnell, Carl Henry, Harold Lindsell, Charles Fuller, Gleason Archer, Everett Harrison, Bernard Ramm, Billy Graham. These are just a few of the names of a group of mostly young, moderate fundamentalists who by the early 1940s had grown weary of their own tradition. After fifteen years of fundamentalist negativity and isolation, this growing network of restless evangelists, scholars, and pastors began to formulate a critique of their own fundamentalist subculture and a vision for its transformation." (Smith and Emerson, 1998) In 1942, some in this group helped to form a national association called the National Association of Evangelicals.

[6] There is no legal connection between Princeton University and Princeton Theological Seminary. They do, however, share faculty and are located next to each other.

[7] They were: Oswald T. Allis, PhD, DD, J. Gresham Machen, Robert Dick Wilson, PhD, and DD, DD, Cornelius Van Til, PhD. For more on a brief history of these transitions, see Richard Mouw's article in Fuller Theological Seminary's journal *Theology News and Notes*. (Mouw, 2007, 31-33)

[8] Among these groups, disagreements arose over issues such as how, if at all, they should relate to organizations that were seeking to integrate Christian fellowship on a broad geographic basis, such as with the National Council of Churches in the U.S. or with the World Council of Churches worldwide. The majority of fundamentalists generally responded to overtures with a clear "no," as did some other Christian sub-groups for their own reasons.

their premillennial urgency to get the job done predisposed them to favor the pragmatic, trade-school approach of Bible school training for their leaders over the more extensive and cosmopolitan approach of college and seminary education. (Carpenter, 1997, 18)

Carpenter also describes how they were "dispossessed" from the colleges and seminaries of their own denominations, where those with liberal theological views held control. Many of these internal battles stemmed from the core issue of how Scripture is viewed and interpreted, as noted above. They believed that properly understood, with the entire Bible in view as the context, Scripture is God's Word for eternity, even if it reflects the culture and perspective of the human authors. Most evangelicals believe Isaiah 40:8 applies to the whole of the Bible, not merely to Isaiah: "The grass dries up, the flowers wither, but the word of our God stands forever."

The growing difference in perspective fueled debates within conservative Christian circles as well. Issues central to these debates included: the person and work of Christ and to what degree it is important to one's life, end time prophecy timelines, and the importance of spreading the gospel message in North America and around the world. Whatever the issues, the need to cling to a particular persuasion was felt, schools, seminaries, and denominations were formed to separate from those deemed in error.

During the 1930s and 1940s, this tension proved to be creative, allowing fundamentalists to establish their identity, consolidate an institutional network, and rethink their mission to America. Ironically, they were freed by their defeats in the antimodernist controversies to concentrate on these more positive tasks. While they were predicting the world's imminent demise, and building a subculture to protect themselves from worldly society, fundamentalists were also retooling their evangelistic techniques and seizing upon inviting cultural trends to mount a renewed public presence. Their goals were time-honored evangelical ones: to bring revival to America and the gospel to the world. (Carpenter, 1997, xxi)

The idea of spreading God's Word around the world through missionary work had been a foundational motivation to Christians in the nineteenth century.

Historically Shaping Concepts: Evangelism vei Social Action

As the desire to evangelize the world came to be a focus, a new debate arose, characterized by "evangelism versus social gospel" or social action. Since around 1900 in the west, the idea of the "social gospel" grew in part out of the work of Charles Sheldon. His books *In His Steps* (Sheldon, 1897) and *The Reformer* (Sheldon, 1902) raised the issue to a popular level. Sheldon asked how being a Christian should make a difference in one's reaction to social issues such as poverty and injustice. Sheldon popularized the phrase "What would Jesus do?" in the book, *In His Steps*, just over a century ago.[9]

For many fundamentalists, the "evangelism versus social gospel" debate that continued into the 1960s and beyond gave another reason to retreat from the world. Instead, they focused on the tasks of being true to the Bible (from their perspective) and outreach. Because liberals increasingly claimed social issues as their own domain in the nineteenth century, fundamentalists increasingly pursued the "winning of souls" or evangelism and missions outreach around the world as the neglected commission of the church. There were, however, many within evangelicalism who engaged in the debate on this issue.[10] Donald McGavran wrote, in the popular magazine, *World Vision Magazine*:

> It is theoretically possible that if the Church were to manifest great concern for social justice and were to redeem some section of society from its bounds, notable growth of the Church would follow. This, however, is not what one usually finds. The social reformations in England did not give rise to the Baptist and Methodist churches. It was the other way around. (McGavran, 1965b, 26)

Because the "evangelism versus social gospel" issue was seen as rooted in one's view of the Bible, it was not quickly resolved. In *The Great Reversal*, David O. Moberg attempted to delineate clearly the issues on both sides to bridge what he perceived as the shortcomings of his own

---

[9] In an article in *Theology Today* evaluating the historical impact of this book, the author noted that, "According to Ralph Gabriel, it did for the 'Social Gospel' movement what T. S. Arthur's *Ten Nights in a Bar Room* and Harriet Beecher Stowe's *Uncle Tom's Cabin* did for the temperance and anti-slavery movements."[9] (Smylie, 1975, 32)

[10] Two especially relevant to this study are Carl F. H. Henry who wrote *The Uneasy Conscience of Modern Fundamentalism* (Henry, 1947) and Donald McGavran who edited a discussion on this topic within mission circles entitled *Eye of the Storm: The Great Debate in Missions.* (McGavran, 1972c)

31

background within evangelicalism. In fact, it is still unresolved in certain circles.[11] (Moberg, 1972)

So, evangelicalism fragmented beginning in the 1920s and early 1930s. They saw modernism continuing to grow in influence on the church and threaten the evangelical view of biblical authority. Fundamentalism decided to separate from any "Christians" who did not hold to their views. In the late 1930s and 1940s, some felt that the only "voice" of evangelicals was from individual pastors or ministry leaders. Yet soon, there were some evangelicals who sought to work together. The National Association of Evangelicals was founded in 1942 to be a voice that sought to engage non-Evangelicals on issues. J. Elwin Wright of the New England Fellowship was the driving force bringing together several known leaders.[12]

The Social Setting in the Mid-1900s in the Western U.S.

The boom of the 1920s was followed by the great depression in the 1930s. The halting of growth and increase in poverty brought a number of global transitions. The U.S. was drawn into World War Two (WWII) as was much of the Western world as well as part of Asia and North Africa. The war transformed a generally depressed U.S. culture and economy, bringing with it resolve and commitment, which was later translated into vibrant growth after 1950.

In some ways the war broke down the barriers intentionally or unintentionally erected by some evangelicals between their sub-culture and the U.S. and, indeed, world culture in general. Following the war many felt drawn back into the wider world they had experienced through the war, in order to serve its people. Among other activities they founded new mission agencies, which focused on parts of the world where they had seen needs.[13]

---

[11] Within some fundamental circles, there is little room for "social work" even as a method for gaining the opportunity to be able to share gospel truth.

[12] From the NAE history found at: http://www.nae.net/about-us/history/62 accessed on November 2, 2009. Two of those involved in the early stages of the formation of the NAE were Charles E. Fuller (1887–1968) and Harold Ockenga (1905-1985), both of whom were intimately involved in the beginning of Fuller Theological Seminary in 1947. They intersect with Winter's life as noted below.

[13] Organizations such as Far Eastern Gospel Crusade and Overseas Crusades began during this period, and engaged in ministries that reflected the conservative evangelical perspective of the need to share the gospel with those who had not heard it clearly in their own culture. These groups were not thinking of the crusades between Islam and Christianity, but about evangelistic meetings, also called crusades, such as Billy Graham and

Many young men, who had "seen the world," returned from WWII and settled in the American West.[14] They were starting out their lives and were drawn either to California's entrepreneurial spirit or to the opportunities that it created.

Winter's Family Background

Father: Hugo Winter

Ralph Winter's father, Hugo Winter, was born on July 18, 1895, in Southern California. Hugo was a self-taught civil engineer and respected civic and church leader. He was the son of a butcher in Los Angeles who had emigrated from Eastern Germany in the 1860s. They settled briefly in the San Diego area, but soon thereafter moved to the Boyle Heights area southeast of Los Angeles. Hugo was the youngest of three children and the best educated: he was able to finish his education at a polytechnic High School. He volunteered to join the army, where he thrived, serving in Belgium and France during World War One. He stayed in the Army reserve after the war, rising to the position of captain. Paul, his oldest son, remembered his father telling positive stories from his experiences and teaching him some of the rousing songs sung in the barracks.[15]

When he returned from the war, Hugo went to work in engineering. Soon after returning from the war, he began working with the city of Los Angeles as a mechanical draftsman. The family later settled in South Pasadena when Ralph, Hugo's middle son, was a young boy.

Hugo worked his way up the chain of command in the field of civil engineering in the L.A. Planning Department. Although he had never gone to college, Hugo took classes, taught himself, and became an instructor part-time at the University of Southern California School of Engineering. In 1936, when Ralph was twelve years old, Hugo was the

---

others began in the 1940s. Most of these agencies changed their names later, in recognition of the offense of the word "crusades" to Muslims, Jews and others.

[14] My own family reflects this trend. My father and his sister and her husband moved from Massachusetts to California during this time, my aunt and uncle coming independently of my father. My father had served in the Navy and my uncle in the Army toward the end of WWII.

[15] Interview with Paul Winter by the author on July 27, 2005, 1. Paul was Ralph Winter's older brother. Transcripts and/or digital audio files are available for all interviews, unless noted otherwise, such as notes from a personal discussion. They will be posted at www.ralphdwinter.org

head of the bridge department for the City of Los Angeles. Later he was the lead in the effort to get agreement on the routes of the freeway system in the greater L.A. area among the almost 80 cities and unincorporated towns.[16]

He was a quiet man, and people knew he was diligent, faithful, and honest more because of his actions than his words. He had a solid work ethic, which characterized many immigrants and their families during that period in U.S. history. Having come to Christian faith at a Billy Sunday[17] meeting, he was very involved in church, and was a stabilizing influence in both his home and church.[18] Ralph could not remember ever seeing his father becoming angry or arguing with Hazel, his mother.[19]

Mother: Hazel Patterson Winter

Hazel Clare Patterson, born December 25, 1894, was the daughter of an engineer whose job was to oversee the construction of icehouses for a company based in Chicago, where she was born. They moved around with her father's job, with her father spending two years each setting up ice storage facilities.

She attended college but did not graduate, much to her disappointment. Hazel, too, was a solid Christian, yet the opposite of Hugo in many ways. Hazel was outgoing, affectionate, and emotional. She may also have been the more intelligent of the two.[20] She was very involved in church throughout her life. She and Hugo met at a Christian Endeavor

---

[16] When Hugo retired in the 1950s, no one had the depth and breadth of relationships he had been able to establish with his peers in so many cities around the L.A. area. To enable the LA Planning Department to continue to leverage those relationships for the freeway projects underway, the Metropolitan Transportation Engineering Board was created. Specifically, it enabled Hugo to continue to draw together the diverse engineering expertise and contribute a sense of common engineering vision to the work, which he did for ten years.

Ironically, South Pasadena, where Hugo and Hazel lived most of the rest of their lives, was the only city that did not agree on the route of the freeway system in the greater L.A. area. Hugo worked with more than 70 cities, but as of 2011, the city has continued to block the completion of a major freeway (known as 710) through their city limits.

[17] Billy Sunday, 1862-1935, was an evangelistic preacher known for a flamboyant style. He turned down a lucrative baseball career after he was saved, and also later turned down a $1 million movie contract (worth approximately $13 million or £7.5 million in 2011) because he did not want to disrupt his preaching. See http://www.billysunday.org

[18] Interview with Paul Winter by the author on July 27, 2005, 2.

[19] Interview with Ralph Winter by the author on July 31, 2005, 2.

[20] Interview with Paul Winter by the author on July 27, 2005, 2.

(CE)[21] youth camp sponsored by the Presbyterian Church in Hollenbeck Heights. Roberta reflected on Hazel by noting:

> This was a time when the women's suffrage movement was struggling in Washington D.C. for the right for women to vote, yet his mother was already the statewide president in Arizona for the co-ed Christian Endeavor Movement. For the rest of her life she always insisted that in her presence the role of women must never be denigrated, whether it had to do with their intelligence, their driving ability, or their leadership ability. (Winter, 2000, 2)

They married on January 1, 1913.[22] They had the solid, stable life and marriage Hazel had wanted, in contrast to the regular moves she had experienced in her childhood. Hazel was thankful that the boys could grow up and remain in the same home. Much of the stability came from Hugo's strong, steady, consistent life, which set the tone for his three sons: Paul, Ralph and David.[23]

The Boys

Paul

Paul was born in July of 1922. By his own admission, while he and Ralph had many traits and interests in common, he was not as inventive as Ralph. Paul's creativity was seen, however, in his approach to his work as a civil engineer. Paul became the engineer of choice when designers had unusual structural features to support in large buildings. Several of the projects he worked on had unique architectural features, which were later used as example for other engineers. During his career, he worked in SE Asia because he, his wife, and another couple sailed the Pacific Ocean

---

[21] See below for more on Christian Endeavor.

[22] According to a speech by Ralph Winter at a staff retreat, July 10, 2007, they were also "members" of the China Inland Mission (now called OMF International) monthly prayer meetings, which often took place in their home. J. Hudson Taylor founded the China Inland Mission in 1865, and emphasized prayer and establishing prayer groups.

[23] Ralph had the same home phone number from the time he was two until he was 72. Ralph was away from that home during portions of his studies, military and missionary service. After he came back from the mission field, his father gave their home to Ralph and his family. In 1996, when his first wife, Roberta, was diagnosed with cancer, they sold the South Pasadena home and moved closer to the ministry headquarters they founded and where they served in Pasadena.

together, stopping for breaks and working to fund the ongoing trip. During that time, he worked as an engineer in Japan, New Zealand and the Hawaiian Islands. At other times he worked in Iran and Afghanistan. After he no longer needed to work, he continued to "volunteer" at Caltech for one dollar per year in exchange for a desk and daily office hours up until late 2007, when he officially retired at age 85.[24]

Paul died just a few months after Ralph in late 2009. At his memorial, his son noted that Paul:

> …was a planner; an analyzer. A profound and deliberate thinker. Someone who, even after he solved a problem, turned it over in his mind, looking for other solutions, for confirmation, for errors, for other ways of solving the problem. Sometimes this can be mistaken for worrying, perhaps unnecessarily, but I think it's part of a simultaneously creative and reductive process which aids in the solution of difficult problems, particularly those with human or other unquantifiable aspects.[25]

Ralph

Ralph Dana Winter was born on December 7, 1924 in Los Angeles, California. He was the middle son and his birth was difficult on Hazel. He was small in stature, and suffered what he called "normal" fever convulsions as a young child.[26] He liked being alone. He was a very intense person with perfectionist tendencies. He enjoyed building model airplanes, some of which had engines and won flying contests. It was something he worked at carefully and he was good at it.[27] Paul and Ralph were close in age and shared the quiet introversion of their father. Ralph remembered having to walk home using an indirect path to avoid the school bully. He was a bit bored with English class in elementary school.[28]

---

[24] Interview with Paul Winter by the author on July 27, 2005, 8,11.

[25] From a transcript of comments by Eric Winter from the November 21, 2009 memorial service. Retained in an email from Tim Lewis to Greg Parsons, November 29, 2009.

[26] Winter's understanding later in life was that four out of five boys have "fever seizures" but grow out of them. February 12, 2009 email from Ralph D. Winter to the author, 1.

[27] Interview with Ralph Winter by the author on August 2, 2006, 6-7.

[28] Interview with Ralph Winter by the author on July 31, 2006, 13-14. In Junior High, he remembered when the junior high principal came onto the campus with a gun and shot and killed five other teachers, including one of Ralph's favorites, a science teacher. Ralph heard this but he was in a different classroom.

Perhaps as a precursor to both of them becoming engineers, he and Paul also enjoyed planning activities and playing together. One annual opportunity for planning came each year when a fireworks catalog arrived. They would add up their allowance and savings to figure out how to get as much as they could from the dollar or two they had, or how to get "as much bang for their buck" as possible—quite literally![29] Occasionally plans went awry, such as the year when their calculations were a little off and an explosion led to Ralph's eyebrows being singed.[30] Ralph worked at any project or activity he put his mind to with diligence. Paul described him as "very competitive and whatever he did, he really had the ability of seeing right through to the basic principles," and this was true of projects in many areas of life. [31]

Ralph also worked at various small jobs. He worked a paper route and delivered the *Saturday Evening Post*. At Christmas one year, he sold Christmas cards door-to-door. He remembers that he started out asking people, "Do you want to buy some Christmas cards?" and they would all politely say "No, thank you." So he rethought his approach and changed it to, "Would you like to see some Christmas cards?" to which everyone said "Yes," and sales ensued.[32]

Younger brother David remembered discussions around the table:

> Ralph was deeply curious about life. He was an experimenter and inventor. He was constantly making something work better than it did—homemade firecrackers, for instance, which practically killed him. He always had a better way to do it. There was hardly anything he didn't think he could improve. (Stafford, 1984, 16)

Ralph came to Christ when a "chalk talk"[33] evangelist somehow was allowed into the Sunday School of the liberal Presbyterian church in Highland Park.[34] (Winter, 2003a, 1) He later confirmed this at a CE

---

[29] Interview with Ralph Winter by the author on August 14, 2006, 4.

[30] Later, in another venture, they saved their allowance for months and received an additional six-month's advance and were able to purchase a wood lathe. They used this to fashion all kinds of wooden bowls and spindles.

[31] Interview with Paul Winter by the author on July 27, 2005, 5.

[32] Interview with Ralph Winter by the author on July 31, 2006, 12.

[33] A "chalk talk" merely meant that the presenter used a chalkboard to diagram and illustrate their points.

[34] Winter seemed to be hinting that the church would not have wanted to allow connections with any "evangelist."

conference at the Long Beach Civic Auditorium. He described his own pilgrimage this way:

> I was born into a devout Christian family, which is one of the most important things in my whole life. My parents were loyal to the local church and loyal to Christian Endeavor, which was a very evangelistic global youth movement (and still is). I gave my life to Christ at about the age of ten, and began sporadically to read through a little Gospel of John. Later at Lake Avenue Church my Sunday School teacher one summer challenged his class of seventh grade boys to read in the New Testament a chapter a day. This had a remarkable effect on me.[35]

He continued, talking about the impact of the verses he noticed later as he read the Bible seriously for the first time:

> ...Verses like these were meat sticking to my ribs. That summer I was really moved by the Bible. That very same summer (between my tenth and eleventh year of high school) I got a job... The first thing I bought with my first paycheck was the most expensive leather bound Scofield Reference Bible available. (1)

Paul remembers Ralph always took his commitments seriously. He described Ralph as, "being from somewhere else," meaning he was different and would think and act in counter-intuitive ways from those around him. Ralph did not feel compelled to be like everyone else. He was certainly not one for conventional thinking or going along with the crowd. At one time he had the idea that every Christian should learn to play the piano so they could accompany someone singing on a moment's notice. But instead of learning to play from a teacher, Ralph went to the library, checked out books on piano theory and basic chords, and taught himself to play. He repeated this pattern of "self-teaching" many times throughout his life.

David

David Winter, born on September 15, 1930, was six years younger than Ralph. Because Ralph's delivery had been especially hard on Hazel, the doctors warned her against having any more children. But when they

---

[35] From Winter's writing file, this is a manuscript for a talk he gave called: "Growing Up with the Bible: Understanding What It Says, Yielding To What It Means" 2005, 1. Writing file number W1345B.3.

were a bit older, Ralph and Paul prayed each night for a little brother. Presumably Hugo and Hazel heard their sons' prayers and, whether for that reason or for others, later decided to have one more child.

David did not participate in the same activities as the older boys because he was so much younger than his next oldest brother. He remembered that Ralph was very thoughtful and purposeful with him. He would "really work hard to come up with something that would mean something special to me" at birthdays or Christmas.[36]

When he was in High School, he remembered when Ralph and another young man were working with the youth group at church that year.[37] They had heard about the RSV version of the Bible and were, "convinced that our generation would profit from the Bible in the contemporary language...what did they do? ... [They] got the money someplace bought a brand new copy of the RSV for every H.S. student in the church. It was transformational. I could hardly stop reading it I was so excited."[38]

He followed his own interests into the field of education. After graduating from the University of California with both a BA and an MA in anthropology, he added a PhD in anthropology and sociology from Michigan State University. David served as the President of Whitworth College in Spokane, Washington.[39] His main service was to Westmont College in Santa Barbara, where he served as President from 1976 until 2001, and again as Interim President for the 2006 to 2007 academic year. He remains President Emeritus.[40]

During Ralph's memorial service, David remembered Ralph challenging him on his life direction:

> When I was just starting college, my first year, I was not doing something dangerous but I was just sort of drifting and he [Ralph] saw that, and he came to me and said 'Dave you are just messing around. You need to get away from here. You need to leave family and friends and have an adventure, an experience, and I know just what you should do,' as he usually

---

[36] Comments made by David Winter at Ralph Winter's memorial, June 28, 2009.

[37] This was probably Dan Fuller, who is introduced later.

[38] Comments made by David Winter at Ralph Winter's memorial, June 28, 2009. Winter later used the Living Bible to encourage reading for his daughters when they were teenagers.

[39] It is now a University.

[40] As of this writing in 2011. Beyond the boundaries of Westmont he also served on many accreditation teams with the Western Association of Schools and Colleges, the regional accrediting association for the west coast and Guam.

did... He said, 'You need to go to Prairie Bible Institute.' This was in Three Hills Alberta Canada, and the three hills were about all that was there. I didn't even hesitate. He was very persuasive and I was also intimidated by his vision, his ideas. I just went. It absolutely changed my life. I came back from that year a different person. I would have never done that except for Ralph.[41]

Additional Major Influences Before College

Early Church Experience

When she was young, her family provided comfortably for Hazel. She, Hugo, and the boys were a committed part of the Presbyterian Church in Highland Park, which had all kinds of social events and was considered a "high-brow" college-professor-type congregation. Yet Hazel was not enamored with high-society "culture." The family members were all involved in numerous events in the church, but Hazel was not happy with the kind of attitudes that she saw displayed at many of the church functions. She often reminded her sons that learning to be "cultured" in the sense they saw displayed at church was no achievement whatsoever. Still, as a family they were committed to their church, regardless of the occasional disappointment, and were faithfully involved in many of its activities.[42]

Christian Endeavor

Beyond a strong sense of faithfulness and commitment, the main reason they continued to attend the Presbyterian Church in Highland Park was because of a youth program called Christian Endeavor. When Hazel attended college in Arizona, she had served as the President of the CE State Union.[43]

Christian Endeavor started in 1881. Founded by Francis E. Clark in Maine as the Young People's Society of Christian Endeavor, CE is a youth ministry, providing a solid foundation in both Christianity and leadership. The program was student led, requiring adult sponsors to be involved, but

---

[41] Comments made by David Winter at Ralph Winter's memorial, June 28, 2009.

[42] Interview with Ralph Winter by the author on July 31, 2006, 8.

[43] As previously noted, Hugo and Hazel had met at a CE meeting at a Presbyterian Church in Hollenbeck Heights.

the adults remained in the background of the weekly meetings, thus encouraging the young people in the group to plan and lead the meetings. The CE movement steadily grew, and at their twenty-fifth anniversary in 1906, there were 67,000 groups with participation estimates ranging up to four million.[44]

Crucial to CE was the commitment participants had to make, affirmed in a simple pledge:

> Trusting in the Lord Jesus Christ for strength, I promise Him that I will strive to do whatever He would like to have me do; that I will make it the rule of my life to pray and to read the Bible every day, and to support the work and worship of my own church in every way, especially by attending all her regular Sunday and mid-week services, unless prevented by some reason which I conscientiously give to my Saviour:[45] and that just so far as I know how, throughout my whole life, I will endeavour to lead a Christian life.[46] (Clark, 1903, 26)

Training in service is how an Endeavorer learns to live out four principles:

1. Confession of Christ (Romans 10:9)
2. Service in Christ's Church (John 12:26)
3. Loyalty to Christ's Church (Romans 12:4, 5)
4. Fellowship with Christ's people (1 John 1: 3, 7)[47]

(Clark, 1903, 26)

CE was very strong in the Los Angeles area. Almost every year from the late 1920s into the 1950s there were city, county and/or statewide gatherings in the various regions. Planning and leading these meetings gave Ralph and his friends great leadership experience.[48]

A few years after making the basic commitment to Christ, Ralph's life was "turned around into an intense commitment" which involved and was then fueled by memorizing 500 verses in the Bible during a period both before and after enlistment in the Navy. All of a sudden, he was no longer interested in making model airplanes. He was, as he often said later, captured by "the expulsive power of a new affection."[49] (Winter, 2003a, 1)

---

[44] See: http://www.christianendeavor.com/ under "About us" accessed on February 23, 2009.

[45] Later versions included here: to tell others the good news of Jesus Christ.

[46] This is a reprint of the 1903 edition of this book.

[47] A later version added the verse references.

[48] Interview with Ralph Winter by the author on August 2, 2006, 3.

[49] This is the correct spelling of this word. It is not "explosive."

Lake Avenue Congregational Church

Though normally the kind of people who would remain devoted to one church, Hugo and Hazel felt compelled to leave Highland Park Presbyterian Church when, in about 1935, the denomination decided to run its own regional programs for youth on the same nights as the CE program. This effectively ended the CE program in their church. Lake Avenue Congregational Church was one nearby that had one of the strongest CE programs in the region. It was a hard decision for Hugo and Hazel, but they felt compelled to meet the needs of their two older sons who were in the program. The Winter family joined the LACC on May 8, 1940.[50]

LACC had connections with a broad range of ministries, some of them with nationwide connections. Charles E. Fuller headed one of those ministries and also attended LACC. Fuller led and hosted one of the most popular radio programs on the air at the time. In 1942 and 1943 his nationwide radio broadcasts *The Pilgrim Hour* and especially *The Old Fashioned Revival Hour* were on the Mutual Broadcasting System, and had audiences surpassing in size those of the most popular secular shows, including Bob Hope and Charlie McCarthy. (Fuller, 1972, 149-152)

Harold Ockenga, Pastor of the Park Street Church in Boston, was also a regular at LACC. Park Street and LACC were like sister churches, and Ockenga was to play a crucial role in the establishment of the seminary Charles Fuller would start about six years after the Winters began attending LACC. The church had many well-known Christian leaders come through and speak, and also sent out many missionaries.[51]

James Henry Hutchins, the senior pastor of LACC during that time, was not known as a great teacher or preacher, but he was a solid pastor and he really built the church.[52] He was thrilled to see the youth involved in

---

[50] Ralph would turn 16 later that year.

[51] A large percentage of their budget, sometimes as much as fifty percent, went to missions. The church sent out a number of classmates and students near Ralph's age as missionaries. Some of the missionaries that LACC sent out during this time included Al Kline, a roommate of Ralph's at Caltech, who went to Taiwan as a missionary; Ernie and Barbara Behr, who also went to Taiwan; Phyllis Chamberlain, who went to Japan; Cyril and Francis Faulkner, who went to China; Dale and Harriet Kietzman, who went to Brazil with Wycliffe/SIL; and David Woodward, the LACC missionary with the longest involvement in one area, who worked with Tibetans and was still involved with them to some degree as late as 2006, though living in the U.S. According to an interview with Ralph Winter by the author on August 14, 2006, 2.

[52] Interview with Paul Winter by the author on July 27, 2005, 3.

various activities, and was passionate to send them around the world as missionaries.[53] Hutchins regularly taught that Christ could return at any time, which injected a sense of urgency.[54]

When Ralph was just starting college at Caltech, he went to Oaxaca Mexico on a short-term visit with others from LACC. The group visited different missionaries, and Ralph began to see what missionaries actually do. That trip, as well as the many Sunday night missions speakers at the church, "made an indelible impression on Ralph, and permanently turned his attention to the mission cause." (Winter, 2000, 2)

In 1959, when Ralph was 34 years old and serving in Guatemala, he wrote a letter to Dr. Hutchins, expressing his indebtedness to Dr. Hutchins and reflecting his inner self-perception. "I think that it is unquestionable that no man outside of my father has had a greater influence and blessing, living or dead. The Bible itself is made alive by lives today. And yours, Dr. Hutchins, has been the foremost." Winter mentioned Hutchins' counsel, lending him books to counter "rationalistic Bible courses at Caltech" and a pen Hutchins gave Ralph expressing a desire to see Ralph "write many fine sermons…." Ralph continued, "I did not turn out to be any great producer of sermons. But you, Dr. Hutchins, yourself have taught me that a ministry is much, much more than the writing of sermons. Yet I do pray that writing will continue in some ways and various ways to be in my life a means of bringing glory to the Name above every name." Winter closed the letter, expressing regret at, "the cycles of unrest and confusion through which my life went, and the degree to which they were disturbances in the life of the church. These were in no way something for which you were responsible! I only seek to know and do His will."[55]

The Navigators

Ralph Winter's closest connection with the Fuller family was Dan Fuller, the only son of Charles and Grace (Payton). Ralph and Dan met in high school and both of them had been involved in CE.[56] Their spiritual

---

[53] Ralph remembered one high school Sunday school teacher who led the class in a study of the Abrahamic covenant, which Ralph thought at the time would not be interesting, but which turned out to be very stimulating.

[54] Interview with Ralph Winter by the author on August 2, 2006, 3.

[55] August 8, 1959 letter from Ralph D. Winter to Dr. and Mrs. Hutchins, 1.

[56] In fact, Dan's father had been the President of the CE chapter in Orange County. (Fuller, 1972, 45)

lives began to change even more when they became part of a Bible study group called Dunamis—based on the Greek word dunamis meaning power or might.[57] Dunamis was a high school age ministry started by a group named the Navigators, or "Navs" for short. This was another ministry the Winters became connected with through their involvement at LACC.

> Dunamis meetings included hearty singing of choruses, oral checkout on memory, and reports on the weekly assignment, called TnT for Trust 'n Tackle. Reports could be only "complete" or "failed" with no partial successes acknowledged. Then followed a Bible study discussion and a challenge by the leader, sometimes a personal evangelism clinic, the meeting ending with a salute 'All for Christ!' (Skinner, 1974, 142)

So the Dunamis groups met in homes with a handful of young men in each. Dan Fuller encouraged Ralph and his brother Paul to join the group, which was held in the Winter home for the next three years or so. Lorne Sanny led the group. This is when Ralph learned 500 verses and Dan learned about 1,000 during his somewhat longer involvement with the Navigators and Dunamis. Another young man involved in the group was Richard (or Dick) Soderberg. Dick was an outgoing high school student body president who was respected by the church and the family.[58]

The Winters' home was at 533 Hermosa Street in South Pasadena, about one mile from the first headquarters of the Navigators. The ministry began in the 1930s and was officially incorporated in 1943. The main ministry began as an outreach to Navy sailors at ports in Long Beach California. All of the Navigator ministries from the military to high school and college men and women were seeking to take the Bible seriously, both in interpretation and in application to daily life. They were interested in accountability to the disciplines they believed a Christian should be involved in including Bible study and specific application to life each day. You had to be prepared to share your progress in each of these areas each week with the group.[59]

The founder, Dawson Trotman, had a heart to share the gospel and was an engaging speaker.[60] Both Ralph and Paul remembered hearing him

---

[57] Interview with Daniel Fuller by the author on March 7, 2005, 1.

[58] He would later be involved with Ralph in a global project in Afghanistan.

[59] Interview with Ralph Winter by the author on August 2, 2006, 5.

[60] Dawson Trotman was the founder of the Navigators. He died prematurely, in 1956, while successfully saving a girl who had fallen out of a boat. He did not make it. The second leader was Lorne Sanny, who everyone believed was the natural person to take over. Lorne

speak. Ralph noted that he "was a very very compelling speaker. He didn't ever have an outline. He never had any consecutive order to what he said. But he always said things that were very challenging and inspiring." Trotman would often accent his message with a memorable saying, which pushed toward deeper commitment, such as, "You can go into a Christian bookstore and buy a Bible that has all the promises tinted in blue, but you can't buy one that has all the difficult commands tinted in blue!" or "If you can't see very far ahead, go ahead as far as you can see" or "Always ask yourself why you are doing what you are doing the way you are doing it." The last two became mottos Ralph used in his own life and with others.[61]

While this kind of speaking may be considered folksy or trite, at the time, from the perspective of Ralph and Dan, Trotman was challenging them to think outside their own cultural, traditional, and mental framework when it came to spiritual matters. They were not interested in a Christianity that was for Sundays only. Trotman's approach may have been attractive to Ralph because he reflected some aspects of the non-traditional Ralph tended to think himself.[62]

With their newfound interest in taking Christ and His word seriously, Dan and Ralph also became students of revivals to see the impact of believers who had walked before them and who were also serious about their faith. Later, when they were both at Fuller Theological Seminary during its first year, they would study a particular revival and type up a summary of what happened and pass it out at every door of LACC, to encourage the church towards revival. They were "quite a pair" with their interest in this subject, but Ralph remembered that it was a bit

---

led the ministry of the Navigators for 30 years, seeing their vision broaden beyond the Military work to college campuses and their staff grew from 171 in a dozen countries, to 2580 in 71 countries. In 2007, according to their web site, they have more than 4,000 staff in 110 countries working with some 214 different people groups in 161 languages (www.navigators.org).

[61] Interview with Ralph Winter by the author on August 2, 2006, 3-4.

[62] As his brother noted previously, Ralph was always seeking to improve how something was done, whether it was a project that needed an engineer's perspective, or his own spiritual walk, or reaching out to the world. Ralph explained, "Even more influential than reading one chapter a day for my Sunday School class was my encounter with Dan Fuller and becoming part of a little Lake Ave Church Navigators 'Dunamis' group which met at my house for three years running right up to Pearl Harbor in December of 1941 and the second World War. Both before that and during the WWII I memorized 500 verses in the King James Version (of course), shading in each verse in my treasured Scofield Bible." (Winter, 2005, 1)

disconcerting to the pastors and professors, who were also interested in other subjects.[63] Dan recalled:

> Ralph Winter felt that the great impediment to foreign missions was the nominalism of Lake Avenue Church and every other church as far as he was concerned. So he started us all studying the history of revivals. And seeing these histories of revivals I think that confirmed in me that something was radically wrong with Lake Avenue, Covenant theology, Reform theology.[64]

Perhaps the biggest reason Ralph and Dan were such good friends was that they were growing in their faith together. Ralph felt, "Dan was a very very serious believer …he is probably the most conscientious believer I have ever met."[65]

Ali Asghar

LACC family friend, Dick Soderberg introduced the Winter family to Ali Asghar, who was from Afghanistan. Dick made initial contact with Ali, and Ali lived with the Winter family in South Pasadena for six months. Ralph described their on-going relationship as, "…fine fellowship – if at time perplexing – through eight years with a keen foreign student from Afghanistan."[66]

Ali was more of a communist than a Muslim in ideology. Initially, he was in favor of the USSR's taking over of Afghanistan, until he saw how they devastated the country and its people. During his time with Ralph and the family, he became a vivid example to Ralph of how someone from the outside looks at church and Christianity. Ralph noted of Ali that, "He was not impressed with the superficialities of Islam, and he was not impressed by the superficialities of evangelicalism, either. He could see right through anything."[67]

Later, Ali "followed" Ralph to Cornell and majored in engineering. Ralph remembered the long talks he, Ali and Roberta had on Sunday afternoon over a meal cooked the way Ali liked it. The discussion was often about what was wrong with Afghanistan, and Ali seemed to disagree

---

[63] Interview with Ralph Winter by the author on August 2, 2006, 12.

[64] Interview with Daniel Fuller by the author on March 7, 2005, 7.

[65] Interview with Ralph Winter by the author on August 2, 2006, 9.

[66] *Shoptalk,* May 18, 1959, a newsletter from the Winters to churches interested in their missionary work, 1.

[67] Interview with Ralph Winter by the author on August 7, 2006, 11.

with all of the other students from that nation who were at Cornell. Ralph and Ali were good friends, but, as Ralph noted, "we just didn't agree on anything whatsoever."[68] Later Ali, who was afraid to return to Afghanistan, migrated to Canada and worked as an engineer, and the family lost touch with him.

For Ralph, Ali brought a broader perspective on issues he had only seen at a distance up to that point. The relationship undoubtedly fed into Ralph's interest in Afghanistan, but even more his interest in understanding cultural differences and their importance in relating to people from different backgrounds.

Summary

The background and character of their parents provided the setting within which the Winter boys could grow and mature. Their upbringing and location on the west coast created an environment that an open-minded spirit could thrive in. At first, Ralph tended to be quiet and a loner. However, the influence of his brother and a solid church fellowship helped balance his natural inclination to withdraw. His family grounded him seriously in the basic Christian lifestyle, and later the CE program and the Navigators exposed him to accountability, high-level commitment, and discipline. Together, these factors shifted Ralph's sense of purpose and calling. His mother's perspective on church during Ralph's formative years and the move from Highland Park Presbyterian to LACC seems to have influenced Ralph's view of church and the average "Christian," which should become clearer later in his life and work. The Bible itself became the foundation for commitment and discipline as well as the source of direction for the many life choices that lay ahead.

The discipline forced upon the nation during the post-depression and post-war periods also contributed to Ralph's character development. The frugality initially imposed by external circumstances of the period may have helped to shape his views on money and the use of limited resources. In the midst of this, an inventive and "tinkering" mentality was fed by opportunities such as model airplane building and the lathe work.

As Ralph developed spiritually as a young man, new questions were raised about life and the Bible, such as how our relationships and careers fit in with following God or "our life's purpose." Trying to follow God as best he understood it became the growing focus in Ralph's mind and actions.

---

[68] Interview with Ralph Winter by the author on August 7, 2006, 12.

While his calling was far from focused, it was becoming clear that he would do what he thought God wanted him to do, no matter what the world around him thought.

Education: Formal, Non-Formal and Informal

Formal Education Begins

While the three boys do not remember their parents talking to them about going to college, there was an underlying assumption that they would. Based on the way Hugo and Hazel lived, getting a good education was second only to doing what seemed right as a faithful Christian. Both Paul and Ralph went to Caltech. Paul received a Masters in Engineering from USC and worked for the City of Los Angeles for a brief time. Both Ralph and David earned PhDs.

For Ralph, however, it was not a straight path. By the end of high school, war was expanding globally. He graduated in the spring of 1942. But just one day before Ralph turned seventeen, in December 1941, the Japanese bombed Pearl Harbor and the U.S.A. finally was forced or drawn into World War II.

> Ralph was ... still too young to be drafted into the army. After graduating, he followed his older brother's footsteps by matriculating at Caltech where he completed his freshman year before being caught up in the war. (Winter, 2000, 2)

Caltech — Fall 1942—1944

Ralph started at Caltech in the fall of 1942. He was not sure what field of study to choose, and opted for civil engineering, as his brother Paul had, because it would most likely apply to a broader range of issues and problems that needed to be solved.[69]

By the time Ralph had finished his first year at Caltech, he was 18 and eligible to enlist. Ralph followed his brother's lead again and signed up for the Navy. Because the Navy needed engineers, especially in the Pacific

---

[69] Interview with Ralph Winter by the author on July 31, 2006, 16. He remembered taking chemistry from Linus Pauling, the two-time Nobel Prize winner and expert in quantum chemistry and biochemistry. Pauling was, "the best teacher I ever had. He prepared so thoroughly, he had everything worked out in advance, he was a brilliant, brilliant guy."

Rim, they sent him back to finish his studies at their expense! Since Ralph had completed all of his lab courses, he could finish his studies by taking the last two semesters concurrently. He finished mid-year. During that last sprint, he signed up for a Navy pilot's program offered to Caltech students who met certain requirements. He finished his undergraduate studies at Caltech in a total of two-and-a-half years and graduated with a B.S. in Civil Engineering. Following graduation, he entered Navy Air Corps Officers Training. He was twenty. (Winter, 2000, 2-3)

World War Two

U.S. Navy — January 1945—August 1945

The Navy's discipline has a way of purging areas of frivolity out of sailors' lives, especially during war. Ralph was in very good physical shape before getting to the Navy, so the discipline "wasn't a shock to me because I had already been in a very accountable system before I went into the Navy."[70]

The War ended abruptly in August of 1945, while Ralph was still an Air Cadet at St. Mary's Pre-Flight school.[71] There were eleven million soldiers and sailors dispersed all over the world, so it took years for some to be released. For Paul, who was doing his military service based in the Philippines when the war ended, it took almost a year to get home.[72] Ralph had had no combat experience, but he was released early, not because he had the status or "points" to get out, but because the pilot training program was too expensive to be continued.[73] (Winter, 2000, 3)

---

[70] Interview with Ralph Winter by the author on August 2, 2006, 8. Referring to the discipline of the Navs before the Navy. He also noted, "the Navigators and the Navy were very close together, the Navigators was built out of Navy people."

[71] He never participated in the flying portion of the training.

[72] Interview with Paul Winter by the author on July 27, 2005, 3, 7.

[73] Interview with Ralph Winter by the author on August 2, 2006, 12. Fortunately, the Navy put him and others from the pilot training program on "inactive duty," so they could not be drafted by the Army to help in the demobilization. Paul remembers that Ralph could have stayed in the service and obtained further flight training and experience, but he understood that Ralph was "becoming much more interested in tending toward a career in some full-time Christian service." Ralph did not imagine that such service would be in a traditional missionary or pastoral role.

Reflecting on this period of development, Ralph mentioned the line from the hymn, *Turn Your Eyes Upon Jesus,* "the things of earth will grow strangely dim in the light of His glory and grace." He noted:

> If you're already an intense person, questions arise as to what books you read, what places you go, your interests just change. I just didn't have any interests. I have to admit, I'm sort of an anti-social person anyway. I didn't go to Boy Scouts. I could get along fine without palling around with other people.[74]

Formal and Non-Formal Education Continued

Westmont College — Fall 1945–Spring 1946

Westmont College had just purchased property near Santa Barbara and consequently delayed the start of school until October 1945. Ralph was back from Navy training and trying to decide what the next step would be. With the encouragement of Dr. Hutchins at LACC, he decided at the last minute to matriculate at Westmont. He wanted to take some Bible and Greek courses, but he was not sure how he would pay for it. Having lived on a "shoestring" for years with the Navy paying for everything, he had not been able to save much. He could not quickly get funding through the GI bill.[75] Because the campus had just moved to a large property, Ralph began to think of creative ways to leverage the college's situation into funding options:

> Here Winter's natural bent in looking for the unusual answer came to the fore. He learned that the college needed someone qualified to teach a class on remedial math[76] to incoming freshmen. And for legal reasons it also needed to have its new campus surveyed and a topographical map drawn. As a graduate civil engineer, Winter knew that he could do both. But he would need assistants to help with the surveying. So he suggested that to cover his costs there he be allowed to teach the course in math as well as a class in

---

[74] Interview with Ralph Winter by the author on August 2, 2006, 7.

[75] This is the U.S. government's help for college expenses for returning military.

[76] Here, and later in this paragraph, the word "math" was used, which is the word used in the United States for what is called "maths" in the UK.

surveying, which in turn would produce the required topographical map.[77] (Winter, 2000, 4)

Ralph also took classes in Greek, Bible, and Church History. While at Westmont, major events and experiences continued to shape Ralph. One experience had to do with the way the Greek class was taught.

Dr. Elbert McCleary, a retired missionary, for the first few weeks taught the course in New Testament Greek by an oral method. Dr McCleary was a real linguist and was convinced that a language cannot be effectively learned unless you can talk it. He was familiar with the famous WW II "Army Language Training Program" located during the war in Monterey, California. He knew that instead of the usual language-learning course of several years, the Army was able to teach conversational ability in just a matter of a few months. Dr. McCleary agreed with the methodology they used and felt that above all the Biblical languages deserved to be taught properly. So, for the first six weeks, he designed his Greek lessons around an oral method. (Winter, 2000, 4-5)

Another thing that made an impact on Ralph were the chapel services. Each day the chapel speakers were drawn from people involved in various kinds of ministries. This helped him to realize that, while God did not need just one more engineer, his engineering education could be leveraged for God's purposes. He also began to consider the impact of teaching languages orally, not only for Biblical languages, but also for missionary language learning.

But perhaps the thing that made the most impact on Ralph during his time at Westmont came through his exposure to "inductive" Bible study.

Inductive Bible Study

The woman who taught Inductive Bible Study at Westmont had studied under the best professor on the subject: Howard Tilman Kuist. It was Kuist who wrote *These Words Upon My Heart* (Kuist, 1947) focusing on careful Bible study with an emphasis on character development for believers.

Inductive Bible Study (IBS) does not follow a particular method of interpretation, nor does it lead to a particular theological system.[78] It is the

---

[77] The topographical surveying class had four students. That small group surveyed the entire campus of 142 acres and produced a ten-foot topographical map.

practice of focusing on the study of the text of the Bible itself and letting it speak. While each person naturally brings their own background and perspective to their study of the Bible, IBS sought to avoid, at least in the initial stages of study, consulting what had been written in commentaries, and what theology or church history "expected" a passage to say. The approach focused on the student reading a particular passage in the Bible as follows:[79]

> 1. Observe the text closely and in depth, and ask "What does the text say?" Ask as many questions as you can and seek to get all your questions from the Bible itself within the context of the passage as well as, ultimately, the whole Bible. Only then, after in-depth study, should one move to;
> 2. Interpretation, asking, "What does the text mean?" and;
> 3. Application, asking, "What does this mean to my life?" What am I going to do about it? Then, one can consider what others have found, or check against strange interpretations that no one has ever held.

As he did with many areas of interest, Ralph desired to share his newfound passion for IBS with his good friend Dan Fuller. Dan also became captured by this idea, later describing it in the Fuller Theological Seminary newsletter:

> This method is characterized as "inductive" because the procedure involves a mastery of the particulars of the Bible text before coming to any general conclusions as to its meaning. By the particulars is meant the basic data of the text, stripped of all interpretative aids that men have added. Hence we are not bound to the punctuation, versification, paragraphing, or chapter divisions. In fact we must go behind the English translations to that text in the original which represents the best results of textual criticism to find the starting point for the inductive method. (Fuller, 1955, 6)

---

[78] IBS differs from other forms of study or categorization of Scripture in that it does not force passages into systems or theories of textual transmission.

[79] Another key book on the subject is called *Methodical Bible Study.* (Traina, 1952) In it, Traina describes the contrast of two approaches: "...deduction, which begins with generalization and moves for their support to the particulars. By its very nature deduction tends to be subjective and prejudicial. ... induction, is objective and impartial; for it demands that one first examine the particulars of the Scriptures and that one's conclusions be based on those particulars. Such an approach is sound because, being objective, it corresponds to the objective nature of the Scriptures." (Traina, 1952, 7)

For his part, Ralph took these ideas and began to think in various creative directions. He envisioned the idea of creating a motion picture approach to teaching the Bible visually. This would be a way to excite people about getting into the Bible in serious study. "You could teach the book of Matthew in an hour and people would learn more than a year long Sunday School study." [80]

Princeton Theological Seminary — Fall 1946— Spring 1947

Because of his growing interest and application of IBS, Ralph was certain that he needed to go to Princeton to study under Kuist, who had joined the Princeton faculty. Ralph sought to convince Dan Fuller to go with him. Dan had also been in the Navy and was stationed in the San Francisco Bay Area. He had not yet had any exposure to studying inductively, but, as in other situations, because Ralph was excited about it and could articulate the importance of going to the source to study, the fall of 1946 found both enrolled at Princeton for a year's study.

While Ralph and Dan's parents allowed them go, they were concerned. They had heard about the challenges to conservative Biblical perspectives at Princeton Theological Seminary (PTS) and were concerned because of the changes that had taken place.[81] They knew about the issues and debates that precipitated four well-known faculty members leaving the school in 1929. Despite the expense associated with long distance calls, Ralph remembered Dan's parents calling him every week. And while Ralph and Dan were aware of the controversy, they were focused in being at PTS for Inductive Bible Study. They also felt they could help keep each other accountable during their time there, and not let each other "stray" from the Bible as the final authority of faith and practice.

---

[80] Interview with Ralph Winter by the author on August 2, 2006, 13.

[81] As mentioned earlier in this chapter, in 1929, the administration of PTS changed. They had previously had a board of directors, which controlled the educational program, and a board of trustees which held the real property in trust, but that was altered so that a single board of trustees was placed in charge of the seminary. This arrangement allowed for a change to take place in the educational program, which shifted the theological emphasis from historic Calvinism to twentieth-century Barthianism. A foundational difference is that Barthian theology does not hold to the infallibility of holy Scripture, while the old Princeton was noted for its insistence on this doctrine. See: http://www.americanpresbyterianchurch.org/princeton.htm accessed December 18, 2007.

The year at Princeton was a year that changed Dan's entire life focus. Dan described in detail what it was like to be around Ralph, the infectious nature of Ralph's interests, and the influence of Ralph's life on his:

> He was this person who liked to be doing as useful and wonderful things as he could with his time. And had an unusual intelligence. ... somehow I really enjoyed being around Ralph. He always had something interesting to say, some new idea. ... I said, "I would like to be with that kind of person at seminary." I think that eighty percent of the direction that my life has taken comes from that picnic at the Winters' house when I decided to send my application to Princeton. ... He felt the importance of learning the inductive Bible study [method]. And that's the thing that I gave my whole life to, and that all traces back to Ralph Winter who caught on to it.[82] ... And there was some hope in those days that if we just study the Bible inductively, we won't have to tear it apart as higher criticism was doing. We don't have to tear the Pentateuch apart. If you study this inductive way then you'll see it's all put together for a reason. ... This is my life workup. ...this [inductive Bible study method] has been the governing force in my whole life, and I owe it to Ralph.[83]

Neither Ralph nor Dan were interested in becoming pastors, or even finishing a degree at Princeton at that time. They did not even plan to stay more than a year there. Roberta later wrote about Ralph that:

> He had come to believe that it was illegitimate to decide on your own to be ordained; that that kind of a call should come from a church body. He felt that to be a minister was a very special gift. Later he was to study anthropology and recognize that in every society there are responsible people who are legitimate "religious" leaders. Thus it later appeared to him that becoming a minister was in actual fact a socially defined category into which any person seriously willing to accept the responsibilities involved could move, and that in the Christian world you were much more likely to be believed in the area of religious things if you carried those credentials. (Winter, 2000, 6)

---

[82] He continued, "He [Ralph] was reading so much and knew all about early people in Church history. He knew about various theological journals..."

[83] Interview with Daniel Fuller by the author on March 7, 2005, 3-4.

While Dan and Ralph studied under Kuist, they were also exposed to Bruce Metzger, world-renowned NT scholar. Ralph remembered hearing about students who were not registered for Metzger's classes who would go just to hear him pray as each class session started.[84]

By the time Ralph and Dan went to Princeton, the U.S. Congress had passed the "GI Bill," which provided for tuition and textbooks plus 75 dollars per month for college or graduate school. Metzger used that to the students' advantage, "requiring" as many books as the money would allow. This is what first exposed Ralph to Kenneth Scott Latourette, the respected mission historian at Yale. Ralph did not have the time that year to study some of the required books from Metzger's NT class, including the seven volume *History of Expansion of Christianity* (Latourette, 1937), but he held on to them and came back to them later in his life.

Before Dan and Ralph returned from Princeton, they also met others who would be a part of their lives in the future. One of these was Bill Bright. Bill was a successful businessman in L.A. who had been connected with the Hollywood Presbyterian Church. He had a candy factory in the L.A. area, but left that in the hands of others to study at Princeton. Bill went on to found Campus Crusade for Christ in 1951.[85] Another was James Emery. He and Ralph would meet up again ten years later in Guatemala.

Also at Princeton was J. Christy Wilson.[86] He was the InterVarsity representative covering that campus and others in the area. In December, 1946, Ralph and J. Christy recruited several students to drive to Toronto to attend a conference for students put on there by InterVarsity Christian Fellowship. The event brought together almost 575 students from fifty-two different denominations at the University of Toronto.[87] (Klein, 1947, 5-6)

Ralph connected ideas that others might not consider. J. Christy and Ralph planned and formed a student mission conference at Princeton, and as they were deciding on speakers, Ralph suggested Eugene Nida, whom

---

[84] Interview with Ralph Winter by the author on August 7, 2006, 3.

[85] CCCI is now a large, multinational ministry with thousands of staff in many countries. For more information, see: www.ccci.org

[86] Wilson when on to Afghanistan and became a mobilizer, trainer, professor at Gordon-Conwell Theological Seminary and mentor of missionaries.

[87] Some of the speakers included: Robert C. McQuilkin, President of Columbia Bible College; Harold Ockenga, of Park Street Church in Boston; Samuel Zwemer, missionary to Islam; Bakht Singh, Indian evangelist and Bible teacher; and L.E. Maxwell of the Prairie Bible Institute in Alberta, Canada, where Ralph would end up a few years later to study inductive Bible study more in depth.

he had met at the Summer Institute of Linguistics (SIL).[88] Nida was a linguistic expert with connections to SIL as well as the American and United Bible Societies. Because of that relationship, Ralph helped to get both Bruce Metzger and Nida to speak at the conference. Ralph felt that learning from each other's area of scholarship would further advance their own understanding.

The Afghanistan Project

During his time at Princeton he also read a news item in *United Evangelical Action* that "Afghanistan, a country which has been visited by few Americans in its history, has requested the Department of State to find thirty-one American male instructors to teach at universities in Afghanistan to implement that Government's recently announced policy of making English a curricular requirement." [89] (Action, 1947, 11) These teachers would also teach other subjects such as mathematics, physics, chemistry, biology, geography, and geology. Ralph's interest was also fueled by his relationship with J. Christy Wilson, who had grown up in Persia, so Ralph assumed that he would be interested in the effort in Afghanistan.

Ralph and others planned to go to teach English, not because they wanted people to learn English, but because the people themselves wanted to learn it.[90] To recruit twenty-two teachers who were committed Christians, Christy sent out a letter to 70 of the InterVarsity Christian Fellowship (IVCF) staff. Only one single man and a married couple responded. Some from other Christian circles also signed up. To Ralph, who was twenty-two at the time, it seemed like a great way both to serve the society for the good and to be "light and salt" in the world. Though the initial count was modest, over the next several years more than 100 ended up going to Afghanistan to serve.[91] (Winter, 2000, 6-7)

---

[88] Winter also met Kenneth Pike that summer, another world-renowned linguist.

[89] This was not a case of teaching English to people so they could hear the gospel in English or become Americanized. The government of Afghanistan wanted this help, perhaps as a step in the globalization process, whereby English use brings connections to the world in various ways, both good and bad.

[90] Much later, Ralph noticed China's call for thousands of English teachers as a similar opportunity. When he founded a University in 1977, one of the early programs was an MA in Teaching English to Speakers of Other Languages and Applied Linguistics. (Winter, 1979a, 8)

[91] Later, Ralph intended to return to Afghanistan, with his wife Roberta.

Fuller Theological Seminary — Fall 1947—Spring 1948

During the year Ralph and Dan were at Princeton, and partly because of it, Dan's father, Charles Fuller, increased his contact with Harold John Ockenga (June 6, 1905 to February 8, 1985) to fulfill his desire to establish a training school for missionaries and evangelists on the west coast. (Fuller, 1972, 193) But he also realized that to have evangelists who were respected and prepared, they would need more than just a Bible and some money. Ockenga had been well respected both at Park Street Church and at Christian Endeavor events as well. His connections with potential faculty and staff and his administrative skills opened doors that began to bring this dream to fruition.[92] But there were larger factors involved in the decision to found a seminary beyond the desires of the individual personalities.[93]

In his book *Reforming Fundamentalism*, George Marsden wrote:

> In the history of Fuller Theological Seminary, founded in 1947 by such new evangelical reformers, we can trace the renewal of America's nineteenth-century evangelical heritage as it developed from a reform within fundamentalism into a separate movement. By the late 1950s, the movement's advocates, strengthened by the popularity of Billy Graham, broke with the dispensationalist-separatist right wing of fundamentalism. This momentous schism immediately raised the question as to what the "new evangelicalism" stood for. Nowhere was this question contested more dramatically than at Fuller Seminary, the intellectual center of the movement. (Marsden, 1987, 8-9)

Ralph and Dan returned from Princeton having accomplished their goal to study the Bible inductively with Kuist, and were part of the first class at Fuller that fall. Bill Bright returned to keep his eye on his candy business in the area and continue his studies.

During this year, Ralph was also exploring the issue of faith and science further. He "continued to learn things not taught in secular schools about the relationship of the story of the Faith and the unfolding of Western civilization." (Winter, 2000, 7) He had learned at Caltech about the academic achievements of great scientists such as Isaac Newton,

---

[92] Interview with Ralph Winter by the author on August 7, 2006, 2.

[93] For more on the inside of the development of FTS, and in particular the impact of their presidents, see also "Reflections on the Journey of Fuller Seminary," by Merlin W. Call, longtime friend, board member and donor to FTS. (Call, 2007)

Michael Faraday, William Thompson (Lord Kelvin), James Clerk Maxwell and Sir Humphrey Davy. However, he had not learned that each of them were also clearly men of faith. He came across a book while at Princeton which said, for example, that Newton had spent twenty years studying the life of St. Paul. Faraday was an ordained preacher who taught from the Bible every Sunday:

> ...it became very apparent that it was because of their faith that they began their scientific investigations in the first place: the God of creation had to be a god of order. And if that were true, He intended for us to find and understand that order. Science and faith were not really in opposition to each other, as many on both sides had claimed. (Winter, 2000, 7-8)

Roberta wrote, "Ralph considered this a second conversion, a conversion 'back' to science and carried this discovery with him" to the first year at Fuller.[94] (Winter, 2000, 7-8)

Summer Institute of Linguistics — Summer 1948

In the summer of 1948, Ralph continued to pursue his interest in language and language learning—especially the Biblical languages. "He was also interested in how a foreign non-Biblical language could be more readily learned, this having value both to the cause of missions and to the

---

[94] Ralph's growing interest led to a marginally helpful attempt to infuse "secular" science textbooks with faith by telling the additional story of the history of men and women like these. Why, he wondered, was this kind of separation so pervasive. Even when science was taught at Christian colleges, there was no clear connection with the faith of those involved, no matter what kind of faith it was.

In the midst of his studies at Fuller, he discovered a major textbook used in teaching history, which half of the colleges in America were using at the time. The co-author was a University of Southern California (USC) professor and Ralph thought that students in the InterVarsity Christian Fellowship (IVCF) group at USC, perhaps fifteen of them, would be taking a course using that book. He wondered, "What would a regular 'secular' history course look like if also studied from 'God's' perspective?" (Winter 2000, 8) He had surmised that fifteen out of seventeen Evangelical students were in secular schools. How would that huge percentage of students learn this additional information? He decided to prepare history lessons from a Christian perspective and meet with a handful of willing students at USC each week. Five students were interested and they started meeting. Unfortunately, he was not able to mobilize any additional help to prepare and teach the sessions and after a while, could not continue. Winter learned a great deal and this led to an ongoing vision to meld together not only faith and science but faith and other disciplines, which served him well in his teaching of "God's story" later. But at the time "it was simply a good idea which one seminary student could not implement all by himself." (Winter 2000, 8)

global need to teach English." (Winter, 2000, 9) The SIL course, done in conjunction with Wycliffe Bible Translators, was designed for those going out to translate the Bible in remote, tribal areas. While there, Ralph was introduced to linguistic scholars who were soon recognized worldwide.[95] This took him further on a path to major in linguistics for his main graduate studies." (Winter, 2000, 9)

It was during this time that Winter was reading the classic by Brother Lawrence, *Practicing the Presence of God*. He began to wonder if his Navigator derived pattern of Bible reading, memorization, and prayer were from the discipline itself or produced by the prompting of the Holy Spirit, so he stopped doing them for a while just to see what would happen. His room-mate at the time was concerned that he might go astray. In the end, Winter developed his own spiritual disciplines by fitting them to his life and needs rather than by adopting a regimented system. The previous discipline system, which he started while he was in the Navigators and which was reinforced by the Navy, had served him well and enabled him to grow beyond the issues of boyhood and to become a contributing member of society. His new, simple pattern of reading the Bible each morning at breakfast, continued throughout his life.

Fuller Theological Seminary — Fall 1948—Spring 1949

Now at the age of twenty-three, Ralph returned to Fuller for another year. During that year, he sought to convince Fuller professors to try out what he had learned about inductive study as well as language and linguistics at SIL on the teaching of Biblical languages. Up till now, Ralph had learned Greek the normal way—by memorizing all kinds of rules, word endings, and exceptions. Why, he thought, learn all that and end up not knowing enough for it to be useful in a few years? Instead, why not learn in a way that gives one the ability to have the "immediate recognition" of a native speaker, rather than associating a new, unknown word in the new language with a word in his own.[96] This idea would play a key role in Ralph's doctoral work a few years later.[97] Although the Fuller

---

[95] For example, Eugene Nida and Kenneth Pike are names found in books on the subject of linguistics. Both are referred to in *Linguistic Theory in America* by Frederick J. Newmeyer. (1986)

[96] Which, Winter pointed out often, is almost never a fully accurate meaning.

[97] Interview with Ralph Winter by the author on August 2, 2006, 13. While this approach has never been developed fully, it has been used in part in the World Christian

professors were not interested in the idea, Dr. Mayfield, a professor at the nearby Pasadena Nazarene College, was willing to try this out. So in addition to his Greek studies at Fuller, Ralph taught eight students Greek via an oral method, which he was developing along the way. He was excited because his students were learning to actually speak Greek, but about mid-year he wondered if his charges would learn the grammar necessary to pass the same final as the other students—a strict requirement of Mayfield. "He was confident that the Apostle Paul probably could not have passed that test either, but his students had to." (Winter, 2000, 10) He finished the semester using more traditional methods:

> It took this experience, however, for him to realize that redesigning language teaching technique was not easy, to say the least. He felt it was difficult in part because the outcomes measured (in this case, an exam of the grammar) had less importance than real language learning goals (namely to be able to communicate in the language). (Winter, 2000, 10)

Linguistic Society of America at the University of Michigan — Summer 1949

Ralph heard about the meeting of this Society and, while considering what he should do next, decided to attend. While there he learned that two top U.S. professors in the field of teaching English to non-native speakers of English were offering a course following the Society meeting there at the Ann Arbor campus. He stayed on to take the course, which fed into his growing interest in language, linguistics, and how people learn and teach language. (Winter, 2000, 10-11)

Prairie Bible Institute — Fall 1949

Ralph had learned of Prairie Bible Institute when he heard the president Dr. L.E. Maxwell speak.[98] He had also heard of the unique way

---

Foundations program, of which Winter is the General Editor. This approach introduces the new language alphabet letter such as Greek till the student can easily read the sentence using Greek, but pronouncing words (such as the familiar English "word" being ωορδ in Greek letters). In the process, new Greek words are introduced and learned till one can read the NT and catch more and more of the vocabulary. See Appendix A for sample lessons of this pattern.

[98] Maxwell had spoken at the IVCF convention in Toronto in 1946, but Ralph was not used to Maxwell's style of preaching, which was very animated and "dramatic," and was a little put off by it.

of teaching the Bible used at Prairie Bible Institute, which might be called "group inductive study."

Every day the teacher would assign a new set of "search" questions, which the student would have to answer to the best of his ability after reading the passage assigned. These sheets were divided longitudinally, with three or four questions on the left with room for the student's answers below each one, and on the right with room for the student to add new insight which he received in class, either from another student or from the professor. His grade would not be related simply to his own answers but to what he had added in class as well. Ralph was so impressed by this methodology that he later adapted it to the classes he taught in history at Fuller.[99] (Winter, 2000, 11)

A Semester Off — Spring 1950

Dick Soderberg had gone to Afghanistan as an engineer. During his time there, he helped persuade the Ministry of Education to open a technical school, the Afghan Institute of Technology (AIT), modeled roughly on Cal Tech. They sought to get scientific and technical equipment and training together to assist the country in raising their own skills in development and science.[100]

Dick took a furlough to recruit for AIT. Paul Winter, who knew Dick well also and was an engineer, responded to the opportunity and, along with his wife Betty, served two years. After arriving in the country Paul ended up serving as president of AIT with his position funded by UNESCO.[101] Another LACC friend, Maynard Eyestone, and his wife also went.[102]

Ralph's father Hugo was also involved. Now a respected engineer in L.A. working on the freeway system master plan, he became President of the Afghan Institute of Technology, Inc. Ralph set up a U.S. corporation so that companies or schools in the U.S. could donate books and equipment for AIT. For six months that winter and spring, Ralph lived in

---

[99] This was later adapted or portions of the idea were used in courses developed by Winter, including the World Christian Foundations MA curriculum and the Perspectives on the World Christian Movement lesson assignments. A sample lesson of this pattern from these courses can be found in Appendix B.

[100] Interview with Ralph Winter by the author on August 14, 2006, 2.

[101] United Nations Education and Scientific Organization.

[102] Interview with Paul Winter by the author on July 27, 2005, 7-8.

a missionary apartment at the Hawthorne Gospel Church in Hawthorne, New Jersey, while calling on technical schools up and down the east coast for donations of anything they could give to help the new effort. Roberta noted, "He was certainly not overwhelmed with equipment—nor books— but what he did get enabled the school to get started. For Winter this time was in a real sense a training for him in diplomacy and in working with secular entities." (Winter, 2000, 12)

Columbia University-Teachers College — Fall 1950—Spring 1951

All this time, Ralph was planning on joining those he had worked with or recruited by going to Afghanistan as a teacher of English. To further prepare himself, he attended the well-respected and largest teacher school of education in the world: Columbia University Teachers College. Two others from LACC joined him, including his good friend, Maynard Eyestone. On a limited budget, they lived as cheaply as they could.[103] (Winter, 2000, 13) In June of 1951, Ralph received his MA in Teaching English as a Second Language.

An Eventful Summer at home — 1951

Ralph was home for the summer after Columbia. He was planning on returning to Columbia to work on a PhD in anthropology. However, his summer plans would be altered by the start of a new relationship. There was a group of girls at LACC who were studying to be nurses. The LA General Hospital had a student nurses' chapel and they were looking for speakers for their chapel. Because of Ralph's involvement as a student leader in Christian Endeavor and since he had been to seminary, he was invited to speak. But a conflicting event nearly precluded his participation: Frank Charles Laubach (1884-1970) was speaking at the First Congregational Church of Hollywood shortly after Ralph was to speak. (Winter, 2000, 13)

Laubach was well known around the world in the area of literacy. His methods were used to teach "more than 60 million people speaking 200

---

[103] Starting with a publication Maynard had from the U.S. Department of Agriculture, they calculated with Ralph's slide rule how they could get the most food/nutrients out of the least amount of money and still stay healthy.

languages and dialects" to read.[104] In recognition of his work, the U.S. Postal Service produced a .30 cent stamp in his honor in 1984.[105] Among the many books Laubach had written, Ralph was especially interested in *The Silent Billion Speak*.[106] (1943)

On July 20, 1951, Ralph went to the chapel and spoke to the student nurses, intending afterwards to continue on to the church meeting where Laubach would be speaking. At the conclusion of his message, he asked the girls if any of them wanted to go hear this missionary speak. He said he had room for five girls, and had no trouble filling up his car. On the way back after hearing Laubach speak, some of the girls who were very conservative expressed doubt as to whether Laubach was "a real Christian" or not. The questions arose less from what Laubach had to say, and more due to the fact that he had a Church of Christ background, and that the church where he had spoken was considered a "liberal" church. Ralph asked the girls directly whether they thought Laubach was a real Christian, and only one was willing to say so: Roberta Helm.

Roberta, born January 8, 1930, was not technically part of the LACC group, but did come from an extremely conservative wing of the Nazarene Church that tended to separatism. Partly because her background emphasized the experiential more than the theological, and partly because of her own strong intuitions, she was able to sense what kind of person Laubach was. That spiritual perception attracted Ralph to Roberta. He was also impressed that, though she was from a narrow Christian background, she was willing to buck peer pressure in the car rather than side with the other girls who disagreed with her.[107]

---

[104] From the dust jacket of his later book, (Laubach, 1958). Also see the Christian History Institute web site article "Good-bye to Frank Laubach, Apostle of Literacy" accessed April 23, 2007, URL: http://chi.gospelcom.net/DAILYF/2002/06/daily-06-11-2002.shtml

[105] Worth approximately $.65 or £.40 in 2011.

[106] Laubach also wrote *Teaching the World to Read: A Handbook for Literacy Campaigns* (Laubach, 1947) and *Wake up or blow up! America: Lift the world or lose it!* (Laubach, 1951)

[107] Interview with Ralph Winter by the author on August 7, 2006, 7. Roberta later recorded it in the third person:

Among these [girls in the car/chapel] was Roberta Helm, a "Nazarene of the Nazarenes," someone said, because she had long hair and was very conscientious in doing what she felt was right. That Ralph would ever become interested in her was not even an option as far as she was concerned. Their theological backgrounds were different. She "looked" different with her long hair, etc. But he had taught for a year at Pasadena (Nazarene) College and had a great respect for Nazarenes.

To Roberta's amazement, Ralph asked her out. He made a list of issues to talk with her about and on their first date they went through his list. On the second date, he announced that he thought they should talk seriously about the possibility of getting married. She was not prepared for that since her family was opposed to anyone from a different Christian background, so after two or three dates, Ralph thought it was over.[108]

Roberta's family was large. She had grown up with two brothers and four sisters. They had moved from the Ohio area to South Texas. Her father, Leroy Helm, had been a cowboy and later was a leather worker. He but was not very interested in study and reading. Her mother Rose Etta (Dewey), was a solid believer and a godly woman. She was well read, and "ruled the roost." The whole family was very musical. They also followed the conservative constraints of the Nazarene Church at that time and did not have much to do with people from other Christian backgrounds.

Once when Ralph was talking with Rose Etta, she mentioned the five Christian authors she appreciated the most. The list included A.T. Pierson, A.B. Simpson, and Oswald Chambers. Ralph could not resist the opportunity to "stretch" her thinking a bit, so he pointed out the fact that four of the five were Calvinists, an assertion which Rose could not believe and which greatly upset her. Later, Ralph realized how stupid his comment was, teaching him one of many lessons he would learn regarding challenging other people's assumptions.[109] His "salvation" in gaining Rose Etta's approval came because he knew much about and greatly admired John Wesley.[110]

At age 28, Ralph had begun to reconsider his views about marriage. He had originally concluded that he would never marry. When he was rooming with his good friend Maynard Eyestone at Columbia, Maynard was interested in a mutual LACC friend, Phyllis Chamberlain. Maynard and Phyllis wrote to each other during that year and became engaged. Even though both were committed to getting into missions, Ralph was convinced that it was not practical for a dedicated Christian missionary to be married. Maynard ended up breaking off his engagement less than one month before the wedding, which had been planned for the summer of

---

Also, her obvious and unembarrassed willingness to be "different" appealed to him. He had long known that whomever he married would have to be willing not to fit into the usual mold. (Winter 2000, 14)

[108] Interview with Ralph Winter by the author on August 7, 2006, 7.

[109] Interview with Ralph Winter by the author on August 7, 2006, 8.

[110] Interview with Ralph Winter by the author on August 7, 2006, 8.

1951.[111] Ralph's influence was in fact part of the reason they broke up. Even though he did not think so, "Ralph got caught up in things and was a tremendous motivator."[112]

Ralph reasoned that:

> ...the world didn't need more children, it needed more missionaries who could devote their full time to the gospel. Not missionaries but lay people.[113] And that was just an idea. But I began to listen to my own self, and I also studied, and I realized that most of the Christians in history were generated biologically, not evangelistically. ...and I realized that the children of pastors often have a tremendous advantage and are more influential because of their background, and so I was able to persuade myself intellectually, and that dove-tailed with my own biological yearnings, and it's funny to say it like this, but it occurred to me again and again that I have the capacity to be a husband, to be the husband of a wife, and to be a father. And so I decided to get married. So I looked around for the first girl, and that was it.[114]

Ralph seemed to be approaching the issue like an engineer and thus, as problems to be solved. At the same time, he was more of an engineering theoretician than an applied engineer, who enjoys seeing all the details of a problem worked out. Roberta reflected later on her husband's desire to identify a solution and then move on:

> By no stretch of the imagination could everything that Winter initiated over the previous years retain his personal involvement over a long period of time. He always hoped that others would pick up his ideas and maybe his start and follow through on it. He considered himself as basically an engineer—one who designs and leaves it to someone else to build. (Winter, 2000, 11-12)

---

[111] Maynard ended up marrying another woman, just one day before Ralph and Roberta were married. Phyllis Chamberlain served in Japan as a single missionary for 41 years, sent out by LACC under The Evangelical Alliance Mission. She married later in life.

[112] Interview with Paul Winter by the author on July 27, 2005, 7-8.

[113] Not missionaries in the traditional sense necessarily, but non-ordained engineers or other professionals.

[114] Interview with Ralph Winter by the author on August 7, 2006, 6.

Winter was not a determinist with regard to marriage or life in general. His factual consideration of a marriage partner is more a reflection of his practical, engineering nature than anything else.[115]

When Ralph returned to school that fall he wrote Roberta a letter a day for ninety days, some 90,000 words. Her interest grew and she asked all kinds of questions. After that fall semester, a short five months and a week after they met, Ralph and Roberta were married at the Bresee Avenue Nazarene Church chapel, in Pasadena, California, on December 28, 1951. Ralph was 28 and Roberta was 22.[116]

Cornell University — Fall 1951—Summer 1953

Just before they were married, Ralph returned to Columbia to pursue his doctorate in anthropology. However, he had heard about top tier faculty in the field of linguistics researching at Cornell, teaching something called "structural linguistics."[117] Cornell was willing to take Ralph's M.A. at Columbia towards PhD work at Cornell, so in 36 hours, Ralph transferred and started the program, moving to Cornell some 225 miles away. His major was descriptive linguistics with a double minor in cultural anthropology and mathematical statistics.[118] While there, he studied under Charles F. Hockett, well known for his work as a structural linguistic theorist. A number of people connected with SIL had studied under Hockett, and Ralph respected them.[119]

---

[115] While he and Roberta were briefly courting, he shared with her his views of frugal living for the Lord. This was later expressed in different ways by each of them: "Reconsecration to a Wartime, Not a Peacetime, Lifestyle" by Ralph (in, Winter et al. 2009, 722-724) and "The Non-Essentials of Life" by Roberta, where she tells the story of how she and Ralph worked through issues of finances in their marriage and with their children. See: williamcareylibrary.com/ebooks/Non-Essentials_of_Life.pdf accessed on February 2, 2009.

[116] For more about their courtship, see: *Five Weeks and a Month*. (Winter, 2001)

[117] Also known as structuralist linguistics. This is an "approach to linguistics which stresses the importance of language as a system and which investigates the place that linguistic units such as sounds, words, sentences have within this system." "They defined some sounds in a language as distinctive and used the identification of words, and some as variants." (Richards et al., 1985, 276)

[118] A double minor was required for this program. Descriptive linguistics is "to describe the facts of linguistic usage as they are, and not how they ought to be, with reference to some imagined ideal state." It is contrasted with prescriptive aims of much of traditional grammar. (Crystal, 1991, 100)

[119] Interview with Ralph Winter by the author on August 7, 2006, 5.

Hockett, following in the footsteps of Leonard Bloomfield who wrote *Language* (Bloomfield, 1933), pioneered the field of structuralist linguistics, which "did much to define linguistics as a science." (Gair, 2006, 1) Hockett added basic "concepts and issues" to Bloomfield's, and he also "firmly believed linguistics to be a branch of anthropology, to which he also made serious contributions." (Gair, 2006, 1)

Ralph went home and he and Roberta were married over the Christmas break and returned to Cornell. Roberta became Ralph's partner in many ways, sitting in on his classes when possible, helping in library research, and "counting the types of words in three vastly different documents that provided the raw material for his study." (Winter, 2000, 14) At times, when money ran low, she would also work as a nurse. The pattern of helping Ralph in his studies and later in his teaching and grading began in that first year of marriage.[120]

To SIL Again — Summer 1952

The summer after that first six months of marriage and the end of the first year of PhD studies proved crucial for Ralph's continuation in the program. Ralph wanted Roberta to experience the SIL program that summer in Norman, Oklahoma, as he had. But he wondered what he would do with his time. He suggested to Kenneth Pike, director of the program, that he would be willing to help teach that summer. By now his skills and training were beyond even the second year SIL offered.

Ralph's civil engineering approach to his research seemed to irk Hockett, but Ralph did not know why, not understanding academic protocol in a different field. Being creative and generating many ideas as well as being an engineer, Ralph tended to challenge everything.[121] As a result, Ralph was constantly challenging Hockett one-on-one or before others in a seminar. "It took months before he realized that now he had to give reasons why a thesis was good rather than why it might fail."[122] In fact, by the end of the first year, Hockett's frustration with Winter had reached the point that Hockett was ready to drop Ralph from the program.

---

[120] They were a team like few others. Working hand-in-hand, even when they returned from mission fieldwork and he began to teach at Fuller Seminary, Roberta would sit in on his classes or fill in for him if he were out-of-town. She graded papers throughout the year.

[121] In engineering design every possible issue and potential situation must be taken into account, making absolutely sure, for example, that a structure will not fail.

[122] Roberta gave the illustration of how an engineer approached the design of a bridge. The engineer had to prove that it would stand up to a wide variety of stresses and loads before he could be sure his work was done.

But Hockett knew and respected Pike. According to Roberta's later writing, Hockett had decided that unless Pike hired him, he would drop Ralph. Fortunately for Ralph, Pike did bring him on to teach phonemics that summer and Roberta took the SIL course. She loved every minute of the course work as well as the fellowship with the missionaries. (Winter, 2000, 15)

The Dissertation

Ralph's specific PhD work brought together several of his ideas about language learning and language teaching. His dissertation was "English Content Words and Function Words: a Quantitative Analysis." It blended linguistics, statistics, and "set the stage for a revolutionary new approach to language learning—teaching two artificial languages first, one combining the vocabulary of the learner's language, and the other the opposite."[123] (Winter, 2000, 14)

"Call" to Ministry?

Ralph finished his dissertation in late August 1953 and graduated with a PhD. Up to then, Ralph had believed that ministry was a calling, not a merely a vocation, so the "call to ministry" was a special call of the Holy Spirit. But he did not feel called that way:

> To me, it [becoming a minister] was a very special, sort of like a second work of grace, it was a very special experience, which I hadn't had. But anthropology persuaded me that it really wasn't a special experience, it was a cultural norm.[124]

That exposure to anthropology began in his late teens when Winter read the book *The Missionary and Anthropology* by Gordon Hedderly Smith. (1942) Smith, a Christian and Missionary Alliance missionary to French Indo-China wrote, "The purpose of this book is twofold—first to show the importance of the study of anthropology for missionaries; secondly, to make an approach to the science of man and his culture from the standpoint of the missionary who works especially among so-called primitive people." (Smith, 1945, 5) Smith had served in a remote area where he experienced significant cultural differences. He then had

---

[123] As noted previously, see Appendix A for an example from the Greek language learning lessons from the World Christian Foundations course, of which Winter was the designer and editor-in-chief.

[124] Interview with Ralph Winter by the author on August 7, 2006, 6. Certainly, Winter would have understood those who felt they had received "a call" to ministry.

opportunity to share in evangelical circles how much the study of anthropology had helped him understand cultural issues and thus enabled him to have a more positive impact for the Christian faith where he worked. For Winter, this created a continued interest in the "study of man."[125]

Winter decided that since he had studied at Princeton and Fuller already, he might as well follow the cultural pattern understood by Christians, go back, finish the seminary degree and be ordained in an identifiable denomination. That way, no matter what he actually did in ministry, it would make sense to folks back home.[126]

It was late in the summer, and there was little likelihood that he could get in to PTS that fall. He wrote a note to the registrar and he and Roberta returned to Pasadena, "...where Ralph applied for a job with the Rand Corporation, a government-related think tank in Santa Monica, California. He still hadn't heard from Princeton, and told the corporation that he could not yet say what he would do." (Winter, 2000, 15)

He was offered an excellent job related to language and computers and it was a real temptation to him. But within a week Princeton wrote saying that one student had backed out, so they had room for him. Ralph declined the job with the Rand Corporation, and within three weeks they were off to the east coast to finish his seminary degree. Ralph's father, Hugo, was a little disappointed. While he and Hazel were behind him in all his endeavors, it was a little hard for them to see him pass up the Rand job to go back to a seminary after earning a PhD.[127] While it is not clear

---

[125] Per conversation with Ralph Winter on July 8, 2008. Moody Press published the book with a foreword by the then current anthropology professor at Wheaton College, who had a grasp of the leader in the field. Winter felt he had an interesting if not engaging writing style.

Much more recently, Ralph saw a similar impact reflected in more recent books, demonstrating the positive impact of Christianity on civilization. Such books include: Christopher Dawson's *Religion and the Rise of Western Culture* (1991), Rodney Stark's *The Rise of Christianity* (1997) and *For the Glory of God* (Stark, 2003), and Thomas Cahill's *How the Irish Saved Civilization* (Cahill, 1995). These books, and others, include recently discovered evidence of the positive impact of Christianity on civilization throughout history. Later, Ralph used such books in the MA level curriculum called World Christian Foundations, of which he was the editor. See sample pages in Appendix B.

[126] For him, the ease of finishing there took priority over any denominational loyalties he might have had through LACC. Of course, his family had been Presbyterian before starting at LACC. Perhaps because of its Southern California location and its affiliations with Fuller, Christian Endeavor, and other ministries, LACC was more open to other groups, as long as they held to the same basic tenets of the faith.

[127] Interview with Paul Winter by the author on July 27, 2005, 9.

what they expected of their 29-year-old son, it would be understandable that they might want him to be finished with formal education.

Back to Princeton — Fall 1953—Spring 1956

Ralph was back at Princeton to finish a degree that Christians would understand: a Bachelor of Divinity. It seemed to him that merely being a student would not teach him all he needed to learn. He heard about a historic church of fifty in Lamington, New Jersey, thirty miles away from the Seminary, which was looking for a pastor, so he applied. It provided 100 dollars per month and a home. Roberta noted, "the experience of preaching and administrating a small church on a weekly basis was invaluable. Also, in this setting he worked closely with people who were mainly older and quite different from himself." (Winter, 2000, 16)

With a PhD in Linguistics from Cornell behind him, he knew enough about language structure and linguistics that, after a few days in the first year Hebrew class, he decided he did not want to learn language the traditional way. He had not taken Hebrew when he was there before so he had to catch up with second year students. He asked if he could be allowed to teach himself first year Hebrew, as long as he could pass the same final as the other students. Roberta wrote:

> We memorized certain passages. We looked up in the century-old, but rarely used *The Englishman's Hebrew Concordance* by Charles Wigram. We learned the definitions of the most common words in Genesis, purposely ignoring the "once words." Ralph figured out what the original grammar must have been: were vowel points really essential; if not, why not? And learned to read and understand Hebrew without reference to them... (Winter, 2000, 16)

He easily passed the test and started second year Hebrew with the other students.

Another significant change occurred in Winter's life during these Princeton years: he became a father. Because their first two children arrived during the first year-and-a-half at Princeton, they decided they should extend the originally anticipated two years into three.[128]

---

[128] Interview with Ralph Winter by the author on August 7, 2006, 6.

Additional Influences: Books

One of the books that had a great impact on Ralph's life was *This Freedom Whence?* by John Wesley Bready (Bready, 1942). While Ralph knew something about John Wesley and the results of his ministry, he commented that he "knew Wesley as an evangelist. I had no idea that the whole country would change because of his preaching."[129] Winter first saw Bready's book in the late 1940s and learned from it the power of the gospel to transform society and to right social ills.

In a similar vein, he had not realized the extent to which the history of the American West was carved by the gospel, with the implication that Christianity was not just something for religious or church people; it was a force for truth and good and has in it the power to transform society. While this idea "just shocked me to the core...[it] proved to me that religion makes a difference in society...."[130]

Perhaps Kenneth Scott Latourette's work most impacted Winter. Latourette had served briefly in China, but returned for health reasons and his main life work was as a historian, most notably on the Yale faculty from 1921 until his untimely death in 1968.[131] While he wrote about China, Japan, and the Far East, and was one of the first to start an East Asian studies program in the west, it was his approach to history that left the greatest impact on Ralph. Over time, Ralph absorbed Latourette's work. Ralph remembered that Latourette summarized both the influence of Christianity on the culture and the influence of the culture on Christianity.[132]

Ralph had not had much time to read Latourette before beginning the Presbyterian's high-quality, six-month training program for field missionaries. Latourette was one of the instructors during that course and Ralph grew in his appreciation of Latourette's work.[133] After Latourette's

---

[129] Interview with Ralph Winter by the author on August 14, 2006, 1.

[130] Interview with Ralph Winter by the author on August 14, 2006, 1.

[131] From 1953 to 1968 he was a Professor Emeritus.

[132] Interview with Ralph Winter by the author on August 23, 2006, 1. He is referring to the individual chapters within each of the seven volumes of Latourette's work, *A History of the Expansion of Christianity*. (Latourette, 1937) There, Latourette used the phrase "Effect on the environment: effect of the environment."

[133] Some ten years later, when he returned from the field and began teaching at Fuller SWM, Latourette's works were "one of the rock solid foundations upon which I built." Later, Ralph had Latourette's two-volume *A History of Christianity* (Latourette, 1953) reprinted inexpensively enough so that missionaries, pastors and students could afford them. Ralph wrote an explanation of this set to promote them as the books to use in Christian

death in 1968, Ralph proposed to publisher Harper and Row that he write a final chapter to bring one of his multi-volume sets up to date. Winter had already written the book, *The 25 Unbelievable Years* (1970) which covered the expansion of Christianity from 1945 to 1970. He revised it for the 1975 reprint of Latourette's work.

It was Latourette's take on the culture of Christianity that had the greatest impact on Ralph:

> ...the only history book that tells you what kind of devotions the monks had.... Most history books talk about ecclesiastical developments, but he is talking about the culture of Christianity very clearly, as well as the theology. So he wrote a very different book when he wrote the History of Christianity. It's now a story of the believing people and what they believed, not just what happened.[134]

Ralph wrote a final tribute to Latourette, who died after a car struck him while on a walk on December 26, 1968. Winter noted, "Many seminary professors have not yet come to grips with his major insight, though he produced for them a scholarly book a year for the last fifty-two years. His latest book is not yet off the press, and another is only half finished." (Winter, 1969b, 4) And, "It's those 10,000 printed pages of books and articles he wrote on the story of Christianity. But it's not *how much* he wrote. That alone, of course, is little short of a miracle (when added to his students, his classes, his boards and committees). Rather it is *what* he wrote. ... He was the first man to undertake the *whole* story of the Christian movement..." (Winter, 1969b, 5)

Ralph would return to that idea in his own teaching.

Analysis

Naturally, Ralph Winter's life was molded by elements common to people of his generation. Hereditary and environmental influences created fundamental, life-shaping factors in his life. Ralph had parents with above-average intelligence, and grew up in a disciplined environment. This

---

colleges: "It would seem quite feasible for Christian colleges to utilize these two sets of books as the historical backbone of an education in the liberal arts. That is how comprehensive they are. Rather than trying to add a Christian supplement to some secular work which grossly down-plays or completely ignores the role of the Christian movement in Western Civilization, it might be better to let the Christian movement be the backbone of Western Civilization—as it really was—and supplement this story with secular accounts where necessary." (Winter and Latourette, 1970, 93-94)

[134] Interview with Ralph Winter by the author on August 23, 2006, 3.

produced a basic resolve in Ralph and his brothers to make a positive contribution for good. In Ralph, that contribution might have been generally articulated as seeking to fulfill God's mission in the world. By this point in his life, his understanding and definitions of how he might be involved in fulfilling that mission had progressed beyond his early exposure at LACC.[135]

Heredity and Family Influence

With engineering in Hugo's life and Hazel's background, we can surmise that Ralph and his brothers were blessed with above-average IQs. This, combined with the character of loving parents who worked hard, provided for the boys' basic physical needs in a comfortable neighborhood. Hugo and Hazel garnered respect for their hard work, involvement in church and community as well as his position in society. Yet none of the Winters seemed to expect respect merely because of their past, their degrees, or their positions.[136]

Perhaps because of his small stature and health issues as a young child, Ralph was a calm, quiet, determined child. Some would call him an introvert who enjoyed working with his hands and keeping to himself. He was competitive, yet not in order to beat others or "win," but instead to succeed in what he did (such as memorizing Bible verses or getting engineering supplies to a tech school in Afghanistan) as a part of fulfilling God's purposes.

While these and other hereditary factors undoubtedly played a role in the development of Ralph's character and personality, the focus of this analysis is on environmental factors.

---

[135] Reflecting on those factors that most shaped his life, Winter recalled: "...becoming a believer put me out of whack with society, which enabled me to look at society as an outsider. That's what an inventor has to do; he has to conceive of what isn't. And if you're swimming in the society, you can't do that so well..." It remains to be seen if this continued into his field experiences.

[136] I talked with Hugo a number of times in the 1980s, and with David a few times. I've talked with Paul many times, in various situations, over a number of years. None of them are pretentious.

Environment

Below are several environmental factors that contributed to shape Ralph Winter during his younger life and his period of formal education.[137]

One major contributing factor was a combination of the post-World War I era and the Great Depression. In general, this period contributed to a mentality of working together through difficulty and frugality, as well as a cognizance that they were helping to rebuild and grow the country.

The Winter family did not seem to suffer need during the post-depression years, but they, like others, needed to be frugal and careful (a characteristic Ralph picked up). While there were tough times during this period, Hugo had a solid job throughout his life, and they were careful about spending money and handling money wisely with the boys. Paul and Ralph getting an advance on future allowances to purchase a lathe illustrates this. Careful financial planning (for example, saving for fireworks each year) did not give Ralph or Paul any sense of being poor or needy, but of treating limited funds carefully.

Another major contributing factor impacting Ralph's spiritual life was the nature and focus of evangelicalism in the 1920s to 1950s. Because one of evangelicalism's deeply held beliefs is a commitment to evangelism, Ralph was exposed to role models with a focus on evangelism in general and world evangelization in particular. His parents (during CIM prayer meetings), Christian leaders, and guest speakers at church (such as Dawson Trotman and Charles Fuller) all contributed to his perspective. As Ralph's faith began to grow because of his parents and the accountability of the CE and the Navigators, he became centered on faith (like his father and mother) and committed to the furtherance of the gospel (like those in his church at LACC such as Pastor Hutchins), as did his brothers, friends (such as Dan Fuller), and later peers (such as Maynard Eyestone and Bill Bright).

A third major contributing factor was World War Two and the post-war environment, which fostered a climate of problem solving and creativity.[138] This environment also contributed to frugality and a personal clarity of purpose. During his last year and a half at Caltech, before

---

[137] The factors listed here are not in any particular order. Examples from the preceding material are in parentheses.

[138] The west coast has historically been linked to the generation of new ideas and entrepreneurial activities, especially in technological arenas. Two well-known examples of successful companies that both started with two men in a garage are: Hewlett Packard, which started in 1939 (incorporated in 1945), and, much later, Apple Computer, which was founded in 1976.

participating in Navy pilot training, he was conscious of the powerful impact of a whole country conserving and serving in the War effort. The general attitude in the country was opposed to self-centeredness, and instead on serving the country and helping in the War. These lessons shaped an entire generation. For some, the lessons learned lasted only through the war, but for others, like Ralph, they lasted a lifetime.[139]

In particular, Ralph's time at Caltech was conducive to tinkering and problem solving. His experiences there during the war caused that to take shape in his mind because "they look at things with brand new eyes to try to invent solutions to engineering problems..."[140]

Although not directly connected to the war itself, other examples of how he applied his creative thinking include: rethinking how to teach a language (by merging the grammar of one and the vocabulary of the other in the early stages); how to teach yourself music/piano (by having a sliding, modulating keyboard); and, how to bridge the divide between faith and science in college students (when he returned to study at Fuller, including the idea of creating textbooks that integrate faith and science).

The American war effort in WWII required massive mobilization. Many were mobilized to become part of the armed forces, including Ralph and Paul. However, the idea of everyone contributing to the "war cause," whether directly or indirectly, was something that Ralph and many other Christians later connected with the evangelical imperative of spreading the faith. Ralph used illustrations from the war in his own mobilization efforts. Beyond these lessons within the nation's mobilization effort, an indirect result was the founding of many mission organizations after the war, as soldiers saw first-hand the needs and opportunities around the world.

Ralph sought to motivate and draw others into what he was interested in or excited about at the time, not to further his own interests, but because he believed these skills and practices (such as IBS or memorizing scripture) should be the concern of all Christians. As he matured, he sought to involve others by leveraging a person's gifts, position, or prestige and connecting them appropriately with others to take strategic advantage of unique opportunities. He was connecting people with ministries to obtain more effective results or deepen relationships, (such as with Eugene Nida in linguistics and Bruce Metzger in NT studies at the Princeton retreat).

Another example of his mobilizing to a cause was the project in Afghanistan where several from LACC became deeply involved. While

---

[139] Some have written about this, such as the popular book, *The Greatest Generation* (2005).
[140] Interview with Ralph Winter by the author on August 14, 2006, 4.

Ralph did not have much success obtaining donations from business for the technical school, he mobilized his brother (who went to Afghanistan) and father (whose position in the City of L.A. lent credibility to the project) in addition to others, (such as the good family friend, Dick Soderberg).

Other mobilization lessons came from basic life experiences, (such as learning a more effective sales pitch for selling Christmas cards), which contributed to Ralph's effective involvement with adults he did not know.

Socialization

Ralph did not always seem to fit in socially. Sometimes, from his perspective, this was on purpose. As he said above, he was "out of whack with society." His brother Paul said "he was from somewhere else," meaning that Ralph thought differently about almost everything and everyone around him, including Paul and David his brothers. Paul also noted that Ralph could "sort of take over," in part because of his "ability of seeing right through to the basic principles" of any given issue or situation.[141] Dan Fuller saw this positively (as Ralph motivated him to get involved in IBS), as did Paul for the most part. As Dan Fuller put it, "People felt that about Ralph, that he always had exciting things to say. And I said I would like to be with that kind of person at seminary."[142]

But, at times, his influence upon people sometimes introduced a social awkwardness. One example was his early opinions about marriage, which were very matter of fact and logical but did not fully take into account issues of accountability or the input of more mature believers. Since he believed a Christian should not be distracted from the task at hand with the things of this world, to a point, he believed that marriage was not a good idea for the serious Christian worker (which ended up breaking the engagement of his LACC friends). Later he realized that view was immature and changed his views. At the time, he apparently did not understand the impact of his opinions on others, nor the forcefulness with which he must have communicated through his example of focused discipline.[143]

---

[141] Interview with Paul Winter by the author on July 27, 2005, 5.

[142] Interview with Daniel Fuller by the author on March 7, 2005, 3.

[143] Ralph called Phyllis Chamberlin, whose engagement was broken off, and she asked him why he did not consult Pastor Hutches before writing the letter suggesting his friend remain single. Ralph said, "He would not have agreed with me." (According to a verbal

The social disconnect was reflected again when he was almost expelled from the Cornell PhD program after the first year. His engineering training that put the responsibility on the part of an engineer to suggest why a structure might fail, did not apply in this new field of study. Ralph confronted the professor as he would one of his own peers, and needed to learn the intricacies of east coast academic protocol in a new field of study.

Ralph's initial relational difficulties in the field of linguistics and missions may have led him to be more cognizant than most people that there are many activities they do in their lives merely because of their background, or because of the sub-culture of the evangelical church. He observed specific issues in both "cultures" that needed to be challenged, such as when he and Dan Fuller handed out copies on the impact of various revivals in Christian history at LACC. But he also understood that he needed to use the prevailing system in order to fit in enough to challenge or change it:

"...somewhere along the line I gained the impression that you can't change a structure without going along with it. So, getting a PhD might have, in my mind, been the best way to fight the system."[144]

Perhaps his weaknesses in social skills and understanding people's emotions, enabled him to more effectively challenge the status quo and to encourage or mobilize others to do the same. This is illustrated during this period in various lifestyle factors, such as how money is spent or conserved. Probably due to a combination of frugality during the post-depression era and Ralph's focus on the task ahead, he was always very frugal, and did not spend money on any non-necessary items (like purchasing the minimum amount of food while at Columbia).

Education — Informal and Formal

Beyond the input from the churches in his background, Christian Endeavor profoundly impacted Ralph. CE provided a place to learn about planning and leading meetings, and was a motivation to his spiritual life. The organized youth-led ministry Ralph was exposed to in CE and the Navigator Dunamis ministry gave him an early start on accountability and discipline, which would deepen in college and in the military.

---

discussion with Phyllis at Ralph Winter's memorial service on June 28, 2009.) Ralph did not think that the engagement was broken off because of his influence.

[144] Interview with Ralph Winter by the author on August 14, 2006, 5.

The Dunamis accountability groups and learning 500 verses also fed into Ralph's faith. They shaped his upbringing and were foundational to his spiritual life to the end. He would often quote from one of those verses, such as, "do not grow weary in well doing," (2 Thess. 3:13) or in prayers, "I believe; help thou mine unbelief." (Mark 9:24).

Another part of Ralph's informal education was the relationship he and his family had with Ali Asghar. Ali's background from Afghanistan fed a different culture's thinking into Ralph and, later, Roberta.

Ralph described his time learning and growing in college and graduate school, which included seven schools and two study programs, as a period when he had "the expulsive power of a new affection."[145] Each of these were turning points in some way.

That new affection included a number of paths, each shaping a different area of Ralph's broadly growing interests. Ralph did not follow a typical student's path. Caltech was a first step. It was a place where problem solving and understanding how worked from the perspective of the maths and sciences. Caltech helped to develop Ralph's creative approach to life. Exposure to people such as Linus Pauling in the context of the growing global problems reflected in WWII created a drive and discipline in Ralph. The war and the rushed course of study were considered an aspect of "doing their part" for the cause of the war.

Ralph's time at Westmont was possible, in part, because there was no time to enroll in another program at the time and he was not sure what he wanted to study. He continued to have an interest in a broad range of issues. And the time at Westmont reflected his multi-faceted interests. He blended studying the Bible, Greek and Church History with teaching maths, and topographic surveying. While future studies for Ralph would necessarily be focused, this interest in a wide range of subjects began to emerge as a pattern. Even his doctoral studies combined linguistics with anthropology and statistics.

As early as his year at Westmont he was evaluating the way Greek was taught.[146] His perspective on the subject of how best to learn a language continued throughout his life. Two of his major complaints were that (1) Since NT Greek was not a spoken language, teaching it like you might Spanish or French would not work, and; (2) Learning vocabulary with one

---

[145] Interview with Ralph Winter by the author on August 2, 2006, 5. He did not say "explosive."

[146] At the time of this writing, no language program I have found incorporates his approach to beginning language learning.

or two word definitions could give the wrong impression or, eventually, the wrong interpretation of a passage.[147]

The path to Princeton the first time, with Dan Fuller, was because of IBS and the desire to study the word in as unencumbered a way as possible. Various connections (including Bill Bright, J. Christy Wilson, and James Emery) added new dimensions through lifelong relationships, as well as possibilities for future studies on the east coast.

The Afghanistan project (which Winter learned about while at Princeton), the summer at SIL studying linguistics, along with the linguistics conference a summer later, added new elements to Ralph's learning and direction. Some of the mobilization implications of the Afghanistan project were discussed above. Through SIL, and beginning at Columbia (and continuing at Cornell), Ralph could see the application of language learning, language teaching, the technical study of language, and language analysis.

Marriage

Marriage changed Ralph's life and study patterns, as would be expected. Having children also slowed the speed with which Ralph finished study programs, but Roberta and Ralph began the pattern of an extremely close relationship blending life, children, learning and working in a shared experience. Roberta's gifts also included considering varying perspectives that others might not, and envisaging what might be added to Ralph's creative approaches. Those who were exposed to them could see their unique relationship.

With this background and now married, he and Roberta were about to take their next step to apply what they were learning to minister in another culture as missionaries.

---

[147] However, he was never able to focus his attention on this problem. Once he arrived on the mission field, his attentions were riveted elsewhere. He did try to recruit others to get behind these ideas, but many of Ralph's other ideas, including his approach to Greek and Hebrew language learning, remain untried on a broad scale.

Chapter 3

To the field: Guatemala — 1956—1966

Introduction

After seven schools and two summer study programs, Ralph was ready to apply what he had learned. Ralph was a bit older than some missionaries and wondered how he might best contribute. The Winters heard of an open missionary post in Guatemala that seemed to fit them well. During language school, after a visit to the village where he and Roberta would serve, Winter described his reflections on the next phase of their lives to his parents:

> In one sense the Mam Center is the worst place in the world for us. It is an absolutely fixed pattern that we'll be unable to soon, or ever to change. On the other hand, it in one small respect is a good place for the very reason that it is established. We'll not be forced to decide what to do (and you know how hard that is for me – I've got to study the whole thing down theoretically and through involved analysis decide the path of optimum value, etc.) and [we] won't be blamed– [we] may even be praised – for doing what was done before. This will, more than any other job, perhaps, enable us to follow up other side-line ideas and projects. And that I've got to be able to do or I'll die of ulcers. It's a fact. I've felt and responded to the call of the ministry and missions. I have surely much more certainly felt and responded to what I believe is a call (no matter what everyone else may think) to the studied application of modest ingenuity to the Christian cause in general. The ingenuity I have is not imagined, but the concern to apply it in a call is, nearly so. Yet while the inventor's role is partially recognized in the secular world it is not about to be in the ecclesiastical. Too bad.[1]

---

[1] Undated letter (fall of 1957) from Ralph D. Winter to Hugo and Hazel Winter, 1.

Pre-Field Orientation and Training — 1956—57

Ten years before Ralph Winter graduated from his last formal degree program at Princeton Seminary, the Presbyterian Foreign Mission Board (PFMB) received a request for a missionary to serve in Guatemala.[2] They were looking for an ordained minister with training in both linguistics and anthropology, and a spouse who was a Registered Nurse.[3]

Ralph was ordained in the United Presbyterian Church on June 20, 1956, at the Lamington, New Jersey church where he had served as a student minister. Dudley Peck[4] gave the "Charge to the Evangelist" during the service. Ralph and Roberta went from there to six months of missionary orientation called a "Study Fellowship." This included four months of lectures, term papers, and logistical details (such as writing their wills) that rounded out the half-year. Roberta described it as a very busy but rewarding time, "Kind of like a graduate school of missions. Ralph, at the end in the feedback session, was the only one who suggested it might be longer." (Winter, 2000, 19) Even after all the schools and programs Ralph had attended, he noted that, "We had never been in an educational program designed by veteran mission personnel." (Winter, 1995a, 1)

The Winters helped teach one month of linguistic training, and, with the other appointees, visited mining communities in Pennsylvania, and worked for a month with the poor in the Bronx in New York helping to rebuild damaged buildings and take a census of the community. One paper Ralph wrote during this training was on the Roman Catholic mission

---

[2] The Presbyterian Board called these "fraternal" workers to focus on the aspect of the missionary coming along side an existing national church.

[3] Samuel Moffett, whose parents were well-known missionaries in Korea, had become the interim Personnel Secretary for the PFMB in New York. He was also teaching mission courses at Princeton, so he knew Ralph and Roberta and likely was the one who connected them with the request from the field.

[4] The Pecks headed the work in the highlands of Guatemala for the PFMB and probably made the request for the position the Winters filled.

orders.[5] Winter called this an uneasy concept, which was never far from his mind during his first five-year term in Guatemala.[6]

Language School: Costa Rica — 1957

Following their initial training, the Winters departed for Costa Rica for a year of language school. Winter had requested permission to learn the tribal Indian language of Mam first rather than focusing on Spanish. But the mission was not ready for such an approach, and felt the Winters would need Spanish for basic in-country communications and logistics. Once involved in learning Spanish, they then asked to be allowed to locate to a more remote Mam area initially, in order to avoid the use of Spanish as much as possible. But the mission was concerned about this approach and potential health issues for one of their daughters and denied that request also.[7]

Language school was frustrating to Ralph because the way they taught language did not take into account what he had learned in his previous linguistic training.[8] In several letters to his parents in South Pasadena, he described many other projects he was working on, such as helping to mobilize and inform churches back in the U.S. about work with indigenous populations, and "to produce [a] Greek Textual Lexicon, the hybrid-test

---

[5] He had noted that the Presbyterians were reluctant to allow or encourage mission initiatives not started by the denomination itself. Much later Winter wrote about this and noted that Charles Leber, Sr., who headed the Presbyterian Board of Foreign Missions of the Northern Church, said, "something which sounded very strange to my Protestant ears. He suggested that he felt it was time for the Presbyterian tradition to develop *religious orders* of the kind the Anglican and Catholic traditions had spawned." (Winter, 1995a, 1) Winter's 1995 paper was presented to an informal meeting in the Worldwide Ministries Division of the PC(USA) in October, of that year.

[6] Roberta wrote that the Presbyterians' concern about starting religious orders grew out of the fundamentalist/modernist controversy at Princeton Theological Seminary in the 1920s. J. Gresham Machen, one of the four who had left in the split, started a mission agency that would cater to the more conservative portion of the Presbyterian denomination. Within the existing Presbyterian mission, his efforts were seen as divisive and, as a result, the board discouraged the establishment of new structures within the denomination. (Winter 2000, 20)

[7] The Winters' oldest daughter had had some health struggles, including seizures, as an infant.

[8] The ideas Winter had about language learning trace back to his learning of Biblical languages. Perhaps, as Roberta noted, he was wondering out loud if advancing his theories in this area might "solve a problem" that many missionaries and others had in learning languages by ineffective methods. (Winter 2000, 21)

project for English and Spanish leaders...."[9] In July, several months into the program, he wrote, "The only fly in the ointment now is the fact that I'm not learning Spanish except in a really harmful way."[10] Three months later he wrote:

> I'm not learning to speak Spanish at all. In fact I am learning, first, the sight of the words, and I find myself having to visualize what I hear or speak in order to understand. This is terrible! Just one carefully designed class (taught by someone besides me) could be a great help – ten times as valuable as all we are doing.[11]

A few years later in 1961, Robert C. Thorp, the Acting Secretary for Latin America, must have heard about this from a distance and wrote:

> Their career as missionaries began with their year in language school in Costa Rica, where Dr. Winter could not conform to the pattern of language study as established by the school at the time and, consequently, did not attend a majority of his classes but, rather, devised his own system for learning the language at home and spent much time trying to develop a plan for the reorganization of the language school and its language teaching methods.[12]

In 1958 Winter was asked by mission leadership to give his suggestions for the language school. In a five-page letter, he outlined steps for possible improvement:[13]

1. Interpersonal Relationships: There was a general disconnect between the faculty and administration and the brightest students. Winter sided with the students and suggested, "their complaining is more often the result of maturity rather than the opposite; the brighter, better trained group does the most

---

[9] August 25, (1957, the year was not written) letter from Ralph D. Winter to Hugo and Hazel Winter, 1. These letters were retained by Hugo and Hazel, and later Ralph and Roberta.

[10] July 4, (1957) letter from Ralph D. Winter to Hugo and Hazel Winter, 2.

[11] Undated letter (probably October 1957) from Ralph D. Winter to Hugo and Hazel Winter, 2.

[12] February 2, 1961 letter from Robert C. Thorp to Nathaniel Bercovitz, M.D. 1. Copies of many letters and reports used in this section were procured from Presbyterian mission work related to Guatemala at the Presbyterian Historical Society, 425 Lombard Street, Philadelphia, PA 19147, with appreciation.

[13] Summarized from an October 27, 1958 letter from Ralph D. Winter to Don Fletcher, Latin American secretary on the Board of Foreign Missions, Presbyterian Church USA.

complaining," but the students' reactions were interpreted by the leadership of the school as, "loose and undisciplined upbringing."[14]

2. Administration: The program needed more staff. The main leader of the program at the time did almost no teaching or curriculum writing, but was hampered by the details of running the program. Even that job was too much for one person, in Winter's opinion.

3. Academics: The substance was weak because there was no ongoing teacher training. Winter argued that this would be extremely valuable to the program, and would improve things as well as encourage the students to work hard in what they might then see was a quality program. He outlined how those costs could be covered, noting several details about educational costs in the U.S. as well as the teaching methods used at programs such as Cornell University or the University of Michigan. These included both teaching students the language and teaching teachers how to teach it. He noted that some of this top-notch "unquestioned record and experience in teaching teachers" needed to "appear on the scene in Costa Rica."

He concluded the letter by describing the shift that had taken place after World War II related to language learning and the lessons learned in the military. In this area the Army was way beyond the methods taught in most universities, yet, Winter argued, most of the universities had accepted newer ideas. In fact, "very recently the Modern Language Association (dominated by traditional teachers) published their detailed recommendations for a beginning course in Spanish, and it is mainly the older Army approach. Even so, it is a great contrast to the past (and to Costa Rica)."[15]

Part of the reason Winter struggled so much was because he believed strongly in the potential impact of the program, which served such a large number of missionaries working in the Western world. Fourteen months later, after reviewing an official report on the language school produced by noted linguist Eugene Nida, Winter wrote another letter stating, "Whatever I say must be seen in terms of my personal estimate of the role

---

[14] October 27, 1958 letter from Ralph D. Winter to Don Fletcher, 2. Winter had read in *TIME magazine* about this issue, and quoted from the October 27, 1958 issue in his letter (page 48 in the Latin American edition).

[15] October 27, 1958 letter from Ralph D. Winter to Don Fletcher, 4.

and importance of this school. … this school is th
training institution in the Christian Mission the world
school effects so strategically the majority of all the missionai.
an area so large."[16]

After the year in Costa Rica, the Winters arrived in Guatemala, whe.
the political situation had at times been tense. This setting was the seedbed
for Winter to see if some of his ideas and approaches might take root and
flourish.

Guatemala in the 1950s

Guatemala is almost exactly the size of the state of Tennessee. It is
approximately forty-four percent the size of the United Kingdom. In 1954,
it had approximately 3 million people, with 293,000 in the capital city of
Guatemala City. The second largest city was Quezaltenango, west of the
capital, with approximately 36,000. During the 1950s, virtually the whole
country was in turmoil. Up to that point, the Liberal party that had ruled
Guatemala was made up of developmentalists pursuing modernization of
the national economy by seeking foreign investors and other changes.
(TIME Staff, 1954, 38) This included the attempt "…to mold the nation's
large and isolated Indian populations into a compliant work force. By 1870
Liberal thinkers had identified the Protestant religion, and its
accompanying body of ethics and values, as a force that might help in this
modernization process." (Burnett, 1989, 127)

Justo Rufino Barrios (1835-1885) was president of Guatemala from
1873 to 1885 and was instrumental in pursuing this kind of modernization
process, which led to "Protestant missionaries entering the country to
establish a decades-long union between a foreign faith and the secular
Liberal state."[17] (Burnett, 1989, 128)

The election of Jacobo Arbenz Guzman (1913-1971) to the
Presidency in 1950, however "brought the happy alliance of the Protestant

---

[16] January 3, 1960 letter from Ralph D. Winter to Don Fletcher, 1.

[17] In order to see the missionaries come, Barrios traveled to New York and convinced
the Presbyterian Board of Missions to send their first missionary to Guatemala, John Clark
Hill. Barrios' visit actually helped to change Hill's direction from China to Guatemala.
Once in Guatemala, Hill established a work in the capital and by the time Hill left there
was a small church in Quezaltenango. But almost no other church or mission work occurred
outside of Guatemala City. The friendliness of the government continued even after
Barrios' death, and new missions joined the efforts, the largest (eventually) being the
Central American Mission (CAM) headquartered in Dallas. (Burnett, 1989, 128)

ssionaries and the revolutionary government to a hasty close." (Burnett, 1989, 136) During his rule until 1954, "Guatemala moved sharply toward the left and into a friendlier relationship with the Soviet Union." (Woodward, 2005, 136) U.S. concerns grew with Arbenz's legalization of the Communist party for fears it could lead to increasing favorability to Communism in the region.

The pro-Soviet and anti-American declarations of the Guatemalans had, by 1953 elicited strong reactions in the U.S. Extravagant eulogies from the Guatemalan press and Congress upon the death of Joseph Stalin, for example, prompted virulent verbal attacks in the United States on the Guatemalan government, with calls for intervention to suppress Communism there. (Woodward, 2005, 139)

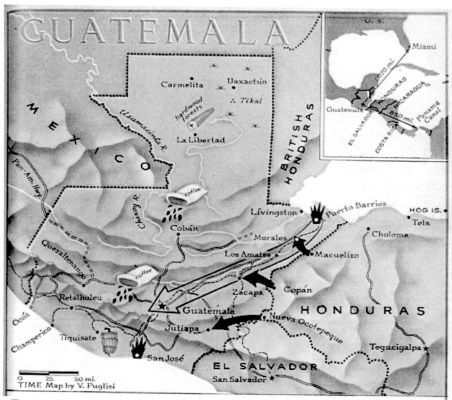

Figure 1 – Guatemala in the 1950s as Armas Returned to Overthrow Arbenz (TIME Magazine, June 28, 1954, 38)

The U.S. even dropped anti-Arbenz leaflets over the capital and produced radio broadcasts warning of a large invasion that could soon come, "creating a climate of fear and apprehension in Guatemala." (Woodward, 2005, 140) "By 1952 the flow of new missionaries into the country had slowed to a trickle." (Burnett, 1989, 137)

Carlos Castillo Armas was the main officer responsible for the overthrow of the Arbenz government (See Figure 1). This changed the government to a military dictatorship. The involvement of religious groups within the country added to tensions and strained relationships. The active and powerful Catholic Church leadership was opposed to the growing communist connections and put pressure on Arbenz. The Archbishop, Rossell y Arellano, "called for Guatemalans to rise up and throw out the Communists." (Woodward, 2005, 140)

The annual field report produced for the leadership of the Presbyterian work in Guatemala noted that the Catholic Church "played an important part in assisting Castillo Armas to come to power."[18] Protestants seemed neutral in the takeover, or perhaps too small to register much attention in the debate. In October of 1954 the new leadership led by Armas opted for religious freedom of worship for all, to the relief of Protestants, who were concerned about Catholic control of all religion in the country.

Even with the Communist leanings of Arbenz,

> Guatemala was clearly becoming more prosperous and more socially equitable. The revolutionary goals of democracy, justice, and economic growth, if not totally fulfilled, were clearly making progress before the overthrow of Arbenz. Caught up in the Cold War, with which it had little to do initially, the Guatemala Revolution had also alienated powerful segments of the country—the Army, the coffee oligarchy, the Church, and foreign enterprise—which would successfully conspire with the United States to end the ten years of Spring.[19] (Woodward, 2005, 141-142)

Because of the devastation of the immediate conflict in the 1950s, including accusations that the outbound leadership took all it could "on the way out the door," the new Guatemalan government was left scarce

---

[18] 1955 Field Report: Guatemala, from the Presbyterian mission, author not named, 1.

[19] This is the period beginning in about 1944, at the end of the leadership of José Ubico Castañeda. Ubico had ruled the country as a dictator since 1931. The "ten years of Spring" references the period after his leadership, brought on by a revolution by those who were initially seeking a broader freedom and improvement of life in the country.

resources, and therefore increased taxes to make up for it. This did not help the already high unemployment and yet there seemed to be general popular support for the Armas regime, even with the Communist underground still active: "Mornings find hand bills and Communist slogans pasted on telegraph poles or scribbled on walls."[20]

Armas ruled only a short time, until he was assassinated in 1957. He outlawed the Communist Party and a wave of arrests, assassinations, and exiles followed. This period began thirty years of guerrilla warfare, ending only after what some estimate to be 100,000 civilians killed. Certainly, the country was in a state of turmoil throughout the 1960s. (Woodward, 2005, 143-146)

Burnett concludes that "...it was during the 1950s that native believers began to chart their own course and to create the momentum for the meteoric trajectory of Guatemalan Protestantism during the 1960s, 1970s, and 1980s." (Burnett, 1989, 140) Even though turmoil was increasing in the 1950s, or perhaps because of it, the Presbyterian Church in Guatemala had become well established in some parts of the country. Civil war continued in different forms and intensity until official agreements to end hostilities were signed between the major factions in 1996. (Woodward, 2005, 159)

Presbyterian Mission Work in Guatemala to the Mid-1900s

Following a long history of Catholic missions dating back to the sixteenth century, Protestant missions had begun work in the late 1800s. At first the work was exclusively among the Spanish-speaking minority, thus it entailed work mainly with Catholics or nominal Catholics. Eventually, however, work among the native, non-Latin groups grew in importance.

The long-term work of Paul and Dora Burgess (who served from 1913 to 1959) and Dudley and Dorothy Peck (1922 to 1970) laid a foundation. The Presbyterian work grew, as did the work by the non-denominational Central American Mission (CAM).[21] All of that laid the foundation for the church and for future mission work. (Coke, 1978, 170-174) The Presbyterians started translation work there in 1923 and the CAM in 1934.

---

[20] 1955 Field Report: Guatemala, from the Presbyterian mission, author not named, 2.

[21] CAM's work started in Guatemala in 1890.

By the 1950s, the Presbyterian mission work was consistently developing indigenous Guatemalan leaders. At that point, missionaries' duties included working as "moderators of sessions," but only when they did not yet have Guatemalan pastors. Paul Burgess noted in his 1956 report that he preached in the Quiché[22] dialect in two churches in which he was Moderator of the Session.[23] There were a number of indigenous leaders in the major towns and cities, especially in Guatemala City. There was solid youth, women's, and men's work, with regular events and gatherings. The Presbyterians were, in fact, celebrating seventy-five years of mission work in a "Diamond Jubilee" by 1957, with a goal of reviving and strengthening the church "that it may enter the last quarter of its first century better able to witness for Christ."[24]

While political instability was not new in the region, in the 1950s mission leadership became concerned about the potential impact of the political situation on the whole mission community. In 1954, a cable from Robert Thorp, head of the Presbyterian mission work in Guatemala, to W.S. Rycroft at the New York office, reflected the heightened level of concern for the field missionaries: "If United States authorities order evacuation should we leave?"[25]

National Church Leadership

In Presbyterian churches both the leadership and the funding at the local church level came from within the country.[26] There was minimal funding for institutions such as seminaries or other programs, schools, and events. No external funds went to pastors or church buildings.

The Presbyterian seminary—Seminario Evangelico Presbiteriano—had named a Guatemalan pastor as the dean two years before in 1953 (his name is not recorded). Subsequently, enrollment had doubled in 1954 and 1955. A report of the period noted issues being considered:

1. How to extend the leadership training service to meet the needs of the whole country—of the churches in the coastal jungles and mountain towns as well as those in and near Guatemala City; and,

---

[22] The English spelling is K'iche'.

[23] 1956 Annual Meeting report by Paul Burgess, 3.

[24] 1955 Field Report: Guatemala, from the Presbyterian mission, author not named, 4.

[25] Cable from Thorp to Rycroft, June 23, 1954, 1.

[26] According to an interview of Winter by the author on August 14, 2006, 9. During the mid 1950s, Guatemalans pastored the churches and "no one could remember the time that any pastor had ever been paid anything" (meaning with outside funds).

2. How to challenge the Guatemalan Synod to a larger measure of responsibility for the direction and financial support of this institution.[27]

At the same time, there were problems as one of the missionaries reported in 1956:

> In the Presbytery where I work there are great differences. ... there are almost as many pastors as churches but only one pastor has a full time church, the rest being occupied in secular work and only visiting in the capacity of interim pastors. The result is that except for one or two bright spots much of the work is stagnant and needs new life.[28]

During this period, the Presbyterians in the U.S. were making detailed plans for full "integration." This entailed a process of turning over all control, property, and assignments of foreign workers (if any remained) into the hands of the Guatemalan Synod. Fraternal workers (missionaries from the U.S.) would be without vote in the ecclesiastical organizations of the Presbyterian Church of Guatemala.[29] The official integration took place on May 20, 1962.[30] (Burgess, 1962, 4)

Native Population Mission Work

Much of the Presbyterian work was focused on those who spoke Spanish as their first language. About sixty percent of the population, categorized as "Indians" in Guatemala, was given considerably less attention.[31] They were defined as those "living in the old Indian villages, wearing tribal costume, speaking its language and living according to its

---

[27] 1955 Field Report: Guatemala, from the Presbyterian mission, author not named, 5.

[28] Annual Meeting Report from James Emery, 1956, 2.

[29] According to an October 1960 two-page document, updated in 1962 by the Executive Committee of the Presbyterian Synod of Guatemala, the plan was to fully integrate the work by 1960. Reasonable delays kept that from full implementation until 1962, (according to the "Report of R.H. Baird to the Commission on Ecumenical Mission and Relations on the meetings in May, 1961 with the Synod of Guatemala on problems Relative to Integration of Mission and Synod" dated received on October 19, 1961).

[30] In *Guatemala News* in June 1962, an article named, "Integration – Rethinking Our Task" reflected the views of a missionary rethinking his role. (Shackelford, 1962)

[31] There were many other distinct people groups based on their language and culture. Milton Coke's PhD study (1978) of translation included twenty-seven language groups, twenty-three of which had thirty-eight distinct dialects, each having at least one published book of the Bible by that time.

customs"[32] as opposed to Ladinos,[33] who speak Spanish and live according to their cultures.[34]

Both the major Protestant mission agencies had established ministry in the country for decades and were now involved in translation work. The Presbyterians had work among the Quiché and Mam tribes, and the missionaries engaged in the work were "necessarily involved in Bible translation and the preparation of hymnbooks and Sunday School literature, since the Indian churches are for the most part not able to use the Spanish language materials available."[35]

Winter's opinion was that, "Of all the Indian tribes in Guatemala, the Mam had been oppressed by the Quiché. So when the Spanish came the Mam were liberated...they were very friendly with the Spanish."[36] The Mam often assumed Spanish names as a way of showing how they appreciated those who had liberated them.

There were approximately 250,000 Mam spread throughout Western Guatemala, and by some reports an additional 250,000 in Chiapas, Mexico.[37] (Coke, 1978, 12) In 1923, Dudley and Dorothy Peck arrived as the first Presbyterians to start the work among the Mam. The Pecks were still on the field when Ralph and Roberta arrived in 1957. Dudley worked establishing the Mam Christian Center (MCC) and Dorothy started language study of the Mam language the day she arrived! The Pecks produced a draft New Testament by their first furlough in 1927. (Coke, 1978, 18) Dorothy was a linguist and the main translator, but she did not have much training, in part because there was not much available at that time. The translation she produced was fairly wooden or, as one report

---

[32] 1955 Field Report: Guatemala, from the Presbyterian mission, author not named, 5.

[33] By local definition in Guatemala and Chiapas, the Spanish term *Ladino* was used for any person who is non-Indian. The term is similar to mestizo, which is used in parts of Mexico meaning "mixed" and "referring to the mixture of Indian and Spanish in both the biological and the cultural sense." (Wonderly, 1959, 56) Here, Ladino does not have the implication of racial mixture.

[34] Winter noted that, "most of the so called 'Latins' are Ladinos, which means they were mainly Indian themselves. The difference between an Indian and a Latin is not genetic but what kind of shoes he wears...whether you choose to be a Latin." Based on an interview with Ralph Winter by the author on July 26, 2006, 5.

[35] 1955 Field Report: Guatemala, from the Presbyterian mission, author not named, 5. The Hymnbook produced by the Pecks was also mentioned in 1956 Annual Meeting report by Paul Burgess, 4.

[36] Interview with Ralph Winter by the author on July 26, 2006, 5.

[37] Some figures are much lower in Mexico.

noted, "studiously literal," and was not used much.[38] The Pecks may have realized this, and with Ralph's training in linguistics and Roberta's in nursing, they looked forward to their arrival.

Five years before the Winters arrived in 1952, missionary couple Jim and Gennet Emery landed in Guatemala.[39] Jim and Ralph had met previously in 1946 when Ralph and Dan Fuller were attending Princeton Seminary. Both from an engineering background, they were able to be engaged in the immediate ministry situation and yet ponder the larger, sometimes global ramifications, often thinking outside of the usual categories. In part because of this similar mind set, they became close co-workers and lifelong friends. Emery worked "closely with the local churches in evangelistic efforts, visiting new fields, helping in training institutes and retreats." But that shifted in 1962, when he began to work largely with the seminary.[40] Later, Winter included an article by Emery as editor of the book, *Theological Education by Extension*. (1969c) He wrote an introduction that described their close working relationship, noting, "Many long late-night conversations between old friends went into the plans the following article presents."[41] (Winter, 1969d, 9)

The article that Emery wrote had been published in the journal *Practical Anthropology* and was called, "The Preparation of Leaders in a Ladino-Indian Church." Emery had "made an analysis of the differing leadership patterns at different levels." (Emery, 1963, 127) Figure 2 shows a chart from that article, which represents his thinking regarding how the culture was changing at that time.[42]

---

[38] World-renowned linguistic scholar Eugene Nida filed a confidential report, under the work of the American Bible Society. He noted that the New Testament that the Pecks translated was not used much. Out of 3,000 copies printed seven years before his report, only 550 have been distributed, and "not more than two-thirds have gone to Indians." This was because of orthographic problems in the translation, a reading/primer program that was too rapid "for teaching the average person to read" and practically no supporting literature of any kind. Nida noted that the Pecks "seem to feel that they should push the N.T. to the exclusion of other supplementary types of literature, which might have a broader appeal, or which might be in other dialects." Based on the *Report on Mam Translation Work* by Eugene Nida, 1947, 1-2.

[39] Emery did his PhD at Michigan State, graduating in 1978, after more than twenty years of missionary service. His topic was, *A search for Alternative Theory for "Cognitive Style"*.

[40] Annual Meeting Report from James Emery, 1962, 1.

[41] Winter wrote this comment while introducing a reprint of Emery's article.

[42] He also saw the clear group leadership pattern in the highland Indians, where, "...elders are not self-chosen, but arrive at their place of leadership by a process of training in successive responsibilities. (Emery, 1963, 128) The article also pointed out differences

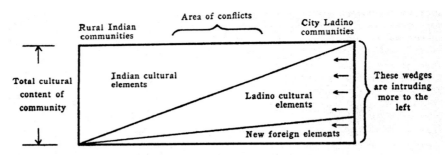

Figure 2 – Cultural Gradations in Guatemala Communities[43]

The town nearest to the Winters was Ostuncalco, with a population around 4,000, half of which was Indian. In 1960, there was a small Presbyterian church in Ostuncalco with less than six active families. Twelve Mam groups or congregations were in outlying areas nearby. The total evangelical (Presbyterian) community in the area of that town was between 400 and 500.[44]

The Presbyterians continued to move toward fully handing over the work to native leadership in the late 1950s and early 1960s. Initially, the Pecks were not assigned to Mam work exclusively because of the Presbyterian church's commitment to Spanish work. At times there was also pressure to unify church work between the Spanish and the Indians. As a result, the Pecks worked with both Mam and Ladinos, emphasizing the unity of this work and urging joint worship services. The Mam deferred to the Ladinos on matters within the church and life in general because of the nature of their relationship.[45] (Coke, 1978, 271)

between city culture, where participation in church or city life is up to choice, and Indian or rural Ladino cultures, where it is expected that everyone participate in both the church and the community. (Emery, 1963, 130)

[43] Taken from Emery, James, "The Preparation of Leaders in an Ladino-Indian Church", *Practical Anthropology* X, 1963, 127. (Emery, 1963)

[44] A Report on the Work and Personnel of the Mam Christian Center, by F.G. Scovell and Wm. L. Wonderly, Ostuncalco, Guatemala, July 16 to 27, 1960, 4.

[45] It may be that these perspectives on how the different subcultures related led to differences in approach to the Mam, especially in determining which language the missionaries should learn and use in the long run.

Arrival on the Field — 1958

The Winters first arrived in the rural highlands of Guatemala on July 22, 1958.[46] Winter's anthropological and engineering perspective on life caused him to absorb all he could about cultural and social issues such as the role of the witch doctor or shaman in society and the problem of alcoholism, and also behavioral assumptions about engagement, marriage, and many other issues. (Winter, 2000, 22) Senior missionary Dudley Peck observed:

> They questioned us about every phase of the work. Their keen analysis of the local situation and anthropologically orientated understanding of the cultural differences between the Indian and the Latino neighbors has contributed to their finding themselves as members of the community. It has been a delightful and stimulating experience to rethink with them the community service approach in winning the Mam-speaking people to faith in Christ as Savior and Lord.[47]

Roberta Winter described her perspective in 1959:

> It has also been a year of getting acquainted—of visiting in Indian homes, of attendance at Indian birth and harvest culto-festivals, of learning to know well the leaders in the Mam Center. We have taken part in the weekly services, the graduation program of the Institute, and the Christmas gatherings in all the surrounding communities. In all this we have learned much about the culture and as well as listening constantly to spoken Mam. More and more we feel an accepted part of the Mam Christian community. …I am looking forward to the day when we will really be one with the people.[48]

Because the Mam people relied on subsistence farming, they were spread out over a large area in the mountainous region. Family plots were broken up as father divided up land and passed it on to several sons, decreasing the size of the plots with each generation and often forcing men to travel a distance to get to a portion of their land. The cost of one tortilla

---

[46] Calculated from the Winter's *Shoptalk* newsletter #3, April 13, 1959, where they note they have been on the field for 265 days.

[47] According to the Guatemala Mission, Personal Report Annual Meeting, Dudley H. Peck, 1959, 1.

[48] Annual Meeting report by Roberta Winter, 1959, 1-2.

was about one cent and a man's average salary was less than forty cents (US$) per day.[49] Roberta described it this way:

> They were—and are—very poor, probably the most impoverished group of their size in the entire hemisphere. Thus, missionary outreach to them had to combine not only evangelism and church planting but also agricultural, medical, economic, and educational work. Since none of them had more than three grades of school, there were no ordained Mam Indian pastors at this point, nor was there any way that they could get the necessary entry-level education, much less afford the time necessary to go away to seminary.
>
> Their one-room huts were made of mud with dirt floors and three stones strategically placed in the middle of the floor to serve as a fireplace-stove. Their clothes (of which they had only one change) were patched and repatched; in fact, where the women carried their babies on their back, the patch itself was very often patched. The Mam diet was almost completely corn with a bit of black beans once a week perhaps and a tiny bit of meat for a very special and somewhat rare occasion. They had no milk, no eggs, no other vegetables or fruits— there was just no money for these. They raised chickens but could not afford to eat either their eggs or the chickens themselves. (Winter 2000, 24) (Winter, 2000, 20)

Focus of Ministry

At the time Winter arrived on the field, there were less than 200 Mam church members. Ten years later, one Mam pastor unofficially estimated that only eighty of the former members were active. "Integration" was complete in the 1950s and church work was in the hands of national leadership, which made counting of Mam church members difficult. Winter remembered attending a synod gathering with some seventy people present, with only four missionaries, who were not running the meeting. The missionaries were there to serve the Indians in any way they could. "The point is that practically, [the church itself] did not make a distinction between the Indians and the Spanish. And the church was both. The church has always been both, it's still both."[50]

---

[49] About US$ 3.32 or £2.06 in 2011.

[50] After Winter left the field, his replacement, David Scotchmer, would organize a Mam Presbytery that could set its own standards for ordination and practice. Much later,

When Winter first arrived, he followed the pattern of meeting with and discipling several young men in the area. He also followed this pattern at the Mam Center, which was like a Bible School curriculum approach. He soon realized that teaching these young men outlines of books of the Bible was not what they needed, so he moved the meeting from the classroom to his own living room, as he had done with the Navigators. They would study a passage and seek to apply it to their lives. This forced the men to understand the passages more accurately and to clearly see how the Bible applied to real life. (Winter, 2000, 22-23)

As Winter learned more, he realized there was a problem with the men he was meeting with regularly: they were not mainstream members of society. Some were orphans, or otherwise "outsiders" to everyday life for one reason or another. He was quoted in a field-wide report as referring to these kinds of students as "social outcasts."[51] He could continue to work with them and see them fully trained, ready to be leaders of churches and other ministries, but would the locals accept them in that role? Winter continued to work with some of them, but began to rethink what he should do to see other recognized leaders gain the equipping they needed. (Winter, 2000, 23)

Thinking more seriously about equipping recognized leaders began to feed into the idea of getting theological training to pastors and leaders rather than requiring them to come to residential training. Winter continued to increase his involvement in the on-site pastoral training at the Mam Christian Center, which the Pecks had established. And yet, Winter and others with him saw numerous disadvantages in sending leaders away to the city for training. Most could not afford the time or money to go. In the end, several of these men became involved in full time ministry, and one became a pastor of a large church of 1,000. This is also how Winter met Ruben Dias, who was very bright, understood both Mam and Spanish, and soon became a key person in Winter's language work.

Language Learning: Different Approaches

The Pecks had hoped Winter would quickly learn Mam so he could work on translation projects, including the improvement of the NT

---

when Winter returned to Guatemala after 39 years, three churches had increased to thirty. According to interviews with Ralph Winter by the author on July 26, 2006, 4, and August 30, 2006, 6.

[51] A Report on the Work and Personnel of the Mam Christian Center, by F.G. Scovell and Wm. L. Wonderly, Ostuncalco, Guatemala, July 16 to 27, 1960, 11.

translation that Dorothy had done. However, it was difficult to learn Mam from the younger Mam men, who preferred to speak Spanish because of their need to fit in economically and socially. In many ways, Winter continued the approach Peck and the mission had started, and served both Ladino and Mam society. (Coke, 1978, 280)

When the Winters first arrived, there were only a few basic primers produced to help with language learning. Having the NT was helpful, but only for understanding certain concepts. Winter wanted to be sure that anything new he did be written down for future missionaries who might be learning Mam. Another reason Winter did not focus on learning the language himself was because his training was in language analysis, not specifically in language learning.[52]

Winter never learned the Mam language well, which some of the Presbyterian mission leaders did not understand. They did appreciate that he was gifted and did "some rather extensive technical analysis and collation of materials."[53] Earlier, Dorothy Peck (but not Dudley) had learned Mam because the Mam women could not speak Spanish well and it was essential if she were to communicate with them directly. Winter himself did work on a dictionary of the Mam language. But as Winter noted, "it was not that useful, because nobody that I dealt with ever needed to talk Mam."[54]

Along with his other work Winter had been working personally with Ruben Dias. Winter thought that if Dias could develop dramas using everyday language, Winter could memorize these in Mam. Since Dias

---

[52] According to an interview with Ralph Winter by the author on July 26, 2006, 19, and an email from Henry (Harry) McArthur, with the Summer Institute of Linguistics (SIL) for the Aguacatec people, dated January 19, 2007, an example of Winter's language analysis skills occurred one day when he talked with McArthur, who was one of several SIL translators working in a nearby language. Winter and McArthur talked about the complicated language structure in which McArthur was working. Winter explained the complicated three-dimensional pronominal structure for this dialect, which McArthur had been struggling with for years. McArthur recalled the conversation: "There were several sets of pronouns on the verbs depending on whether they were active, passive, or middle, and also depending on whether the root commenced with a vowel or consonant. One day I was discussing this with Ralph as we waited outside the kids' school in Quezaltenango. He took out a paper and pencil and on the hood of a car drew me a rather complicated-looking diagram, but that showed how the whole system worked in a nutshell. He had understood the system perfectly and was able to draw a diagram that showed how it really worked." He added that Winter, "had a good grasp of the Mayan religious [system] and culture and taught classes in one of the university extension courses in Quez."

[53] A Report on the Work and Personnel of the Mam Christian Center, by F.G. Scovell and Wm. L. Wonderly, Ostuncalco, Guatemala, July 16 to 27, 1960, 16.

[54] Interview with Ralph Winter by the author on July 26, 2006, 9.

could understand both the language and the culture enough to help develop an effective story line for these dramas, it would help Ralph better understand cultural issues related to day-to-day life. And he would learn some of the language. So Winter would share the outline of an idea with Ruben, who quickly caught on and produced the story in Mam. According to Winter, Ruben "could listen to a tape and transcribe the Indian language in phonemic script without batting an eye."[55] To Winter's surprise, Ruben produced three stories the first day. Winter would give him something to translate from Spanish into Mam, and he would just type it out, "just like that," on the typewriter. The two men would spend hours together discussing how to communicate within the culture as well as wording and rewording passages. Later, Ruben went on to produce a second edition of the New Testament in Mam. But Mam material was not used much as the Spanish continued to increase in use.[56]

Winter was urged if not "commanded" by the mission leadership to focus on learning Mam when he and Roberta returned after their furlough in 1962. When expressing this in a letter to Winter, John H. Sinclair attached the motions of the Joint Committee (Guatemala), which also noted "I know that there will be many demands made upon you immediately upon your arrival to get into other activities, but I trust you will have the good judgment and the grace to put aside all other tasks, perhaps even some needful projects that challenge your fertile imagination, and give yourselves to the task of learning well the language."[57]

In April 1959, Winter outlined 21 weeks of his work since their arrival in Guatemala. Only nine and one half weeks were available "for anything like language learning."[58] How many of those "assignments" were self-assigned projects of Winter's choosing is not clear from the record.

Winter recognized that someone would need to learn the Mam language to truly help the people and the church leadership. But he continued to believe anyone who wanted to learn Mam, should learn Mam first before Spanish. Later, when the Winters recruited a replacement, he urged the board that the new couple learn Mam first.

The Winters understood from their own experience that new missionaries would need to learn Man in order to minister effectively. They recruited David and Sarah

---

[55] Interview with Ralph Winter by the author on August 30, 2006, 6.

[56] Interview with Ralph Winter by the author on July 26, 2006, 9. Dias was still involved in the church as of 2008.

[57] July 10, 1961 letter from John H. Sinclair to Ralph and Roberta Winter, 1.

[58] *Shoptalk* news letter, April 13, 1959, 2.

Scotchmer and convinced the Presbyterian mission to assign them to Mam language study before Spanish study. (Coke, 1978, 284)[59]

A Different Approach to Everything?

Recalling the Winters' delays in learning Mam, Thorp noted that Winter:

> ...apparently was involving himself in too many other activities and was not learning the language. At least he was not apparently following the usual patterns of learning a language but rather dabbling in new methods and techniques which he himself had devised.
>
> After three years he has still not learned the language but has amassed a dictionary and recorded several hours of conversation in dialect and with his helper has written the conversations with inter-linear Spanish translation.
>
> When asked about his lack of progress in mastering the dialect he replied on one occasion, "Just because I am a linguist does not mean that my specialty is learning languages. I am also an engineer and like an engineer I might devise language learning techniques without ever learning the languages, much as an engineer would design an assembly line without ever building a car himself."[60]

Thorp gave his opinion as to why this might be happening, writing, "Dr. Winter is undoubtedly bothered by the fact that at the age of 36 he still has not found his niche. He rationalizes his failure to learn the Mam language on the basis that he is basically an engineer or that he might not stay on at the Mam Center or that he has too many other responsibilities." [61] Thorp also wrote:

> A great deal could be written about his transient ideas and schemes, many of them inpracticable and not founded

---

[59] At Winter's suggestion, the Scotchmers learned Mam before Spanish, even though that was very difficult, because of the proximity of Spanish speakers and the need to know some Spanish to deal with the everyday issues of life. Sara Scotchmer struggled especially, not knowing even a little Spanish when she arrived. Yet, they did learn Mam, and were able to help the churches there in a number of ways and the ministry transitioned. See, (First) Annual Report of the Scotchmers in Guatemala, November 1, 1970, 2. Also, Interview with Ralph Winter by the author on July 26, 2007, 8.

[60] February 2, 1961 letter from Robert C. Thorp to Nathaniel Bercovitz, M.D., 2.

[61] February 2, 1961 letter from Robert C. Thorp to Nathaniel Bercovitz, M.D., 2.

upon careful planning. Others of them are actually brilliant. (Most of them are not taken seriously by his fellow workers, which must increase his frustrations.) He is almost a genius, with a versatile, productive mind, and his time and activity cannot keep pace with it.[62]

Winter was involved in many other activities and had ministry responsibilities as soon as he arrived in Guatemala. Some of these included administration of a Bible School, administration of a Spanish program for elementary children, and the building of relationships with people, which included birth celebrations, funerals, and baptisms in lakes at 3,400 meters elevation. While Winter learned Spanish well, it was difficult for him to focus on Mam language-learning or any one specific task with so many other ideas, projects and responsibilities.[63]

While the Winters were in language school, Ralph wrote many letters to his parents describing how he was feeling about his work and sharing ideas for new problems or issues that needed someone's attention. He also wrote to some in his mission leadership about his ideas for informing and motivating greater involvement in churches back home. Interacting with church and mission leadership, Winter describes four ways he desired to communicate with churches who were interested in their work:

1. *Shoptalk* – A letter to pastors, the leaders of mission committees, and a few others. This was to be every two weeks, seeking to elicit questions, ideas, and input from these leaders which could be put into the next letter. Winter felt that an every-two-week communication would be necessary to keep churches informed and engaged.

2. *Missionfotos* – A series of photos which would go to each of the churches to post or otherwise display. The photos would show the work and would each have a caption explaining what was happening. Winter had planned on a thirty-week period during which he hoped for fifteen "installments" which would

---

[62] February 2, 1961 letter from Robert C. Thorp to Nathaniel Bercovitz, M.D., 2. In the letter Thorp uses the word, inpracticable.

[63] While Winter helped to keep things going that the Pecks and others had begun, he often thought of new ways to do old things as well as additional things that needed to be done. In fact, Winter's way of initiating and reexamining everything irked others. One missionary, who apparently preferred things to be stable and consistent, was quoted as saying, "It doesn't matter what is suggested. If Winter is involved, I'm automatically against it." (Winter 2000, 27)

be showing up at the church every two weeks, keeping church bulletin boards updated every third Sunday.[64]

3. *Slidetape Programs* – This would include about sixty 35mm slides with a twenty-minute commentary. It would be updated every three months, with one church lending it to other churches.

4. *Slidefile* – This would be a letter sent to the broadest audience, sometimes with photos. It was to be sent twice a year.[65]

Winter summarized the purpose of all this as follows:

> Our fundamental purpose is to make the world mission more real to the people back home. This means that we must strive constantly to wean the people away from mere interest in us and fasten their gaze upon the people to whom we are going. Travelogues and family details will not enter at all except where we feel that thereby contact will be made more definite with the people who constitute the objective of the Mission, or where the general role of the missionary can be helpfully explained to folks whose concept is out of date.[66]

Ultimately, records contain only a few issues of *Shoptalk* and it quickly broadened in focus to include anyone who was interested, presumably because there was not time to produce all the other projects as well. Winter did take many photos, but it is not known how many photographs or slide shows he produced and sent to churches after the first sent out in September 1957 from Costa Rica.[67]

---

[64] Winter was on the planning committee and attended a communications fair in San Jose, Costa Rica on April 10, 1958 called Organizing for Impact. This was targeted at "foreign missionaries." The mimeographed booklet from the event included a three page article called "Welcome to the Fair" which Winter wrote, encouraging participants to work at impacting "those who are consigned to remain in the hubbub of modern America" with stories that motivate and mobilize them toward involvement at some level. There is also and description of a seminar he co-led with Bill Douce called, "Use of Photographs."

[65] September 28, 1957 letter from Ralph D. Winter to Dr. Rycroft (copy to Mae Ross Taylor and Archie Crouch), 1-2.

[66] September 28, 1957 letter from Ralph D. Winter to Dr. Rycroft (copy to Mae Ross Taylor and Archie Crouch), 2.

[67] September 16, 1957 letter from Ralph D. Winter to Rev. Stevens (copy to Mrs. Clewett), 1.

Mam Christian Center

Because there were established churches and pastors in the area, much of the involvement of the missionaries was related to mentoring, training and leadership development. The Mam Christian Center (MCC), was located about fifteen miles from the end of the nearest paved road and public electricity at the time. It was a place for people to come and receive instruction in areas such as evangelism, Bible teaching, agriculture, and public health.

By the time Winter was on the field two months, he noticed that with more than a dozen areas of work and ministry, accounting for the funds for each ministry could get confusing. He believed it was essential to learn basic accounting, so he purchased a 500-page standard textbook on accounting and studied from seven to midnight each night for three months.[68]

In his mind, this was an area of ministry and activity that needed accuracy and understanding in order to keep the work going. He would later train pastors in accounting and basic bookkeeping for the running of small businesses.[69]

Over time and by necessity, the ministry of the Mam Center changed. When the Pecks retired in 1962, Winter linked the institute training program with a seminary program that used Spanish. The institute had formerly worked in Mam and Spanish. New missionaries David and Sara Scotchmer, came to replace the Winters in 1970.[70] David wrote:

---

[68] He became the most knowledgeable missionary in the country on the subject, according to Roberta. (Winter 2000, 20-21) Soon he was dealing with the accounting of their local schools, training programs, and clinics. Fellow missionaries, like Jim Emery, routinely had Winter check their books at the seminary, and he would be counted on to find any error in the books for the whole field of Guatemala. Several reports and letters during this period demonstrate Winter's involvement in the accounting for many areas.

[69] Some of the accounting lessons Winter learned were applied to multiple projects over time, such as the idea of a revolving fund. Rather than spend money whenever they got it, Winter encouraged the investment of funds to repay the source of funds or reinvest in the business, even if it was donated money. This way, they would not merely be looking at income and expenses, but also the assets, liabilities and net worth of a particular project. (Winter 2000, 25)

[70] David and Sara Scotchmer served from September 1969 until 1982. In their first annual report, (First) Annual Report of the Scotchmers in Guatemala, November 1, 1970, 15, in 1970, David Scotchmer noted that the Mam Center seemed to be drifting, to the point where people not living on the property or daily involved in the Center did not know what it was there for. He wrote about this and the role of the fraternal worker (expatriate): "Confronted with the stamina of the 'founding-pioneering' Pecks and the zeal of the 'inspiring-innovating' Winters, we are rather challenged to define our own role and [the

With the ministry of the Winters the [Mam Christian] Center no longer was a place to which people came for instruction, but rather it became a center from which various ministries radiated to strengthen the already growing church—extension institutes, adult education, projects in small industries, seminary extension courses. The Winters sought to minister among the Mam by providing connecting links to the world outside their own. ...

With the departure of both the Pecks and the Winters, today we see a Mam Center not so much a servant of the church and community as much as an institution without inspired leadership, direction, or vision. The essential struggle of the Center at present is one of survival for the sake of a few who benefit from its continued existence.[71]

Indians lived below the poverty level and were on the edge of starvation most of the time, so medical issues were a part of everyday life. The church was already established among this people group, so a main ministry need was the training of pastors. Winter was involved in this training from the beginning, but also saw the need for pastors to get instruction not usually included in the typical seminary, including medical training. An unintended side effect of this instruction was increased tension with a senior missionary by the name of Ruth Wardell.

Field Relational Issues

Even before the Winters were assigned to Guatemala, there were relational problems on the field.[72] The request to the mission board for missionaries with anthropology and linguistics and nursing fit the Winters but, Roberta wrote:

We found out later that many of the missionaries in the Guatemala Presbyterian mission had real reservations about this request because of the personnel problems that existed at the Mam Christian Center. But they passed the request on

---

Presbyterian] fraternal workers within the Mam church and community. One word seems best to describe both our self-understanding and to fit the situation: the role of the ENABLER." (Note: During that period of time, the word "enabler" referred to one who served, helped, and encouraged. It was not seen as negative.)

[71] Both quotes from: (First) Annual Report of the Scotchmers in Guatemala, November 1, 1970, 6.

[72] For more details of this relationship issue, see Appendix C.

because they thought it would never be filled. (Winter, 2000, 18)

The struggle seems to have centered on a single missionary named Ruth Wardell. Ruth was a nurse from Jim Emery's home church and was brought in to staff a medical clinic that the Pecks had started as part of the MCC. She arrived in 1949 and remained faithful to the work until 1980. She was a strong person, a perfectionist who was determined to suffer hardship if and when necessary. Jim Emery's son, Paul, remembered hearing stories of Ruth riding a mule up into the mountains for days to provide medical service in remote areas.[73]

It was difficult for many of the missionaries to get along with her since she had set ways of doing the work and did not seem to be open to others' opinions. She carefully controlled the clinic and did not allow either other missionaries or Indians to participate in that work.[74] As a result, she was not able to multiply the work of the clinic. Although Roberta was a trained nurse and at the top of her class at the USC nursing school, Ruth would not let her use the clinic in Ruth's absence. When reporting on her work in a 1962 report, Roberta wrote an indirect reference to this, noting that, "Other responsibilities have included helping those emergencies who come to my door in the absence of Ruth Wardell. I have used medicines from our personal supply in order to not infringe on clinic funds."[75]

The longstanding relational strain between the Pecks and Wardell and the shorter one with the Winters was never resolved. Winter believed that it could not have been resolved at the field level, because no one had ultimate supervisory control over the others.[76] In the end, Wardell's line of reporting was merely transferred to a different structure. This saved everyone time. Board meetings for the various ministries had become a struggle between conventional approaches and creative ones.[77] While Wardell had verbally resigned, it did not stick, and, instead of leaving, the clinic was run under a different board as of January 1963.[78] It appears that the clinic continued to run the way Ruth wanted it to until she retired.[79]

---

[73] According to a March 9, 2011 email from Paul Emery to the author, 1.

[74] There were two or three Mam who gave out the medicine and shots she ordered.

[75] Annual Meeting Report by Roberta H. Winter, 1962, 2.

[76] There was seniority, but no real management structure. February 12, 2009 email from Ralph D. Winter to the author, 1.

[77] October 15, 1958 letter from Ralph D. Winter to Don Fletcher, 1.

[78] January 25, 1963 letter from Ruth E. Wardell to John Sinclair.

[79] In the (First) Annual Report of the Scotchmers, November 1, 1970, 10, Scotchmer commented on Ruth, noting the difficulty of working with Ruth because she did not take

Serving Pastors

Foundational to Guatemala's poor economy was their land inheritance system previously mentioned. The land was divided up between the sons, with the youngest son receiving a larger portion so he could care for his parents until their death. By the 1950s, the plots of land were so often subdivided that they were small, spread apart and thus a long way from the new owners' housing. Churches could not substantially support their pastors, if at all, so in order to make a living, a pastor might have to walk for hours to travel between his land, church, and home. Pastors could not even consider going across the mountains to establish a new church. Often, to get work, young men would take seasonal jobs down on the coast, where the tropical climate brought illnesses such as malaria, dysentery, or other diseases. (Winter, 2000, 23-24)

The Winters saw the problem and planned to help them provide services in ways that drew in resources by producing and selling desirable products to markets outside the Mam areas. There was no way to meet the most basic needs of the people by selling one another goods or services, even if some of these Indians received help from outsiders.[80] As a result, Winter tried: 1) to help them establish and run small, portable businesses; and, 2) to link the role and perception of the pastor with that of the shaman.

Portable Businesses

These small, portable businesses were intended to help sustain pastors and give them the freedom to expand their ministries. With the bulk of the Presbyterian churches and mission offices in major cities, the priority of the mission funds available was weighted toward the cities' needs. Since Winter's work budget was only $650 per year, he personally sought to raise additional funds to "invest" in these small businesses.[81] Winter kept the funds he raised separate from any other accounts, and used them to set up the businesses and train the young men in the skills they needed, both for the work itself and for the administration, government registration and

---

into account the voice of the Mam clinic workers, did not allow them to work afterhours, and showed a lack of interest in prevention as anything more than a "token effort."

[80] Funding this from Mam resources would merely circulate money, help one or two families, but could not lift the region out of poverty.

[81] $650 in US$ in 1960 was worth £415. In 2011, it would be worth $4962 or about £3090.

other business requirements.[82] He sought to start businesses that were portable to allow the pastor/businessman to travel as necessary.[83] (Winter, 2000, 25)

Ruben Diaz was in charge of the largest of the business ventures in which Ralph was involved, a furniture-making business.[84] They made folding chairs and church pews, and later closets and doors for housing developments. These were sold to the second largest city in the country, Quezaltenango, fifteen miles away. It eventually handled thousands of dollars a month. Other businesses included itinerant photography with a photo lab, a weaving business using the best, color-fast thread; a print shop with mimeograph machines; and silk-screening services.[85] There was also basic dentistry to pull rotting teeth and even make plates, and a fluorescent light-assembly factory. Winter also taught several men to drive a jeep, which became the first "ambulance" service for the mission clinic.[86] (Winter, 2000, 25)

In each case, except weaving,[87] Winter taught them to do the different kinds of work necessary to run the business. In the process, Winter also taught them to "use" money without spending it: in other words, to invest in businesses to create revolving funding. The money that went into any business had to be paid back (or reinvested for growth), so that it could be invested in another project. Usually it would take a few cycles of the business to see them get paid off, but every business had to actually make a profit or it was shut down. There was no room for subsidizing something for the long run. The reinvestment of funds was crucial for building the businesses and solving the longer-term problems.

It was often difficult to run these businesses:

> ...one of the givens was the strong prejudice against Indians on the part of the Ladino (Spanish-speaking) minority. Winter found that he could not simply give the money to the young man in charge of the furniture factory and send him 100 miles to the capital city to buy a quantity of special screws, for example. Winter himself had to accompany

---

[82] Winter used his newly acquired accounting skills for these businesses and trained the nationals to do accounting as well.

[83] Like the apostle Paul had done when he made tents as noted in New Testament.

[84] This was not a portable business.

[85] The latter two were also used to produce adult education books being used locally.

[86] A Report on the Work and Personnel of the Mam Christian Center, by F.G. Scovell and Wm. L. Wonderly, Ostuncalco, Guatemala, July 16 to 27, 1960, 15. The value of the car was $300, which was worth just over $2290 in 2011, or about £1426.

[87] There was a government-run school the Mam could attend.

him because store owners there simply could not believe that a poor Indian in rubber-tire sandals could legitimately have the funds necessary to buy the bolts and screws necessary for the factory. (Winter, 2000, 25-26)

The Winters spent some of their own salary to support what the women were doing as well, especially with weaving. The Winters had excess personal income because they tried not to spend money on non-essentials such as soda pop, knowing that if the Indians did what they did, buying a Coke would take food out of the mouths of their families, not to mention fail to nourish them, and rot their teeth. Similar problems already existed due to alcohol consumption.

Winter had workers set up not only production but also distribution for the textiles they made. At first, as they made and sold products, the Winters hoped that the women could make enough to pay to have their corn milled at a local mill and use their time for weaving or other activities, but, "it soon became evident that their husbands took the money they earned from their weaving and as a result they were burdened with one more job. The idea was not a bad one; it just didn't take into consideration the cultural factors of the husbands toward their wives." (Winter, 2000, 26)

While most Mam were not formally educated beyond three grades of school, they were bright, eager to learn and worked hard. They learned all the skills needed for running the businesses, accounting for thousands of dollars a month down to the penny. At one point, Winter was delayed in writing a letter in response to Sinclair because, he wrote "we landed a 50,000 [unit] contract, and I had to spend five straight weeks night and day in one of our shops to help engineer the product and its production. [Otherwise] I have not even been in the shop for more than ten minutes for the last five weeks."[88]

Years later, David Scotchmer noted a decline in the use of the woodworking business:

It is the best-equipped shop in the area west of Quezaltenango, and many find it advantageous to use because of reasonable costs of the work due to lower rent and labor costs compared to city prices. ... The missing key, however, in terms of the shop's contribution to the needs of human and economic development is the lack of an entrepreneur—that person who can instruct and organize the workers by relating to them, as well as act as mediator for those workers within the larger, impenetrable Spanish world (e.g. the problem of

---

[88] October 20, 1964 letter from Ralph D. Winter to John H. Sinclair, 1.

securing contracts for semi-skilled Indian Labor within a Ladino-dominated economy).[89]

The small businesses helped the church planting efforts succeed, increased the ability of the pastors to serve their church(es), and provided for their families. The village near the Winters' home had about 200 inhabitants, with a "market" population of close to 1,000 from the region. At the request of the mayor and town leadership, Winter also started a local junior high school that is still in operation. (Winter, 2000, 26, 28)

Pastors as Shamans

Considerable medical work was undertaken by Presbyterians in Guatemala. The largest included the American Hospital in Guatemala City, which worked at full capacity "for some time," and had a school of nursing attached. Furthermore, a "very valuable service is being given by the Mam clinic and by a clinic in San Felipe on the western slopes of the country."[90] Because the Mam center adopted the broader training approach, the medical work had "been especially successful in reaching the needs of the Mam people and in combating the domination of the witch doctors who combine religion, healing and a lot of psychology (of a kind) for their purpose."[91]

Winter sought to enhance the work of the church and its pastors by training the pastors in basic medical work. When observing the shamans of this animistic people, Winter noticed they did not just deal with spiritual issues, but physical needs as well. For example, shamans or witchdoctors offered the people a mixture of both "teaching" and medical work, while a Pastor only taught. Missionaries who did medical work were not highly respected by the people because they did not teach or preach, and pastors were also looked down upon because they could not do medical work. Winter's point was that to gain the respect of the people and open more doors of opportunity, pastors should be trained to deal with basic, physical needs of the people they were serving and seeking to reach, and medical people should be trained to deal with the spiritual.[92] A report about Winter's thinking written from one field supervisor in the capital city differed:

---

[89] (First) Annual Report of the Scotchmers in Guatemala, November 1, 1970, 9.

[90] 1955 Field Report: Guatemala, from the Presbyterian mission, author not named, 6-8.

[91] 1955 Field Report: Guatemala, from the Presbyterian mission, author not named, 6.

[92] Interview with Ralph Winter by the author on July 26, 2006, 12.

... Dr. Winter feels that no Christian leader can have the respect of a Mam community unless he also is a healer, since this is the role of the shaman or witch doctor, who is looked to as the leader in the non-evangelical community. However, the three most capable Mam workers ... each say that the witch doctors are losing their influence today (partly due to the current missionary efforts of orthodox Catholicism), and these workers have given us the impression that this factor can easily be over-estimated. Nevertheless, it would be very valuable if the clinic could help give certain medical and health concepts to as many students as possible, but not with the intention of training them to treat illness except in limited fields and under supervision.[93]

When Winter and Wallstrom worked together, they examined the medical and evangelistic work throughout the Chiapas region in Mexico and produced "The Chiapas Study" of effective, indigenous work in Mexico.[94] Several people from a number of organizations, including Wycliffe, Reformed Church in America, and Presbyterians, participated in the study. Reaction to the study was mixed. Winter and Wallstrom suggested that pastors be trained in the rudiments of medicine. But other missionaries and some of the home office leadership wondered what Winter was trying to accomplish. Some traditional medical workers believed you could never train pastors to do what medical people did. Since many knew of Winter's perspective on these issues and his relational differences with Ruth Wardell, some assumed his study was an excuse to further his agenda. Others saw his study as a distraction from his main assignment of working on the Mam language. Still others felt the pastors could only learn so much, and needed more pastoral training if they were to receive more training in something.

By seeking to transfer the Chiapas model, Winter was trying to solve problems, in this case: how the pastors and Christian leaders were perceived by the people, how the culture was shifting to speaking Spanish and how that impacted his current situation and what he expected in the future. In the case of the Chiapas Study, training pastors to deal with 90% of the health problems they encounter day-to-day was the goal.[95] Reflecting on it later, Winter illustrated the cultural differences between

---

[93] A Report on the Work and Personnel of the Mam Christian Center, by F.G. Scovell and Wm. L. Wonderly, Ostuncalco, Guatemala, July 16 to 27, 1960, 9.

[94] Interview with Ralph Winter by the author on July 26, 2006, 11.

[95] Interview with Ralph Winter by the author on July 26, 2006, 14.

the North American missionary approach to medical work and the Mam's understanding of the role of the shaman within their society:

> ... a man and his wife would go to the clinic and sit through the line...[of some] 40 or 50 people a day. And they'd say:
>
> "What's the problem?"
>
> "It's our daughter."
>
> "Where's your daughter?"
>
> "She's home."
>
> "Why didn't you bring her?"
>
> "Well, she's not sick."
>
> "What are you doing here wasting our time?"
>
> "Well, the problem is whether she should marry this person."
>
> And the person at the clinic, Ruth Wardell, would say, "get out of here."
>
> ...[however] the shaman would say, "hmm" and he would get out his pouch and go through a ceremony [by counting beans]. Of course the shaman didn't know how many beads were in there. But, he was a very wise person, essentially a marriage counselor, and he would decide whether it was a good marriage or not. And even if it didn't work out, the young people knew it was supposed to work and they would make it work. The Christian marriages fell to pieces, and the Mam marriages didn't fall to pieces. ... this happened again and again and again. ... [the Mam] assumed that a clinic worker was like a shaman.[96]

Additionally, Winter had observed the Mam had no concept of "specialization" within the culture. This meant it was a foreign concept for a person to be *only* a pastor or *only* a doctor. The missionaries from the U.S. had that concept. The indigenous people did not. Winter felt that it was a great disadvantage for pastors not to know anything about medicine:

> It wasn't that *we* didn't believe in specialization, but that *they* didn't. So we have to produce a person whose expertise embraces both pastoral and medical, at least to some extent. ... I never ever conceived of a pastor becoming a clinic worker. All I said is we have five kinds of diseases which have easy medical solutions which constitute ninety percent of the problems, and if a pastor knew the answers, he could take a

---

[96] Interview with Ralph Winter by the author on July 26, 2006, 16.

great deal of load off the clinic. And the pastor would then have more or less of the dual function of a shaman.[97]

In 1966, Winter wrote, "Rural people instinctively doubt the feasibility of specializing in any one thing. This is the first reason they are not eager to dig up full-time support for the man who comes to them trained only in an ecclesiastical vocation. Nor will such specialized pastors dare to adopt the part-time pattern which is logical to the rural mind." (Winter, 1966b, 10) Winter also saw that with such low population density, a "rural church movement must be able to survive and grow as a small-group phenomenon." (Winter, 1966b, 11) He was convinced that they needed the skills not only to lead a small church but also to provide for their own needs and family with resources not provided by the church.

As Winter often would, he sought out collaborating ideas to bolster his own views. Besides Wallstrom, he also met with a non-Christian doctor from a well-known clinic in Kansas who would visit the field for a month each year, and they would talk into the night. According to Winter, this doctor, who learned Spanish, agreed with Winter in his idea of eliciting the help of the pastors for basic medical needs.[98]

Other Responsibilities

Winter was involved in a number of different kinds of roles. He wrote a one-page issue of his *Shoptalk* newsletter seeking to answer the question "What actually does a missionary do?" He then listed his assignments under six major headings and included his specific roles related to 1) the New York office of the mission, 2) the Guatemala-wide responsibilities, 3) the Quezaltenango station, 4) the governing board, 5) the administrative council of the Mam Center, 6) the synod of the Guatemala National Church, and 7) international networks.[99]

His roles continued to increase in diversity as Winter continued in the work. This included work related to the farm connected with the Mam Center, as well as helping the nearby city with a technical engineering problem. The Pecks expressed concern for Ralph, writing, "we also have noted how Ralph is tempted to spread himself thin..." In the same report, he noted that he and Roberta were finally getting three hours a day for the

---

[97] Interview with Ralph Winter by the author on July 26, 2006, 16.
[98] Interview with Ralph Winter by the author on July 26, 2006, 17.
[99] For a detailed list, see Appendix D.

study of Mam once they were back on the field, which was their primary assignment. How long that lasted is not known.

As the Winter girls grew, Ralph and Roberta were involved in setting up an Inter-American School where missionary children, Guatemalan children, and children from the U.S. would come to an ideal, bi-cultural educational setting. They later wrote an article together about this school model, without mentioning the school itself, in 1968 called "When School is Half a World Away" (Winter and Winter, 1968) They could see the potential of the school to draw in students even from North America, because the Winters felt "many of our finest Christian families, would give their right arm to see their children grow up bi-lingual," but they did not yet know about the school.[100] While the school may not currently be following the pattern the Winters envisioned, it has been successful and still has 100 students as of 2006. It was another example of Ralph's creativity and innovation, as Roberta noted.

Often, it is a painful thing to be an initiator. Non-initiator personalities often criticize or at times are jealous if some new project which they were against actually succeeds. But for progress to be made, someone has to risk pain from being misunderstood. Not many people are willing to run that risk. (Winter, 2000, 28)

Economic Issues and the Outside World

Certainly, Winter was impacted by the surroundings. Working and living closely with a group that is on the verge of starvation, as both Ralph and Roberta described it after the fact, is the kind of situation that people either leave or attempt to help.[101] In 1958, he wrote one of his earliest articles on this: "Poverty and Christian Mission." First, he included a reference to those who want to provide "hand outs" by writing, "...to obtain outside food donations doesn't really solve the problem. Nor money for food. In our valley of 20,000 Indians a million dollars given outright

---

[100] October 6, 1964 letter from Ralph D. Winter to Dick Wallis, 5. Winter himself was never very involved in the school, but there was opposition from the Presbyterian office in New York, while other missions seemed to like the idea and saw it as helpful and necessary.

[101] Winter used to tell the story of the Mam woman carrying a full basket of corn on her head. If she spilled just one kernel, she would stop, take the large basket off her head and pick up the kernel and put the basket back on her head. Every kernel was either eaten, planted or (rarely) sold.

would supply food for only a few months and then what?" (Winter, 1958, 1)

As mentioned above, the availability of land was a crucial issue and as populations grew, it became a greater and greater issue. The only land still available in the region was where it was too hot and full of disease. But even there, Winter noted, "Relocating people on the coastal land is merely postponing the evil day when there will come in flood tide the inevitable shift from hand agriculture of the masses to mechanized agriculture of a few and the secondary result of large scale technological unemployment. (Who should know this better than those in the U. S.?)" (Winter, 1958, 1)

Winter saw that both the physical and spiritual needs must be addressed:

> As a rule the Johnny come lately missions in Guatemala (e. g. Pentecostal, Southern Baptist...) are all strictly gospel preaching and no nonsense about economic problems. They obviously haven't faced nor stopped to think about the physical conditions of their future constituencies. But the older missions that have raised up thousands of believers over more than half a century are faced with the problems of success: do we help the already Christians in all their problems of development and outreach, individual and church finance? Do we help them to relate to the world as it is today? Or do we let Radio Cuba be the only voice discussing their practical problems? (Winter, 1958, 2)

Missionaries who worked in the capital did not understand and were often shocked by the poverty and difficulties of living when they visited the work in the highlands. At one point, Winter wrote an article called *The Future of the Rural Man*,[102] and somehow got the attention of someone at USAID, which operated in Guatemala City. This person made the four-hour trip to visit Winter in his home and then invited Winter to come to the city and speak to his staff about issues related to rural poverty.

Winter shared his observations about the extreme economic conditions, the lack of local natural resources, and the lack of respect of the Mam by the Spanish-speaking culture. But, what the Mam did have were the skills and, "the will to work and a patient ability to work with their hands." (Winter, 2000, 24)

Winter had a number of ideas about what the Mam could do for export, such as tying fishing flies or producing jewel bearings for military

---

[102] This article has been lost, but Winter remembers writing it to alert people to development issues mentioned earlier in this chapter.

and other applications. Whatever they did, resources would be required from the outside. At the end of his talk to the USAID lead staff asked him what he would do with $10,000 to help the Mam.[103] Ralph did not hesitate: "Advertise in the Wall Street Journal for businesses to come and invest in these people who are so capable with their hands but need funds, wisdom, and markets from the outside more than just a one-time gift."[104] He did not get any funding. From Winter's perspective, USAID was in the business of giving money, but not helping to make more money.[105] (Winter, 2000, 24)

Mobilizing for the Task

Winter always promoted whatever he was interested in at any given time and sought to engage anyone else who might be interested. This was demonstrated on the letterhead of the MCC in 1965. On the left border under the names of the staff/missionaries was a list of services offered by the training and medical work. It reads like a promotional brochure, including allusions to cool mountain beauty that is almost unparalleled in Latin America and fabulously colorful Indian dress that varies from place to place, "unmatched in the whole world." It also detailed the result of 50 years of work, with over 50 congregations, and the good will of the people. Yet, it also noted that these are the poorest group of their size in North America. It closed by stating that visitors are welcome and airmail postage to Guatemala is only 13 cents.[106]

---

[103] $10,000 in 1960 is worth approximately $76,400 in 2010, or £47,585.

[104] This is very similar to ideas popularized since by those who work with the poor, such as the 2007 book, *Creating a World without Poverty* by Muhammad Yunus. (Yunus and Weber, 2007)

[105] In the long run the U.S. AID may have been short sighted. If they had worked at developing the kinds of industries to keep people like this productive, perhaps the illegal immigration "problem" in the developed nations would not be as large. When Ralph Winter returned to Guatemala after being gone for almost 40 years, he found two-storey houses, paved streets, and cars; all funded from money made outside the country. But almost all of the men were gone, working illegally in the U.S. and sending money back home. Crime was rampant among the young men, who have no older brothers or fathers as role models. The church lacked younger leaders, other than those whose fathers served as pastors.

[106] Letterhead from October 29, 1965 letter from Ralph D. Winter to John H. Sinclair. Noting that: "The Mam Indians are Mayan descendants more numerous than all the Indians in the 48 States..." Because of my experiences with Winter, I believe that he was involved in the production of the letterhead and probably wrote it himself.

Winter was also a good speaker so when back in the States, churches wanted him to share what was happening in their ministry in Guatemala and other places in Latin America.[107] One mission leader, Jim Nesbitt, a retired oil man volunteering in the Synod office in the L.A. area, appreciated Winter's concept of the church and its mission. It was the best he had heard from any of the Presbyterian missionaries.[108] Even the Pecks expressed interest in hearing what Winter said at a Presbytery meeting, requesting a copy of the speech.[109]

Roberta's perspective during furlough was slightly different. She was also encouraged by those who were interested in their work, but was discouraged by those who seemed bored with missions and needed a new cause to champion, "There were those who were tired of the same story of need, need, need, turning to some new gimmick or to some anti-communist organization they felt to be the only way to save our world. Mission? What can they do?" Others, she noted, found it hard to believe that the Christians in national churches were actually "growing up" and that the church was "capable in and of itself of providing its leadership, and . . . doing a tremendous job of evangelism on its own."[110]

The Winters were concerned about their girls adjustment back home. They devised a creative way of helping them bridge home and field. During their year at home the girls went to school. Then, each subsequent year, the Winters had a month of vacation, so they would drive seventy-three hours home from Guatemala to South Pasadena and put the girls in school for several weeks then drive back. That way they would keep up with friends and the "feel" of school back home. Winter believed that, "…they never really had any culture shock in reverse…."[111] The girls seem to agree with their parents, even today.

---

[107] The fact that Communism was active in Latin America during a time of unrest also fed the interest on the part of people back home.

[108] June 15, 1961 letter from Archie Crouch to Ted Romig. Crouch was a retired Presbyterian Missionary who had worked in China.

[109] October 8, 1961 letter from Dudley and Dorothy Peck to Ralph and Roberta Winter, 2.

[110] Annual Meeting Report by Roberta H. Winter, 1962, 1.

[111] Interview with Ralph Winter by the author on August 14, 2006, 6-7. Also in a March 9, 1962 letter from Robert C. Thorp to John Sinclair discussing the Executive Committee of the Guatemala Mission minutes.

Educational Work

The need to provide tools to help pastor/leaders in rural areas grow in their knowledge and practice was on the minds of Winter and coworker Jim Emery. Since they both arrived after the ministry with the Mam was established, they could easily see the need for leadership to multiply ministry. One important step was for the Mam to be free to ordain their own clergy. Because the majority power base was in the Spanish speaking Ladinos, this was a crucial step for the future, and one that would give a voice to the Mam and other smaller population groups.

The training at the Mam center was not purely educational. Instead, it was a "whole-of-life" program, including adult literacy, primary education, agriculture, sanitation and a medical clinic, all in addition to Bible, discipleship and traditional church work. Students went out from the Mam Center as teams to hold meetings that could last a few days or even weeks. These ministries included not only evangelistic activities to "reach the unconverted," but also Bible instruction for church members and efforts to improve the life of the people in areas such as sanitation and agriculture.

The educational work included schools for children in various regions, often in temporary and changing situations. Because of the high percentage of Indians in the region, with some fifteen or more distinct languages in a given area, education was far more difficult and probably not as advanced as in other countries or areas within Latin America.

Away from the city, the Spanish language primary education program stopped at the third grade. Because they wanted to see Indians ordained and able to lead their own churches, Winter and Emery began to work to extend the required seminary training down to the post-elementary level and to bring those with only three years of schooling to the point of finishing elementary education at a minimum.[112]

For Winter, this was almost a moral issue:

> ...I believe it to be sound in the fullest Biblical and Presbyterian sense for men to be ordained by [the] Presbytery who have not been called to a professional ministry. The fact that the Apostle Paul and in fact most Presbyterian ministers in history up until recent times have had a hand in agriculture (or other) along with their congregation is not to be sniffed at.

---

[112] An elementary education is the first six years of school in the U.S. The "third grade" is equivalent of year two in the UK.

I fully believe in a professional ministry, but not to the exclusion of other men ministering...[113]

Since he knew it would be a help to most organizations working in rural situations, Winter and Emery worked with many of the denominations and "faith missions" in their region for a year to raise the education level up to that same level so all their leaders could advance.

The government would give the necessary "seven level" (or elementary school) diploma if a person was at least fourteen years old and could pass an exam. So Winter and the many he mobilized from several mission organizations, created primers which put together separate books with all the science, maths, social studies, and history necessary. If the students learned this material, they would know all they needed to finish their schooling and pass the test. These were called "vertical" textbooks, each one covering a different subject through several years. Once they learned this material and passed the exams, then the Mam could go to seminary, get a seminary degree, and then be ordained. (Winter, 2000, 28-9)

When the Winters took the new textbooks for the program to the Minister of Education of Guatemala, he "was a bit surprised, hesitated, and said, 'But we have just now published an entirely new curriculum from the first through the sixth grade.' But Winter had already gotten wind of this and we [both Ralph and Roberta] had followed the new curriculum even before it was published." (Winter, 2000, 29) The Minister seemed relieved and pleased.[114]

Pastoral Training

By this time, a number of the Presbyterian missionaries were focused on training national pastors. To help make that training more accessible, the main Presbyterian seminary was moved from Guatemala City closer to most of the Presbyterian churches in the western part of the country. This was helpful and necessary, but it did not help those in rural areas, nor busy church elders who could not go to school weekly during the day or night because of their heavy responsibilities. Winter and Emery saw these yet-unordained leaders as the functional leaders of many small churches. They

---

[113] February 4, 1963 letter from Ralph D. Winter to John H. Sinclair, 1.

[114] Roberta developed two sample tests to give the students practice. Many of the students were "afraid" of fractions, so Roberta "also wrote a special easy-to-understand text for them." In that first year, almost 1,000 students graduated by taking the test, allowing them to matriculate into the seminary and work towards ordination. (Winter, 2000, 29)

were the ones that people looked to for wisdom, even if they did not have training or ordination as a pastor.

They also looked at how training was done in other nations in Latin America.[115] Winter and Emery were brainstorming or privately pondering, often into the night, how to solve problems for the leaders they were working with. The focus on getting the training to leaders was reflected when Winter later wrote:

> ...the gift of leadership sought by the church is more likely found in a person who is an active, self-directed initiator, rather than the follower-type that will gladly "go along" with others. Indeed, the true leader is often the most successful in extension studies, since with relatively little outside help he is much more likely to be able to effectively discipline his free time and studies at home. Thus the extension system may tend to weed out those who need the more highly controlled environment we seek to find and develop a "leader among men." (Winter, 1969d, 155-156)

Extending Education

These discussions were leading to a clearer direction for Winter and Emery. They remained involved in many ministries as they focused on training leaders where those leaders were serving.[116]

Summary and Analysis

This period of Winter's life included significant transitions. From pre-field training to language school in Costa Rica to arrival in Guatemala, he

---

[115] Interview with Ralph Winter by the author on July 26, 2006, 22-3. They discovered that in Brazil there was a large number of ordained clergy who were "lay" professionals. They were not necessarily pastors per se. Winter would often point out that, since residential training programs took in younger men and women, when they became ordained and began to pastor, people would be nice and polite to them, but they would not get the respect that these true elders got. He later called these the "functional leaders." Winter recognized that the Brazilian model might not have been acceptable to some Presbyterian leaders, but was something to consider seriously, because at that time almost no pastor in Guatemala was "full time." For more detailed information on this program, see Winter's article, "The Problem of Pre-Theological Training" in *Theological Education by Extension* (Winter, 1969d)

[116] The next chapter will explore how this developed into Theological Education by Extension.

began to apply lessons and information learned previously to the new challenges around him. He continued to look for alternative approaches to anything with which he was involved. He asked and pondered questions to understand problems and issues more clearly. His reputation as a pacesetter in his youth group foreshadowed his growth into a leader on the field. His style when approaching new challenges was to learn as much as he could about them, while experimenting with ideas and theories until he found something that worked, even if just passable as a solution at times.

Learning and teaching were patterns he further developed during this period of his life that proved foundational for years to come. He built upon the skills and lessons he had already learned and used his teaching and mentoring as a way to deal with the problems he faced and to motivate others toward involvement. Both he and Roberta, as part of their pre-field orientation, were able to teach language-learning skills they had received at SIL and Cornell. He also continued to study new topics during this time, such as exploring Kenneth Scott Latourette's writings where he was exposed to the Roman Catholic orders and their impact on missions throughout history.[117]

The fact that Winter was aware how he could contribute most effectively bears note. This self understanding, noted in 1957, included his sense of his gift and contribution through what he believed was, "a call (no matter what everyone else may think) to the studied application of modest ingenuity to the Christian cause in general."[118] The application of ingenuity was applied in every area of his life and ministry. It is what frustrated the Ruth Wardells of the world and intrigued, fascinated and stimulated the Jim Emerys. Winter believed this was his gifting and calling, even though it was not understood, for, "while the inventor's role is partially recognized in the secular world it is not about to be in the ecclesiastical. Too bad."[119]

Winter felt it was "too bad" because he believed it was needed even more in the world of the ministry. So, his statements demonstrate an underlying modus operandi or mentality that Winter carried into any task:

---

[117] In the 1990s, because of Winter's research and writing in this area, he was called upon as a professional witness to testify as a subject expert in a legal case in Canada between the government and the Canadian Christian Council regarding this issue and how protestant mission agencies could or should be considered in a similar light to the Roman Catholic Orders in the eyes of the government.

[118] Undated letter (fall of 1957) from Ralph D. Winter to Hugo and Hazel Winter, 1.

[119] Undated letter (fall of 1957) from Ralph D. Winter to Hugo and Hazel Winter, 1.

educational, ministry or business. He was constantly looking to "tinker" or improve whatever system with which he was engaged.

That "ingenuity" was seen during the time he wrote his parents that letter, while in language school. Winter's experiences during language school in Costa Rica demonstrated both an extraordinary gift of insight and problem identification as well as a tendency to over evaluate. Winter's suggestions about how to improve the language school were certainly informed, reasoned, and wise. They were not simply based on personal preference, but, rather, grew out of his education and problem-solving approach. To some, his ideas and suggestions were considered a distraction from the task at hand or threatening, partly because they entailed too much change too fast for people who were responsible for the work, but were deeply invested in current patterns. In part, this may have been connected with his problematic socialization skills. He struggled to connect or empathize emotionally with others and that may have enabled him to strongly press for what seemed right or natural to him. He could not understand why someone (such as Ruth Wardell) would not want to help improve all the ministries in which the Mam Center was involved.

While Winter probably did not normally intend to challenge anyone beyond the extent to which he would challenge himself, at times or with certain people, his input seems to have been either misunderstood or taken as a personal affront. In other situations, such as in Costa Rica, Winter's "refusal" to learn Spanish the same way others did was interpreted by some as a weakness in Winter's character. They wondered if he had the ability to finish something without always trying to critique or improve it.

Once on the field, Winter continued on a path of intensive learning and observation. This included language acquisition, accounting, photography, furniture building, business operations, family- and child-rearing, being part of a multi-facetted team that worked within a poor rural tribal situation, working with pastors and young men involved in the Mam center, and the churches in the region. In the midst of it all, Winter constantly evaluated *what* they were doing and *why* they were doing it the way they were doing it.[120] He was constantly thinking of new projects or ideas that needed attention as well as different ways to accomplish the work more effectively and efficiently.

In light of his obvious linguistic ability and personal energy, it was difficult for mission leadership to understand why Winter did not learn the Mam language. For his part, Winter clearly saw his skills and training in

---

[120] As noted, he had learned this motto from Dawson Trotman. Winter often quoted it throughout his life, but it was also a reflection of his study of anthropology.

language analysis as the best way to contribute to the task. After all, he might have argued, the mission had not allowed the Winters' two specific requests before they arrived in Guatemala: to study Mam first and Spanish later, only as necessary, nor to live in a more remote area, further away from the common use of Spanish. In fact, Winter recognized early on that Mam was not used much among the men, making it difficult to learn and of limited value. In that regard his lack of diligence in Mam language learning would have seemed logical to him. By his own admission, however, Winter's broad interests also played a role in keeping him from language learning. There were also additional ways in which he could use his skills and linguistics training, such as with other linguists in the region and men like Ruben Dias. Winter realized that Ruben had an innate sense of how to communicate in Mam. In a culture where the language was less and less appreciated, Winter would never attain that level of understanding and he knew it. Additionally, the suggestion from the mission that they were working toward the end of "fraternal workers" in that region probably did not help encourage the Winters to learn the language. It is interesting to note that the Scotchmers did learn Mam first and it was a great help to the situation of the church and the region.[121]

It was becoming clear that Winter was neither the kind of engineer who planned everything carefully nor one who was merely content to process the multitude of calculations and details required to bring closure to a major project. Certainly, he could do that kind of work when necessary, and did. But often found himself easily distracted by other good projects or ideas to pursue. In some situations, observations of field leaders seem correct: Winter's ideas were transient and some seemed more like schemes than plans. He was certainly able to work hard at a project until he understood it well (such as his self-taught crash-course to learn accounting). Perhaps accounting drew his attention because it was maths- and data-related, thus it could be clear and orderly in an otherwise disorganized life and surroundings. But Winter said, "it just needed to be done, so I did it."

Winter expressed no "hurt" from the fact that some of his co-workers did not take many of his ideas seriously. He expressed the opinion that the leadership, far removed from the local situation, whether in the capital of Guatemala City or in New York, did not fully understand the situation on the ground. Both the Pecks and Jim Emery greatly valued his contribution,

---

[121] Sara, David Scotchmer's wife, felt the focus on learning Mam first was good, but did not believe it was possible to avoid the use of Spanish, which did make it harder to cope with some of life's basic needs for her.

as he did theirs. The only remorse the Pecks communicated in the materials available was that the Winters did not learn Mam and, thus, were not able to improve the translation Dorothy Peck had done years before. As disappointed as they were, they eventually came to appreciate Ralph's decision not to focus on learning Mam.

Early in this period, Winter regularly wrote to his parents in a transparent, self-evaluating tenor. Many of these letters reveal a man intimately concerned with the details, needs and events of his local situation, as well as his own reactions to what he was experiencing. He observed his own need to work on new "side projects" in the midst of a ministry that was full of fixed patterns and that had a broad range of ministry. He saw his own need to tinker, both mentally and physically, in order to remain "sane."

Part of the struggle he had with Ruth Wardell came because he could not understand why a committed Christian, who felt called to God and missions work, would not be interested in learning and continually improving the ministry. Winter did not consider whether someone (like Ruth) *wanted* to do something or not. It did not matter to him if he *wanted* to do whatever he considered best, so why would it matter to her or anyone else? He undoubtedly wondered why Ruth could not see ways to improve that were so clear to him. If some change or action could help the cause, personal feelings were not important.

The available documents do not shed much light on his relationship with Roberta and their children during this period. There is no sign of tension in their marriage. Certainly, this was a difficult period because of moving the family several times and health issues for both Roberta and Beth, their oldest daughter. Ralph himself had ulcers.[122] It appears that while those early health struggles may have kept Roberta from as deep an engagement in the work, she was still as involved as she could be with the people, seeking to help those in need, learning Mam, and being a part of the missionary team. In the last few years on the field, because of some resolution to the health issues and the increased free time she had as the girls grew older, her involvement increased. In looking back on that period of their childhood, all of the daughters say that they had access to their

---

[122] These continued into his time at Fuller, which follows, until he learned by accident of tetracycline, an inexpensive antibiotic that cured them. Later, he found out that medical researchers had discovered that most ulcers are from infection rather than "nerves" as previously thought by many doctors. However, Winter liked to point out that, even as late as the 1990s, many medical doctors, including his up to that point, continued to treat them as being related to stress or nerves. To Winter, this was an example of things being "entrenched" in a culture or profession (the medical profession in this case).

father at all times. They never felt he "shooed" them away because he was "busy."

Not unlike others within evangelicalism in the 1960s, Winter believed that his actions were the natural application of his faith. The work he was involved in was worthy of engaging other Christians as well, and gaining the support of others was necessary if he were to accomplish what he felt his faith called him to do.

Because Winter saw problems that needed to be addressed and also realized that many of these were too large to solve alone, he naturally sought to involve others in the solutions. Early on, Winter had a growing interest in motivating people toward deeper involvement in whatever he was doing, such as Inductive Bible Study or the history of revivals. Now, from Guatemala, he desired that Christians in churches in the U.S. understand mission work and see that they, too, could be involved at some level. During his field experience, he worked toward mobilizing those at home with his *Shoptalk* letters. He also had a number of other creative projects and ideas for communicating with churches in the U.S. in order to increase their involvement. He took and enlarged many photographs for interested churches and individuals. He promoted not just his own ministry, but whatever was going on in the whole region, hoping to have people come and visit so they could fully understand the work and the potential of helping or investing in the area. The lack of natural resources in the region, and thus the need for outside involvement, seemed to motivate some of this awareness building.[123]

But many of these early broad appeals to Christians in general back home quickly diminished in the face of the day-to-day field realities. He did, however, continue to write and engage leaders. His letters included communications to the Mission Board and local pastors, especially in California. The specific motivation for this is not clear beyond his desire to interest people at all levels in his work. But as he gained more experience and built more relationship with leaders, he sought to involve those with the most appropriate credentials, experience, and connections for any given task. Examples included mobilizing other denominational agencies and churches in the production of the elementary school degree-completion program, and involving Dr. Wallstrom in evaluating the role of medical work in Chiapas. Winter could see how people in influential roles could

---

[123] Winter continued to use this broad appeal to the general Christian audience, in part, because if someone reading his letters or hearing him speak was not interested in his specific work, they could be in some other type of work done by other missionaries on Winter's team or by the church in Guatemala.

make a difference and help to convince others of the ideas and projects he felt important.

Winter saw parallels between the role of the shaman and that of the pastor. He wanted pastors to be viewed more highly by society, which motivated him to do the Chiapas study and consider other radical steps, such as the possibility of going to medical school. In this situation, as well as others, Winter was eager to explain his ideas to other missionaries and mission leadership, convinced that these gifted professionals could help carry the ideas forward more effectively than he could alone. This interaction with other missionaries and mission leaders was not merely a one-way street. Learning from what other Presbyterian missionaries were doing in places like Mexico and Brazil helped Winter refine his ideas and build his case, using evidence from experts in other fields to convince those who were uncertain about his approach.

The difficult relational problems with Ruth Wardell shaped Winter's approach to dealing with conflict between Christian workers. He approached the disagreement with a calm, reasonable "discussion" from his perspective. While not understanding why Ruth would not want to try a different approach, he also did not want the situation to become a bigger problem than it was, and he also respected her role as the senior missionary. By suggesting various solutions for the situation and for Ruth, he was attempting to break the logjam in a way that produced a role for her but did not hinder other creative options.

In the end, however, the "solution" was one where Ruth maintained, or extended, her own independence and the missionary team ministries continued to suffer from a lack of integration between medical and other aspects of ministry at the Mam Christian Center. His creativity in suggesting a change in Ruth's reporting relationship, which Dudley Peck apparently agreed with, allowed the hospital and spiritual ministries to continue on parallel but independent tracks and did not encourage the field leadership to grapple with the realities. Of course, no one wanted to remove her and send home a hard working, committed and medically trained missionary after many years of service, even if that service was limited and limiting on others. It seemed that no one wanted to admit to those back home that they could not get along with other missionaries, and they all felt the Mam who were able to take advantage of the clinic and other activities around the Mam Christian Center would not understand if she left.

Ultimately, having Ruth report to a distant medical hospital in the city seems to have diminished some of the tensions among the missionaries, but it also undermined the ability of the clinic to help the local work. It did not deal with the relational problems Ruth represented. It may have ignored work style issues and character flaws in Ruth and all other parties.

Even though he continued to have many and varied additional responsibilities, and perhaps as a reaction to what he perceived as an unproductive situation, Winter considered how he could continue work on projects he had conceived years ago, such as the *Lexical Handbook of the Hebrew Bible.* In his mind, this also helped make the use of languages in Biblical study more accessible, thus solving a problem for a potentially large group. No one has yet taken on this project and produced the book for the whole of Genesis or the rest of the OT.

Winter's ideas, creativity, and imagination failed to connect with some. For example, his interaction with US AID probably made no impact on his work. He never received a grant from them. According to Roberta's interpretation years later, he was more focused on attempting to influence the staff of US AID and how they approached their work than merely getting more money for projects. It is an example of his attempt to solve a larger problem than his own, but in this case it did neither so far as we know.

Winter seems to have connected with the Mam very well. He understood their situation and identified with them. He understood how poor they were. With his problem-solving perspective, he could not be content giving handouts or simply "living with the people." He knew that would not help in the long run. The Winters lived simply, and naturally had resources the Mam did not have. Winter believed that outside investment was necessary to attract and multiply capital in the area, thus multiplying opportunities for helping the people in the long term. While the businesses Winter started became models and helped a number of pastors and others, there never was any major investment that could take advantage of the skills of the Mam throughout the region and connect more deeply with the world outside the village. In Winter's opinion, labor left the region due a lack of material resources.[124]

Probably the most significant, long-term relationship from Winter's service in Guatemala was with James Emery. While Winter met Emery at Princeton in 1946, it was in Guatemala that their relationship grew deep,

---

[124] As noted earlier, when Winter returned to Guatemala in 2006, he found almost no men between the ages of 15 and 60. Those in between worked illegally in the U.S., sending money back home and improving the village, but impoverishing the family structure. For a report on this trip, see Appendix E.

greatly impacting both of their lives. The friendship with another engineer, improver, and experimenter provided a fertile soil of encouragement and ideas for both men, as well as contributing through them to the development of theological education.[125]

As one would expect, Winter's and Emery's discussions and thinking about how to improve and tinker with the work among the Mam and the Ladinos grew out of the local situation. They saw mature men and women who were not able to get needed and helpful training. In some ways, Winter and Emery were just like most of the other missionaries, who thought about how best to use the limited funds/budgets they had. They felt the money in the budget for the seminary would go further, though, if they used a different approach to training. But at the same time they were unlike others in their willingness to radically alter the way many people were trained for ministry. And though the extension model took more time than simply teaching a class in a residential location, for Winter it did not matter if the new approach involved *more* effort on the part of the missionaries. It was, again, simply what was necessary to make the greatest impact.

Winter and Emery also realized they would eventually be "out of a job" as the Presbyterian Board continued to turned the work over to indigenous staff. All of this fed into their day-to-day work and led to much of what we know today as Theological Education by Extension or TEE.

These experiences, coming as they did after his study of linguistics and learning to deal with the logistics of living in a poor, rural culture of a foreign country, "speeded up the ground fertility of new ideas" for Winter.[126] He was not attempting to think of problems just to exercise his own creativity. Nor could one claim that he always finished the task at hand. Much later in life, he described his approach to life and work in this way:

> I don't work. I just follow my interests. I've never worked a day in my life you might say, in a certain sense. Most of the things I do, I do because I'm interested in them. I don't have a sense of duty. Just look at my desk if you want proof of that. I'm constantly doing something that needs to be done that I am interested in seeing happen. And everything else slides.[127]

---

[125] This will be covered further in the next chapter.

[126] Interview with Ralph Winter by the author on August 14, 2006, 4.

[127] Interview with Ralph Winter by the author on August 2, 2006, 5. Winter's desk was usually stacked high with magazines, papers, works in process, new books just arrived from Amazon on a range of subjects.

Winter, while being seen as one was "almost a genius, with a versatile, productive mind" was seen as not being able to have "his time and activity ... keep pace with it."[128] There were too many areas where he sought to apply modest ingenuity. His interests were broad.

Those interests would take Ralph and Roberta away from Guatemala, as the ideas and application of Theological Education by Extension became widely known and applied. They opened the door for Winter to speak from a much larger platform than the highlands of Guatemala.

---

[128] February 2, 1961 letter from Robert C. Thorp to Nathaniel Bercovitz, M.D., 2.

Chapter 4

Extending Theological Education

Introduction

Undoubtedly, many people have thought about or attempted some form of Theological Education by Extension. Some of the known modern efforts began as early as the 1940s.[1]

The Beginnings of Theological Education by Extension

Theological Education by Extension developed in response to an acute need in rural churches. According to Winter, Jim Emery "made the observation that the real leaders of the church were not becoming pastors."[2] Emery had been working both in leadership training at the seminary and in creative ways to get the local Indian pastors the training they needed. In 1962, Jim Emery wrote in his Annual Meeting Report about his work for the seminary in Guatemala:

> One problem has grown more acute during the year, forcing our thinking toward new solutions. This is the matter of leadership for the rural church. During the year there have been two churches looking for pastors but in spite of much searching, have been disappointed in that no one has been willing to accept the call. They are both small towns on the hot coast, and even though they have offered what many pastors hoped to get a few years ago, have been unable to find someone. It has become obvious that there will be no takers, for churches of this class, and so we will have to look for new ways to provide the needed pastoral care so that these churches will grow and become stronger, and not wither and

---

[1] Examples are given in Appendix F.

[2] Interview with Ralph Winter by the author on August 16, 2006, 1. Here and later, "real leaders" often meant elders or other mature pastors who were already engaged in the leadership in local church situations.

die. This will be the main problem for the Seminary, which we face in the coming years.[3]

During the same year (1962), the Presbyterian Church in Guatemala took inventory and "discovered that in twenty-five years the seminary had prepared only ten pastors who were actively serving the denomination." (Covell and Wagner, 1971, 71) At the time, only five to six students were enrolled, but there were 200 growing churches in the country.

Winter later wrote about the situation in the Mam church, saying:

While there were many congregations of believers in this group already, no one from this [Mam] tribe had ever gone to the Presbyterian Seminary for training, and it was not very likely that the seminary (located far way in the capital city) would be able to contribute anything very soon to the well-being of the far-flung network of mountain Indian churches.[4]

(Winter, 1996, 173)

In his article called "The Preparation of Leaders in a Ladino-Indian Church" in *Practical Anthropology*[5] (1963), Emery observed: "The people who most need the training are not those who traditionally attend the seminary, but those of the larger group who are more mature, and with experience. These, however, cannot attend seminary for economic reasons, even if they could meet the academic requirements."[6] (Emery, 1963, 132)

These and other factors, such as the dispersed population and the rural nature of the region, led Winter and Emery to pursue the idea of pushing training out of set locations to where the existing leaders and pastors were, rather than following the normal pattern of bringing unproven young potential pastors to a residential training program. One of the core reasons Winter and Emery moved in this direction was that they saw that the real leaders of the church in the Mam region were not the young men and women, those who were free from work, family, and

---

[3] Annual Meeting Report by James H. Emery, 1962, 1-2.

[4] Winter continued: "...Jim Emery had arrived five years earlier and had worked extensively down on the coast with Spanish-speaking churches. It was apparent to him that there was a similar problem with the coastal congregations; very few of their actual, local leaders would ever make it to the seminary in the capital city or, therefore, ever be properly ordained as ministers." (Winter, 1996, 173)

[5] The article was reprinted as part of a description of the background of TEE in *Theological Education by Extension*. (Winter, 1969d)

[6] As mentioned in the last chapter, if they never received "the proper training" they could not be ordained or hold positions of leadership and influence beyond their local church as defined by the denominational leadership, which was controlled by the Ladino majority at the time.

ministry responsibilities and able to go to a residential training. Only the younger ones were available for full-time, daytime programs. In contrast almost all of the Pastors at the time, who were older and had multiple responsibilities, worked at a job to make a living, and thus would not be able to attend such classes.[7]

The Guatemala Program

In many ways, Guatemala was the ideal size country to experiment with something like TEE.[8] Mexico would have been too large. Winter and Emery started by building upon the credibility and respect that Emery had earned as a part of the leadership of the existing Presbyterian Seminary of Guatemala. Initially, Winter and Emery established an extension operation for that seminary. Winter contributed a scholarly dimension to the board because of his PhD degree and experience. The underlying assumptions of the Seminary, as they moved into this program, were that there were leadership gifts in operation within the various subcultures of a given church and that you could train those with the gifting where they were. (Winter, 1966b, 12)

But changing the training pattern was not without its struggles. In 1964, Winter and Emery were trying to keep the extension program running, while others were arguing for reopening the Seminary using a traditional model.[9] There was not enough funding for both so they became competitors for scarce resources. Winter and Emery suggested postponing restarting the traditional seminary for a year. That way, they would at least be able to "work one more year with the 100 men in the extension wing [and] find out which of them are really worth it."[10] Winter argued that because the Presbyterian mission planned to hand over the work in the region, most of the older missionaries would be returning to their sending countries in a few years, anyway. He reasoned that by investing in local leaders they might help establish forty solid leaders in ministry in the

---

[7] Interview with Ralph Winter by the author on July 26, 2006, 2. Evening or weekend classes were not a common occurrence at this time, but reflecting back on it in a private undated discussion, Winter believed that such classes would not have solved the problem for those who worked or who lived at a distance. In the Mam and other rural locations, it was still too far away.

[8] Both in population and area.

[9] The fact that that extension model did not represent a tried and tested U.S. strategy for training pastoral leadership at the time, may have been the reason some preferred a traditional approach to training future church leadership.

[10] June 11, 1964 letter from Ralph D. Winter to Jim Emery and Chuck Ainley, 1.

region before the expatriates left. In the same letter, he noted that if the Western Presbytery in Guatemala did not give solid backing to their efforts, "I will no doubt myself be looking for a job. Our furlough comes up in Sept '65 and so it may be then that someone else takes over here anyhow, for good."[11]

Winter and Emery had a refined different goal in sight: training those who were *already* recognized "lay" leaders and elders, rather than developing training programs for future professionals, whose gifts and impact were as yet unknown:

> We can still hope that some of the nationals will catch a vision of the extension approach to the problem. But so long as we, in the U.S., go on for all practical purposes ignoring the Biblical and theological possibility of men in their thirties going into the ministry, we ought not to feel very greatly abused by events here if the U.S. example speaks louder than we can here in the board meetings![12]

Winter later looked back and described what they were seeking to do as they sought to solve a series of problems:[13]

> First Problem Observed: We were not training for the ministry the real leaders of our church.
>
> First Solution Attempted: We moved our seminary from the capital to the rural, geographical center of our field of endeavor.
>
> Second Problem Observed: Our genuine local leadership in the rural areas could not even go a few miles to a residence program - they had jobs, wives, and families.
>
> Second Solution Attempted: We decided to meet these men for three hours once a week and set up "extension centers" where they could readily attend. We also arranged a two-day meeting each month for all students for all centers. This was on the main campus of the seminary.
>
> Third Problem Observed: Their "take-home" studies didn't take [stay with them] because they could not effectively handle assignments in traditional textbooks on a home-study basis.

---

[11] June 11, 1964 letter from Ralph D. Winter to Jim Emery and Chuck Ainley, 1.

[12] June 11, 1964 letter from Ralph D. Winter to Jim Emery and Chuck Ainley, 1.

[13] Not all of these solutions were fully implemented. This list is from Winter, 1969d, 307-308.

Third Solution Attempted: We re-wrote the entire curriculum (over a period of years) in a semi-programmed form, precisely designed for home study.

Fourth Problem Observed: Men of equally keen leadership and spiritual qualifications were found within even our own area in two different Indian tribes, and on three different social levels, as well as with radically different academic backgrounds.

Fourth Solution Attempted: Our decentralized extension center allowed the multi-cultural diversity sufficient breathing space almost automatically, but for the different academic levels we had to build a multi-level structure into our texts. Studies were related to the following secular backgrounds: sixth grade, ninth grade, twelfth grade, and two years of college.

Fifth Problem Observed: We still had many, many keen men who had not had even six grades of public school, and who thus could not take even the lowest level of course work our seminary felt it could offer.

Fifth Solution Attempted: A second extension program, completely separated from the seminary, was established on a nationwide, inter-mission basis, soon having 60 centers and 1,000 students, all working to gain their sixth grade primary diploma. Within two years, half the students in the seminary had come by this route. By careful, diplomatic dealings with the government and by special exams allowed by laws framed for cases where students in public schools got sick, this program helped students to get a regular government-recognized diploma.

Also reflecting back on some specific results of the TEE program in Guatemala, missionary Ken Mulholland, wrote:

With no increase in funds, the student body of the Presbyterian Seminary had increased from 7 to 200 taught by 3 full-time and 12 part-time faculty members. And many of the evident needs of the churches were being met. (Kinsler, 1983, 36)

The Program Expands

One of the reasons the movement continued to grow was because many churches did not have trained pastors. A number who had received this new kind of training were already serving as elders, but those who had been trained by the traditional system resisted the idea. During a Guatemala presbytery meeting, a couple of traditionally trained pastors said that the men in the extension program were not "seminary pastors" but "lay people." Emery mentioned that when he went to seminary, he was a layperson. To further strengthen his point, he turned to the pastor who had made a speech about this issue and asked, "when you went to seminary, weren't you a lay person?"[14]

Winter explained another reason why the program in Guatemala continued:

> Presbyterians have representatives who are both elders and pastors, but if the church doesn't have an ordained pastor, one elder will come from that church. (Normally, a pastor and an elder come to the meeting.) So there were maybe 60 or 70 churches, but there were no ordained pastors yet...[these elders] came and they outvoted all of those capital [city] pastors and sustained the program. [15]

Seeking to mobilize interest and involvement on a broader scale, Winter wrote the first of several popular level articles for *World Vision Magazine* in 1966. At the time, the magazine was focused on missions and broadly covered much more than merely World Vision's work.[16] In Winter's first article, "This Seminary Goes to the Student," he described some of the thinking behind TEE. It was focused in Guatemala and on getting training to the "rural man." He noted that by then the California Friends Mission was also using TEE in Guatemala and Honduras. They had 13 regional centers and 85 students. In Guatemala, the Presbyterians had 100 students and 11 regional centers where students gathered in their

---

[14] Interview with Ralph Winter by the author on August 16, 2006, 5. According to Winter, Emery was the only person with the deep respect of the people to be able to say something like this in that kind of situation.

[15] Interview with Ralph Winter by the author on August 16, 2006, 5.

[16] This magazine was the only popular level magazine that sought both to raise awareness of missions and world issues impacting the evangelical missions movement. From 1957 until 1971, a number of mission leaders from various missions participated by contributing articles, reviews, and news items. In 1971 the name was changed from *World Vision Magazine* to *World Vision* and the magazine began to limit the focus only to their work, and eventually ceased publication in 1998.

own localities, at least once a week. (Winter, 1966b, 12) By mid-1969, he wrote that the seminary in Guatemala had "220 students and has become the catalyst of a whole movement involving more than 50 other schools in Latin America, and there is serious interest around the world." (Winter, 1969c, 8)

In that same article, Winter told the stories of men who had been or were being trained using TEE methods in Guatemala, Bolivia, and Colombia. He was careful to mention other organizations using TEE in addition to Presbyterians such as The West Indies Mission, George Allen Theological Seminary, Evangelism-in-Depth, and United Biblical Seminary.[17] In a later article he mentioned the Conservative Baptist Foreign Mission Society and the joint efforts of the two major North American mission associations (IFMA/EFMA) expressed through the Committee to Assist Missionary Education Overseas[18] (CAMEO) (Winter, 1970d, 16), which sought to bring together Christian educators in the U.S. with mission leaders and education needs on the mission field.[19] (Editorial, 1967, 115)

In "The Acorn that Exploded," Winter wrote that, "more than 3,000 men are pushing forward in seminary extension programs in Latin America. There may well be 20,000 by 1975." (1970d, 15) The article includes subtle hints that established seminaries might be expressing concern over TEE. Winter outlined briefly his view that even established schools could benefit from TEE and could further what they were doing. The TEE program, he noted, focused on the local pastor, not the theological scholar.

---

[17] In a later article, George is spelled, Jorge.

[18] CAMEO sought to bring together "educators and mission leaders as to the responsibilities educators and evangelical institutes in the homeland have for their counterparts on the mission field." (Editorial, 1967, 115)

[19] CAMEO sponsored Winter and others to teach TEE workshops in various places around the world. A letter from Bob Erny, missionary with the Oriental Missionary Society in Hong Kong, sent around this announcement:

The summer CAMEO (Committee to Assist Missionary Education Overseas) is sponsoring Theological Extension Education (TEE) workshops throughout Asia and Africa. Included in Asia are Pakistan, Thailand, Hong Kong, Philippines and Japan. These workshops were designed to be attended by educators and leaders representing a broad range of churches and theological institutions.

Other TEE trainers were sent to Africa that same summer, presenting seminars in Liberia, Ivory Coast, Congo and Swaziland.

Ross Kinsler joins Winter and Emery

Arriving on the field in 1964, Ross Kinsler was the third missionary in Guatemala who worked closely with the developing application of these educational models.[20] When he was on his way to Guatemala in language school, he heard about what Winter and Emery were writing and doing. He wrote letters asking questions about different aspects of the work. Kinsler felt he was merely being inquisitive about Winter and Emery's ideas about TEE, but Winter thought he was *opposed* to what they were doing, until Kinsler arrived and got involved.[21]

In 1964 some were saying that the Seminary in Guatemala was a failure and the Extension Plan was worthless. A meeting held that year to celebrate the seminary yielded merely twenty students and there were no graduates. Kinsler blamed that situation on rain and poor event promotion. Whatever the reasons, a year later the situation had changed dramatically and Kinsler wrote of a gathering at the largest church in the area with between 1200 and 2000, including a Seminary choir of 35. One of those in leadership said, "There's never been anything like it in this part of the country."[22]

Kinsler wrote another letter, a few days after that successful meeting in November of 1965, detailing the successes of the program at that time.[23] But six-months earlier, apparently concerned that Kinsler might be having doubts about the idea of TEE, Winter wrote him, responding to some of the difficult questions about the program that Kinsler, and or others had raised. Winter ended his three-page letter with a set of his own probing questions, whose answers highlighted the strengths and potential impact of the plan. These questions were rhetorical and were intended to engage Kinsler and bring him "up to speed" with Winter and Emery's thinking about the issues:

---

[20] Kinsler received a PhD in NT from the University of Edinburgh, served in Guatemala until 1977. After leaving Guatemala, Kinsler joined the staff of the WCC working with TEE through the Joint Program on Theological Education (formerly the Theological Education Fund) and publishing several books on TEE and related subjects, the most recent being *Diversified Theological Education: Equipping All God's People* (2008).

[21] Interview with Ralph D. Winter by the author, July 26, 2006, 23; and an interview with Ross Kinsler by the author on March 6, 2007, 2. See also, *Theological Education by Extension* (Winter, 1969d) for comments by Winter in his note at the beginning of a letter by Kinsler on page 116.

[22] November 3, 1965 letter from F. Ross Kinsler to John H. Sinclair, 1. Kinsler was quoting others who believed the seminary and the extension program were failures or failing.

[23] November 8, 1965 letter from F. Ross Kinsler to John B. Housley, 1-2.

1. Are you serving candidates for the ministry, which no residence program could possibly reach?
2. Are you moving more men into the ministry than a U.S.-style seminary in Guatemala possibly could?
3. Are many of these men of higher caliber both intellectually and spiritually than the former program was able to reach?
4. Are you able simultaneously to serve men in radically diverse social sub-groups?
5. Is the new approach actually becoming in Guatemala the primary vehicle of ministerial training just as the U.S. method is in the U.S.?
6. Is it likely that the U.S. method here in Guatemala could not actually ever (in the near future) be more than a program for a small part of ministerial needs--either from the standpoint of quantity and also of cultural requirements?
7. Is it true that present, urgent needs in the explosively growing protestant movement in Latin America are 100 times the present capacity of all existing U.S.-style seminaries, and the costly, lumbering, mono-cultural stance of these institutions prevents them from reaching out without making radical transformations of program and personnel?[24]

In early 1964, Winter wrote a letter and attached a four-page explanation of *The Extension-Seminary Plan in Guatemala*.[25] This document detailed their best understanding of the cultural situation in Latin America and how they believed the Extension concept would work out in that situation. Many of the points were expanded upon by Winter, Emery, and Kinsler in other published documents.[26]

---

[24] June 10, 1964 letter from Ralph D. Winter to F. Ross Kinsler, 3.

[25] January 23, 1964 letter and document from Ralph D. Winter to Ray Strong (and a number of others, copied). Winter wrote this as Secretary of the Board of the Seminary.

[26] For example, January 23, 1964 document, *The Extension-Seminary Plan in Guatemala* from Ralph D. Winter to Ray Strong, et. al. On page 3, Winter listed: "Basic outward characteristics: (1) No residential program. (2) Contact with students: maximum daily, minimum weekly in the Regional Centers, two days per month in Central Campus. (3) No subsidy or scholarships to anyone of any kind... [except to cover expenses of the professors traveling to the Regional Centers]. (4) Training both less and more advanced than usual Latin American Seminary, depending on the students. (5) Division of secular education as well as vocational in addition to theological, since for ninety percent of the area covered these first two are not available. (6) No school year. Time taken to complete a B.D. course, for example, might be less, would likely be more than the usual period. It is a fact that more mature students can cover a lot more ground in the same amount of time. (7) Generally far higher competence in the student body, despite far greater enrollment, since the non-

Preparation for Growth

In what proved to be a very significant occurrence, Winter met James F. Hopewell, an Anglican who headed the Theological Education Fund (TEF) under an arm of the WCC.[27] At the time, the TEF was seeking to persuade seminaries around the world to merge in order to deal more effectively with the different churches from one base, enabling faculties (building, libraries, dormitories) to be more efficient.

During the conference where they met, Winter had lunch with Hopewell and explained to him what they were doing in Guatemala. In 1964, TEF gave a $14,000 grant to purchase books for twelve regional extension sites in Guatemala and Mexico.[28] (Winter, 1967, 10) Winter disagreed with the idea of combining seminaries for efficiency because combining locations only made the distance problem worse for rural pastors. Thus, it would not solve the problems they were encountering. Yet his relationship with Hopewell resulted in growing international recognition of TEE and Winter in particular.[29] In 1965, Hopewell was the most experienced "outsider" to observe the activities of the Guatemala "experiment" and positively comment on them. In the introduction to a chapter by Hopewell, Winter wrote: "This document in early 1965 represents the first time an eminent person was willing in a large group to go out on a limb to this extent for the extension concept and to give his words added force by accompanying them with a critique, a serious critique, of traditional methodology." (Hopewell, 1969b, 36)

In April of 1967, a shorter version of Hopewell's verbal presentation was the lead article in an entire issue on the subject of Theological Education in the journal *International Review of Missions*. He also wrote a lengthy guest editorial for that issue, where he expressed his perspective regarding schools suffering "contemporary irrelevance" and schools serving fewer and fewer students. (Hopewell, 1967a, 141) In that article, Hopewell directly addressed the isolation of theological schools, which are physically and educationally removed from the realities of life and real needs. He raised questions about everything from the stereotypical, less-mature

---

residential 'reach' of the seminary brings ten times, perhaps thirty times as many worthy men into potential studies."

[27] Hopewell had been with TEF since it started in 1958, which was before it had any connection with the WCC. Winter wrote, "He had visited more theological institutions on the face of the earth than any other man who has ever lived." (Winter, 1969d, 37)

[28] According to "A Report of Theological Education Fund 1964-1965", 32. $14,000 in 1965 is worth approximately $100,428 in 2010, or £62,773.

[29] It is not known if Winter had this in mind at this point.

student to the questionable validity of teaching to prepare future professors rather than pastors and leaders. He wrote:

> Were it our primary intention in a seminary to equip a man for the profession of witness in the world, I doubt whether we would construct an institution that essentially removed him from that world, giving him a three year vacation, so to speak, from the life he would live before and after. I doubt whether we would be so ready to distract his attention from the world by making him concentrate his entire being upon a programme which dealt largely with ideas and techniques which mainly confirm the given structure of the Church. (Hopewell, 1967b, 158)[30]

Hopewell raised important issues such as the level of scholarship, encouraging a learning that is engaged with the world. He asked: "Is there not possible another dimension of excellence, no less demanding in intellect and discipline, that measures the extent to which a theological program equips the candidate to be the servant of a missionary community which exists within the world at large?" (Hopewell, 1969b, 43)

Hopewell's years of experience observing theological institutions globally resulted in his perspective having great influence. He brought an "outside expert perspective" to the situation and he approved of much of what he saw in the TEE movement. In his article, he described a number of specific, positive examples of new approaches being tried. Regarding the Guatemala example, Hopewell mentioned the move the Presbyterians in Guatemala made to locate their seminary outside the city, closer to the pastors and churches they sought to serve. He described how a few faculty were almost the only ones residing at the physical facilities. The students depended on reading and self-study in place of lectures, but that was turning out to be a help rather than a hindrance. The seminary had also set up twelve regional centers for regular weekend retreats, where faculty met with students face-to-face. Monthly meetings at the main campus were also part of the program. He continued: "One of the most satisfying effects to date has been the dramatic expansion of seminary enrollment. Before the seminary began its decentralized programme five years ago, student enrollment stood at six. Today [1965] it is over one hundred." (Hopewell, 1967b, 161)[31] He also noted that the Society of Friends Bible Institute had

---

[30] Also in: (Winter, 1969d, 40-41) with slight editing.

[31] Also in: (Winter, 1969d, 44-45) which lists the number of early students at five, rather than six.

begun a similar program on the other side of Guatemala, which had fifteen centers and one hundred students.

Hopewell also questioned the methods and content of the teaching and the need for reevaluating. He noted that the best time to teach a person might not be in one intensive block of a few years. The need to understand cultural issues was raised, noting that many faculty at institutions around the world were not native to the culture in which they were teaching. In sum, he was driven to help seminaries produce leaders in ministry who were "capable of being pedestrians with the rest of humanity, ...concerned with the dynamics of walking and the direction in which the world is moving." (Hopewell, 1969b, 53)

That desire could be seen in another article where Hopewell evaluated the Guatemala experiment. In "An Outsider's View" he wrote: "Certainly the most enlightened approach to Bible school education is found in Guatemala where, as explained below, programs for training are being designed for administration by single teachers in remote places." (Hopewell, 1969a, 101) And:

> The teaching of the students within their own environment and in connection with their secular employment is not merely a gimmick. The Presbyterian scheme is drawing a different type of man into the ministry and is equipping him in a way which gives at least some indications of being far superior to that gained in a residential full-time course. (Hopewell, 1969a, 102)

He also mentioned the workbooks the Seminary was already producing, and the plans for more than 100 more to be produced. Hopewell raised the issue whether there was any other way that the following goals could be achieved:

1. Older men established in a profession are given an opportunity to study theology. These men are already tested as leaders in their communities.

2. Their method of study forces them to rely upon reading and self-expression. Passive acceptance of lecture is minimized.

3. The variety of centers permits instructions at different levels— post-sixth grade in some instances, university level course in the capital city.

4. Transition to a tent-making ministry is natural, indeed anticipated. Types of vocational crises that afflict full-time seminary students in other countries are largely avoided.

5. Pastors utilize courses as an effective type of continuing education.
6. Costs are surprisingly low. Because they all work either in churches or secular tasks, or both, students can pay for their courses and require no subsidy for living expenses.
7. Enrollments have increased more than tenfold. (Hopewell, 1969a, 101-102)

Finally, Hopewell noted he was satisfied concerning two major doubts he had held about decentralized education. One concern had been the quality of a decentralized education. The "cost" for the extension model presented itself in a higher commitment of the teachers: a commitment which involved extra travel to visit students, extra preparation, and the additional grading of workbooks. He saw this being addressed by the committed faculty at the seminary, and the fact that, "they are working with students whose intellectual gifts are demonstrably superior to those attracted to the refuge of the residential seminary." (Hopewell, 1969a, 103)

Another concern Hopewell had was related to the sense of community and opportunity for vocational growth. Hopewell "was impressed by the intensity of the fellowship gained in the evening hours by men and women...present at the regional center." Related to a new course of study that Hopewell observed while visiting the seminary, he wrote, "Enrolled in these evenings were about twenty men and women, including a physician, a secondary school principal, a lawyer, a carpenter, a weaver and a manager of a large farm. These desire a new form of Christian service." (Hopewell, 1969a, 103)

Even as Winter sought to include Hopewell's input to bolster the TEE movement, his introduction offered an explanation, perhaps to avoid damaging relationships with the NCC by being overly friendly to conservatives.[32] (Winter, 1969d, 101-187)

Examples from other nations were also included in the early articles and books on the subject of TEE. The experiences of a number of training institutions in Colombia were written up in Part II of *Theological Education by Extension* (Winter, 1969d, 101-187) and other South American nations were written up in Part III (191-258).

---

[32] Winter wrote: "...the reader must understand that this address was intended to be provocative. The National Council of Churches sponsored the consultation at which it was given. There were neither conservative evangelicals nor interdenominational missions represented. This explains the generally critical tenor of his remarks as they were directed to representatives of the older denominations, and the fact that the few references to conservative schools are more friendly." (Winter 1969, 37)

An early newsletter for TEE reiterated some of Hopewell's ideas by suggesting that TEE did answer the following questions for those concerned about ministerial training:

1. How will residence programs alone meet the needs created by the tremendous growth of Protestantism in, for example, Latin America?
2. How can we justify the exclusion of many sectors of society from theological training because of limitations imposed by marriage, finances, and work schedules, including both those with high needs and those with lower needs?
3. How can we justify the use of teaching time for a limited few when quadruple the number could be benefiting from it?[33]

A TEE Movement?

Winter knew that he and Emery were not the inventors of TEE. In his introduction to the first part of the book *Theological Education by Extension*, he wrote:

> Those of us involved in that project didn't dream up any brand new ideas that were not seen already in countless different forms in many other times and places. Nor was there anything so inherently good about the project that would account for it being considered the prime mover in the movement described in this book. The real explanation for the influence of the project is the sheer fact of its existence as a going thing rather than as merely a set of bright ideas. This follows the anthropological dictum that ninety percent of all innovation in human society is copied from somewhere else rather than developed in a given situation through creative thinking. (Winter, 1969d, 3-4)

Winter sensed that the momentum of the movement had reached critical mass. As of the middle of 1969, in the preface of the same book, he wrote, "…we are well aware of the fact that since at least half of the most significant events in this movement have occurred in the previous twelve months, an even greater number of developments are likely to unfold in the next twelve. We do at least now have a movement on our hands." (Winter, 1969d, xvii) The following chart is from the book outlined events, of

---

[33] Extension Seminary Quarterly Bulletin, Number 3, 3, not dated.

various types, connected with or promoting TEE in some way. It also lists, along the left side, the numbers of organizations involved.[34]

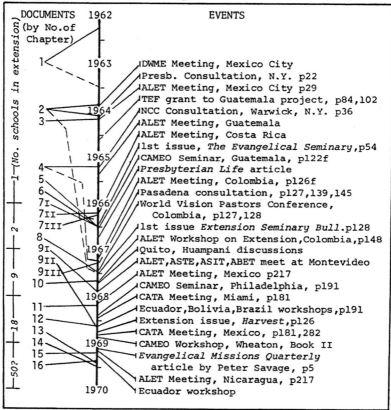

Figure 3 – TEE "Events" as listed in Theological Education by Extension, *(1969d, 6)*

The needs of the pastors and local churches in the region were leading them on a path that others had paved with different models in different parts of the world. The Guatemala team apparently did not know very much if anything about these other programs, either because they were just beginning, or they were for a specific denomination, or because information traveled more slowly at the time.

---

[34] See Abbreviations on pages xiv and xv for details of the initials in Figure 3. Some initials are unknown to this author and not outlined in the book in which they were included.

TEE Defined and Refined

In the *Church Growth Bulletin* of which he was the editor, Donald McGavran wrote about the challenge of getting the right training to the right people:

> The greatest *encouragement* in missions today is that the Christian movement is outrunning the traditional methods of ministerial training, but the great *tragedy*, both in the U.S. and abroad, is that we are ecclesiastically and institutionally arthritic at the point of *bending* to give appropriate, solid, theological education to the real leaders that emerge in the normal outworking of our internal church life. Without this critical retooling of our theological education, church growth may in many areas wander into Mormon-type heresies instead of producing a Biblically-based evangelicalism. In some places this is already happening before our eyes. (McGavran, 1969, 142, emphasis his)

In September 1967, at what he considered the most significant event related to TEE held to that date, Winter gave a simple answer to the question, "What is Extension Education?"[35] "Briefly, it is that method which reaches the student in his own environment rather than pulling him out into a special controlled environment. It isn't necessarily the best method of education for all purposes, it is merely different." (Winter, 1969d, 153) He then described a continuum from the extremes of "extraction" to "extension" to help the readers analyze activities used to "educate" people.[36]

Another way of defining TEE was to describe what it was not. A newsletter produced in Guatemala for the Extension movement in the late 1960s wrote:

What Extension is not:[37]

1. It is NOT the one-and-only answer to the problem of theological education.
2. It is NOT only for low-level training.
3. It is NOT only for laymen.

---

[35] This was the meeting held in Armenia, Colombia. September 4-9, 1967. It was funded by the Theological Education Fund, (probably because of Hopewell's involvement) and sponsored by the Latin American Association of Theological Schools, the Northern Region of which Winter led as the Executive Secretary at the time.

[36] By extraction, Winter meant taking a person out of their current ministry and requiring them to go away to another location for training.

[37] *Extension Seminary Quarterly Bulletin*, Number 3, 1-3, not dated.

4. It is NOT costly.
5. It is NOT educationally inferior.
6. It is NOT correspondence.
7. It is NOT paternalistic.
8. It does NOT prevent theological "community."
9. It does NOT have all the answers.

In 1983, Kinsler defined TEE this way:

> Theological education by extension is not simply an extension or adaptation of what is done in the classrooms of theological seminaries and Bible schools. Some TEE programmes are not even linked to established institutions. Nor does the concept used here embrace all kinds of non-traditional or non-residential theological study. Rather, *TEE is that model of theological education which provides systematic, independent study plus regular, supervised seminars in the context of people's varied life and work and ministry.* From one perspective it opens up a wide range of degree and non-degree theological education options to the whole people of God....[38]
> (Kinsler, 1983, xiii-xiv)

Kinsler also described some of the variety of approaches to TEE programs:

> In 1972 the Theological Education Fund enumerated several types or forms of alternative theological education: study centres, lay training centres, centres for urban mission and training, theological education by extension, other decentralized programmes, clinical pastoral education, community-based theological learning, cell groups for study and mutual care and team ministry, theological reflection in liberation movements, and ad hoc education events (workshops, conferences, short courses, etc.). (Kinsler, 1983, 1)

---

[38] By the time of Kinsler's book, the breadth of structures using TEE at some level was broad:

"One of the extraordinary dimensions of the extension movement evidenced in this book is its ecumenical spectrum and depth...although TEE is a very recent development, it has already been adopted by Anglicans, Baptist, Congregationals, Roman Catholics, Presbyterians, Lutherans, Nazarenes, Methodists, Pentecostals, Orthodox, Independents, united churches and many others." (Kinsler, 1983, xiv)

Lois McKinney offered this definition of TEE: "It is the contextual, experiential development of servant leaders for the church."[39] (McKinney, 1986, 29) McKinney focused on the results: servant leaders. Kinsler focused on the training process. Others were primarily concerned with the more narrow focus of creating tools to help train leadership within their own denominations.

A number of those involved in the early days of TEE saw the value of the interaction between students as well:

> ...you are dealing with a person with a living relationship to a living group, and you have to deal with him little by little. His problems come up when they come up. His schoolwork may have no connection to his problems at a given point. But it can often be related to it and you are dealing with a real person and his interest in his studies depends on his relationship to that group. If the group dies, his interest dies. (Winter, 1969d, 335)

TEE Expands

Other factors fed into this new, growing idea. Winter had helped to found the Association of Latin American Theological Schools. Before leaving for their furlough in 1965, Winter was elected Executive Secretary of the northern region, which allowed him to travel around Latin America, learn more about what was happening in the region, and spread the TEE vision. Winter was also elected the General Secretary of the Theological Accreditation Association for the Northern countries of Latin America, Mexico, and the Caribbean. His three years in that role also contributed to the spread of TEE and to Winter's growing knowledge of the region. (Winter, 2000, 30)

In part because of Winter's diverse roles, TEE was beginning to gain a hearing in broader mission circles. Several had noticed Winter's work in The Evangelical Foreign Missions Association[40] along with the

---

[39] Lois McKinney Douglas taught mission at Trinity Evangelical Divinity School and previously at Wheaton College Graduate School. She served as a missionary for twenty-three years with the Conservative Baptist Foreign Mission Society, teaching at theological seminaries in Portugal and Brazil, and serving internationally as a consultant to theological education programs.

[40] The EFMA is now named The Mission Exchange. The IFMA is now named CrossGlobal Link, each with more than 100 member agencies. In both cases, I will use the older name initials for this historical account.

Committee to Assist Missionary Education Overseas (CAMEO),[41] which sponsored the promotion of TEE around the world. In 1970, C. Peter Wagner[42] and Ralph Covell[43] sought to encourage the expansion of TEE ideas and models into Asia, where Covell had been a missionary. Following a trip to the region they produced a book which was a follow-up to *Theological Education by Extension* (Winter, 1969d) called *An Extension Primer.* (Covell and Wagner, 1971) TEE had grown out of the work in Guatemala into Latin America, where Wagner had his mission field experience. The book they produced takes as its point of departure the impetus the movement received from the work in Guatemala:

> A modest experiment with a new form of ministerial training in Guatemala in 1962 has, within a decade, not only drawn the attention of theological educators worldwide, but also caused many to rethink their patterns and presuppositions for theological education. (Covell and Wagner, 1971, 1)

Covell, who had served as a missionary with the Conservative Baptist Foreign Mission Society in Taiwan and knew the training situation in Asia, wanted to learn about TEE. When he began to teach at the seminary level, he thought he ought to learn more about the training situation in Latin America, so he visited the seminary in Guatemala. But the trip changed his perspective: "I was impressed that with the various movements of TEE that were going on, they were still related to the seminary. In other words, they were not freelance-type TEE movements. They had a base, and that was sort of the way that the work was carried on."[44]

The first workshop to explain and promote the idea of TEE regionally was in Central America in 1963. The first international gathering was in 1967 in Armenia, Colombia. (Kinsler, 1983, 7) By 1977, there were at least 133 programs with some 19,384 students in Latin America and the Caribbean. In Africa, the first workshop was in Kenya in 1969, with one each year for the next four years in other African locations. (Kinsler, 1983, 9) As of 1977, there were fifty-seven programs with 6,869

---

[41] CAMEO was a joint committee of the IFMA and the EFMA to further missionary education worldwide.

[42] Wagner joined the faculty of the SWM at Fuller Theological Seminary in 1971; he was a student at the SWM in 1966-1967. He had been a missionary in Latin America.

[43] Covell had been a missionary in Taiwan and later taught at the Denver Conservative Baptist Theological Seminary, now called Denver Seminary.

[44] Interview with Ralph Covell by the author on January 15, 2007, 4.

students. 1978 was likely the first year Nigeria reported in with ten programs with 5,923 students.

Many places had regional or countrywide associations for TEE. Movements are documented in Asia, Europe, and North America. This went from, "A handful of experiments in Latin America at the end of the 1960s to 300-400 programmes with perhaps 100,000 students around the world at the end of the 1970s..." (Kinsler, 1983, 15) Even in China back in 1981, more than 32,000 members and leaders of the house church movement were reportedly in various kinds of training programs. (Kinsler, 1983, 28)

Over the first ten years, through the efforts of a number of missionaries and leaders, TEE continued to spread.[45] In Brazil, an association of evangelical extension seminaries produced 100 textbooks over the next ten years. It spread in Asia in countries such as Japan, Korea and India.[46]

In India, the program was still strong in 2009. Its structure, called The Association for Theological Education by Extension (TAFTEE), is the largest training entity in the country, with 13,000 active students.[47] Earlier in their history, they produced courses along the Programmed Instruction model. One such degree level course was both theological and practical in design, called *Poverty and Development*. (TAFTEE, 1981) Often TAFTEE's students are professionals and leaders in their communities.[48]

---

[45] Winter and others promoted TEE in Spanish/Portuguese speaking countries such as Brazil, Peru, Ecuador, Mexico, Colombia, Argentina, etc.

[46] As it spread, others identified issues that TEE helped to solve. In a TEE leaflet, Malcolm Bradshaw, a missionary in SE Asia, raised the issue of having enough trained leadership for the growing church in the region: "...full-time ministers will no doubt continue to be needed. Yet the brunt of the responsibility for shepherding the small house congregations will of necessity fall upon the shoulders of a new task force of semi-professional ministers... Self-supporting status will be essential because most flat churches will be too small in numbers to support a full-time pastor." (As quoted in Covell and Wagner 1971, 3)

In Latin America, Mario Rivas, President of the Bolivian Baptist Union, suggested the idea of giving up paid ministry pastorates completely: "Let's forget the idealistic position of a full-time pastorate if the situation so demands. Let's get out into the community and work like other men, earning our daily bread through radio broadcasting, teaching, public offices, and above that offer our talents for the glory of God. Many pastors are doing that already." (As quoted in Covell and Wagner 1971, 3)

[47] Email from the director of TAFTEE, David Samuel to Greg H. Parsons, February 11, 2009.

[48] The TEE movement in India, and elsewhere, remains the subject of research by those evaluating the movement, such as a dissertation on the impact of TEE in India and

In 1972, Winter wrote a four-page paper, published in the English edition of a newsletter called "Seminario de Extension" (Number 2–1973).[49] In it, he defined TEE, explained what it can do, and summarized its major contributions at the ten-year mark. "Let us call extension education any method of education which does not disrupt the learner's productive relation to society. In the case of theological education, it is the seminary that extends (fits into) the life-cycle of the student rather than extracting the student to fit him into the life-cycle of the seminary." (Winter, 1972d, 1)

A major contribution of TEE was that it allowed for superior selection of the leaders to train. Winter noted, "...the overarching significance of extension is the breath-taking new *freedom of selection* which it allows." (Winter, 1972d, 1, underlining is original) Under the section, "What it can do?" Winter wrote: "It can train "minority" church leaders. Here I am not referring to the training of leaders *for* minority churches, but to the training of leaders *in* minority churches." (Winter, 1972d, 2)

Winter wrote that TEE can train the majority of church leaders, but he was not talking about replacing existing seminaries, instead:

> One of the most disruptive tensions in the non-western churches of the world today is the conflict between the natural leaders, who have in many cases pioneered in the early growth of the church, and the new breed of younger ministers who have gone the seminary route. It is a safe generalization that the healthier churches are those that make the best use of the natural leaders. (Winter, 1972d)[50]

In 1970, after an eight-year period, estimates indicated that in Latin America "some 50 institutions ... are using these methods to train something over 2,000 students." (Covell and Wagner, 1971, 5-6) Reflecting back thirty years later in 1996, Winter listed four reasons why

---

its impact on Union Biblical Seminary. *Development of the Theological Education by Extension in India with Special Reference to Extension Education Ministry of Union Biblical Seminary* (Keikung, 1986) and *Missiological Education: An Indian Exploration, Studies in the Gospel Interface with India Contexts* (Arles, 2006) which focuses on missiological education of various types including TEE.

[49] The back page of the newsletter notes that 1,000 copies were distributed in Spanish and 2,100 in English.

[50] Winter knew, based on simple maths and church growth patterns, that seminaries could never train enough pastors and leaders if those churches were growing and multiplying.

there was a continuing need for the training of "lay people."[51] By 1996, Winter wrote the following, showing the focus of his thinking on training for all, not merely those who are in professional ministry:[52]

1. That *missiological education for the lay person* is the best hope of rescuing our generation from a "Great Commission-less" Christianity, a form of Christianity which is a deadly and widespread heresy within the Western churches and as such is a fatal disease striking at the very root of the global Christian mission.

2. That *missiological education for the lay person*, therefore, even outranks the strategic importance of training professional missionaries.

3. That *missiological education for the lay person* can best be achieved by off-campus education, and that—believe it or not—the off-campus education of "lay people" is also the only way that the best selections can be made for the ordinary pastors/evangelists without whom the Christian movement cannot continue.

4. The idea, finally, that the massively growing trend in university circles toward *off-campus education* is also the only way the average post-secondary education institution will survive in the increasingly "on the run" world in which we live.[53] (Winter, 1996)

Peter Wagner wrote of three "Eras" in the history of TEE. The first was the Guatemala "experiment" run by Winter, Emery and Kinsler from 1962 to 1967. Even during that early period there was interest in other Latin American countries as well, linked as they were by the Spanish language. The beginning of the second phase is generally associated with a conference held in Colombia in 1967, after which the movement began to spread globally. A key figure person in this global expansion was Raymond

---

[51] The main distinction was between those who were ordained and those who were not ordained in denominational churches. Being Presbyterians, Winter and Emery were working within that system. They merely wanted to be sure that "lay" people could be trained in a way that would allow them to be ordained, should they be so gifted and desire it.

[52] Also, the emphasis in TEE had shifted to terminology such as "off-campus" or "distance" programs.

[53] The focus of this article was on missiological training because it was part of a *Festschrift* created on the retirement of Paul E. Pierson, the 3rd Dean of the SWM. As the title indicated, that book focused on, *Missiological Education for the 21st Century*. (Woodberry et al., 1996)

Buker, Sr., the coordinator of CAMEO. The third phase, which was being proposed in this Foreword of the book: *Discipling Through Theological Education by Extension*, is focused on content and on clarifying the purpose of TEE and promoting the development of more materials. (Gerber, 1980, 9-10)

Early Factors Debated Within TEE

Several factors were discussed which shaped TEE:

1. The relevance of the training to the cultural and church settings of the pastor: What harm might be caused when people received their training outside of their cultural context? "Many Asian Christians uphold the West as their theological model. Thousands of young people have made an exodus, particularly to the U.S. for their education." (Ro, 1970, 49)

2. The recognition of the influence of Western cultural training patterns in both the theology and the methods of teaching, for example:

> As the insights of cultural anthropology filter down to grass roots, missionary educators have become more aware of patterns of culture and sub-culture all over the world. ... Institutions that are not extended will often require that a student from one culture take his training within another one. Experience has shown that this cultural extraction is not ideal. (Covell and Wagner, 1971, 9)

3. Consideration of the minimal, academic requirements that were prerequisites for ordination, and the related question: how denomination requirements should be weighed against what was actually needed in the context of a local fellowship; and,

4. What does a pastor for a "typical" church in the U.S. need, as opposed to a pastor in a rural tribal group or in the inner city.[54] (Covell and Wagner, 1971, 10-11)

No matter if traditional training methods were used or new TEE type methods, the training needed to fit the context. If leaders were trained in

---

[54] For example: "...academic standards for the ministry are better determined by the academic levels of the people in the pews than by the seminary board. It may be true that college and seminary are basic of a U.S.A. suburban pastor, and that seminaries now need to replace the BD with a professional doctorate to keep their graduates on an academic par with the increasing number of PhD's in their congregations. This standard is not necessary among the mountain peoples of Taiwan, however, nor perhaps even for effective ministry in the black ghettos of the inner cities of the U.S.A." (Covell and Wagner, 1971, 10-11)

such a way that they no longer fit into their context back in their home church, the training was a failure. Winter and others at Fuller and many other seminaries had struggled with one aspect of the problem: international students who came to the U.S. and never returned to their homeland.[55]

TEE had also been called the "humanizing of theological education" (Covell and Wagner, 1971, 6) Pursuing the goal of training leaders that God had already called, TEE sought to help seminaries begin with new ways of identifying leaders and giving them the training, tools, and recognition they needed to be able to serve in their local context.

Improving TEE Effectiveness

All those involved in TEE realized that for it to be effective, they needed to produce appropriate and contextualized resources. With less time in a classroom in front of a professor, students needed to receive information in other ways, in addition to weekly or bi-weekly meeting with teachers. New teaching resources needed to be developed and leaders looked for ways to meet that need.[56]

In Winter's role as the secretary of the Latin American Association of Theological Schools, northern region, he helped both to coordinate presentations as well as presenting at a workshop held in Armenia, Colombia, South America. The twin themes of this workshop were extension education and the design of a new kind of semi-programmed textbook. There were 29 participants including five women and a number of Latin leaders who worked in training institutions in the region. Winter presented four of the seventeen sessions with Kinsler presenting six, and C. Peter Wagner gave two. Louise J. Walker, an educational expert with a Spanish-speaking ministry of the Assembly of God denomination, gave three presentations on how to develop materials for extension education. (Winter, 1967) Her presentations clearly and carefully outlined steps toward the development of programmed instruction, explaining dozens of detailed steps from design, to content considerations and education components, such as immediate testing, checking and feedback.

---

[55] As recounted to this author in various private discussions and public presentations by Ralph D. Winter over many years.

[56] June 10, 1965 letter from F. Ross Kinsler to John H. Sinclair, 1. For example, when Jim Emery was in the United States on an extended furlough for additional study, Kinsler suggested Emery could help develop curriculum and meet a crucial need.

Seeking to illustrate various modes of education, Winter described different kinds of methods used to educate from the perspective of cultural anthropology. He employed two extremes for the sake of illustration: The army, jail and monastery illustrated the extraction method and radio, television and newspaper illustrated the extension method (See Figure 4). (Winter, 1967, 5)

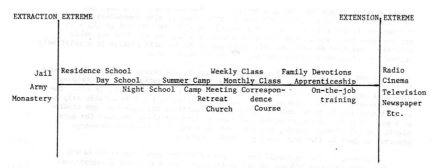

Figure 4 – Education Extremes Illustration by Winter 1967

In the summer of 1971, Winter and Covell made a trip similar to the one Covell and Wagner had made the previous summer. They started in France and went to Pakistan, Thailand, the Philippines, Hong Kong, and Japan. Winter noted they had trained and interacted with 587 seminary leaders that summer. Each of those leaders were included on the initial mailing list of what was typically a four-page monthly newsletter called *Extension*. It was produced from November 1972 to December 1977.

It was published for "those whose responsibilities require them to be right up to date on what is happening in this worldwide movement and who are able to share insights that are turned up in their own activities."[57] (Weld, 1972, 1) It collected information from those who were furthering TEE in their own areas, detailed their events, and gave sample course ideas and success stories. The first edition in late 1972 mentioned the following:[58]

1. An Asia-wide TEE consultation was planned in late November or December in Bangkok.

2. An event in Colombia would be held to discuss how to "accelerate and improve the writing, production and distribution of extension materials."

---

[57] By "turned up" Weld means activities they noticed in the process of training.

[58] For a sample page from this newsletter, called "Extension", see Appendix G.

3. A TEE organization meeting for the Near East and North Africa was planned for January '73 in Beirut.

4. A workshop in Malaysia was held with twenty-one people representing nine evangelical groups.

5. There were 4,879 extension students studying in Latin America in 1971. Two thousand of those were in Brazil, representing thirty different institutions.

6. Twelve centers in India had two hundred students as reported by The Association for Theological Extension Education (TAFTEE).

7. Announcement of a writers' workshop for Pakistan planned by the Committee for Theological Education by Extension in December. (Weld, 1972, 1-2)

Wayne Weld was a missionary from Colombia. For his studies under Winter at Fuller, he produced *The World Directory of Theological Education by Extension*. (Weld) In it, he seeks to report about aspects of TEE programs, including training, which had occurred, materials produced, and locations of programs. He lists the following countries, many with programs in multiple cities. (Weld, 1973, 90)

Argentina	Australia	Bolivia
Brazil	Chile	Colombia
Dominican Republic	Ecuador	England
Ethiopia	France	Guadeloupe
Guatemala	Guyana	Haiti
Honduras	India	Indonesia
Iran	Italy	Jamaica
Niger	Japan	Kenya
Malaysia	Mexico	Nigeria
Pakistan	Panama	Peru
Philippines	Puerto Rico	Rhodesia
Sierra Leone	South Africa	Spain
Taiwan	Tanzania	Trinidad
United States	Uruguay	Zambia

Also in the directory, Weld lists the denominations and mission organizations involved in actual TEE program or training for TEE.[59] Weld, like Winter, talks about TEE being a movement. He notes that it is "the most exciting and widely disseminated innovation in ministerial training certainly in the last ten years and probably in many decades."

---

[59] For a list of almost 200 organizations, see Appendix H.

(Weld, 1973, 1) He also includes many statistics and details about programs ten years into the movement. For example, in a chart comparing TEE programs in Latin America, the Caribbean, Africa and Asia, Asia had a much higher academic level of students in the program. Twenty-five percent of all the students already had a BA, compared with only six percent in Africa, the next highest region. Forty-nine percent were already licensed in ministry, compared to only two percent in Africa, which was the next-highest region. (Weld, 1973, 45)

Weld includes some critiques of TEE. In the context of the chart just mentioned, he notes that many programs were started in English, which greatly influenced who could participate and which countries would more likely have strong programs. (p. 45) He also noted that this was changing and suggested that filling empty positions with local pastors or national leaders was beginning to happen. (Weld, 1973, 67)

Weld makes several observations and recommendations out of his experience in Colombia which he believed might be applicable to other extension programs: (Weld, 1973, 64-69)

1. The denominations must be "sold on" theological education by extension.
2. One way of relating extension training to the work of the denomination is the organization of centers in local congregations.
3. We should not be too concerned with numbers. A fifty percent drop out rate is perfectly acceptable as long as the right people are being attracted to and maintained in extension studies.
4. Pastors should be encouraged to continue and renew their theological education in this way.
5. Even if the pastors cannot always be enlisted, greater dependence on national teachers is necessary.
6. Workshops for teachers are essential.
7. Monthly meetings of students must be stressed.
8. In order to encourage students who see completion of studies as a very distant goal, intermediate goals may be set up.
9. Greater flexibility in the curriculum is essential.
10. In an effort to show that TEE is academically respectable, perhaps insufficient attention has been given to the certificate or lowest-level studies.

Ted Ward of Michigan State University (and later Trinity Evangelical Divinity School, part of Trinity International University) brought education theory and training experience to the TEE movement. He used the analogy of a "split rail fence" (Figure 5) where the first horizontal rail was the field service or experience that a pastor was engaged in, and the second rail was cognitive input from books or other media. The "fence posts" in the illustration were seminars that pastors attended with other pastors where they discussed together with a professor, until the next seminar, represented by the second fence post, in a week or a month. Ward also discussed the use of media such as tape recordings, which could be used to make the learning experience more focused and prepare the student for more effective learning. (Winter, 1969d, 321-322) He said:

> This can help the student understand what he is going to run into in a lecture. A most important part of a good lecture is tuning in an audience. This is usually done by using an introduction, primarily designed to orient your audience to the frame of reference in which succeeding points will make sense and be retained in the hearers' thought processes. (Winter, 1969d, 322)

Figure 5 – Ted Ward's Split Rail Fence Analogy[60]

In 1970, Ward and his wife Margaret produced a book called *Programmed Instruction for Theological Education by Extension.* (1970) Produced in conjunction with CAMEO, it sought to "serve, not impose structure or constraints" and "to provide a first step toward the skills of writing programmed instruction." (Ward and Ward, 1970, vvi) Generally, programmed instruction used a textbook to teach materials in a systematic way that also took into account the culture and language of student. Programmed instruction had been used in business, technology, and the natural sciences, but not as much in humanities, and very little in theological education. It was a way to get information to people incrementally, allowing for immediate feedback. (Ward and Ward, 1970, 41)

The Wards' book described how to produce such a text, and expressed an overarching vision for producing a great number of textbooks in

---

[60] Ted Ward, "The Split-Rail Fence: Analogy for Professional Education," *Extension Seminary*, #2, 5

different languages and cultural settings. They knew it would be a massive effort:

> The Intertext project is the first sizable effort to develop an application of the programmed instruction style for theological education. In promising a way to meet the need for off-campus education of pastors, the Intertext project has quickly become one of the most extensive voluntary non-profit collaborations for the development of instructional materials. (Ward and Ward, 1970, 1)

Some also produced programmed or semi-programmed textbooks where, in its ideal form, as Winter described it, the text "asks a question and if you answer this, then the next question is this; if you answer that, then the next question is that. It does not tell you where to go, it follows you. It's very complex."[61] They also sought to relate what they were doing to existing textbooks where appropriate. Winter wrote, "there needs to be a carefully composed textbook task force that will parcel out to different members of the group all of the various courses deemed necessary in this program." (Winter, 1969d, 143) In *Theological Education by Extension*, Winter included a detailed, if not complicated, "PERT-chart" process from concept to press on a sixteen-step book production process.[62] (Winter, 1969d, 290) The diagram included a number of mission agencies, editorial, and book production processes and the interaction between them all.[63]

However, the development of materials was very slow, and never progressed beyond a few books. Winter and others knew it would be difficult, but continued to promote it at first. He wrote, "We feel 'programmed instruction' is a technique with much to offer us, but it will be a taxing problem to produce all of these materials and also work out the details of the new program as it unfolds."[64]

---

[61] Interview with Ralph Winter by the author on August 16, 2007, 2. See the sample pages in Figures 6 and 7 for an example.

[62] PERT stands for Program Evaluation and Review Technique. It was first used for complicated project management for the U.S. Navy. It was often used in business for projects requiring many steps, approvals, and evaluation.

[63] That process envisioned "one institution to free a faculty member to do a first-class job of one book, knowing that other books constituting the remainder of an interlocking set of theological texts are being undertaken elsewhere. The program is inter-confessional and international as well." (Winter 1970, 18)

[64] January 23, 1964 document, *The Extension-Seminary Plan in Guatemala* from Ralph D. Winter to Ray Strong, et al., 3.

A few books were produced. Wayne Weld produced *Principles of Church Growth* (1974) based on McGavran's writings and conference presentations. The book was originally produced in Spanish for those who had finished primary school in Latin America. It was also produced in English to demonstrate how a programmed textbook worked. Often, it included a paragraph and a chart or graph that illustrated an idea, followed by several questions, which the reader could answer and immediately see if they were correct. See Figures 6 & 7. (Weld and McGavran, 1974)

Figure 6 (marked 5-14 in the image) has a graph of the growth of two congregations with a brief description. Figure 7 (5-15 in the image) has questions related to the chart.

Ralph D. Winter: Early Life and Core Missiology

66. Seeing the success at the beginning of the period, it is possible to believe that the church could have continued to

_____ see /

67. One way to break out of stagnation would be to _____ the program.   see //

It is important to make graphs of every congregation and every region. Graphs based on denominational totals of membership hide more than they reveal. In the graph that follows it can be noted that although the denomination is growing well, there is much difference between the two congregations indicated. If the problem is not studied in detail one would believe that all the churches were enjoying the blessing of God, who gives the growth.

Two Congregations of the Same Denomination 1965-1970

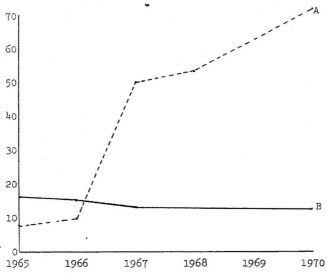

/ grow
// change, modify

Figure 6 – Programmed Instruction Example from Principles of Church Growth by Weld and McGavran, 5-14

68. One of the most effective ways of using graphs is in comparing two or more congregations or denominations. In the graph above the contrast is noted. It is important to prepare graphs for such comparisons. The most useful graph would be of

_____a) Each congregation and region.

_____b) Each nation and continent.

_____c) Each meeting and activity.   see &

69. Graphs of denominational goals of membership.

_____a) Are the only useful graphs.

_____b) Don't indicate the differences between congregations.

_____c) Reveal all that it is necessary to know.   see //

70. Since the congregations compared in the graph are of the same denomination, it is reasonable to believe that the differences between them are because of

_____a) Doctrine.

_____b) Local policy.

_____c) Resources.   see &&

71. It would be interesting to find out what happened in church A in

          _____   see ///

72. Why does this period interest us? _____
                                               see /

73. If you were a member of congregation B, what would you do?

```
/ because the church began to   /// 1966
  grow or SIMILAR WORDS           &  a
// b                             && b
```

Figure 7 – Programmed Instruction Example #2 from Principles of Church Growth by Weld and McGavran, 5-15

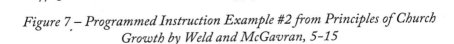

Rev. Jack Wing, of the California Friends Mission working in Chiquimula, Guatemala, produced a workbook on the elementary level for the OT and NT. (Winter, 1969d, 112) Ross Kinsler produced *Inductive*

Study of the Book of Jeremiah in Spanish and English for TEE use. (Kinsler, 1971) It was a tool the student could work through that taught a form of inductive Bible study. It combined the traditional IBS approach with the groups-of-questions-to-be-answered approach Winter learned at Prairie Bible Institute, in a fill-in-the-blank style. (See Figure 8 and 9.)

326 ·   10:B   Lesson X: JEREMIAH'S TRAGIC ROLE

14:1-6	Lord to Judah	Describes the drought
7-9		
10		
11-12		
13-16		
17-18		
19-22		
15:1-4		

C. Jeremiah's Anguish (Jeremiah 15:5-21)

Jer. 15:5-21 contains a variety of materials which are only superficially related to Jer. 14:1-15:4. It includes one of Jeremiah's "confessions" and an extraordinary "private oracle" which echoes some of the words of Jeremiah's call. The dialogue between the Lord and His prophet reaches an almost unbelievable intensity. Jeremiah expresses blasphemous thoughts, and his prophetic office itself is called into question.

As you study this passage, allow the text to speak to your life. Try to experience with Jeremiah the anguish of his calling as God's prophet in a time of great tragedy. And let his experience illumine your role as God's servant and messenger in our own day, which is also a time of great tragedy.

1. Read Jer. 15:5-9. Who is speaking to whom in this paragraph? _____

* _____ *

The Lord is speaking to Jerusalem or to Judah.

2. What is the topic of this paragraph? _____

What situation does it refer to? _____

What specific event does it refer to (give two possibilities)? _____

* _____ *

Figure 8 – Kinsler's Intertext Book on Jeremiah, 326

More specifically, those involved in the Latin American context had begun to promote and produce books in what was called "the Intertext Project." In the front matter of the book, *Inductive Study of the Book of*

Jeremiah, it was noted that an Intertext, "is a theological seminary textbook designed for use with a single weekly seminar and more than usual out-of-class study. It can be used with either residence or extension programs. It is built specifically to fit into a larger matrix, a complete curriculum of other books and courses." (Kinsler, 1971, ii) The description in the book also explained how texts in the project were to be reviewed by institutions and denominations, who would, in turn, develop what was called by some the "largest non-government educational development project in the world today."

Section C: JEREMIAH'S ANGUISH (JEREMIAH 15:5-21)   10:C   327

the destructuin of Jerusalue. It may refer to the fall of Jerusalem in 487 B.C. or to the defeat of Jerusalem in 498 B.C. See your Chronological Chart. The passage is similar to the Lamentations Jeremiah wrote after Jerusalem's fall.

3. Some Bible translators use the past tense in Jeremiah 15:5-9. Others use the future. In the Revised Standard Version it sounds as if Jerusalem had already fallen when Jer. 14:17-18 and 15:5-9 were written. However, Bible prophecy often uses the past tense to describe future events that God has determined to bring about. So we can't tell when these words were written.

Compare these passages in whatever versions you have.

4. Compare in the RSV the topic and tenses of Jer. 15:1-4 with those of Jer. 15:5-9._____

4. Compare in the RSV the topic and tenses of Jer. 15:1-4 with those of

Jer. 15:5-9._____

* _____ *

They both speak of destruction but 15:1-4 is still a warning of impending doom.

5. Write down the Lord's question in v. 5. _____

_____

What is the understood answer to this question? _____

* _____ *

Who will have pity on you, O Jerusalem?
No one. If the Lord has rejected His people, there is no pity.

6. Why does the Lord not have pity on Jerusalem? _____

* _____ *

In v. 6 the Lord repeats His often stated accusation against His people. They have rejected Him. It is only because they have rejected Him that He has now rejected them.

7. Notice what the Lord has done to His people. Read through the paragraph again and circle the personal pronoun "I" each time it is repeated. Underline the phrases that describe what He has done to His people.

8. Describe Jeremiah's role in Jer. 15:5-9. _____

Figure 9 – Kinsler's Intertext Book on Jeremiah, 327

Yet the books were hard to produce in part because to reach the quality everyone recognized was necessary, they needed to be done by native language speakers. Many local tools were developed, but the Intertext project failed to get off the ground.

Evaluating TEE

There were a number of studies done on TEE during the 1970s. Many of them focused on a particular country and the programs run in that country, often under one denomination. For example, Ken Mulholland wrote *Adventures in Training the Ministry: A Honduran Case Study in Theological Education by Extension.* (1976) With a broader subject matter, Cliff Holland's dissertation, called *Theological Education in Context and Change: The Influence of Leadership Training and Anthropology on Ministry for Church Growth* (1978), focused on the combination of leadership training (TEE) and anthropology. Vance R. Field did a masters level study, called *Theological Education by Extension* (1972).[65] It sought to both define and give examples of the movement in Alliance circles in Indonesia.

In the mid-1980s, about twenty years after the "Guatemala experiment," a small consultation was held under the sponsorship of the International Council of Accrediting Agencies and World Evangelical Fellowship (now called the World Evangelical Alliance).[66] The event sought to evaluate the TEE movement and produced a book from the event called, *Cyprus: TEE Come of Age.* (Youngblood, 1986) The lead presentation was by Ken Mulholland titled "TEE Come of Age: A Candid Assessment after Two Decades." (Mulholland, 1986, 9-25) Mulholland had served with the Presbyterian Church in Honduras. He noted that the Guatemala model had "assumed definitive form: self-instructional home-study materials for daily preparations, decentralized weekly seminars of students and teachers, periodic extended meetings at a central location for students from any or all centers."

Mulholland further noted five accomplishments and problems with TEE at this twenty-year point:

1. It made formal theological training available to persons for whom it was previously unavailable.
2. It raised significant issues of educational method.

---

[65] This study was done at Western Evangelical Seminary.

[66] The ICAA was started by and worked closely with but autonomously from the WEF. It began in March of 1980.

3. It unleashed unparalleled creativity in theological education at all levels.
4. It strengthened the church.
5. It brought to the forefront the question of leadership selection. (Mulholland, 1986, 13-17)

The "areas of disappointment" were as follows:

1. It did not communicate the missiological vision of its pioneers. The goal of some programs became filling in the blanks in the lesson, finishing classes, getting grades, etc.
2. It often became fixed at a single academic level. As well, national leadership trained in other models often tended to keep the TEE programs at lower levels, which sometimes meant that it was viewed as second-class education.
3. It depended too heavily, too often, and for too long on expatriate leadership.
4. Thus, it did not always prove institutionally stable nor was it able to maintain continuity through the years.
5. The hope of early TEE pioneers (to establish a high level of coordination to minimize duplication, maximize resources, and establish accreditation standards) has been realized only partially and sporadically. The programmed text idea never took hold for various reasons, and the Intertext project failed, only producing a few books...[67] (Mulholland, 1986, 18-23)

Some of the reasons for these problems were the influence of both educational and cultural issues. The values of those who developed the materials may not have matched the end users. The ability to translate certain ideas and concepts was part of the problem. Certain theological issues were non-issues in other cultures, where other issues were more important, such as poverty in a place like India, or ancestor worship in Asia. (McKinney, 1986, 35)

Some of the models produced quality, appropriate materials. The work with the Conservative Baptist Home Mission Society in Honduras, done by George Patterson, was one such model, where they linked TEE to church planting and church development. (McKinney, 1986, 28-29)

There was also no global network to foster the joint international work desired by the pioneers. Weld, who produced a directory of TEE

---

[67] He continued: "...such as *Principles of Church Growth* (Weld and McGavran 1974) and Kinsler's book on Jeremiah. Both of those were in English and Spanish. Additionally, there were many regional- or language-wide texts and resources produced in many countries of the world, but not as the Intertext project had envisioned it." (Mulholland, 1986, 18-23)

programs while at FTS under Winter, tried to revise the directory and did not hear back from very many of the programs, thus assuming they were no longer operative. (Ferris, 1986, 42)

Robert Ferris, who worked with the TEE program in the Philippines in the mid-1980s, presented a paper on the future of TEE, pointing out the dangers of pursuing excellence to an extreme within a specific TEE program. He wrote, "In the process, we have trained the wrong people. Those who are gifted for ministry have struggled on without training, and the church has suffered. Without anyone's even realizing it, programs which appear to be thriving models of excellence in theological education are, in fact, models of failure." He noted the reason for this was the tendency to give more consideration to schooling attainments than to demonstrated gifts for ministry. (Ferris, 1986, 44)

Noting a survey done by Wayne Weld through the monthly newsletter "Extension," Ferris saw the pattern of (1) self-study, (2) practical work in the students' own congregation, and (3) regular encounters with tutors as too methodologically focused. He argued for a "distinctive context in which ministry formation is undertaken." (Ferris, 1986, 52)

On the positive side, the "experiment" in Guatemala was evaluated later as to its impact on the growth and maturity of the church in the nation. Five denominations in the country were studied and found to have seen their membership doubled from 1970 to 1980. "Theological education by extension, pioneered by the Presbyterians, has had a wide use in each of the groups." (Gerber, 1980, 80)

In the long run, TEE seemed to work in some places and not others. According to Robert Ferris, it took a lot of work to do well, and most trained theological teachers were not trained in effective teaching methods.[68] Ferris also noted that the program became focused on the wrong things:

> TEE assumed that learners were motivated by learning and that their primary interest is in the ministry effectiveness. That's not what I have found. What I found was that, yes, the people who enrolled in these programs wanted to minister more effectively. But they also wanted a certificate.[69]

He observed that the places where TEE continued effectively such as India and Pakistan, was because they agreed on one program within each country. In India:

---

[68] Interview with with Robert Ferris by the author on January 29, 2009, 1.

[69] Interview with with Robert Ferris by the author on January 29, 2009, 3-4.

TAFTEE was one integrated program for all of the churches of India. There was a critical mass that they were able to assemble and there was a relatively large clientele for the programs that were developed. They were only developing one set of programs. There was one curriculum they all were working on.[70]

Winter's files included a number of letters he received in response to a crucial article by James E. Goff (Goff, 1971) that appeared in the WCC journal *RISK* in the Spring of 1971. The files on this article include letters from Winter, Emery, and Kinsler, as well as John Sinclair and the staff at the WCC.

Goff had written an article in *RISK* about TEE as it was beginning to grow beyond Latin America. He expressed serious concerns about the strong Western influence, given the heavy involvement of missionaries from North America. From his reading of materials, he felt TEE was an attempt to repackage North American (or other Anglo-Saxon) theology, avoid local politics and social change, and teach Latin leaders to apply American management skills supporting "the powers that be" rather than empowering local leadership.[71] These were issues that Goff saw as having the consequence of maintaining missionary control over churches and was:

> ...information which can be programmed and fed to the pupil in pill-sized doses. The concern is not so much that budding pastors learn the Bible as that they learn it right, and the technique of programmed learning makes spoon-fed indoctrination possible. There is a right answer to every question because most of the questions are trivial. (Goff, 1971, 36)

Winter apparently wrote or called and asked the WCC editorial team to print a follow-up article.[72] He stated that he did not mind differences of opinion and dialog, but that he did mind being misquoted and taken out of context. The *RISK* reply acknowledged Winter's request, but felt that both Winter and Goff were missing each other's arguments. While they had entertained the idea of producing an issue of *RISK* on this topic during

---

[70] Interview with with Robert Ferris by the author on January 29, 2009, 5.

[71] This is part of a summary introduction to the article on the front page of this issue of RISK.

[72] This letter does not exist in this file. The file includes two letters from the WCC staff. One on December 20, 1971 from Martin Conway, Publications Secretary WCC, and one on February 11, 1972 from Rex Davis, managing editor for *RISK*, both at the WCC offices in Geneva.

1972, they eventually decided not to do so at that time. In another letter on the subject, Winter suggested that Goff had misunderstood his intentions and taken comments out of context, apparently not carefully reading either the large book on TEE (which Winter had edited) or even the context of sections which he quoted.[73]

Apparently, Winter sent the article to his former Presbyterian mission field leader, John Sinclair with a copy of the journal article and a letter he wrote to Gerald Anderson. In his reply to Winter, Sinclair mentioned that he sought to "take a middle position" in the debate, agreeing with most of Winter's arguments as outlined in the Anderson letter, but siding with Goff on the issue of the dominant role of North American missionaries in the planning.[74]

Winter wrote a brief reply to Sinclair, noting that he actually appreciated the fact that he took a middle position, and that he did not mind if people were actually opposed for whatever reason, but:

> What I do mind is for a discussion of the issues of theological education by extension to be derailed by misquotations and imputations of purpose which are wildly misleading. It is one thing, for example, to comment on the relative lack of Latin American participants in the first tentative list of authors for a crash program of book production, it is another thing to quote me as saying that certain North American organizations would have to run this thing in Colombia when as a matter of fact I said the opposite.[75]

Winter concluded this short note back to Sinclair with a phrase similar to what he may have said in his letter to the *RISK* staff. "Goff's treatment in the *RISK* article in my mind is no more dialogue than is Clarence Hall's treatment of the World Council in the Reader's Digest."[76] Hall's article, "Must Our Churches Finance Revolution?" (Hall, 1971) expressed deep concern, some might say hysteria, on the issue of the WCC funding insurrection in the U.S. and Africa. The *RISK* (WCC) staff

---

[73] Letter from Ralph D. Winter in South Pasadena to Gerald H. Anderson in Nashville, December 21, 1971.

[74] Letter from John H. Sinclair in New York to Ralph D. Winter in South Pasadena, December 28, 1971.

[75] Undated note signed by Ralph D. Winter to John Sinclair.

[76] Winter mentions people in the following connections: speaking in the home church of the current moderator of the General Assembly, San Francisco (COEMAR) office who tracked furloughed missionaries' activities, people in the Stewardship and Promotion within the General Mission Interpretation, Ecumenical Mission and Relations Committee.

looked on Winter's negative reference to Hall's one-sided article favorably, as both noted this reference in their reply letters to Winter.[77]

Jim Emery also wrote a 6-page letter to Goff, which carefully and clearly refuted almost every point in Goff's article. After quoting three of Goff's major points against TEE, Emery wrote: "These portions and their apparent lack of understanding of the extension system and its effect on students seem to show that you had decided to tear up the concept and destroy it before ever opening Ralph's book, examining the materials, observing it at work, or discussing the objectives and principles with those involved."[78]

Emery attempted to give the "flavor" of how TEE worked on the ground. Goff had argued that the materials were "programmed" and so were the expected answers and responses from the students. Emery argued that:

> The [TEE] system proposed to present the student not only with information, but to use the time with a teacher to discuss and relate the reading to the actual life experiences, understanding and problems of the student. You should take note here, that in your criticism of the "system" you completely ignore the discussion, which is probably the most important element in it.

> The amount and variety of information accessible to the student is always limited. Especially so to the student with little experience in reading. We solve this problem by forcing the student to read with understanding, so that by the time he finished the program, he has the skills and incentive to continue to read. Most of them do continue, and choose their own books. You can call this thought control if you like, for whoever controls access, to some extent controls thought, be he liberal, conservative, right, left, or center. Ted Ward notes this in Ralph's book (TEE p. 312) "And don't forget, programmed instruction is a virtually amoral tool."[79]

In conclusion, Emery pondered what Goff would put in the place of TEE:

---

[77] It is not clear what Winter felt about the content of Hall's *Reader's Digest* article. He merely hints that it was unfair, making parallels with Goff's article in *RISK*.

[78] Letter from James H. Emery in San Jose, California to James Goff in Cuernavaca, Mexico on December 29, 1971, 1.

[79] Letter from James H. Emery in San Jose, California, to James Goff in Cuernavaca on December 29, 1971, 2.

In residence [seminaries] the students are much more subject to the professors ideology than in extension. (And in the third world most professors of residence institutions are European or North American.) One reason the professor has a greater influence in residence is that since the students lack experience, they depend on the professor to define both the problem and the solution. The extension student knows the problem, and the teacher has to adapt his thought to the problem. He can't just force the student to ask questions he can answer.[80]

Ross Kinsler saw similar problems in Goff's article. He was contacted by Goff and had read Emery's letter. Emery's letter was so astute and direct as to likely make a reply difficult.[81] Kinsler seeks to open a dialog with his letter, perhaps feeling that he can relate to Goff and WCC circles better than others.[82] He argued that the TEE movement was, by then, "widely accepted now on all six continents and that it is staunchly defended by a growing number of participants." It is beyond the "propaganda, for and against. Rather, we are called upon to do what we can to make the movement most useful and least harmful."[83] Kinsler closes his letter with an appeal to Goff's approach to TEE:

How are we ever going to break down the most prominent form of oppression in our churches, the rule of the clergy over the people? Through traditional residential theological education young men who have never earned the right to be heard are given an artificial status (schooling, ordination, ecclesiastical power) which is devastating both to the laymen and to the clergy themselves. In extension all have equal access to education, ordination, and genuine leadership.[84]

As mentioned above, another area of struggle for the TEE movement was the production of programmed texts. There were workshops that promoted and furthered the idea of this kind of textbook for TEE, but few

---

[80] Letter from James H. Emery in San Jose, California, to James Goff in Cuernavaca on December 29, 1971, 5.

[81] There is no correspondence from Goff in reply to any of these letters in this file.

[82] As noted above, he joined the staff of the WCC in TEE and served until retirement in that area.

[83] Letter from F. Ross Kinsler in Guatemala to James E. Goff in Cuernavaca on March 13, 1972, 1.

[84] Letter from F. Ross Kinsler in Guatemala to James E. Goff in Cuernavaca on March 13, 1972, 2.

were produced. While other types of materials were produced, the coordinated effort that Winter and Wagner promoted never took off. According to Edwin Brainerd's article "The 'Myth' of Programmed Texts" (Brainerd, 1974) the idea of a programmed text was furthered by the involvement of Ted Ward, but Brainerd felt that Ward's ideas on how to produce texts were ignored by those in the TEE movement, when it seemed to complicate their plans.

> ...while he [Ward] presented the advantages of programmed instruction, he did not favor the marriage [of TEE with programmed instruction]. In fact, he presented the hypothesis that 'programmed tests cannot be written in a second language.' And postulated a lengthy, involved training program for would-be programmers. But, as was evident in the question and answer sessions that followed, these comments went unheeded.[85] (Brainerd, 1974, 220)

In the next issue of *EMQ*, leaders involved in the TEE movement responded to Brainerd's article in letters to the editor. Peter Wagner pointed out that Brainerd may be comparing the production of programmed text in the U.S. with what is done by missionaries without training or resources. That is why, Wagner felt, they started to use the idea of "semi-programmed" text, a phrase Ward discouraged.[86] Ray B. Buker, Sr., who led CAMEO, wrote two pages expressing his concern that the idea of texts being a "myth" might cause people to think there was nothing going on in TEE book production. While there may not have been fully programmed texts in mass quantity, there were a lot of resources, supplements to existing books in various languages and active production going on in three major programs. He mentioned programs in English speaking Africa, the Philippines and Brazil.[87] Harold Alexander wrote to be sure that people understood there was a clear distinction between TEE and programmed texts. While cognitive input is one of the three of Ted Ward's split rail fence analogy, there was no reason that that had to be via programmed texts.[88] Paul A. Pomerville, who had worked with TEE from 1969 in Indonesia, wrote the longest letter to the editor. He expressed what he felt was Brainerd's actual point was not that it was a "myth" but that there was merely a lack of programmed instruction materials available.

---

[85] This was during an event in Bolivia, and Ted Ward's comments were included in the book Winter edited, *Theological Education by Extension*.

[86] Letter to the Editor in *EMQ*, January 1975, 11:1, 48-49.

[87] Letter to the Editor in *EMQ*, January 1975, 11:1, 49-51.

[88] Letter to the Editor in *EMQ*, January 1975, 11:1, 51-52.

He details Brainerd's misinterpretation of Wagner's comments at the Wheaton workshop, and noted, like others, that programmed texts were not the only way to produce instructional materials. Pomerville also defended Ted Ward's meaning on the issue of producing books in another language, which he felt were misinterpreted by Brainerd.[89]

In the next issue of *EMQ* three months later, one more reader replied to the four above. Samuel F. Rowen pointed to the larger issue of the need for all kinds of instructional materials. He noted that everyone had mentioned Ted Ward and that his role should be appreciated and recognized. Because opinions were strong on all sides, Rowen suggested that Ted could say, "Lord save me from my disciples," and saw that "everyone can claim him [Ward] as the source of their blessing and the rightness of their action." Rowen's last point was an encouragement not to lose "the revolutionary dimensions implicit in TEE."[90] Rowen was involved in promoting and writing about TEE his whole career.

Bolivian missionary of 18 years, William Kornfield, wrote an article in 1976 that sought to encourage extension education to be more culturally relevant. At this point in the movement, he felt TEE needed serious evaluation. He saw the advantages, but pointed out that:

1. Students were not finishing assignments and lacked motivation
2. There were inadequate materials available outside of Spanish (major dialects in Bolivia for example)
3. Materials that were available were produced by non-nationals
4. There were not enough trained teachers in this style of learning
5. Materials were not adapted to the cultural situation
6. Teachers and students were different enough culturally, and limited exposure to each other decreased the effectiveness
7. It took too long to graduate, studies were too spread out
8. Topics, or the application of them, often missed the real needs of the church in the local area (Kornfield, 1976, 13-22)

Ted Ward wrote "What Happened to TEE?"[91] (2011) Written from a professional educator's perspective and with the deep desire still to improve

---

[89] Letter to the Editor in *EMQ*, January 1975, 11:1, 52-56.

[90] Letter to the Editor in *EMQ*, April 1975, 11:2, 129-130.

[91] In response to a request from this author, Ward answered the question: What do you believe to be the reason TEE declined in the West? See the full text of this document in Appendix I.

theological education and the education system,[92] he suggested that the promise and potential of TEE was lost for a number of reasons. The level of deep change suggested was too big a stretch for established educators. Strategies required teachers to become writers and designers and then have little face-to-face interaction with students. The need to develop appropriate resources, such as programmed instruction, "demanded for the design and writing of programmed instruction [and] was well beyond the majority of missionary-volunteers. Whatever was assumed about TEE, the coupling with programmed instruction was ill-conceived. It proved to be an Achilles heel." (2011, 2)

The systems proposed proved difficult to implement and while TEE leaders sought to convince established institutions that it was workable, some were undoubtedly threatened by the massive changes necessary. Additionally, Ward notes that serious engagement with "the education community" might have resulted in lasting change in the status quo. "In retrospect, a successful introduction of the innovative features could have resulted from a more careful, orderly, and less vigorously promoted attack on the time-honored traditions of the academy." (2011, 2)

We further examine the relationship between TEE and the Fuller Theological Seminary School of World Mission in the next chapter. The transition of Ralph and Roberta Winter from Guatemala to Fuller occurred as they were in the midst of a broad range of ministries involving both the growing TEE movement and the activities of the Mam Center.

Multiplying Connections

After their first five-year term on the field, the Winters had a one-year furlough. Seven months after returning in 1962, Winter wrote his Annual Meeting report, describing what happened during their time in the Southern California area the previous year. He carefully mentions many important leaders in the Presbyterian Church with whom he was involved during the year. He remarks, in a self-deprecating way, concerning the openness of churches in the "whole Southern California" that "there must have been a dearth of missionary speakers. By merely expressing willingness to speak, invitations (mainly through the efficient General

---

[92] Ward also noted: "Surely a more effective approach to leadership education is still needed. Seminaries seem handicapped by rapturous infatuation with an accumulated mass of erudite information. Pastors seem to be dissatisfied with the way they have been trained: too much information, too little attention to applications to real human needs, inadequate emphasis on the formation of understanding and the nurture of spirituality." (2011, 3)

Mission Interpretation office of the Los Angeles Presbytery) began rolling in to the point that this became a nearly full-time job in itself." That year, he spoke in 152 different churches to 14,800 people in the total audience, and met with many Presbyterian leaders in both Southern and Northern California.[93] This experience and growing exposure brought increased ministry connections with both local church and regional denominational leadership: more churches, pastors and mission leaders knew of the Winters and their work.

Winter also described a new committee that was formed to help church folks get more involved in mission work, helping long-term workers with "tasks either too simple or too technical."[94]

During this furlough, Winter also participated in a three-week trip to Mexico with Dr. Wallstrom, who had served the Presbyterian Board in Iran. That trip and Winter's interaction with Max Lathrop who had been planning a conference for Mexico led to them convening the First Christian Indian Congress held in October 1961 at Lake Patzcuaro Mexico. Winter wrote of the significance of this event in the March-April 1962 issue of *Practical Anthropology*. This had grown out of a network of those who worked with Indians in the Latin context. Winter noted the various Indian groups represented were using Spanish to communicate, had similar local church issues and problems, and struggled to both "compare notes" but also recognize differences between their different cultural expressions of Christianity, the church and the Bible. (Winter, 1962)[95]

Transitions

Towards the end of Ralph and Roberta's second five-year term in Guatemala, they could see how God was using their experiences to spread TEE globally. Ralph had been traveling around the region and new opportunities were opening around the world. During the same time, Winter had edited a Presbyterian-wide newsletter in both Spanish and English. It was distributed to both the church leadership and the missionaries in Guatemala. He also wrote a series in the publication called the "Seven Deadly Missionary Sins." One of those sins he called

---

[93] Annual Meeting Report by Ralph D. Winter, 1962, 1.

[94] Annual Meeting Report by Ralph D. Winter, 1962, 2.

[95] Email to the author from Ralph D. Winter, April 13, 2009 and April 14, 2009. Max Lathrop worked on the Mexico portion and Winter helped organize and mobilize for the rest of the indigenous populations.

"Gimmickitis." which referred to the tendency of missionaries to get into various good activities that might keep them from the best thing. Winter had read Donald McGavran's classic work *The Bridges of God* at the six-month missionary training course he took just before going to the field in 1956. He remembered that book when he heard that McGavran would be heading a new School of World Mission at Fuller. With his past Fuller connections and his childhood friend, Dan Fuller (who was a key player at Fuller for years), Winter decided to send the "Gimmickitis" article to McGavran, apparently feeling that McGavran would be interested because of its focus on how missionaries get distracted from the basic job of establishing and growing churches. McGavran published it in the *Church Growth Bulletin* in January 1966.[96]

The list of items in the article included: medicine, agriculture, airplanes, schools, and literacy. Winter noted:

> ...all these can become (and by themselves <u>are</u>) no more than gimmicks. Medical work can become as sterile spiritually as it is clinically. Agriculture can go dead. Airplanes can be misused. No matter how good a job is done in any of these lines, none of them is adequate in itself, and the honest people involved in all these programs tell you so themselves. (Winter, 1966a, 127)[97]

In the same article, he wrote: "Nothing you devise ought to stray far from a program that can be 'owned and operated' by Colombians in this present day." (Winter, 1966a, 128) And, "For over 30 years Guatemalan churches have built all their own buildings and paid all their own pastors' salaries with no help from abroad." (Winter, 1966a, 129)

When they left Guatemala for their second furlough, the Winters were planning on returning. They left their belongings in their home as they had five years before. But after Winter sent the "Gimmickitis" article to Donald McGavran, unexpected doors of opportunity began to open.

In his personal report in 1965, Winter reflected on his gifting which seemed to be setting the stage in his mind for a potential shift in focus to a broader ministry:

> My life revolves around planning and scheming. My forte is less that of following through doggedly in routine

---

[96] Interview with Ralph D. Winter by the author, August 30, 2006, 1.

[97] The *Church Growth Bulletin* was consolidated and reprinted in three volumes. Volume I-V covered September 1964 through July 1969 and was printed in 1969, volume two covered September 1969 through July 1975 and was printed in 1977, and volume 3 covered September 1975 through November 1979 and was printed in 1982.

details. Yet one of my greatest natural bents is struggling together with individuals in their personal problems. These two poles of theory and practice keep me intensely busy. Books flow endlessly into this house and ideas pour ceaselessly out of my heart and life.

Laying aside from discussion all the ideas fantastic and unfulfillable, there still remain many insights that are safe and solid opportunities for arduous and gratifying work. If I suffer, then, it is because I cannot, even now at 41 to 42, depend on assistants (except almost illiterate Indians) to help me fulfill what knowledge and experience lead me legitimately to expect to be able to do.[98]

Field leaders in the Presbyterian mission noticed this in Winter during his first term. They wrote, "Dr. Winter possesses a wealth of information on a wide variety of subjects, and has a very versatile mind and the ideas come so fast that his time and activity cannot keep pace with them. It is interesting to note, however, that Ralph seems to consider himself an inventor of ideas, rather than one to carry them out."[99]

Beyond the busyness of fieldwork, language learning, and the difficulties of life, Winter seems to be expressing a sense of responsibility to the natural and spiritual gifts he had been given and nurtured. While there was no hint of asking for release from any assignment or responsibility, there is a hint that he may not have been satisfied in the long run. And he and Jim Emery were aware that the Presbyterian leadership could move to close the field.

As the TEE movement grew, there was a sense in Winter's reflections, that the highlands of Guatemala were too small a place to experiment. Yet with the strong non-residential training idea behind the growing TEE movement, why would the Winters move to a residential seminary? Ultimately having a platform from which to share ideas to a significantly large and well positioned audience became the reason. It gave the opportunity to influence on a broader scale, both with TEE and with other issues of interest to the Winters, which we shall consider in the next chapter.[100]

---

[98] Personal Report Outline, "half filled out in 1964 for 1963, then completed in 1965", 4. Signed, September 17, 1965.

[99] A Report on the Work and Personnel of the Mam Christian Center, by F.G. Scovell and Wm. L. Wonderly, Ostuncalco, Guatemala, July 16 to 27, 1960, 16.

[100] Interview with Ralph D. Winter by the author, August 16, 2006, 5-6.

Analysis

TEE was the major connecting factor between Guatemala and the next phase of Winter's work at the School of World Mission at Fuller Theological Seminary in Pasadena. Winter, Emery and Kinsler brainstormed and developed a program for their situation related to the seminary in Guatemala. It was not until late 1963, toward the end of the Winters' time in Guatemala, that interest had grown to the point where conferences that included discussion about TEE began to occur. (Winter, 1969d, 6)

Winter and Emery had observed what was happening within the current programs as well as the needs of the pastors with whom they worked. With the Seminary making no measurable progress in producing pastors and leaders, they developed the ideas behind TEE and, subsequently, models for students in the region. At first, they needed to "sell" the idea to other missionaries and mission leadership. In order for TEE programs to be accepted as legitimate by non-missionary leaders and trainers around the world, they needed some level of acceptance from recognized leaders in the field and from North America. They believed that TEE could help seminaries also.

While statistics and data factored heavily into many of Winter's ideas, it was not because he was impressed by large numbers of people doing or not doing something. To Winter, the numbers pointed to underlying issues. The fact that the seminary had seven students when they started the TEE program could point to a number of problems to be solved, as could the fact that the TEE program quickly grew to 200. Another factor in pushing forward with TEE was that no Mam had ever been to the seminary and the number of graduates who were serving as pastors was small.

Winter's questions to Ross Kinsler just before Ross arrived were a reflection on Winter and Emery's goals and activities at the time: How can they all serve more and higher quality candidates from various backgrounds and with differing educational experiences that no one else was reaching?

One reason TEE spread initially was that it was working on the local level. Winter learned from anthropology that new ideas were not adopted merely because they were good ideas but because they were "borrowed" from somewhere else, where people saw they worked. Guatemala became an example, first to other countries in Latin America, and then to other parts of the world.[101] There was also growing conviction that this approach

---

[101] Interview with Ralph Winter by the author on August 16, 2006, 5.

to training could greatly help in areas of the world where churches were growing rapidly, such as in parts of Africa, Latin America and Asia.

Much later, Winter expressed his conviction that TEE faltered where it did, eventually failed in many locations and did not become *the* global pattern of theological education because it was not widely used in the Western world. TEE did adapt and is widely used in some countries.[102]

Winter wanted to help solve the problems he saw by mobilizing others toward involvement. Earlier, this was reflected in the Afghanistan project. It was also reflected in his approach to the US AID officers who asked how they might get involved in the remote parts of Guatemala. His trying to mobilize Dr. Wallstrom to switch fields and go to Guatemala is another example.[103] For TEE, he mobilized people such as Kinsler, Hopewell and Ward.

During this period, it becomes clearer that Winter not only was mobilizing others to get involved, but he was building a case as to why he and others believed that TEE was crucial for the training of pastors and leaders in the church worldwide. In his work promoting and arguing for using the model of the shaman in the Mam region, Winter pursued and enlisted various experts (such as Dr. Wallstrom) to establish and build his case. He took the same approach with TEE.

It is unmistakable, both from Winter's comments and from the available materials, that the involvement of James Hopewell was an immense boost to the expansion of TEE. Hopewell's position in the Theological Education Fund of the WCC had provided him vast exposure to many seminaries in various situations all over the world. Winter says of him:

> Not only is he a well-trained, keen observer with mission field experience of his own, but he has simply traveled farther and visited more theological institutions on the face of the earth than any other man who has ever lived. Not only so, but his reason for those hundreds and hundreds of visitations has been specific and professional. Probably no other man can as expertly walk into an institution and cut through its

---

[102] It should be noted that TEE is a precursor to other types of extension education as well as distance education. Naturally, those current programs are greatly helped by advances in technology that Winter, Emery and Kinsler did not have access to, such as email and the internet. Also, the establishment of the William Carey International University was another application of TEE.

[103] Wallstrom was at a point of deciding what field he might serve after leaving Iran.

superficial appearances to the core of its mission and ministry. (Winter, 1969d, 37)

That depth of exposure and information concerning the quality of various training programs gave Hopewell a depth of credibility, probably beyond any other person at the time. Winter and Emery added other significantly placed people, such as Ralph Covell and Ted Ward. These men and women helped broaden the acceptability of the idea and brought recognition to TEE. Each of them brought respect and connections within different circles of influence. For example, Covell served and taught in Conservative Baptist circles and had served in Asia. Ward, who taught education at Michigan State University, brought credibility from academic circles. His specific field was education.

Through these people, Winter was building a case for TEE. He also built a case in writing. His extensive editorial work, including one to two page introductions for most of the chapters of the 600-page book, *Theological Education by Extension* (1969d), is another example. In these, he not only explains how they fit into the flow of the book, the movement and its history, but he uses them to introduce the significance of the people involved, as noted above with Hopewell.[104]

Just as he had earlier promoted the general work of missionaries and the church in Guatemala, Winter wrote about TEE at the popular level in magazines such as *World Vision Magazine*. He also contributed to academic publications like *Practical Anthropology* and *Evangelical Missions Quarterly* with a more technical approach. In these articles and presentations, he included the names of various mission agencies or denominational groups and specific leaders. For example, he wrote about what non-Presbyterian groups were doing with TEE in other parts of Guatemala or other countries.

Winter tried to state the arguments for the usefulness and validity of TEE in ways that would not offend traditional seminaries and might allow them to consider making use of the method. He saw the value of recognizable institutions while pointing out their shortcomings. An inverse example of this point, a new university in Guatemala asked Winter to lend

---

[104] Winter was the editor of this book yet his name does not appear on the main introduction or these article introductions. The writing is consistent with his other writings and his approach to a joint work such as this book, not to make the book overly appear to be his work more than the authors. Given this author's experiences, the style of these introductions, details included in them that only Winter or Emery could have experienced, and the fact that Winter was the editor, there is no question that he wrote these.

his name to give them credibility.[105] Winter believed he was only asked because of his PhD.[106]

Part of his reason for casting vision and working on the idea of TEE was that he believed in what it could do to help people who would never be able to go to a residential program. In order to fill in the education gap between the average education level and what they needed to get started in theological training, Winter cast a vision which helped motivate other missionaries' involvement in the elementary education diploma program. They all helped produce the materials needed to see 60 centers open around the country with 1,000 students enrolled. Winter cast a vision, with Ted Ward and others, for the Intertext project. But that was a point of failure, in part, because of the complexity of the texts as well as the need for leadership from both missionaries and nationals to sustain the project or even produce more than a few books in a few languages.[107] With growing opportunities to promote the idea globally, time for Winter to produce curriculum was limited.

On a personal level, Winter continued his interest in a broad range of subjects. Outsiders evaluating the Mam Center noted, "His personal library, with all kinds of technical and religious books, reflects his incredibly diverse fields of interest."[108] He consistently sought to learn from whatever field of study possible. His personal letters to his mother and father include details for them to purchase books and other items to ship to Guatemala. Yet this was a point of conflict as well. The regional and home field leadership wanted Winter to focus on language learning, as noted previously.

Some people thought of Winter's approach as countercultural. More accurately, he was willing to approach solving problems in unconventional ways if it would accomplish the goal and be a model useable by others: Mam leaders, missionaries or church leaders back home. The development of elementary education curriculum (above) was so that the Mam could get further seminary training and be ordained in the Presbyterian church. Ordination was not countercultural, but rather part of the subculture of the church. But Winter identified a problem (in this case, lack of pre-requisites

---

[105] This was the first evangelical University in Guatemala, the Universidad Mariano Galvez. Much later, Winter discovered that the school had grown to some 40,000 students.

[106] Winter said that all he did was stand up for the photo during the founding ceremony.

[107] Of course, as time has passed, programs that are still thriving, such as in India, have produced a number of tools for their operation.

[108] A Report on the Work and Personnel of the Mam Christian Center, by F.G. Scovell and Wm. L. Wonderly, Ostuncalco, Guatemala, July 16 to 27, 1960, 16.

for seminary and thus ordination) and sought to solve it via unconventional means.

Up to this point in his ministry Winter does not question the need for seminary as a pre-requisite for ordination. Much later, he would state that, "once seminary is required for ordination the church stops growing."[109]

Winter's self-perception of his gifts and passions was refined during this period. His personal reflections in his Personal Reports and in letters to his parents, demonstrate his desire to ideate and learn new skills, but at the same time reflect his struggle with follow-through with an ever-increasing number of good ideas. Regional field leaders noticed this as well. Winter started in Guatemala in traditional discipleship, but realized there were other problems derailing the lives and ministries of the men with whom he worked. From various education programs to raise learning and qualifications, to the establishment of businesses to free up leaders from a dispersed agricultural lifestyle, to what became TEE, Winter was focused on what might help these men and women grow and learn in ways that would provide for their livelihood and make their ministry more effective. Then, TEE was growing and seemed to be working well. Programs were started beyond Latin America, extending as far as Asia and Africa.

Winter continued to take a negotiating approach to relational issues, as happened with Ruth Wardell. This time, when some within the mission were suggesting they return the seminary to a traditional program like they had before starting TEE, Winter and Emery suggested a middle position of postponing the traditional program for one more year.

In the end, the unexpected move to a traditional, residential seminary became an opportunity to influence what was becoming the largest evangelical seminary in the U.S., and through that platform, many others globally. While TEE became the focus of Winter's work in Guatemala, its expansion and growing popularity became a part of the reason for the transition he made back to the U.S. to teach at Fuller SWM.[110]

---

[109] This was something this author heard Winter say a number of times in various settings after 1983.

[110] It is interesting that TEE seems to have thrived long-term in locations, such as India, where the massive size of the training need along with the cost of traditional seminaries, has shown the model can work.

Assessment and Contribution

Winter and Emery contributed several core ideas to TEE, in the process creating a tool that trainers, pastors and missionaries can use. They had discussed together how to train pastors in a deep and profound way, implementing a productive program in Guatemala. TEE raised crucial issues for those involved in training Christian leaders:

1. It brought training to those who could not afford the time or money and who could not travel a long distance to obtain training, also allowing them to remain involved in their ministry.

2. It mobilized missionaries, church and mission leaders, giving them a tool they could shape for their local situation.

3. It helped seminaries expand training offerings, increasing the pool of potential students without increasing facilities.

Yet, as it spread, it was uneven in its application, succeeding in some places while struggling in others.[111]

At the beginning of any project of serious interest to Winter, he could easily focus on details. While Winter was deeply involved with the conceptualization and design of the TEE program in Guatemala, as the movement gained momentum, he spent more and more time encouraging others to use the TEE model. He minimized some potential problems within the TEE model, hoping that others would work out implementation details. He was usually considering the broader issue or underlying problem, considering the broadest audience that might be helped by a solution.[112] The description of Winter by a Presbyterian field leader as, "…almost a genius, with a versatile, productive mind, and his time and activity cannot keep pace with it,"[113] reflects the fact that

---

[111] Early on it was probably most developed in Spanish, where many Christians and missionaries in different countries were dealing with similar problems and, because of the similar language, where resources could more likely be used in other locations with only minor modification.

[112] His fertile mind and constant ideating allowed only a few ideas to gain his full attention, and often, even then, only for a season. Later in life, Winter implemented less and focused more on spreading ideas through speaking and writing. Throughout my 26-year exposure to him, he could easily be so intensely focused on an idea or specific project that he would easily forget something he was scheduled to do, and yet move onto another major idea or project the next day.

[113] February 2, 1961 letter from Robert C. Thorp to Nathaniel Bercovitz, M.D., 2.

unfinished ideas or projects were as evident as the ground-breaking ideas he would eventually contribute.

James Goff's critiques of TEE speculate as to the specific situation in Guatemala. Goff correctly sought to remove unhelpful North American influences from TEE. And he believed it needed a much stronger element of social change and uplift. But he did not seriously look at the TEE book Winter edited. Nor did he seem to clearly understand the TEE model or personally witness the results in Guatemala. He also may not have realized the extent to which the Presbyterians had already handed over the work and were involved in raising the economic and educational levels of local people. Goff assumed the North American bias would be very strong and influential beyond helpfulness. Certainly, Winter and Emery were products of their Christian exposure in North America, and that colored their experiences, ideas and implementation. But they seem to have been fairly self-aware and cognizant of much within the local cultural situation. Emery was correct in his reply to Goff, noting that influence or bias was even stronger in the typical residential pattern, where students are shaped daily or weekly through exposure to professors.[114]

Winter, Emery and Kinsler had also encouraged existing leaders to develop their own tools. They had seen their mission continue to turn most things over to national leadership. They knew they might not be able to continue with the mission as "fraternal workers." And they were focused on empowering the Mam through education and businesses so the pastors could effectively lead their churches and see them grow.

Winter realized and agreed that in an impoverished rural tribal setting, one ultimate goal was local ownership of the program. While Ruben Dias and others were very involved, the local pastors themselves did not have the time or resources to produce materials, run a program, pastor churches and run businesses for income. Additionally, having native Spanish speakers produce materials would not necessarily solve the problem of materials being from "outside" the Mam worldview.[115] Each setting needed TEE to be customized to the local culture, which was one of the major difficulties in its implementation.

---

[114] Of course, as professors have become non-North American, this problem is ameliorated to some degree, although other problems can be introduced due to local cultural differences, such as the distinction between a native Spanish speaking professor and a young Mam student.

[115] I am not suggesting that this was part of Goff's critique or position. This may be one reason Winter worked so closely with several of the men in the village, including Ruben Dias. It was his work that helped to bridge the gap between the outside perspective and the village.

Ted Ward suggested they engage more educational experts and slow down the expansion of TEE in order to refine it. He wanted a training model that took into account educational factors along with cultural sensitivity. In Winter's experience, "experts" tended to overcomplicate things.[116] In this situation, he was intent to release a "beta" version, get further input from experts and adjust along the way. He believed that as more programs began globally, experts would naturally be drawn in to assist and improve the methods. Pouring effort into designing a refined prototype first would not result in a viable growing program. Winter's approach sought to keep the movement expanding.

Yet there were valid critiques, as I have noted earlier. Ward's assessment included the problems associated with complexities of producing regionally appropriate programmed texts. Ward felt the programmed approach would work because those within the culture inherently understood the issues. To Winter, the move to "semi-programmed text" made the work a more readily reproducible pattern. Full "programmed texts" would be very helpful tools, but could not be produced by the average seminary professor or missionary. Winter believed that was a worthy goal but it was too idealistic to wait for professionally produced texts before promoting the TEE concept more broadly. It would have killed the movement.

In the end, Ward was convinced that the lack of appropriate materials was the Achilles heel of the movement. In contrast, Winter believed it was because TEE was not adopted on a broad scale in the west. I believe that both were factors. Where TEE has continued, such as India, program leaders have produced textbooks appropriate for their context and are able to provide affordable training for the pastors and leaders using TEE. But in other locations, the lack of effective, local materials made it difficult to continue.

TEE significantly contributed to the growing distance education movement for theological training. As the recent book, *International Handbook of Protestant Education* noted: "Theological Education by Extension (TEE) is regarded as one of the greatest advancements in Protestant education." (Jeynes and Robinson, 2012, 371) It seems to thrive in situations, such as India and Africa, where the funding challenges for training remain. Where it thrives, local leadership and resources production has been crucial. The core ideas addressed by TEE provide a foundation for modern day distance programs. With the advent of the

---

[116] Certainly, Winter could do this as well. He could obsess over details in the process of implementing a project or task.

Internet, programs continue to grow, particularly as residential programs became more expensive in the west. But it remains unclear if these newer Internet-based programs have effectively taken into account the local situation any better than early TEE efforts.

Chapter 5

Training Field-Experienced Missionaries: Fuller Theological Seminary – 1967—1976

Introduction

During the period after WWII, an increasing number of ministries were founded that grew out of the experiences of soldiers returning to the U.S. From 1900 through 1945, there had been a total of 113 mission organizations founded in North America, 36 (32%) of which were denominationally affiliated.[1] From 1945 until 1976[2] there were 426 new organizations founded, 28 (7%) of which were denominationally affiliated.[3]

---

[1] Denominational affiliation means they are either the mission arm of the denomination or they have a denominational name in the organization name. Many of the groups founded mid-century were branches from a larger "parent" denomination.

[2] This is when Ralph Winter left Fuller's SWM and founded the U.S. Center for World Mission, which was one of the 426 new organizations founded during the latter period.

[3] From the electronic database used to produce *Mission Handbook: U.S. and Canadian Protestant Ministries Overseas 21st Edition*. (Weber, 2010) Provided by A. Scott Moreau via an email on April 22, 2010. Dr. Moreau provided data that included the founding dates of all organizations that fit the criteria above. Some of the organizations in the database no longer exist and are not included in the print edition, thus the electronic version was used rather than the book.

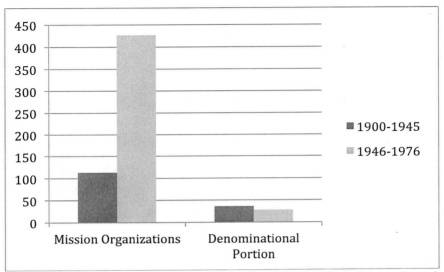

Figure 10 – North American Missions Founded During Two 45-year Periods

In part, this reflects differences within evangelicalism in theology and practice.[4] Major streams within evangelicalism took different approaches to engaging the culture around them. Some were called new or neo-evangelical. One of those was Fuller Theological Seminary (FTS), which was founded in the fall of 1947.[5]

George Marsden's book on the history of FTS, *Reforming Fundamentalism: Fuller Seminary and the New Evangelicalism,* (Marsden, 1987) tells the story of a seminary that transitioned from what was originally one man, Charles Fuller's, dream to what it eventually became: a school whose educational philosophy and breadth of Biblical interpretation have been attributed to its desire to engage both theology and culture. In 2003, the *Los Angeles Times Magazine* noted this ongoing distinction in a cover article titled "The New Believers: The 'Post-Evangelicals' embrace both science and the Bible, oppose war and abortion, and believe Right can meet Left." (Rifkin, 2003)

---

[4] It may also reflect positively and negatively on American independence and/or entrepreneurialism.

[5] Rolland McCune defined new evangelicalism as, "...a strain of conservative, traditional, Protestant, religious thoughts that coalesced into a movement in the mid-twentieth century, purporting to avoid the fundamentalist right and the neo-orthodox/neo-liberal left." (McCune, 2004, xvi) McCune argues that the movement failed because in its attempt to become relevant, it gave up basic fundamental truths.

FTS's voice, both to the evangelical movement and to the world, had a wide-ranging impact and produced many results. These were interpreted by some conservative evangelicals as failure and weakness, but by those seeking a different path from fundamentalism or trying to reform evangelicalism, as success and strength.[6]

Ralph Winter returned from ten years in Guatemala and entered this evangelical academic scene as a professor in 1965. Historical events, such as the war in Vietnam and the counter-cultural social transformation of the 1960s, impacted evangelicalism and helped to shape the theology and debates of the period. It is important to understand FTS's changing role in the evangelical missiological community in order to understand Winter's role and contribution during this period of his life.

Birth of an Idea: A School of Evangelism

Charles E. Fuller wanted a high quality seminary on the west coast. Since he was an evangelist, his original vision was that the seminary be a place to train evangelists and missionaries in the Bible and provide them with the "tools" necessary to spread the faith. He had been a "lay person" who had received training at the Bible Institute of Los Angeles, so he sought to replicate that pattern at a deeper level.[7] But this idea of a school of evangelism did not fully materialize until the mid-1960s, shortly before his death in 1968. Reflecting back on the founding of what was initially called the School of World Mission and Institute of Church Growth, Ralph Winter wrote about the original vision for the school. Winter believed that when the School of World Mission (SWM) was established in 1965, it was a "mid-course correction" to get back to what Charles Fuller originally had in mind for the whole of FTS:

> He was the one who decided there ought to be a Fuller School of World Mission. His concerns set in motion the search for a founding dean for the projected school. I still recall the lengthy search process and the serious energy invested in it long before McGavran was chosen. ... He [Fuller] was himself a lay person ... who, like Dwight Moody, did not get his theological training in what we consider "the proper way." Earlier, of course, Charles Fuller was the

---

[6] Likely because of differences in their interpretation of Scripture.

[7] The Bible Institute of Los Angeles became Biola University.

founder of Fuller Seminary itself, a temporary compromise of his original intention ...[8] (Winter, 1996, 170)

Winter had known Fuller longer than many because of his childhood friendship with Fuller's son, Dan. Charles Fuller had worked with Harold Ockenga, senior pastor at Park Street Church in Boston. Ockenga led Fuller Seminary as an institution focused on scholarly pastoral and theological training, but he did so from Boston and never moved to California.

In the 1960s, Dan Fuller was the dean at Fuller, and was involved in the beginning of the SWM. He wrote to the renowned linguist Eugene Nida, whom he wished to be on the Steering Committee:

> We are impressed by the great need for such a school as the Christian church faces a variety of complex tasks in attempting to carry out the Great Commission. ... to serve as a center for grappling with the issues that confront Christians as they seek to establish churches throughout the world. Here research into these problems can be pursued and the results made available not only to the students but also to the Church at large.[9]

Donald A McGavran

Donald Anderson McGavran was born on December 15, 1897 in Damoh, India. He died in Pasadena on July 10, 1990 at 92 years of age. McGavran's grandparents were Agnes Anderson and James Henry, people who had followed William Carey's example and set sail for India in 1854 with the English Baptist Mission. "Because of the close historical identity between the Christian Churches of the U.S.A. and the Baptist denomination in England, Anderson assisted the missionaries of the Christian Church in getting established." (Middleton, 1990, 2)[10] James Henry also served as the principal of Serampore College.[11]

---

[8] Fuller attended the Bible Institute of Los Angles, which was founded during the Bible institute movement in the U.S. during the early 1900s. Winter continued: "Charles E. Fuller was a layperson who had been able to get a bit of Bible and mission education in a school of a type that no longer exists, The Bible Institute of Los Angeles. Note that if he had not gained biblical education as a lay person there never would have been a Fuller School of World Mission much less a Fuller Seminary, or a global Old Fashioned Revival Hour." (Winter, 1996, 170)

[9] Letter from Daniel P. Fuller to Eugene Nida, December 17, 1964, 1.

[10] Vern Middleton is Donald McGavran's biographer. His dissertation, which I quote in this section, was later produced into a more popular version. While the quotes I use may

During college, when Donald thought about what he wanted to do with his life, he felt he had "done his time" in India and was not interested in going back as a missionary. But in the summer of 1919, he attended an event where John R Mott[12] spoke, where the direction of his life was changed. McGavran recalled:

> Till then, while being a reasonably good Christian, I had determined that my life work would be in some field other than the ministry. "My family has done enough for the Lord." I said, "I shall make money." I looked to law, geology or forestry as fields of work which were attractive to me. At Lake Geneva, day after day we were challenged to complete surrender to Christ. Let Him decide everything. Everything included making money and my life work. For several days I resisted, but finally I yielded and said simply, "Very well. Lord. It is clear to me; either I give up all claim to being a Christian, or I go all the way. Since that is the situation I choose to go all the way. . ." From then on I was sure that if God called me to the ministry or the mission field I would go. (Middleton, 1990, 11)

After further training at Yale, a year at the College of Missions was required of those going out with the United Christian Missionary Society

---

or may not be in this newer version. Readers who wish to learn more about McGavran should consult Middleton's biography called: *Donald McGavran: His Early Life and Ministry, An Apostolic Vision for Reaching the Nations.* (Middleton, 2011)

[11] According to Herbert M. Works, Associate Professor of History, Northwest Christian College, who wrote a short biographical sketch on McGavran for a register of McGavran's papers produced by Northwest Christian College Library. McGavran's father was John Grafton McGavran, who married Helen Anderson, the second daughter of James and Agnes. John's grandparents were among the early converts and followers of Alexander Campbell, the founder of the Disciples of Christ movement. John first set sail in 1891 and when he married Helen, they pioneered work in India. John was directly responsible for opening a region in India for the Disciples of Christ. (Middleton, 1990, 5-6)Most of McGavran's letters quoted in this thesis are held in Fuller Seminary's Hubbard Library Archives.

[12] Mott was a key figure in the mobilization efforts of the early 20th Century. He won a Nobel Peace Prize in 1946, and was a part of the Executive Committee of the Student Volunteer Movement for Foreign Missions, the presiding officer of the World Missionary Conference in Edinburgh in 1910. He was also the chairman of the International Missionary Council. McGavran was the last surviving person to attend the 1910 meeting. (Mulholland, 1991, 65) He was 12 at the time, attending with his father. For a short biography on Mott, see: http://nobelprize.org/nobel_prizes/peace/laureates/1946/mott-bio.html accessed on November 9, 2009.

(UCMS). Then, in November 1923, he returned to India as a third generation missionary with his new wife Mary.

Vernon Middleton summarized McGavran's life in his PhD thesis:

> McGavran's life has been one long search for effective evangelism. He is a missiologist with a rich and varied background of experience and research in virtually every aspect of missionary endeavor. Utilizing the historical approach, the aim of this dissertation was to explore the various phases of his life so as to discover the multiple facets which have contributed to the development of the brilliant principles which have revolutionized the missionary movement in the second half of the twentieth century. (Middleton, 1990, ix)

That missionary career grew out of his varied experiences growing up and serving in India. Once back in India, McGavran was able to quickly build upon his family's history in the country. He was soon deployed in an administrative role in established Christian schools there, where little Hindu boys and girls would come to the school for an education, "learn their verses, but never become Christians."[13] He served his first seven years as the administrator of the mission's entire education system, yet he seemed frustrated by his mission activities, and desired to see more happen than merely keeping a school running. (McCready, 1977, 3-4) Before new doors of opportunity opened, he worked hard at developing teachers and resources skills, which he later put to good use in passing on church growth ideas to others.[14]

McGavran was fully involved in the work of the mission and observed many different patterns of mission efforts, but later he would say that it was the publication of a book by J. Waskom Pickett[15] that most

---

[13] This is a paraphrase of a story McGavran told many times. I heard it first in about 1986. It is interesting that McGavran never knew that apparently many of them did come to Christ, in part, because of Christian schools of all kinds. Through the schools, they had gained a deep respect for Jesus Christ and some, later, became followers of Christ, so that by the 1980s there were millions of followers of Jesus who would not call themselves "Christians." See *Churchless Christianity*, (Hoefer, 1991) a book which was researched and written by 1982, but published in 1991 in India, just a year after McGavran died. It was almost 10 years later when Winter heard of this significant account and subsequently published a U.S. Edition in 2002 at William Carey Library.

[14] Email from Vern Middleton to the author on November 10, 2009.

[15] Pickett (1890-1981) was a Methodist Bishop recruited by Asbury College classmate E. Stanley Jones to go to India. He was a personal friend of Jawahirlal Nehru, the first Prime Minister of India, and Mahatma Gandhi. Two days before Gandhi's assassination,

profoundly influenced his missionary career. The book was called *Christian Mass Movements in India: A study with recommendations.* (1933) Pickett was older than McGavran and had a much broader experience in India studying churches that were growing and multiplying there. McGavran saw Pickett as his mentor and motivator. As McGavran explored the ideas he read about and visited some of these "mass movements to Christ," his whole perspective changed and shaped the focus for the rest of his life.

Many people have been involved in the discovery of church growth. While God has granted me a part in the process, I neither invented church growth nor am solely responsible for it. Indeed, I owe my interest in church growth to a great Methodist bishop, Jerrell Waskom Pickett. In 1934, he kindled my concern that the Church grow. I lit my candle at Pickett's fire. (McGavran and Hunter, 1980, 14)

At first, McGavran had significant reservations about the idea that large numbers of people were coming to Christ. He worked with Pickett and conducted his own independent studies of these movements to see if they could be verified. For twenty years he continued to work as a missionary in his own mission while at the same time studying and working alongside Pickett. McGavran documented the principles behind the growth he had observed in the book *Bridges of God.* (1955) That book played a large part in increasing his influence both outside of India and outside of his own denomination. While Pickett stimulated McGavran and certainly altered the course of his life work, it is McGavran who is known as the father of the modern church growth movement.

Pickett's biographer wrote:

For McGavran, the mid-India survey proved to be "most revealing," by which he meant that it revealed many fresh opportunities. But the experience also confirmed that Pickett was onto something, that by questioning old assumptions, he had managed to blaze a fresh path. Although it would be nearly two decades until McGavran published his *Bridges of God*, the book with which he began to stir the missiological world, had he not realized the value of Pickett's insights, and had he not, later on, discovered their international relevance, and had he not tirelessly worked at refining and

---

Pickett spent 45 minutes with Gandhi at Nehru's urging, pleading unsuccessfully with him to leave Delhi.

This is according to: http://www.asbury.edu/offices/library/archives/biographies/j-waskom-pickett accessed on July 11, 2011.

communicating the concepts until the missiological world could no longer ignore them, Pickett's powerful ideas would probably have died in 1930s India. (McPhee, 2001, 443)

McGavran thought much about how the denominations and mission organizations around the world would view the ideas embodied in Pickett's work, suggesting changes in terminology when he felt Pickett's original usage would be an impediment. For example, McGavran convinced Pickett to change terminology from "mass movements" to "people movements."[16]

According to Middleton, McGavran knew this little book "would launch him into the public eye of the international missionary community, because of its revolutionary proposal." (Middleton, 1990, 126) According to Middleton, Fred Price, librarian of the Missionary Research Library at Yale, said that *Bridges of God* was the "most read missionary book in 1956." (Middleton, 1990, 129)

Training Others in Church Growth

McGavran had been in India a total of forty-four years, including thirty-one as a missionary. He returned at age 57, intent on passing on his wisdom and insights through writing, speaking and especially through more in-depth missionary training. Towards the end of his work in India with the United Christian Missionary Society Division of World Mission (UCMS),[17] McGavran had experienced enough to realize that there needed to be a place where the ideas he had observed about how the church grows could be further studied. He believed that principles he and others had observed at work in India and later in Africa could have a great impact on missionary work and needed to be shared. (Middleton, 1990,

---

[16] Letter from McGavran in New Haven to Pickett in New Delhi on February 20, 1955. He also notes in this letter that there really were no "mass movements" in mid-India, so the title of one of Pickett's books, *The Mass-Movement Survey of Mid-India*, was not accurate. McGavran found what he considered to be mass movements or people movements in other parts of India. He also wrote to Pickett about changing the title of two of his books when they were reprinted, noting, "Mass movements throughout the rest of the Christian world have a bad name. Any mishandled people movement is called a mass movement!! Which is part of the problem."

[17] This was a joint effort of several denominations working together overseas. It was formed as a merger of The American Christian Missionary Society (1849), The Christian Woman's Board of Mission (1874), and The Foreign Christian Missionary Society (1875), it carried out the ministries of these former bodies until restructured in 1968. These were all part of the Christian Church (Disciples of Christ). See:
http://www.disciples.org/internal/ucms.htm accessed on 8/1/07

150-51) This desire of McGavran provided impetus for the establishment of the Institute of Church Growth (ICG).

He continued to think through what should be included in a research and training organization focused on church growth. He wrote a confidential letter to Vergil Sly, a leader within the UCMS structure, suggesting that he change the focus of his service from field service in India to a potentially global focus promoting ideas and practical lessons he had learned. He strongly believed these would help many missionaries. He suggested his proposed role be backed by the UCMS. In this new capacity he would do the following:

1. Continue the study of People Movements through (library research) and surveys abroad.
2. Found a People Movement committee under the International Missionary Committee with a branch in England and a quarterly paper.
3. Secure People Movement studies in all courses for new missionaries and nationals at home and abroad. Get the newer theology, methodology and philosophy widely known by the younger generation.
4. Fit into any plans of our folk to fatten up our People Movements. Help raise a half a million for a real Growing Church Fund.
5. Publish a book a year on some phase of People Movements.
6. Teach special course on church growth in Bible Colleges and Seminaries for those interested in younger churches.[18]

Institute of Church Growth

As McGavran continued to research and to speak, teach, and write, he kept looking for others who were doing research of the nature that he and Pickett had done in India. He sought to encourage any he found doing it. In 1961, the ICG was founded at the Northwest Christian College in Eugene, Oregon, for that purpose. A few years later, a quasi-quarterly

---

[18] Letter from McGavran in New Haven to V. Sly in Indianapolis, November 3, 1954. Middleton added this comment to the above 6-point outline: "Although the position never materialized, of the six major concepts in the above job description almost everyone of them was fulfilled either through the establishment of the Institute of Church Growth at Eugene, Oregon, or later the development of the School of World Mission at Fuller Theological Seminary at Pasadena, California." (Middleton 1990, 161)

Church Growth Bulletin spread the word about the movement. By 1965, ICG had engaged some fifty missionaries in research.[19]

In the view of Arthur Glasser,[20] this was the beginning of the church growth movement. "In my judgment the church growth movement actually began in January, 1961, when McGavran founded what he called the *Institute of Church Growth* (ICG) in an unused corner of the library of a small Christian college in remote Eugene, Oregon." (Glasser, 1987)

Each student at ICG was required to write a case history of the development of the church in the mission in which he labored, producing a "considerable volume of factual information documenting church growth around the world." (Middleton, 1990, 175)

Moving ICG to Fuller Theological Seminary

FTS was growing and developing during the 1960s. Dan Fuller had finished his studies and received a ThD from Northern Baptist Seminary and a DTheol at the University of Basel in the early 1960s.[21] He returned to FTS to teach, and held various academic leadership roles, including Dean of the Divinity school. David Hubbard became the President in 1963 and served until 1993. He led an expansion beyond Fuller's School of Divinity, later called the School of Theology, by adding both the School of Psychology and the School of World Mission in 1965.

In addition to *Bridges of God*, Donald McGavran had also written *How Churches Grow* (1959) and *Church Growth and Christian Mission*. (1965a) When Hubbard heard about McGavran and his Institute for Church Growth in Oregon, he took a board member with him and visited McGavran at the ICS in Oregon to see the program and perhaps recruit McGavran to start a School of World Mission at Fuller. Alan Tippett was also teaching there with him while finishing his PhD in anthropology.

---

[19] The *Church Growth Bulletin* was produced with McGavran as editor from September 1964 until November 1979. In 1965, it was published every other month. Later this was published in book form in two volumes: (McGavran, 1969) and (McGavran, 1977)

[20] Glasser served in China with OMF, formerly the China Inland Mission started by J. Hudson Taylor. He served as the Home Director for OMF in the US until 1970. In 1971, he succeeded McGavran as Dean of the SWM.

[21] His dissertation was called: *Easter Faith and History*. When it was published as a book in 1965, *Christianity Today* included it as one of the 25 most significant books published that year.

Tippett was an experienced missionary with a sharp, scholarly focus seeking to apply anthropology to missiology and mission practice. [22]

An announcement in the *Church Growth Bulletin* noted, "The School of World Mission at Fuller envisages ultimately a faculty of six and a student body made up of missionaries on furlough and missionary candidates under appointment. Graduate fellows from younger churches in Asia, Africa, and Latin Africa will strengthen the research arm of the School." (McGavran, 1969, 70)

In March of 1965, before the SWM started, F. Carlton Booth[23] wrote to Eugene A. Nida about the aspects of the school that could be highlighted on Charles Fuller's radio program. Billy Graham had recorded a message about Fuller starting the SWM, and Booth was writing to Nida to explain some of the details of the school so he might make a similar recording to promote it.[24]

While the first class of the SWM was held on September 28, 1965,[25] McGavran was not inaugurated as dean of the SWM until September 27, 1966.

---

[22] Which he did at the University of Oregon in 1965, doing a PhD called *Fijian Material Culture*. (Tippett, 1968)

[23] Booth was a long time friend of Charles E. Fuller, and came to FTS in 1955. He taught Evangelism classes before the SWM was started and was involved in helping FTS recruit McGavran to head the SWM.

[24] Letter from F. Carlton Booth to Eugene A. Nida, March 15, 1965, 1. In this letter, Booth was asking Nida to make a similar audio recording to be played on the Old Fashioned Revival Hour as the SWM was launched. Booth wrote: "Some of the aspects of this School which we have felt should be highlighted from time to time on the tapes are: (1) the importance of missionary fellowship whereby nationals are brought to the School for study, (2) the building of an adequate library, (3) the proposed international house where students from other lands can live and/or study at the Seminary and thus have opportunity for interaction with Christians and the Christian Gospel, (4) the plan of having the teachers in the classroom for a year or so, then out on the mission field for a period of research and study, returning again to the classroom, (5) the advantage of having a constant stream of visiting missionary lecturers at the School with all the stimulation this will bring, (6) the importance of church planting and the high priority this will have in this School, (7) the possibility of missionary conferences being conducted using both faculty and missionary personnel, (8) providing advanced training for missionaries home on furlough."

[25] In the early days, the SWM was called the School of World Missions and Institute for Church Growth. Middleton's PhD dissertation on McGavran, finished in 1990, had that full name on the cover page, perhaps in part to honor McGavran's desire and the original agreement with FTS. Institute for Church Growth was dropped at some point.

The School of World Mission and Institute for Church Growth

Fuller's Bulletin listed the following purposes of the "Graduate School of World Mission":

1. Prepare men to fulfill the Great Commission in the midst of change peculiar to our age.

2. Provide a theology of missions for all seminary students looking toward a pastorate.

3. Bring Christian nationals to the school as students and teachers to provide opportunities for mutual exchange.

4. Develop a team of research specialists to study and provide a center of thought and information regarding World Mission.[26]

McGavran brought Alan Tippett with him when he moved to Fuller.[27] Tippett's strong background in anthropology added a crucial dimension and scholarship to McGavran's church growth ideas. He was a brilliant scholar, a capable researcher, and writer who was always well organized and prepared. At times, Tippett's teaching was over the students' heads in areas where they did not have his depth of background and experience.[28] (Kraft, 2005, 80-85)

As the SWM developed, it grew even more diverse in global expertise, adding faculty with experience from Latin America, Africa, and Asia. The students themselves contributed much of the content of the learning. They were almost all field-experienced missionaries and were appropriately called "associates." Faculty and associates would meet regularly just to discuss ideas, often totally unconnected to any particular assignment. When asked by professors at other institutions how many students the SWM had, Winter, half joking, would reply, "four to five," pause for a shocked reaction, and add, "but we have 100 teachers." He would add that he was not sure what the students learned, but he and the other faculty learned a great deal about the world where the students had served as missionaries.

A summary article describing current missiological studies in North America in the *Evangelical Missions Quarterly* (*EMQ*) in about 1973 noted

---

[26] The Bulletin of Fuller Theological Seminary, Spring 1965, 1, 3.

[27] Tippett served as a missionary on the Fiji islands for more than 20 years. He was working on his PhD while teaching with McGavran at the ICG.

[28] Since Tippett's death, materials for approximately 10 books are being edited for publication through William Carey Library publishers.

that, "Fuller appeals to missionaries on furlough and specializes in church growth ... Fuller is the only school granting the Doctor of Missiology."[29] (Kane, 1974, 56) It also noted that:

> In Evangelical circles no issue has commanded more attention than church growth, whose pioneer and prophet is Dr. Donald A. McGavran, who founded the Institute of Church Growth in 1960 and ever since has been calling mission leaders back to the prime purpose of world missions – preaching the gospel, discipling the nations, and multiplying churches. Scores of books and hundreds of articles have been written on the subject – with still more to come. (Kane, 1974, 59)

Also in the early days, and as other faculty were added, they would often meet evenings with the students, and two or three students would tell the story of the works with which they had been involved on the field. They would draw graphs and critique what they were doing. When students first arrived to begin the program, McGavran would interview them for an hour or more, asking questions to learn about their part of the world. He was the kind of person who wanted to learn and grow in his awareness of the world, not just his own fields of interest or experience.[30]

Not everyone agreed with the approach of the SWM. Discussions on issues such as People Movements and the Homogeneous Unit Principle were frequent topics of articles and discussions during this time. Reflecting back on the early period of the SWM, Glasser noted one reason for this was that "Tippett and Kraft both were talking anthropology, and that was a great new factor in mission thinking and missiology."[31]

Eugene Nida, noted linguist with the American Bible Society, had been a co-editor with McGavran (and others) on the book *Church Growth and Christian Missions.* (McGavran, 1965a) He had been asked to serve on the Steering Committee for the SWM, and had verbally agreed.[32] But after some communication about the course names or topics McGavran had proposed, Nida was not convinced that it was best. He wrote to McGavran in 1965, "My general impression of the list of courses and topics which you

---

[29] This is of late 1973, the SWM later added the PhD as well.

[30] Interview with Ralph Winter by the author, August 30, 2006, 12. For a partial list of those who taught courses at Fuller's SWM in those two years, see Appendix K.

[31] Interview with Arthur Glasser by the author on Feb. 10, 2005, 5. Kraft arrived a few years later than Tippett and Winter.

[32] Letter from F. Carlton Booth to Eugene A. Nida, March 15, 1965, 1, and a letter from Daniel P. Fuller to Eugene A. Nida on February 22, 1965.

have offered is that this is somewhat 'more of the same thing' as far as the School of Missions is concerned. Would it not be possible to approach these problems in a somewhat more graduate level rather than as a kind of 'glorified seminary' or 'elaborated Bible school program.'"[33] He continued, "Moreover, 'the growth of the church' is hardly a topic by itself. It is, of course, a significant concern at several points in any discussion of missions, but I would not think that you would want to make it a particular subject, for it is too closely tied up with the theory of mission and the dynamics of communication."[34]

Others felt the focus on Church Growth represented a western, pragmatic approach. They believe it reduced the missionary task "to a 'manageable enterprise' through the use of information technology, marketing techniques, and managerial leadership."[35] (Escobar, 2002, 18)

While McGavran remained involved at Fuller up until the last weeks of his life, Glasser replaced him as Dean of the SWM in 1971, specifically because he was solidly evangelical, Biblical and from a respected conservative mission.

Church Growth Basics

Central to McGavran's thinking was his definition of mission, found in the first edition of *Understanding Church Growth*, as "an enterprise devoted to proclaiming the Good News of Jesus Christ and persuading men to become his disciples and dependable members of His Church." (McGavran, 1970)

The core idea in *Bridges of God* was that people prefer to come to Christ with people who are similar to them in cultural background. McGavran's thesis statement for *Bridges of God* noted:

...the normal way in which peoples are Christianized is by group action. The individual acceptance of Jesus Christ as

---

[33] Letter from Eugene A. Nida to Donald McGavran, December 7, 1965, 1.

[34] Letter from Eugene A. Nida to Donald McGavran, December 7, 1965, 2.

[35] Escobar articulated this idea beginning in the late 1990s. He described more of his thinking at that time: "Movements such as Dawn, AD 2000 and Beyond, Church Growth, and Spiritual Warfare are expressions of a missiology whose main features are as follows: First, there is an emphasis on quantity that seeks to reduce everything to statistics. The aim is to visualize the missionary task with precision, thereby giving rise to concepts such as 'unreached peoples,' 'homogeneous units,' 'open fields,' '10-40 window,' or 'Adopt-a-People.'" ... "Second, this missiology is distinguished by its pragmatic emphasis, which *reduces the concept of mission to forms of proclamation that can be quantified.*" (Escobar, 2002, 18-19)

Lord and Savior, which is what the individualistic Western Church now believes is the only correct, orthodox, and meaningful way, is not the way in which peoples, societies, races, castes, and clans turn to Christ. Peoples (as opposed to individuals) turn to Christ in group action, by consultation among themselves, by following some convinced leaders, by religious migration, so to speak. After that, sanctification can proceed through individual conversion and meaningful dedication by individuals. (Middleton, 1990, 371)

McGavran realized that talking about "mass movements" might not sit well with some of his fellow missionaries or denominational leaders. Some might confuse the terminology with an emphasis on crusades or only on evangelistic events focused on decisions. Since he was part of the Christian Church (Disciples of Christ), which was a member of the World Council of Churches, McGavran processed his ideas in terms that would make sense to them. While many of his own church were not conservative in their views on the Bible and on the need for evangelism or missions as defined by evangelicals, McGavran knew that it would be difficult for someone to be a part of any denominational church and be opposed to the idea of wanting to see the church grow.[36]

What some later called "evangelistic opportunity" grew out of McGavran's idea of working with those who were open to the gospel. (Shenk, 1973, 16) The reverse idea, the concept of resistance to the gospel, was raised in McGavran's observations and comparisons between church growth in India and Africa. These ideas became clearer to him when he traversed Africa on his way home for a furlough. (Middleton, 1990, 150) Why, he wondered, did the church grow amazingly in places in Africa south of the Sahara? Why did it fail to grow similarly in India, or grow only in select people groups?[37]

Donald M. Wodarz, Priest of the Society of Saint Columban, wrote a dissertation on the missiology of McGavran.[38] Even though an outsider to evangelical Christianity, he captured the essence of McGavran and his

---

[36] According to Winter in a private, undated conversation.

[37] McGavran was not suggesting that people should avoid reaching out to people groups that seem to the missionary to be resistant to the gospel, although many of his followers, and detractors, have failed to recognize that point.

[38] *Church Growth: The Missiology of Donald Anderson McGavran* (Wodarz, 1979) This was for a DMiss at Pontificia Università Gregoriana, Rome. The university's web site spells it: Università.

church growth missiology in his summary of the book, *Understanding Church Growth.*[39] (McGavran, 1970)

> Churches grow in those places where Christians involve themselves in seeking and finding the lost sheep, bringing them into the master's fold, and feeding, pasturing those brought into the fold. Faithfulness in proclamation, calling to repentence, or finding the lost is not enough; those who have heard, who have repented must be brought into congregations, they must be taken into folds where they are nourished and fed with the Word of God.[40] (Wodarz, 1979, 185)

While McGavran knew that family relationships were central to the church growth within a people, the core idea was that people prefer to come to Christ with others like themselves. This became known as the Homogeneous Unit Principle.

Homogeneous Unit Principle

This core idea undergirding McGavran's understanding of church growth became known as the Homogeneous Unit Principle (HUP). McGavran used the phrases "people movements to Christ" and "Christward movements." The HUP was based on the idea that people are made up of distinct cultural groupings or homogeneous units of peoples or people groups. If the gospel makes sense in terms of their cultural context, people tend to come to Christ in larger numbers. This is what he had seen in India when he worked with J. Waskom Pickett. (Pickett, 1933) McGavran had observed this in Africa as well, which was a great contrast to most of what he had seen in mission work in India, with the exception of Pickett's work. McGavran defined the HUP as "a section of society in which all members have some characteristic in common."

---

[39] Certainly, some have been skeptical about the idea of People Movements. Much of the data of the research was available only in India, making it difficult for others to access. In an interview with Arthur Glasser by the author on Feb. 10, 2005, 5, he reflected back that, "McGavran's people movement was a real people movement." He was referring to the fact that these movements in India, and those in the first studies done with Pickett, were not only valid movements of people coming to Christ, but they were also well-researched and substantiated. McGavran himself had been skeptical when he first began to work with Pickett. Glasser was the 2nd Dean at the SWM, replacing McGavran.

[40] "Repentence" was the spelling used in Wodarz's dissertation for the word often spelled "repentance."

There were those who questioned these ideas.[41] A primary issue was the unity of the body of Christ and how that would be practiced in churches of different cultural backgrounds, if each were choosing forms natural for their own culture. The Lausanne Committee for World Evangelization convened a consultation on HUP, held in Pasadena from May 31 to June 2, 1977. John Stott moderated this gathering, and many of the FTS-SWM faculty presented, including McGavran and Winter.[42]

Winter's presentation was consistent with both the theme of the conference and the church history he had taught for years by that time, "The Homogeneous Unit Principle in Historical Perspective." In it, Winter argued from a historical view of the gospel impacting culture. He noticed that what individuals within any culture consider to be normative for them becomes a basis of spreading the gospel, a foundation of how they practice Christianity from that point on, and how they might expect other Christians to live out their faith. Arguing from Paul in Galatians, he wrote:

> Thus while we do not have any record of his forcing people to meet separately, we do encounter all of Paul's holy boldness set in opposition to anyone who would try to preserve a single normative pattern of Christian life through a cultural imperialism that would prevent people from employing their own language and culture as a vehicle for worship and witness. Here, then, is a clear case of a man with cross-cultural evangelistic perspective doing everything within his power to guarantee liberty in Christ to converts who were different from his own social background. (Winter, 1977, 6)

To those who felt this was "setting aside" the goal of unity for the sake of evangelism, Winter wrote:

> It is quite the opposite: we are willing to do evangelism in the world as it is, in the highly divided world in which we live believing wholeheartedly that in the long run the working of the Holy Spirit through true evangelism is the only way to melt down the high walls of prejudice and thus produce true unity with or without diversity where no true enmity at all existed before. (Winter, 1977, 8-9)

---

[41] This will be noted later in the chapter.

[42] See Appendix J for a list of presenters and topics at this event. About 6 months before this time during his sabbatical from FTS, Winter decided to found the U.S. Center for World Mission. He continued to teach some classes at Fuller through the spring of 1979.

The responder to Winter was Victor E.W. Hayward.[43] While agreeing with Winter on a number of points, he argued from the concept of an overarching value of Christian unity. He agreed with the idea of HUP being an evangelistic strategy in which forming separate congregations fit into the area of Christian liberty, as Winter had suggested. But he felt that this was only half of the truth. To Hayward, worship where "the universal nature of the church is denied neither virtually nor by implication" is as important as evangelism. (Hayward, 1977, 3) Hayward admitted that he was not a historian, and so relied upon others in a broad discussion of history. He outlined the kind of situation in which a HUP strategy could be useful:

> Only after the universal nature of the Church has been demonstrated, only after the Gospel has been brought, more or less simultaneously, to several different homogeneous units within a given locality, is it safe to utilize the insights of the homogeneous unity principle for rapid growth without compromising the very nature of the Church itself. And even then, every opportunity of making manifest the fundamental unity and universality of the Church must be deliberately seized. (Hayward, 1977, 7)

The Church Growth Concept and Select Perspectives

Based on his experience in India and his observations in more than 70 countries, McGavran was convinced that if you focus on presenting the gospel to people within their own cultural patterns, the church would grow. Behind all of his thinking were his years in India. Its way of life had made a profound impact on him. India's strong distinctions of community within and outside of the caste system influenced him greatly.

The American Society for Church Growth defines church growth as follows:

> Church growth is that careful discipline which investigates the nature, the function, and the health of

---

[43] Hayward was a missionary to China for five years starting in 1934. He then served the British secretary of the NCC in Shanghai during the closing era of missionary work there. He served as the general foreign secretary of the Baptist Missionary Society (now, BMS World Mission) from 1951-1959. In 1959 he moved to the WCC headquarters in Geneva and served as executive secretary of the Department of Missionary Studies and starting in 1969 as associate general secretary of the WCC.

Christian churches, as they relate to the effective implementation of the Lord's Great Commission to make disciples of all peoples (Matthew 28:19-20). It is a spiritual conviction, yet it is practical, combining the eternal principles of God's Word with the practical insights of social and behavioral sciences.[44]

There were many who characterize the church growth movement as being focused mainly on numerical growth without regard to discipleship and depth. They believe church growth promoters such as McGavran and later C. Peter Wagner were mainly trying to build bigger churches or church movements, and were willing to justify anything that worked. Most of that perspective seems to have grown from the application of McGavran's church growth principles to established churches in North America as well as places such as Korea, where church growth became popular and effective in its application.[45]

In the late 1960s, apparently in order to deal with this concern, Winter wrote an outline for a lecture titled "Quality or Quantity." These rough handwritten notes, presumably for a lecture by Winter, include hints at the debate that was occurring.[46]

"Church Growth" – phrase emphasizes the quality of corporate life beyond the quantity of individual decisions.

Capacity to multiply congregations

A booby trap: making theoretical distinction between quantity and quality.

Jesus → preached [to] crowds – superficially heard

→ trained [the] twelve – solidly established

Every Task ... properly understood has dimensions of Qu[ality] and Qu[antity]

Can't take qualitative growth and say it is not countable because people are countable...

---

[44] From: http://www.ascg.org/ Accessed on 11/25/08.

[45] Wagner was very involved in this movement and published extensively on it and, later, on other subjects. For examples of various views on this see the book, *Evaluating the Church Growth Movement: 5 Views* (McIntosh, 2004). For details on perceived excesses within the U.S. church growth movement see: *Confessions of a Reformed Church Growth Consultant* (Brady, 2007). Brady evaluates the ramifications of the CG movement in the Western world, a topic which interested McGavran little.

[46] I have sought to duplicate these notes, adding words in [brackets] for clarity. Indentations seem to indicate subordinate points.

Clues (we are interested in changes in membership, not amounts but rates).[47]

A bit later, Winter wrote a chapter with the same title in McGavran's book *Crucial Issues in Missions Tomorrow.* (1972b, 175-187) Winter challenges those who suggested the church growth movement was only, or mainly, interested in numbers. He wrote:

Those who emphasize "church growth" are sometimes accused of being more interested in quantities of church members than in their quality. This is despite the fact that the very phrase *church growth* implies an additional dimension of emphasis beyond conversion, since it focuses not on how many raise their hands at an evangelistic service but on the *incorporation* of the new believer into *church* life. Other religions may consist of individuals worshiping at shrines, but the essence of Christianity goes beyond individual experience. Thus, the very concept of *church* growth is an attempt to emphasize the quality of corporate life beyond the quantity of individual decisions. (Winter, 1972b, 175-176)

Winter further argued that "… all quantities are measurements of certain qualities." (Winter, 1972b, 177)

There were also those who disagreed with the HUP, which was foundational to the church growth model. In the extreme, some felt that the HUP was racist.[48] The misunderstanding or misinterpretation of McGavran's core idea often grows from those who desire an integrated church fellowship sooner than new believers may be ready for it. (McIntosh, 2004) As early as *The Bridges of God*, McGavran hinted at the idea of spreading Christ to those groups that were on the fringe of an existing church, not merely spreading the message through more effective evangelism (however helpful and necessary that is).[49] Embedded in the title *The Bridges of God* was the idea that a person who was from another culture, who expressed interest in the gospel and the things of God, was a

---

[47] I have included the first half of Winter's handwritten undated notes, which are in the general Fuller Seminary archives for the School of World Mission. Arrows, indentations and brackets are in the original. By "clues" I presume he means they were looking for clues from the rate of the growth of the church.

[48] In a dissertation, Bruce W. Fong evaluates the HUP and discusses with the issue of ethnicity in the church concludes that, "It is clear that neither McGavran nor Wagner are perpetuating a racist ideal. Neither are racists. Also, their concern is not 'numbers' for numbers sake. Neither of these criticisms are legitimate." (Fong, 1996, n 18., 180)

[49] This is the title of one of McGavran's later books, *Effective Evangelism: A theological mandate.* (McGavran, 1988)

bridge of God back to that people. Winter often noted McGavran's illustration of this: if you have someone from a tribe "hanging around" in the back of a Spanish-speaking church in Latin America, then focus on that tribal person, which will enable the gospel to go back to the tribe that is without a gospel witness via this man or woman, who is a "bridge of God." Thus, HUP was a method for evangelistic growth, not a long-term approach for structuring a church.

McGavran's heart for evangelism came out in many other ways. In a letter to Winter giving input for the book Winter was editing on TEE, McGavran said:

> I note that in two chapters you are uniting the idea of extension seminary training to the Christian mission, i.e., to giving every man on earth the chance to say yes to Jesus Christ. I hope you will make these powerful chapters. At all costs, the extension seminary must avoid directing the attention of its students away from effective evangelism into sterile academic routines. On the contrary, it must become a means whereby only those already engaging in church planting are recognized as fully qualified candidates and only those who learn church planting, engage in it as a part of the courses, and teach it to others, have any chance of a first class diploma.[50]

While they used statistics to measure progress, Glasser, like Winter, did not feel it was fair.[51] At the SWM, McGavran questioned new students, all experienced field missionaries, about the situation where they served. He often used investigative techniques and asked, "How is the Church growing, how has it grown, and why is it growing, where and why has it stopped growing, what mission procedures help and hinder church growth, and how can we get more church growth."[52]

As far back as 1955, he suggested the need for "real faith" of individuals, not just people becoming what are called "cultural Christians." (McGavran, 1955, 96) Part of the more recent critique comes from the current desire to see true Christians living out their faith. In 2007, Douglas

---

[50] Letter from McGavran to Winter, January 19, 1969, one page, in Winter's E-File #45 Book III.

[51] He said it was not "fair to what the Church Growth Movement is to say that we're just interested in statistics...." Interview with Arthur Glasser by the author on February 10, 2005, 11.

[52] Letter from McGavran in New Haven to Elfers, Publisher, on September 5, 1956.

McConnell, Dean of the School of Intercultural studies[53] at Fuller, noted the need for maturity in addition to church growth: "McGavran used to say that what was needed is a mighty multiplication of churches. Today I would say what is needed is a mighty maturation of that witness in the world, so we can impact effectively, in wisdom." (McConnell, 2007, 18) Some would argue that was what McGavran had in mind, even if many of his followers focused on numbers or appeared to, especially in western situations. Many arguments have been made on both sides of this issue. As can also be seen in many theses from the early days of the SWM, it was a sensitive point.

In an early article on the nature of church structures and mission structures, Winter examined views of theologians about the church and their concerns about church growth. They wanted to "slim down" churches to a core of the truly committed. Winter wrote, "Thus McGavran's church growth analysis is for them precisely the wrong thing at the wrong time. And, for them and their churches it may well be, unless they discover (1) that McGavran does not merely mean numerical growth by his famous phrase, and (2) he certainly is not talking about multiplying dead churches." (Winter, 1969a, 76)

A major figure in the church growth debate at the time was Orlando Costas. His book, *The Church and its Mission: a Shattering Critique from the Third World* (1974) outlines both the contributions to as well as problems of the Church Growth Movement.[54] He recognized the positive contributions of church growth as: (1) challenging or standing against the negative view of missions "that has characterized so much missionary thinking in the last decades of the twentieth Century" with an "optimistic, forward looking approach to the missionary enterprise" (124-127); (2) providing insight into evangelism, conversion, and church (127-129); and, (3) stimulating the study of mission. (129-131)

He also identified what he considered to be some problems in the church growth movement, and noted that the movement: (1) Had a shallow hermeneutic, as a thorough Scriptural basis had not yet been achieved (131-134); (2) Sought to have its theological locus in only a partial ecclesiology, focusing on the Church and not on the redemptive action of Christ, the basis of the church (134-137); (3) Had a truncated

---

[53] Formerly SWM. As of Spring 2011, McConnell is also Provost of the entire Seminary.

[54] Costas defines the church growth movement as what was being written and studied at the SWM at FTS under Donald McGavran, Alan Tippett, Winter, Peter Wagner, Arthur Glasser, Charles Kraft, etc. (Costas, 1974, 103-4)

concept of mission, of not seeing mission in its wholeness, including incarnational witness, proclamation of the gospel, and discipling in an ethical context (138-143); (4) Held an ambiguous concept of man and sin, reflecting various views in work by Tippett and McGavran related to how the church should minister to the whole man (144-145); and that it (5) Had too heavy a reliance on anthropology, without looking enough into sociology or psychology, thus skewing their perspective on the broader range of relating the gospel to man and his situation (145-149). (Barro, 1993, 100-101)

Others observed different aspects of McGavran's emphasis.[55] When McGavran died, Edwin L. Frizen,[56] who had seen McGavran in action on many occasions, noted, "He decried the many 'good works' that missionaries get involved with that dull the cutting edge of effective evangelism and discipling of new believers." (Frizen Jr., 1991, 62)

Arthur F. Glasser wrote about his last visit with McGavran in 1991. They talked about various issues, and McGavran asked Glasser, "What part of the Great Commission are we most prone to forget?" (Glasser, 1991, 59) Glasser landed on the answer, "All authority in heaven and on earth has been given to me." That, McGavran noted, was what would motivate Christians to do the ministry they were called to.

An article by Kenneth Mulholland on the impact of McGavran's life recounted core ideas that had surfaced during the course of McGavran's life:

1. McGavran was convinced that the church should grow. Recounting a discussion between McGavran and J. Robertson McQuilkin after a church growth conference in Japan, McQuilkin asked, "Dr. McGavran, among the denominations which are growing, each attributed their growth to a different cause. One claimed it was due to prayer, another that it was a

---

[55] Still others found perceived weaknesses in what was called "managerial missiology." "Its basic tenet is that Christian mission can be reduced to a 'manageable enterprise' thanks to the use of information technology, marketing techniques and managerial leadership." (Escobar, 2003) Escobar continued by listing some of the concepts that grew out of such thinking, including HUP and "unreached peoples." While he noted he, "had great respect for his zeal and his pragmatic approach to mission issues, and I admired his hard working habits," he "could not accept the complete disregard he had for theological aspects of mission studies, about which he was very vocal in missiological gatherings." According to an email from J. Samuel Escobar to the author January 15, 2011.

[56] Frizen had served in the Philippines with Far Eastern Gospel Crusade after seeing the great needs there as a soldier in WWII. He then became the Executive Director of one of the two main mission associations in the U.S., the IFMA (currently called CrossGlobal Link).

movement of the Holy Spirit, and another to their strategy, and still another to their organization." Responded McGavran, "What do they all have in common?" "They all expected to grow. They believe the church should grow and they are going out and doing it." (Mulholland, 1991, 65)

2. Church growth is a legitimate measuring rod for theological extension. Mulholland connected the fact that Winter was asked to come to Fuller SWM as a sign of McGavran's sense "that TEE was a vital instrument for church growth." (Mulholland, 1991, 67)

3. Missionary expansion must be understood principally as crossing cultural rather than geographic barriers. Examining cultural distinctions much smaller than at the national level lead to the people movement in India, which Pickett and later McGavran researched. McGavran's idea, which summarized his perspective on People Movement and later church growth, was that people like to become Christian without crossing racial, linguistic or class barriers. (Mulholland, 1991, 68) In other words, with people like them.

4. Urban populations must be given priority. McGavran saw that missionaries tend to avoid cities and work in rural areas. (Mulholland, 1991, 69-70)

5. Research is a vital part of missions strategy. Naturally, this grew from his experiences with Pickett in India. (Mulholland, 1991, 66-70)

In February 1973, the Missionary Study Fellowship of the Institute of Mennonite Studies hosted an event made up of those with "transcultural outreach" responsibilities to gather; 1) to talk about the concepts surrounding various approaches to church growth; and, 2) "to raise questions concerning the nature and mission of the church as these relate to church growth from their viewpoint of a particular theological tradition." (Shenk, 1973, 3) The editor of this book, who would later come to teach at Fuller's SWM, wrote about the impact of McGavran and the SWM on this issue, noting that the ICG/SWM, "has already produced some 60 studies around the world."[57] (Shenk, 1973, 9)

---

[57] Also presented at this Mennonite gathering was the idea that the church growth concepts had made inroads in certain circles and, as a result, faced closed doors with others. Church growth "found a clientele in the EFMA, IFMA, [and] National Association of Evangelical-related churches, and has therefore taken on the polar relationship to the

The debates concerning church growth issues continue. Many other voices have contributed to that debate, and while it is not the purpose of this thesis to critique these, I have sought to include the major issues and voices at the time of the SWM as a context for Winter's involvement at the SWM.[58]

McGavran's Influence on Missiological Awareness

It would be easy for the uninitiated to underestimate the impact of Donald McGavran. His ideas clearly focused on helping the church to grow by the careful, hard work of missionaries who shared their faith and expected God to work to bring people to Christ and into the church. As Wodarz concluded in his dissertation:

> One constant aim of Dr. McGavran has been to spread knowledge of Christ and the ways that men become his disciples and enter into responsible relationship into His Church. Church Growth Missiology has as its purpose the growth of the Church—in all ways—not merely in numbers of persons who are members of churches—though at no time is it proper to speak of mere number of church members—but also in the ways that these members grow in responsible discipleship of Christ and because of that relationship to their Master desire to bring others to share in the riches of discipleship. The burden of the two, now nearly three billion rest heavily on McGavran's thought, and this must always be kept in mind when considering his missiology. (Wodarz, 1979, 340)

Earlier in his work, Wodarz had summarized three ideas of "particular merit" from McGavran: 1) placing emphasis on the specific role that missionaries have "in the process by which churches grow," 2) initiating serious research "into the processes by which peoples come into Christianity," and 3) insisting that "missionary strategy be based on facts resulting from research." Part of what he argues in the latter point is that the diffusion or dissemination of research was also crucial in the broad

---

World Council of Churches, and ecumenical politics in general, which they have held." (Yoder, 1973, 28) Yoder argued that this was not necessary.

[58] No matter what one's view is on issues such as church growth or the Homogeneous Unit Principle, it would be very difficult if not impossible to suggest that the SWM under McGavran had little impact on the shape of evangelical mission efforts both in the U.S. and around the world.

recognition of McGavran's work and the work of others in the church growth movement.[59] (Wodarz, 1979, 289, 297)

The SWM and McGavran's church growth principles influenced mission organizations. Various SWM faculty spoke at meetings of the U.S. mission associations IFMA and EFMA, and through joint committees and special events, exposure to church growth ideas was spreading. In 1961 there were two member missions of the IFMA who listed opportunities for church planting work. By 1971, that number increased to twenty member missions, representing a change from 6 percent of the agencies to 73 percent. During the same ten-year period, the listing of "general mission" opportunities declined from 79 percent to 12 percent. (McGavran, 1977, 200) Perhaps the focus from mission-experienced professors at places like the SWM and missionary-practitioners studying how churches globally were growing helped to sharpen the focus of mission efforts.

In January of 1973, McGavran spoke of his expectations for the SWM at a banquet which included a surprise 75th birthday celebration and a Festschrift in his honor.[60] In his introduction, he noted that the SWM "is closely tied to the future of the whole missionary enterprise. So the five expectations I voice will begin with those for Christian missions and shift gradually to those for this school." (McGavran, 1973, 6) McGavran talked about and desired the following:

1. the importance of salvation, even in the midst of change,
2. that receptivity to the gospel would increase,
3. that the SWM would "multiply the export of missionary ideas,"
4. that the SWM would establish a PhD program, and
5. that while the SWM had focused on church growth abroad, that an American Institute for Church Growth would take shape at Fuller.[61] (McGavran, 1973, 6-7)

Winter's Arrival to Teach—1967

Initially, when Winter was still in Guatemala, he was asked to come as a visiting professor and lecture during weekly gatherings of all the

---

[59] Wodarz also pointed out the role of William Carey Library publishers in the quick economical publishing of books with a focus on a missionary audience. (1979, 297)

[60] His talk was transcribed and published in Fuller's journal, *Theology News and Notes*, 19:2, June 1973, 6-7.

[61] He also notes that this has been largely because of C. Peter Wagner's initiative.

students.[62] Dan Fuller recalled his father, Charles, was reading and hearing about Ralph Winter shortly before Winter joined the SWM faculty as the third faculty member:

> I had been talking with a friend of my father and he said 'your father was talking about having Ralph Winter for the School of World Mission.' I had never heard that before. So my father knew about Ralph and people could see that there was really a person who was going somewhere and going to do something big and great in the Christian world movement.[63]

The Winters were not thinking of leaving the field. Winter recalled that when they invited him to come back and teach, he suggested that he could teach six months a year and live six months a year in Guatemala. At first, McGavran said that was fine, but then he became gravely ill and many wondered if he would survive. He challenged Winter to stay on arguing that you could not really mentor students in an MA or a doctorate if you were only there for six months of the year. Winter felt a bit surprised and somewhat "betrayed." They had left their home in Guatemala for furlough planning on returning in six months, so it was a major decision for them to suddenly be forced to choose whether to leave the field (and the relationships with people and work they had developed there) permanently. In the end they went back to Guatemala after the six months, packed up and returned to Pasadena.[64]

At the same time, while feeling "jarred" by the situation, Winter saw potential in the move because he believed he would be able to accomplish more for the cause of missions, and that was more important than merely

---

[62] As an announcement, the *Church Growth Bulletin* mentioned "added Faculty" for the fall of 1966 and spring of 1967. This included visiting faculty from Asbury Seminary, J.T. Seamands, who would teach two courses in the fall quarter, and "Rev. Ralph D. Winter, Ph.D., United Presbyterian missionary in Guatemala, who will teach two courses in the first quarter of 1967 stressing promising new systems of theological education abroad." (McGavran, 1969, 191)

[63] Interview with Daniel Fuller by the author on March 7, 2005, 8. He continued: "I heard that Ralph wanted very much to come. And he came and I remember going down to talk to him and he (Ralph) said, 'boy what an opportunity this is for me to come under the faculty of the greatest living missiologist and to be able to talk missions with somebody who knows more about it than any living person now.' So, at the outset I saw a Ralph Winter that was very happy to come."

[64] Interview with Ralph Winter by the author, August 30, 2006, 2. Because of the long lasting guerilla warfare in Guatemala, even writing letters to someone in the highland tribal area could put them in danger during certain periods. As a result, communications were cut off by necessity and not he was able to return to the Mam area for thirty-nine years.

thinking about his own career as a missionary. When asked why someone passionate about TEE would go to a residential school, Winter was ready with a one-word response: "platform." This meant that the SWM was a larger "soapbox" or pulpit from which the TEE ideas could expand and grow around the world. The rate at which TEE was spreading continued to increase.

Winter's esteem of McGavran continued to grow as a result of their interaction. McGavran's extensive field experience, both as a third generation missionary in India and as a result of all the places he had traveled globally after India, provided a wealth of information from which he could draw. Winter noted, "...he just had a practical sense of what's important and what isn't important. And [that] didn't jive with anybody's traditional thinking at all...he was really a no-nonsense guy."[65]

The first full-time faculty members (McGavran, Tippett and Winter) were close and worked well together. McGavran was very practical and fairly private. He was the diplomat, the activist. Tippett was the scholar, the academic. McGavran did not joke much, except about the British, because of his experiences in India and in order to tease Tippett. Since Tippett was from Australia, he felt he needed to defend the British.[66]

The Presbyterian board was willing to "loan" Winter to Fuller, and continued his funding. Fuller insisted on paying the board what they would have paid Winter as a faculty member. Winter began to teach subjects other than TEE, such as the expansion of Christianity.[67] He preferred that title to "church history," favoring Kenneth Scott Latourette's approach. As noted previously, Latourette's work expanded Winter's thinking and learning even more now and was an important additional factor for the experienced missionary associates at the SWM.

Winter's title was, "Professor of the Historical Development of the Christian Movement". This was reduced to, "Professor of the History of the Christian Movement" in the printed version of his presentation at Lausanne in 1974. In one of Fuller's undated promotional materials, Winter is called a "professor of missionary techniques and methods." He also taught a course called, "The Emergence of the Western Christian Tradition".[68]

---

[65] Interview with Ralph Winter by the author, August 30, 2006, 7.

[66] Interview with Ralph Winter by the author, August 30, 2006, 9.

[67] For a partial listing of course descriptions by Winter, see Appendix L.

[68] While teaching was necessary, Winter very much enjoyed the many other projects that were begun during the ten years at the SWM. As Roberta noted, "Always Winter's main concern (and his gifting) was discovering the missing links in what is necessary for

Both Ralph and Roberta were involved in the work at the SWM together, just as they were in Guatemala. It was difficult to keep track of all their activities. Glenn Schwartz, assistant to Dean Arthur Glasser, wrote about jobs that incoming students' spouses might consider: "Dr. Winter, for instance, needs someone who can type ... who can keep financial records of a very simple sort for the American Society of Missiology, and who can keep track of him—which is the hardest job of all, but the most fun."[69]

Winter's Focus at the SWM from 1967–1976

The Growing TEE Movement

Naturally, because of Winter's involvement as a professor, there was a growing interest and engagement in issues related to leadership development and TEE at Fuller. Often, as students evaluated how the church was growing in both quality and quantity, they were challenged to consider how to train leaders locally. The fact that most of the students or "associates" had mission field experience enhanced the quality of their work and their collaboration with other students. Missionaries in other parts of the world heard about this research or read about it in the *Church Growth Bulletin*. This increased participation in the missiological discussion and increased the cross-fertilization of ideas and actions.[70]

Winter believed that the church in America was suffering and would continue to suffer if it could not deal with the issue of how leaders are trained for ministry here and internationally. He would often trace the

---

missionary advance and then working to produce what is necessary to fill that need. Perhaps this is why the theology faculty in 1975 nominated him for a Templeton prize." (Winter 2000, 31) No further details are available about this nomination. It is interesting that according to Roberta it was the School of Theology that nominated him.

[69] July 27, 1973 letter from Glenn Schwartz to incoming students and their spouses.

[70] A small sampling of the many theses done at Fuller SWM on TEE includes the following:

Stephen L. Chen, *Church Growth - Textbook for Theological Education by Extension.* (Chen, 1977) This was produced as a project for an MA of Theology in Missiology. Chen surveys various issues in Taiwan, and writes a manual in Chinese for use there.

David L. Hill, *Theological Education in Missions as a Factor in Baptist Church Growth with Special Emphasis on the Philippines.* (Hill, 1979)

Daniel Ward, *Theological Education by Extension: A Proposal for India's Free Methodist Church.* (Ward, 1982) Ward wrote this MA in Theology thesis to propose a form of TEE that would work in the Indian context. He evaluated several existing seminaries, and lay leadership-training programs before proposing extension solutions.

history of the church in different places in the world, noting the problems created in churches when real local leaders were replaced with foreign, seminary-trained and ordained pastors, who were either not leaders in gifts or who were not recognized as such.[71]

While models of TEE have shifted over the year, the emphasis has grown as modeled in the distance education methods used by many schools, especially for degree completion programs.[72]

There are still, as of this writing in 2011, TEE programs in operation. As mentioned, India has the largest called: The Association for Theological Education by Extension TAFTEE. The seventh edition of the global prayer book, *Operation World* noted that in Africa, "TEE programmes, modular training and training-in-service are all key for training both lay leadership and the many overworked and bivocational pastors. Several hundred TEE programmes now operate in Africa, accounting for over 100,000 students. Despite past obstacles, TEE is establishing itself as an effective alternative for theological training." (Mandryk, 2010, 37)

Defending Church Growth Issues

As Winter taught courses on the expansion of Christianity and learned from the "associates" and other faculty, his interests continued to broaden. He, like others on faculty, wrote on various issues related to church growth around the world. Wodarz noted:

> Dr. Winter's projects have had a large influence on the promotion of Dr. McGavran's ideas. Winter's work with the systems of extension education led to his publishing *Theological Education by Extension*, which is a method whereby church leaders can be training in their own communities. (Wodarz, 1979, 124)

Winter's statistical background from his doctoral studies meant he could easily understand quantitative research. But his ongoing study and teaching of history began to be increasingly reflected in his writing and speaking.

In 1970, he wrote the lead article, which combined these in the *Church Growth Bulletin*. The title of the article, showing the typical Winter

---

[71] This, he believed, was the major failure of the Student Volunteer Movement.

[72] In 2008, Ross Kinsler published the book *Diversified Theological Education: Equipping All God's People* that included articles from experts in this kind of training in different parts of the world. (Kinsler 2008)

flair, grabbed the readers' attention in the lead ten-page, two-part article: "Jesuits Yes, Presbyterians No!" (Winter, 1970c) In it, he starts by commenting on a book review written by Presbyterian James E. Goff.[73] He had written an extensive nine-page review (Goff, 1970) of the book, *Latin American Church Growth*. (Read et al., 1969) The book was the product of some SWM associates and was an attempt to give countrywide data on 17 nations in the region. According to Winter, this was the first detailed statistical information coming out of a non-European region since William Carey's *"Enquiry"*.[74] The goal of the book was to inform and challenge current church and mission leadership with regard to the status of the church in Latin America.

Goff wrote a strongly negative review, pointing out errors in both arithmetic and theology. He gave his opinion of church growth in the area of the lack of awareness on the part of missionaries of the political and economic injustice.

There were mistakes in some of the calculations in the book. For example, one chart was mislabeled, which Winter realized may have accounted for some of Goff's errors. Because of the significance of this study of the growth of the church in 17 countries over two and a half years, Winter argued that you do not throw out the premise of the entire book because of small errors.[75]

Winter's statistical background allowed him to easily detect errors in Goff's analysis. Goff failed to "think that the current annual growth rate (of either the general population or the evangelical church) cannot and must not be derived by computing an <u>average growth rate over a seven-year period</u>." (Winter, 1970c, 63)

Goff also criticized the underlying theology of the book, suggesting there was little interest in helping serve the poor or dealing with social issues. Winter countered that Goff had misquoted, making some statements of the authors seem more extreme to argue his point. Beyond that, Winter closed by musing, "Is it appropriate for him to belittle the

---

[73] This is the same James E Goff who had written a critique of TEE in the WCC's *RISK* magazine, mentioned earlier.

[74] Winter pointed out that Carey had errors in his information, as did this book reporting on the situation in Latin America. Those kinds of minor errors do not mean that the whole thesis of the book is invalid. Carey's book was originally published in 1792 and several editions now circulate. (Carey, 1891)

[75] Winter had written another short article in *CGB* titled, "Church Growth Calculations: Facts and Fallacies, No. 1". (Winter, 1970b) He would follow that up with similar articles as well, in part to deflect some of the stereotypes included in reviews of church growth theory such as Goff's.

Pentecostals who – far more than Presbyterian missionaries – are out in those slums demonstrating first-century Christian individual concern for the confused newcomers to the megalopolis?" (Winter, 1970c, 65)

Winter's growing exposure to different mission situations around the world gave him hope in the continued progress of the church, so he compared the book on Latin America to Carey's in two areas: (1) statistics pointing to success for Latin Americans in the 60s-70s; and, (2) the need to send more missionaries. Yet he realized that additional study and research and corrections needed to be undertaken.

In the second part of his article, Winter examined *Observations in Lower California* in 1771 by the German Jesuit Johann Baegert, S.J.[76] In it, he included a chapter aimed at Protestant pastors in particular, asking why they did not send missionaries to "convert heathen." This chapter was reprinted following Winter's critique of Goff's review in the *CGB*. Winter noted that he felt there was no difference between Baegert's underlying purpose (to see Protestants sending) and William Carey's.

This article provides insight into Winter's thinking, combining several areas of his interest and experience. Naturally, the articles and the book that it refers to are focused on church growth according to a very broad definition. But the reference to Carey's establishment of mission structures and the Jesuit structures for sending workers shows Winter's growing interest in the importance of mission structures and how they hinder or help the mission effort. Just a year later, in the *Church Growth Bulletin*, Winter would argue for the role of mission organizations as crucial for the church to reach out, especially in pioneering work. He argued for this in the article "Churches Instead of Missions?"[77] (Winter, 1971a)

He mentions two "errors" encountered in the current thinking about church/mission discussions. These reflect his growing emphasis on the need for mission structures in the missionary task:

> The first error wars against the Western-based missionary society and says it isn't needed. The second error is the strange assumption that not even the younger churches need missionary societies. Illogically, it is assumed that once an overseas national church is well planted, it will just as naturally grow and reach out and finish the job. (Winter, 1971a, 158-159)

Winter also furthered his thinking concerning the need for the gospel to impact areas it had not touched. Beginning in 1969, he began to write

---

[76] University of California Press Berkeley reprinted this book in 1952.

[77] This article will be discussed more fully in Chapter 6.

more about the differences between church organizational structures and mission structures.[78]

Select Students' Reaction to Winter's Teaching

Winter engaged with students on several levels. Because the associates (students) were generally mature missionaries and mission leaders, he engaged them in a number of subjects, which he saw as connected, even if the students did not. He shared his broad perspective on history and the expansion of Christianity. He continued to mobilize people with ideas and toward involvement in work he considered substantial, such as the 1980 commemoration of the Edinburgh 1910 meeting to which he inadvertently recruited one student to lead, or the need for cross-cultural experience even for a pastor, by which at least one pastor was challenged.[79]

Select Additional Initiatives During the Fuller Years

Presbyterian Structures

Just as in Guatemala, Winter was involved in a number of initiatives in addition to his teaching. Years before, in his pre-field orientation program during the last six months of 1956, Winter had heard a leading executive of the Presbyterian mission board speak of the unique values of the "order" pattern, seen not only in the Catholic church but also in some Lutheran and European denominations. Winter was fascinated with the concept of committed groups of men or women who would organize themselves for service. He was encouraged by this Presbyterian leader to continue thinking and writing about it, which he did. This early historical study of the "orders" had started him thinking about how to organize efforts to further God's purposes and the work of others around him, whether missionary or pastor. (Winter, 2000, 28)

A section in their governing document facilitated Winter's efforts within the framework of the Presbyterian Church. In 1902, a section of *The Government, Discipline and Worship of the Presbyterian Church (USA)*

---

[78] This was leading to a second major insight of Winter's life: church organizational structures as different from mission organizational structures. We will return to this subject in the next chapter.

[79] Many individual associates tell stories of how Winter's approach to teaching left a mark on them as students. I have included several student reflections on their experiences in Winter's classroom in Appendix M.

was amended to include what was known as Chapter 28 of the Book of Order.[80] This made a provision, which clearly allowed for presbytery, synod or national mission initiatives without the need of a majority vote in the General Assembly. These would be officially recognized within the denomination, but not under denominational control. Winter helped initiate four groups that were organized under Chapter 28.

Winter founded the United Presbyterian Center for Mission Studies (UPCMS, later known as the PCMS) in 1972. He saw this as a "non-threatening study center" which would "talk up the very concept of mission orders." (Winter, 1995a, 2) He wrote:

> I felt that our church could not go on being blind to the massive involvement of our local churches in non-Presbyterian mission activities. I felt that the wisdom of our board ought, in part, to be employed in the evaluation of these other types of mission—for the benefit of our membership. I did not think it was reasonable for our people at the local church level to be exposed to every conceivable fly-by-night mission activity and not be able to draw upon the decades of wisdom and field experience, which our own people abroad had accumulated. (Winter, 1995a, 2)

It was recognized without any question by the General Assembly as a legitimate Chapter 28 organization. (Winter, 2000, 28) The PCMS had two purposes: 1) analyzing the needs and opportunities for Christian mission in today's world, and 2) suggesting additional methods and structures for mission.

One of the first ministries the PCMS created was a mission education and mobilization arm called Presbyterians United for Mission Advance (PUMA). It was "to encourage in every way possible popular, pew-level education in mission." (Winter, 1995a, 2)

In 1974, the General Assembly Mission Council recognized another organization Winter helped to start: the Presbyterian Order for World Evangelization (POWE). The POWE has two main purposes: 1) the evangelization of all the world's people groups, especially those that remain

---

[80] It was originally Chapter 23, but was changed to Chapter 28 some time after 1912. In 1995, Winter noted that this became a sub-point under Chapter 9, and then was "dragged completely into the dust, no doubt by well-meaning people for whom history was not an enlightening resource." (Winter, 1995a, 3)

outside any active evangelistic effort, and 2) the cultivation of a lifestyle that prioritizes world evangelization.[81] (Blincoe, 2012, 9)

Finally, shortly after leaving Fuller, Winter helped found the Presbyterian Frontier Fellowship (PFF) in 1977. PFF's Mission Statement is as follows:

> We challenge, mobilize, and empower Presbyterian congregations into global partnerships that establish indigenous churches among unreached people groups.[82]

Through these organizations Winter was enlisting evangelical Presbyterians who were globally-focused toward a deeper involvement in the mission task.[83]

William Carey Library

The SWM faculty was aware the work of their students would be helpful to others doing mission work. Because the students were all experienced field workers, their theses tended to have more practical applications.

Initially McGavran and others connected with SWM used their influence to convince Eerdmans Publishing Company to publish some of the theses coming out of the SWM. A sampling of titles includes the following:

1. *Church Growth in Mexico* by Donald McGavran, John Huegel, and Jack Taylor (1963)
2. *Wildfire—Church Growth in Korea* by Roy E. Shearer (1966)
3. *New Patterns of Church Growth in Brazil* by William R. Read (1965)
4. *Church Growth in Central and Southern Nigeria* by John B. Grimley and Gordon E. Robinson (1966)
5. *God's Impatience in Liberia* by Joseph Conrad Wold (1968)
6. *Tinder in Tabasco* by Charles Bennett (Bennett, 1968)
7. *Latin American Church Growth* by William R. Read, Victor M. Monterroso and Harmon A. Johnson (1969)

---

[81] The POWE's website www.reconsecration.org includes Winter's paper, "Reconsecration to a Wartime Lifestyle."

[82] From: http://www.pff.net/who-we-are/missionvision.html accessed on November 9, 2009. For a number of years, the PFF has annually raised more than $1 million U.S. specifically for work among unreached peoples.

[83] The PCMS and the PFF functionally merged in 2005.

SWM faculty discussed the idea of publishing the work of the students and urged Winter to try to implement this, which he did with Roberta and their four daughters.[84] William Carey Library (WCL) was established in 1969. WCL produced and published the work of the students and faculty but they were not merely interested in publishing. They also worked with other publishers to produce books and get them into markets to which WCL did not have access. This activity also drew attention to what was being discussed and written at the SWM. Later, WCL expanded their offerings and began distributing mission books from other publishers.[85]

Roberta was very involved in the day-to-day work of WCL as was Marguerite Kraft. It helped that Winter had learning accounting and started 17 businesses in Guatemala. Later, in seeking a new student spouse to take Marguerite's role, Assistant to the Dean, Glenn Schwartz wrote:

> The William Carey Library, which is a publishing venture operating cooperatively with the School of World Mission, needs someone to take Marguerite Kraft's place, who is going on the missions staff at Biola College. She [currently] processes orders, places orders for more books, answers problem correspondence, etc. Her job requires some typing, but, more than that, a great deal of ability to learn quickly. She works jointly with Mrs. Ralph Winter, and it is fun work, directly associated with missions and the school.[86]

As previously noted, Winter edited the 600-page book *Theological Education by Extension* (1969d). He also wrote *The Twenty Five Unbelievable Years* (1970) and *Warp and Woof* (1970) during his time at the SWM. In addition, many church growth studies were produced and sold by WCL.[87]

Ralph Covell wrote an article describing mission book publishing from the mid-1960s to late 1973.[88] The WCL was mentioned as one of two institutions begun during the last decade and many books published by

---

[84] All of the family had a part in the business. At various times, this included book preparation to receiving books in the garage and shipping orders.

[85] At one point, WCL distributed mission books from almost 100 publishers.

[86] Letter from Glenn Schwartz to incoming students and their spouses, July 27, 1973.

[87] See the list of the books produced by WCL from 1969-1980 in Appendix N. By its 40th anniversary in 2009, WCL had published over 700 titles and sold more than one million books.

[88] Covell was serving as an associate professor of missions at Conservative Baptist Theological Seminary (now, Denver Seminary) in Denver, Colorado.

WCL were mentioned.[89] (Covell, 1974, 116) Covell also mentioned the idea of "mini-publishing" as something that would likely increase. Mini-publishing includes the development of "demand publishing of books and the use of cassettes and other techniques to facilitate inter-communication among those interested in the world mission of the church." (Covell, 1974, 116) He refers to Winter's article on the subject: "Minipublishing: New Hope for Strategic Dialogue."

A few of the books Covell mentions include:

> *Theological Education by Extension* by Ralph D. Winter, (1969d)

> *Bibliography for Cross-Cultural Workers* by Alan R. Tippett (1971b)

> *Crossroads in Missions* Edited by Arthur Glasser (a reprint of five mission books) (1971b)

> *The Gospel and Frontiers Peoples* by R. Pierce Beaver, (1973)

> *The World Directory of Theological Education by Extension* by Wayne Weld, (1973)

> *Evangelical Response to Bangkok* by Ralph D. Winter, (1973b)

Wodarz noted that WCL was one way that Winter helped McGavran and the SWM get its message out: "But the most important contribution by Ralph Winter to the School of World Mission was the establishment of William Carey Library. ...which handles low-volume publications at reasonable prices and quickly makes available the publication of research carried on at the School of World Mission."[90] (Wodarz, 1979, 124)

American Society of Missiology and Missiology: An International Review

When McGavran was in negotiations to move the Institute of Church Growth to Fuller, he was promised that they would be able to offer a PhD through the SWM, which was something the college in Oregon could not do. However, it took years to accomplish. Fuller President Hubbard had argued that there were two reasons that prevented FTS from offering the

---

[89] The other organization he mentioned which was established during the 10 years up to 1974 was the Mission Advanced Research and Communications Center.

[90] He continued, "In the three years from its founding in 1968, the William Carey Library published 37 works of missionary interest. In the first fourteen months it printed 26,000 books and 22,000 smaller publications."

degree: 1) there was no scholarly society that was engaging the community of scholars on the subject and, 2) there was no journal. At the time, missiology was considered an interdisciplinary subject. (Winter, 2000, 33) Winter and a few others changed that.

Background to the ASM: Scholarly Missions Studies in the 19th Century

As early as the World Missionary Conference at Edinburgh in 1910, there were only four full professorships in the U.S. in missions. Soon after, four more were added. The *International Review of Missions* began in 1912, but after mid-century it had shifted focus to broader ecumenical concerns when it was taken over by the WCC.

In 1952, the Association of Professors of Missions (APM) was organized. It built upon the Fellowship of Professors of Missions, which started and was focused on the east coast. The journal, *Practical Anthropology*, started in 1953, but was focused on only one area of the social sciences. (Shenk and Hunsberger, 1998, 6-7)

Gerald H. Anderson[91] returned from serving in the Philippines in 1970 to become President of Scarritt College for Christian Workers. He attended the APM meetings. He was "astonished that only about fourteen persons showed up for that meeting" and was dismayed because "if this represented the future of mission studies in the United States, then we're in very serious trouble." (Shenk and Hunsberger, 1998, 9) When Winter attended his first meeting of the APM, he "immediately perceived an absence of the main bulk of mission teaching and research in the meeting for so simple a reason as the original definition of membership excluded Bible college and other undergraduate schools where a host of active professors has been teaching hundreds of students for years." (Shenk and Hunsberger, 1998, 9)

Founding of the American Society of Missiology

Winter and George Peters of Dallas Theological Seminary convened a meeting to discuss the idea of having a broader group than the APM, which could draw from evangelical, ecumenical and Roman Catholic

---

[91] Anderson was Director of the Overseas Ministries Study Center in New Haven, Connecticut and formerly Academic Dean and Professor of Church History at Union Theological Seminary, Philippines. He also served as President of Scarritt College in Nashville, Tennessee and Senior Research Associate in the Southeast Asia Studies Program at Cornell University.

scholarship. They then wrote to a select group of well-known missiologists for their input, and subsequently broadened the group and announced a meeting for June 9 through 10, 1972, at Anderson's Scarritt College in Nashville, Tennessee. They would meet just before the APM and found the American Society of Missiology (ASM). Shenk wrote:

> The timing of the call to form a new missiological society seemed quite wrong to a number of people, especially some APM members. After all, the APM had its own evaluation under way and intended to receive a report only two days after the ad hoc group was to meet. To some it seemed that the initiative to found ASM was calculated to put an end to the APM, despite all assurances to the contrary.[92] (Shenk and Hunsberger, 1998, 11)

Indeed, Winter and Anderson believed that the APM was in need of refocusing, but they thought starting the broader-purposed ASM could actually help the APM. Their proposal suggested that the new society:

> 1. Be comprehensive by including members (a) from all Christian traditions, (b) from all missions-related scholarly fields, and (c) from groups of mission executives and missionaries, along with the scholars.
>
> 2. Be a professional society, to counteract the "bad press" that had plagued mission studies.
>
> 3. Produce a scholarly journal as well as high-caliber monographs. (Shenk and Hunsberger, 1998, 12)

One of the points of discussion was related to how to balance the continuum of practical versus pure scholarship:

> Should the new society define its purpose as that of fulfilling our Lord's final command or, rather, the study of missiology without reference to doctrine? The latter stance, a non-confessional stance, was the only one likely to win acceptance among the other academic disciplines. In the end the latter position prevailed. Indeed, it was the conservative evangelicals who argued that only if the new organization

---

[92] According to a letter from Per Hassing of Boston University School of Theology and Donald M. Wodarz, St. John's Seminary, who wrote on behalf of the Boston Theological Institute on March 9, 1972. They agreed that a society such as was proposed was needed, but the timing and rush of the process and decision was of concern.

were strictly scientific could they participate at all. (Shenk and Hunsberger, 1998)

In 1972, the society was established with Gerald Anderson, Winter, and Donald M. Wodarz authorized to help run it until the next meeting. With that, the ASM began a pattern it continues until this day, having representatives from each of the three major Christian traditions: Roman Catholic, ecumenical, and evangelical. In 1976, the ASM was admitted into membership in the Council on the Study of Religion, apparently in part due to Winter's involvement in publishing (through William Carey Library) and a chapter he wrote for a book titled *Scholarly Communication and Publication* by George W. MacRae in 1972. Winter's chapter was called "The Economics of Minipublishing" and was a slight revision of his article "Minipublishing: New Hope for Strategic Dialogue" (Winter, 1972a) describing the value and potential of short run publishing.

Founding of Missiology: An International Review

In 1972, with growing publishing experience, Winter heard that the small, quality journal *Practical Anthropology* (PA) was reconsidering its role and audience. Winter negotiated transfer of it to the ASM and continued as the business manager of the new journal for the first six years, seeking to fill the remaining commitments of *PA* with the new journal.[93]

Eugene A. Nida was a major player in *PA*, and wrote about their evaluation of their audience, wondering out loud if the new, national translators around the world were "not journal-reading type people." In that same letter to Winter and Tippett, Nida wrote, "We would be very reluctant to simply cease publication of *PA*, for obviously it has performed an important function and can continue to do so. But we do feel that people such as yourselves are in a much better position than we are to carry forward this emphasis."[94]

The new journal was named *Missiology: An International Review* and its first issue came out in January 1973.[95] During its first years, various

---

[93] This is another situation where Winter's accounting experience came in handy, as *PA* was some $4000 in debt, not realizing they had spent money "due" to subscribers for future issues.

[94] September 5, 1972 letter from Eugene Nida to Dr. Winter and Mr. Tippett, (error on Nida's part, apparently not knowing that Tippett was also a PhD), 2. From the Fuller SWM Archives, Box 1-2.

[95] Interview with Ralph Winter by the author, August 30, 2006, 14-15. *Missiology* started on the base of the journal, *Practical Anthropology*, which had run out of money. Alan Tippett was the first editor of *Missiology* and Winter was the secretary/business manager.

Fuller SWM faculty were editors, including Tippett and Glasser. Tippett was a perfect choice for the first three years because of the respect he had in anthropological circles, although according to an unpublished autobiography by Tippett, he was upset at Winter for suggesting his name without asking him first.[96]

A Follow up Course for the Urbana Student Convention

Winter had attended a student mission convention in Toronto in 1946 when he was at Princeton. That was the first such North American event sponsored by the InterVarsity Christian Fellowship, which continued to call students together around the theme of discipleship and world mission. It was held the week between Christmas and New Year every three years. Winter attended most of the conventions, except when he was in Guatemala.

Over the years, the convention would challenge students to various commitments, including being willing to serve "overseas" if God called them. The number who signed those cards was dropping, perhaps as a result of the 1960s, where protest and individuality reigned. Whatever the reasons, in 1970, only eight percent signed. But in 1973, twenty-eight percent signed, saying they were willing to become missionaries should God direct. Since there was a record audience that year of 14,000, that meant thousands had signed the cards.

Winter wanted to help those students get the information they would need to make wise decisions about their future. After the 1973 event, he asked the leadership of the convention if, as a part of their follow up to the event, they would allow him to write a letter inviting students to a special summer training course. David Howard, Urbana director, asked several questions about who would be teaching, what they would teach, where it would be held, who would sponsor it and who would take financial responsibility. Winter promised to get the backing of various professors, and called some 200 of them. In the end, after shaping a sponsoring body of fifteen mission executives and getting Harold Lindsell, editor of *Christianity Today*, to run a full page "article-announcement," twenty-nine students showed up for the first of two weeks of class, but only two to three

---

[96] Chuck Kraft and Doug Priest have copies of this long manuscript. This author has only seen two pages, which include this idea.

from the IVCF Urbana contacts.[97] Most were from LACC and its sister Park Street Church in Boston.[98]

Select Additional Writings During the Fuller Years

Beyond TEE and church growth, Winter also continued to write and speak to other leaders and to inform and mobilize churches and students. A number of his writings related to Sodalities and Modalities will be covered in Chapter 6.

In 1970, he published the book *The 25 Unbelievable Years: 1945–1969*.[99] (Winter and Latourette, 1970) It was originally done as a chapter to close out Latourette's two-volume *History of Christianity* (Latourette, 1953) when publisher Harper and Row reprinted it in 1975. [100]

In mid-1973, he wrote the mobilization booklet *Say Yes to Missions*, which eventually came to be used for the 1973 Urbana Student Convention. In it, he was attempting to counter the usual assumptions young people have about the world and their role in it, and "patch up [their] somewhat brainwashed American education." He noted that one way to patch it up would be to read about the Christian movement through the centuries, such as in the book written by Latourette.

Also in this booklet are early signs of Winter's interest in large populations of the unevangelized. He mentions the Muslim and Hindu worlds and counters the oft-repeated "missionary go home" cries. He also mentions, perhaps for the first time, the concept of cultural distance by referring to the M-Scale. "M" represented the cultural distance of the missionary from the target culture. Later, Winter changed this to the E-Scale.[101]

---

[97] Lindsell had been involved at FTS almost from the beginning up until the 1970s.

[98] The course would be further developed and an extension program established by the newly established U.S. Center for World Mission. The name of the course was Institute of International Studies and later changed to Perspectives on the World Christian Movement. This is also the name of the book and Study Guide used in the course.

[99] Winter only published a few books. Much more of his writing is in journals and papers he presented formally and informally.

[100] Winter actually wrote two versions of this book. One was more acceptable to non-evangelicals and one was to evangelicals. The "toned down" version was printed in Latourette's book. The other was printed by WCL as a stand-alone book by the title above.

[101] See Appendix O for the full, original description of the E-Scale. Winter said that this was done because the Billy Graham Evangelistic Association, who was sponsoring the meeting, preferred the word "evangelism" to "missions."

This led naturally to another subject that was taking up more and more of Winter's thinking: what were the "gaps" in mission around the world.

Applying The Missiology: Leaving Fuller

As a result of his writing, teaching, and engagement with students while at the SWM at Fuller, Winter and his wife Roberta were being challenged themselves. Discussions and instruction about church growth, anthropology, cultural understanding, and the expansion of Christianity were all helping experienced missionaries learn and grow in ways that should further their work back on the field. Winter's work in TEE and the expansion of Christianity had challenged many, directly and indirectly, all over the world. There was something about "usual missiology" that was not satisfying for Winter. As an initiator and problem identifier, he may have been looking for just how to identify the core of the issues being raised from those around him at Fuller and in the ASM. And the Winters had a growing involvement with the younger generation of future missionaries.

He began to notice that there were certain places around the world from which the faculty of the SWM was not getting any information, or at least not very much. Western missions and the national church seemed to be overlooking certain religious or cultural segments. These included groups such as Muslims and Hindus and places such as China (which he later changed to Buddhists). When later describing his tenure at Fuller and the "gap" he was observing in the church growth reports being produced at the SWM, Winter often said, "I was sitting there and realized that I could have 1,000 more missionaries come through my classroom and I would never have a missionary from a place where no missionary had ever gone."

This got Ralph and Roberta thinking about what needed to be done. Winter's writings contain descriptions of the issues and suggestions on how they might be approached.

In the process of working through these issues, discussing them with faculty and presenting his paper, the Winters began to be drawn into a broader ministry.[102]

---

[102] In an Interview with Arthur Glasser by the author on Feb. 10, 2005, 3, he said, "...Ralph always was intensely loyal, intensely helpful, always friendly, etc.... We realize that there was a lot more there than we knew about. He had to be free from his schedule of courses to initiate things of one sort or another. And so, it was the greatest gift to Fuller and to the missionary movement when Ralph Winter broke away."

Winter had tried to talk Fuller into starting its own center focused on world missions. It would be more than the SWM. It would seek a closer connection with the sending agencies and would seek to collaborate with them and others involved in mission. It would not be more academics, but would be modeled after the coordinating offices of a number of denominational mission sending organizations in New York City at 475 Riverside Drive. That building housed the mission arm of a number of denominational sending organizations. Winter had hoped that Fuller would open such an office building or "implementation annex" nearby. During those discussions, a church property became available, and Winter had hoped Fuller would purchase that space. In the end they were not interested in the property or in the idea of supporting a missions coordinating office. After many discussions with key faculty and administers, Fuller decided they were not going in this direction. That increased Winter's sense that he needed to do something about what he and Roberta had been thinking and writing about.

There were many reasons for such a building or quasi-independent organization, as Kraft noted:

> ...we talked often of setting up another organization that would not be hampered by academic rules and regulations. It would be lean, mobile, flexible and adaptable to carry out the "activist" ideas we generated that didn't fit into our academic programs.
>
> We even had more or less formal discussions over a two-year period involving both outsiders and Fuller insiders. In these meetings our ideas began to converge into the concept of a major 'annex' to SWM that would implement new strategies and functions essential to the things we were talking about in class.[103] (Kraft, 2005, 132-133)

Fuller Seminary had a certain "face" it presented to the missions world, and the associated limitations of that face was something Winter realized.[104] In a number of conservative non-denominational mission circles, there were growing questions about Fuller and where the SWM

---

[103] According to Kraft, this is the last part of the quote in an email from Winter to Kraft on 7/5/02, 2

[104] In the 1970s, the seminary was going through several transitions, one of which led to changes in their doctrinal statement related to their view of Scripture. Even some from Fuller's faculty were involved in arguing against the change, including Harold Lindsell, who wrote: *The Battle for the Bible*. (1976)

stood.[105] Many participated in the SWM by sending their missionaries there but others held back. While the SWM was almost ten years old and had attracted some 1,000 missionaries who passed through its classrooms, there were still some who had questions about what was going on there.[106]

When Winter finally left in 1976, some at Fuller thought he was intending to start a competing university.[107] Hubbard was not concerned about possible competition, nor fear of losing students, but a major part of his job was to represent Fuller and what the SWM was doing to new students and donors. Winter's presence at the school had provided a good argument for why students should come and, as Hubbard pointed out, professors do not leave a tenured position unless there is a problem. So donors might think that Hubbard pushed Winter out for some reason. Hubbard also realized that if Winter failed in this new initiative, it might reflect poorly on Fuller. So Winter was given a leave of absence. (Winter, 2000, 35)

In the end, the Winters believed that God was leading them.[108]

Analysis

The period at Fuller Seminary began with an unexpected transition from Guatemala, brought increased influence and change in Ralph Winter's life and work, and ended with an unexpected transition ten years later.

Winter's early experiences related to TEE helped to open the door to his involvement at Fuller and led toward deeper engagement with issues related to how churches grow. The in-depth exposure to faculty, associates (students) and mission leaders from around the world led him to expand his knowledge beyond his field experiences in Latin America. It augmented his familiarity with church planting and church growth issues in numerous new contexts. Combining these experiences and data brought

---

[105] Some may have wondered how distinct the SWM was from the School of Theology.

[106] This round number, which Winter used, of 1,000 missionaries in his classroom, likely includes some of the students from the School of Theology who were required to take one course at the SWM as well. There were also a number of courses which could be taken for credit in either school.

[107] Winter did found the William Carey International University in early 1977, focused under a very different mandate of international development, by which he meant anything that will help the effective development of cultures globally rather than theological training.

[108] According to their own explanation, that leading came through their experience at the Lausanne Congress on World Evangelism in 1974, which will be discussed in chapter 7.

an increase in Winter's interest and study in the subject of cultures around the world. The SWM seedbed of the ideas and global relationships launched him into a broader leadership role within evangelical missions in North America and globally.

Winter's interaction with the North American mission associations (EFMA/IFMA) increased the "audience" who would consider his ideas. He had the opportunity to communicate his ideas about TEE, and he learned from those he respected (such as SIL/Wycliffe). While those around him greatly influenced him, his time at Fuller also enhanced his influence. It was the platform he thought it would be.

The scholarly interaction with people like McGavran, Tippett, and later anthropologist Chuck Kraft, as well as with associates, was a tributary into Winter's thinking, writing, and teaching. Beyond his obvious engagement with issues such as TEE, he made use of other skills in numerous areas including statistics and analysis. The SWM provided a small, cohesive, effective team, each with different skills and experience. Naturally, books from scholars like Latourette also informed his teaching and influenced his approach to Christian history and the spread of the gospel.

Undoubtedly, McGavran had the single greatest influence on Winter during this period. Twenty-Seven years older than Winter, and with an ever-growing number of countries where he had first-hand knowledge, McGavran was greatly respected by Winter. McGavran had a laser-focus on church growth, considering all aspects of it. He continued to learn from any and every source. As we have seen, Winter attempted to be a "lifelong learner" himself. McGavran also saw the problems and issues that could keep a missionary from focusing on what he believed was crucial. That seems to be why Winter's series of writings from Guatemala called "Seven Deadly Missionary Sins" (in particular the one called "Gimmickitis") drew McGavran's attention to Winter.

The unexpected shift to the SWM full-time (instead of remaining on the field and teaching part-time) was initially a shock to Winter, yet he already respected, and soon became a strong proponent of, McGavran's missiology and insights. The passion of McGavran's focus on church growth influenced Winter's own vision and shaped his approach to missiology.

A number of the side projects and ministries begun while teaching (starting WCL, ASM, and *Missiology*), as well as his initiatives within Presbyterian circles, demonstrated Winter's inclination to focus on gaps or identify and solve problems in the "system" of evangelical missions or

Christianity in the west. During his time at the SWM, he worked on a number of those problems. This peculiar approach to the issues Winter was aware of had roots back in his way of dealing with young people at LACC (should young, committed believers remain single, for example) and his development of the Hebrew language tool for Genesis. Winter continued to leverage other people's skills to promote the SWM agenda, such as when he suggested Tippett edit the new journal, *Missiology*. Another can be seen in the mission leaders he involved as projects like the ASM were conceived.

The combination of Winter's Guatemala/TEE and his Fuller/SWM experiences were leading him to recognize that true leaders were engaged in ministry and were not free to leave those ministries and move to Pasadena. Thus, seminaries like Fuller tended to attract people who were younger and unproven in ministry, in the hopes that they would indeed be gifted and called. Certainly, the SWM's requirement that "associates" have field experience greatly helped this, but Fuller began a gradual "drift" toward allowing younger, pre-field students into the various programs.[109]

Another factor that influenced Winter's leaving Fuller was his growing desire to implement many of the ideas discussed at the SWM. His discussions with leaders at Fuller were moving in that direction, but the decision not to have an "implementation annex" connected to Fuller was another component in the Winters moving on. The central factor for this transition will be covered in Chapter 7. Now we will turn to a major theme that arose before Winter's tenure at Fuller and continued until he left: mission organizations and church organizations.

---

[109] According to an email from Charles Kraft to the author, 9/2/10, 1.

Chapter 6

Sodalities and Modalities

Introduction

The role and distinction between church and mission structures was a growing theme of Ralph Winter's writing. He had written on the related subject of the catholic orders during his six months "Study Fellowship" before heading to Guatemala. While serving at Fuller, he presented six major and several minor papers on the subject, a selection of which are detailed below.

There was a proliferation of Protestant mission organizations after William Carey sailed to India,[1] and another increase that began after World War II. Figure 11 below shows Protestant organizations begun before and after William Carey.[2]

---

[1] Carey himself talked about it in a way that suggests he was proposing the establishment of structures parallel to existing church structures, but for mission work by Christians: "Suppose a company of serious Christians, ministers and private persons, were to form themselves into a society, and make a number of rules respecting the regulation of the plan, and the persons who are to be employed as missionaries, the means of defraying the expense, etc. etc. This society must consist of persons whose hearts are in the work, men of serious religion, and possessing a spirit of perseverance; there must be a determination not to admit any person who is not of this description, or to retain him longer than he answers to it." (Carey, 1891, 82-83) or (Carey, 1988, 62-63)

[2] University of Edinburgh historian Andrew Walls presented one analysis regarding the genesis of modern mission societies in his book *The Missionary Movement in Christian History : Studies in the Transmission of Faith.* (Walls, 1996) In the chapter "Mission Societies and the Fortunate Subversion of the Church," Walls claims that, "The origins of the modern voluntary society lie in the last years of the seventeenth century. It was put to new uses in the eighteenth century and in the nineteenth developed new ways of influencing, supplementing, and by-passing the life of Church and State alike." (241)

Rufus Anderson, an American missionary statesman, who served as the secretary of the American Board of Commissioners for Foreign Missions from 1832-1866, also contributed an analysis of the start of modern missionary societies. He wrote, "The *Protestant* form is what we see in Missionary, Bible, Tract and other kindred societies, not restricted to ecclesiastics, nor to any one profession, but combining all classes, embracing the masses of the people; and all free, open and responsible... it is the *contributors of the funds*, who are the real association; not the American Board, not the General Assembly's Board, nor any other, but the individuals, churches, congregations, who freely act together, *through such agencies* for an object of common interest... This Protestant form of association–free, open

Some, including Winter, have conjectured that the more recent increase in mission organizations after World War II resulted from young Christian soldiers being exposed to various parts of the world, seeing people in need, and thus catching a vision for reaching them. He wrote, "Yet 145 new mission agencies have come into existence in the U.S.A. since 1945, as well as over 100 or more in India." (Winter, 1971b, 194)

---

responsible, embracing all classes, both sexes, all ages, the masses of the people–is peculiar to modern times, and almost to our age." (Anderson and Beaver, 1967, 65) Walls interprets Anderson to be suggesting that "the voluntary society subverted the old Church structures: it altered their power base." (Walls, 1996)

Brian Stanley, Professor of World Christianity, Director of the Centre for the Study of World Christianity at the University of Edinburgh, discussed different kinds of relationships of mission structures from the Moravians on, with a focus on modern structures in: "Where Have Our Mission Structures Come From?" (Stanley, 2003) He describes differences between (1) communitarian-institutional, (2) voluntarist-ecclesiastical, (3) denominational-nondenominational, (4) national-international and, (5) unidirectional-multidirectional. (Stanley, 2003)

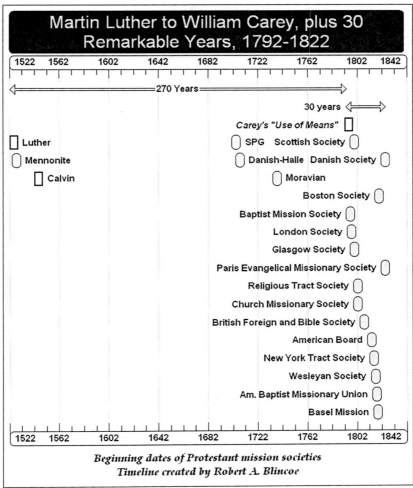

Figure 11 – Luther to Carey, plus 30 Remarkable Years, 1792-1822[3]

These organizations became involved in a wide range of ministries, from establishing churches to doing "mass" evangelism as well as literature distribution, broadcasting, theological training, medical work, agricultural relief and development, aviation, camping, orphanages, translation, etc.

---

[3] In a dissertation focused on the issue of ecclesiastical structures and voluntary structures, Bob Blincoe charted the voluntary or mission structures. This chart was in an early draft of his dissertation, but was not included in the final version. (Blincoe, 2012)

(White, 1983, 53) A few of the organizations founded directly after WW II were as follows:[4]

1. Youth for Christ, youth work, established 1945
2. Mission Aviation Fellowship, aviation, established 1945
3. Far East Broadcasting Company, broadcasting, established 1945
4. United World Mission, evangelism, church planting, established 1946
5. Far Eastern Gospel Crusade (now SEND International), evangelism, church planting, established 1946
6. Greater Europe Mission, evangelism, church planting, established 1949
7. World Vision, relief and development, established 1950

Winter's progression of thought, which is outlined below, grew from his increasing exposure to the evangelical missions movement in North America through (1) multi-agency relationships in Guatemala; (2) with students at FTS-SWM and the organizations they worked with globally; (3) through teaching and training he performed around the world; and, (4) through presentations to mission-related audiences of various types. In this section, each heading below is the title of a paper Winter wrote. As he had in the past, he also includes the writings of others in various ways.

Vertical and Horizontal Structures: The Anatomy of the Christian Mission - 1969

In 1969, Winter wrote "The Anatomy of the Christian Mission." (Winter, 1969a, 76) His stated purpose was "to emphasize that further conversation about the mission of missions must be based upon a clear idea of what the fundamental structures of mission are." He then proposed "as a tentative vocabulary of discussion the use of two terms: vertical structures and horizontal structures." (76) He took those phases from a labor union discussion, a current topic in politics at the time. The horizontal structure or organizations included people across the country from the perspective of a "craft" (such as all the carpenters). The vertical approach included all the workers in one company (such as General Motors). This contrast

---

[4] This is from the current list maintained for the MARC Mission Handbook by the Evangelical Missions Information Service at Wheaton College, courtesy of A. Scott Moreau. The full list includes approximately 7 organizations founded between 1946-1950 with clear denominational origins and another 38 organizations founded during the same period without denominational connections.

demonstrated the difference between denominational and non-denominational structures.[5] Applied to mission organization, the IFMA (a non-denominational association) "runs horizontally across the whole country, and even to other countries, expressing the concerns of a missions-minded minority within many different Christian denominations."[6] (77) In Winter's model, global or regional structures like the WCC or NCC would be vertical. An individual non-denominational organization such as Mission Aviation Fellowship or Christian Endeavor is a horizontal mission organization because "their money and people come from many denominations and their activities on the field are services to many denominations." (79)

Winter also compared the work a mission did on the home front to support the effort on the field. At home, a non-denominational organization might cross denominations, while on the field it could be a mixture of a vertical and horizontal structure. He made a distinction in the potential benefits of vertical and horizontal structures:

> The vertical structure has greater internal diversity and may thus tend to have greater objectivity and overall perspective, but less mobility. It may tend to bureaucracy due to the "distance" between the donor and the final function. It may tend to be a caretaker structure that, again, due to great internal diversity, finds it difficult to gain broad support for anything, especially enterprises beyond its immediate internal needs. The church as church finds it difficult to become excited about the spiritual fate of the urban masses in Calcutta.

> The horizontal structure tends to have a more specific objective and the direct support of those behind it. It has greater potential mobility and efficiency. But it typically sees only its own goals and therefore needs overall perspective. Citizens of the Kingdom may even need protection against its capacity to oversell its cause. Yet it offers a healthy escape valve for the differing visions of the diverse elements of a heterogeneous church. (88)

---

[5] Some use the phrase "inter-denomination" as well. Here, I mean they work both with a number of different denominations as well as with organizations which were not denominational.

[6] Winter was referring to individual denominational churches that might send a missionary to an inter-denominational agency (such as Wycliffe Bible Translators). The IFMA did not have denominational members of any kind at this time. The EFMA included denominational and non-denominational members.

Warp and Woof - 1970

Winter continued to think through the best way to illustrate and discuss the idea of two different structures. He combined several ideas in *The Warp and Woof: Organizing for Mission*, (Winter and Beaver, 1970, 3-4).[7] The terms "Warp" and "Woof" are borrowed from the craft of weaving and illustrated in Figure 12.[8]

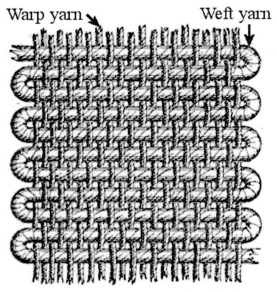

Figure 12 – Warp and Weft or Woof

The very *fabric* of the Christian movement will be torn apart if either the warp or the woof does not play its essential purpose. The warp of a fabric is the longitudinal threading and the woof is the lateral threading, and (depending upon the weaving technique employed) one may be more visible than the other, carrying the design, etc. But *both are utterly essential.* In a word, they are interdependent. (Winter and Beaver, 1970, 3-4)

---

[7] The title was used both for the whole booklet and for one of the chapters in the booklet. It has a publication date of 1970, but includes articles from 1971. It may be that there was an earlier version without the 1970 material and when it was reprinted or copied, the publication date for the entire booklet was not updated.

[8] From: http://www.sarkisian.com/images/warpweft.jpg accessed on January 19, 2011

The booklet's five chapters are reprints from various sources. Four of them were written by Winter, and one by R. Pierce Beaver. The first chapter is the article discussed above, "The Anatomy of the Christian Mission." In the second chapter was a talk Winter presented at the Chicago Furloughed Missionary Conference held by the Commission on Ecumenical Mission and Relations in August 1970 called a "Plea for Mission Orders." In it, Winter argued for the establishment of a vertical organization to "serve United Presbyterian churches and church men" by analyzing world needs and opportunities, gathering and distributing information on existing mission activities, suggesting methods and structures for mission, and reporting on its studies to United Presbyterian mission agencies. (Winter and Beaver, 1970, 30)[9] In an earlier version of his "A Plea for Mission Orders" Winter wrote:

> WHEREAS the world God created is urgently in need today as never before, and these needs are accompanied by unprecedented opportunities in many new forms, both at home and abroad, and
>
> WHEREAS God in His sovereign grace has seen fit in recent years to engender in our midst a great deal of repentance and faith and dedication to mission, and
>
> WHEREAS this grace in our midst bears marks of both unity and profound diversity, and
>
> WHEREAS the fullest release of these human resources for mission seems to require strikingly greater organizational decentralization than we now have,
>
> We do, therefore, countenance and encourage the development of such mission orders within our church as will loyally express the energies now lying unmined within significant horizontal veins of common interest and concern.[10]

(Winter, 1970a, 1)

In the third chapter, "The New Mission and the Mission of the Church," Winter details the large increase in mission organizations and discusses the interrelationship between those connected with

---

[9] An organization was started called "United Presbyterian Center for Mission Studies" and twelve men are listed as the Administrative Board. The one page referenced here is the 2nd edition or printing. The 1st edition lists the organization's potential name as, United Presbyterian Mission Information Service and four names of the leadership are listed.

[10] This is from a typed paper in Winter "E Files" under E-00, the first folder after he started his formal writing files. He wrote this after dialog during a furlough missionary conference, Commission on Ecumenical Mission and Relations of the United Presbyterian Church in the USA (COEMAR).

denominations, with global bodies like the WCC and independent or "faith" missions.[11] He discusses how each type of organization deals with issues of structure versus spontaneity, stability, and change. (Winter and Beaver, 1970, 32)

R. Pierce Beaver, who was professor emeritus of missions in the Divinity School of the University of Chicago, wrote a chapter called, "A Plea for a New Voluntarism." In it, he states there is a "crisis in Mission" which is deepening.[12]

The last chapter by Winter carried the same title as the name of the booklet, "The Warp and the Woof of the Christian Movement." Winter sought to strengthen his argument and introduce new terminology to clarify the concept of horizontal and vertical structures. A church is different from a club or a campus ministry in that its membership includes whole families. These other groups limit by age or sex, as in the Roman Catholic orders. Normally a person is only part of one local church, where they could be part of several vertical organizations.

For the first time, Winter introduces new terms: local churches he called "modalities" and mission societies "sodalities." Winter recognized that these terms were technical terms. He notes that he took the term sodality from the Roman Catholic tradition, but that modality had:

> ...a very vague definition in the dictionary, seemingly being used for several different things. And since there were some technical reasons for that *root* to be valid, I sort of adopted the word and gave it a special twist of its own in order to pair it up with 'sodality.' So to that extent I am responsible for the term 'modality,' but I'm really not to be blamed for the term "sodality." (Winter, 1980, 1)

---

[11] This is reprinted from its appearance in the journal, *International Review of Mission*. (Winter, 1971c, 89-100)

[12] Beaver wrote, "The crisis is the product of an abysmal decline in faith and concern; ... the crisis is in part a consequence of the merger of the International Missionary Council into the World Council of Churches, as was foreseen by such persons as Max Warren and Helen Kim. They feared that local concerns, ecclesiastical bureaucrats, confessional politicking, ... and growing parochialism would conspire together drastically to reduce commitment to witness 'to the ends of the earth' and to the discipling of the nations." (Winter and Beaver 1970, 43) He argues that "'sending missions' are not outdated and missiologists, theologians, and mission administrators need to call for continued outreach and need to challenge people to 'volunteer to go.'"

Beaver closed his chapter with a challenge for national churches to realize they are not self-sufficient, and to realize that experimentation in pioneering methods was still necessary as they sought to give shape to missions in the days ahead.

Churches, or modalities, grew mainly through biological growth. Sodalities were selective and grew out of a desire to accomplish specific tasks. Modalities "are characteristically impotent apart from careful maintenance of consensus, whether they are civil or ecclesiastical structures. Not all sodalities are prophetic, but prophetic influences will likely derive mainly from sodalities, not modalities." He continued, "...churches as churches have never in history cut a very impressive prophetic role, either at home or abroad. Many church leaders have been great souls, and prophetic at times. But, as with a hammer, they have worn themselves out on the anvil when they have not acknowledged and fostered the mobility and striking power of mission sodalities."[13] (Winter and Beaver, 1970, 60)

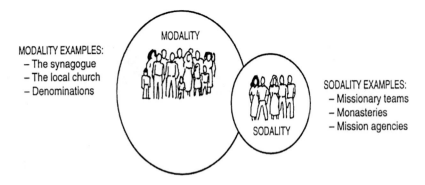

MODALITY EXAMPLES:
– The synagogue
– The local church
– Denominations

MODALITY

SODALITY

SODALITY EXAMPLES:
– Missionary teams
– Monasteries
– Mission agencies

Figure 13 – Modality and Sodality[14]

Winter then summarizes the impact of the sodalities of the Christian mission in history in the Western world. Even in the United States since WWII, a "maze of voluntary societies gained momentum" and at the same time, "church governments began zealously soliciting and demanding control over them." (Winter and Beaver, 1970, 57-58) He was arguing that both were crucial, as in the warp and woof analogy, not only to hold the cloth together but also to carry the design in the pattern.[15]

---

[13] This section and quote are similar to what he wrote in "Churches Need Missions Because Modalities Need Sodalities" in *EMQ*, Summer, 1971, 195-200.

[14] Figure 13 is from a mission introduction course, *World Mission : An Analysis of the World Christian Movement* first produced in Spanish and later back-translated into English. (Lewis, 1994, 28)

[15] The illustrations from Winter's previous article were used here again. Civil government is the "horizontal" or "warp" (the church or modality) and private enterprise or the "vertical" are the woof (the mission society or sodality).

The booklet argues that mission structures are needed. Missions were struggling with what to do with the growing churches their missionaries had started. Winter illustrated this from his experience in Guatemala. "Well-known is the example of the United Presbyterians who have tried to eliminate the colonial posture of the older mission in favor of a church-to-church relationship involving the mutual exchange of not 'missionaries' but 'fraternal workers.'" (Winter and Beaver, 1970, 53) However, later in the booklet he added, "...we may need only 'fraternal workers' in church-to-church relationships, and yet still need missionaries in mission-to-mission relationships." (Winter and Beaver, 1970, 61)

Some were questioning the need for missions at all:

> But all these details are not worth the effort of analysis if the category of the mission agencies is itself in question. Thus one reason for the apparent neglect of the subject is the strong feeling on the part of many that the church is the central and basic structure, whereas the mission is somehow secondary or perhaps merely a temporary aid in establishing churches: the scaffolding must come down when the building is done. But is this an adequate analogy? (Winter and Beaver, 1970, 53)

Winter raised the question that resides at the very core of the issue of church/mission relationships: "Can we say that, as a seed gives up its life to a new plant, the mission must die when the church is born? At this point we must try to get at some underlying distinctions, even if we end up with two new terms." (Winter and Beaver, 1970, 53)

He answered his own question with a plea in the last paragraph of the article:[16]

> The existence of a national church, here or there, merely proves that mission sodalities can be successful, not that they should be dismantled. Church-to-church "relations" are appropriate for those peoples within whose midst an active, evangelizing national church exists. But "missions" are no less appropriate for the vast ethnic groups in whose midst there is not yet any adequate national church, much less internal mission sodalities reaching out to understand the specialized tasks of mission. Churches need missions, because modalities need sodalities. This fact has the gravest consequences for our fullest response in mission in this hour. (Winter and Beaver, 1970, 61-62)

---

[16] Winter here also hints at a burden that was growing in his mind.

Churches Instead of Missions? - 1971

In 1971, a mission leaders' event to be held in Green Lake, Wisconsin, was being planned. It was organized by the Evangelical Missions Information Service and sponsored by the two major missions associations, the EFMA and IFMA, as a part of their joint, triennial mission executives' retreat. The theme of the event, referred to as GL 71, was related to Church/Mission issues.

The topic of the gathering was a "serious issue facing world missions in the '70s: mission/church relationships." (Gerber, 1972, 16 n1) The meeting sought to deal with the issues surrounding churches established around the world by North American mission organizations. The details from the meeting were chronicled in a compendium published by WCL called *Missions in Creative Tension*. (Gerber, 1971) Its preface noted:

> Missions in the 70s find themselves at the very heart of severe tensions swirling around church/mission/church relations. They spring largely from a fact unique to our times: A VIRILE, DYNAMIC CHURCH WORLDWIDE. Firmly rooted in national soil. Maturing in uneven patterns and at varying stages. But experiencing unprecedented growth. Struggling for national identity. Assuming forms compatible with indigenous cultures. Independent yet interdependent. (Gerber, 1971, 11)

Prior to that event, at least two publications were produced which sought to influence the focus and outcome of the gathering. William Carey Library published a 908 page "multibook" titled *Crossroads in Missions*, (Glasser, 1971b) which was a reprint of five books.[17] Arthur Glasser wrote

---

[17] The five books included in Crossroads in Missions were:

1. *The Missionary Nature* of the Church by Johannes Blauw (1962), which, Glasser noted, "contends against the heresy of developing a 'theology of missions' that transforms the missionary task into one of the activities of the church rather than 'the criterion for all its activities.'" (Glasser, 1971b, 153)

2. *Missionary, Go Home!* by James A. Scherer (1964), which "contends that 'under the traditional politico-geographical definition (of mission), the task could be considered nearly over; but under the new interpretation (the reintegration of the total human family under the Lordship of Jesus Christ), it has just begun'" (Glasser 1971b, 153)

3. *The Responsible Church and the Foreign Mission* by Peter Beyerhaus and Henry Lefever (1964) which: "...wants us to get beyond bowing to the immaturity of those who argue that we should encourage the younger churches to seek the sort of self-sufficiency that will make them not only independent of any other Church but isolate them from the total stream of God's life in the world. We must get beyond the tension between the local church autonomy and the unity and catholicity of the whole Church, and seek responsible

the introduction to the book specifically targeting the Green Lake study conference and noting the "uncertainty and intense debate over the nature and mission of the Church." (Glasser, 1971b, vii)

In his introduction as editor, Glasser recounted a number of "massive congresses on evangelism" throughout the world and quotes the objective of GL 71 as, "to identify points of tension which exist between missions and churches around the world and to discover guidelines for constructively coping with them in fulfillment of the missionary mandate."[18] (Glasser, 1971b, viii)

In addition to *Crossroads in Missions*, the *Church Growth Bulletin* dedicated a full issue to Church/Mission relationships in preparation for GL 71. As the editor, McGavran wrote a letter to the SWM faculty, asking each of them to write an article related to this issue in time for a mission leaders event. He mentions that the *CGB* had done this in the past, noting that, "The goal is to get into the hands of all secretaries and missionaries going to 'GL 71' an issue which will <u>play the same definitive part which our SPECIAL UPPSALA ISSUE played at the General Assembly of the World Council of Churches.</u>"[19] He included a two-page description of their topic and suggested points they should include in their brief article. He discussed his concern related to national church tensions with missionaries:

---

participation in the greater task of proclaiming the Lordship of Jesus Christ, directed towards every nation and to every aspect of the nation's life." (Glasser 1971b, 153)

4. *On the Growing Edge of the Church* by T. Watson Street (1965), which "calls for younger churches 'coveting the higher gifts' and thereby extending the apostolate until the whole Christian corpus participates in the work of Mission." (Glasser 1971b, 153-154)

5. *The Missionary Between the Times* by R. Pierce Beaver (1968) which: "...calls for the rejection of Willingen's (1952) [a reference to the WCC meeting in a city by that name in Germany] exaggerated declaration that 'Every Christian is a Missionary.'" There is an apostolate of God. He also presses us to examine critically all our old methods. "New forms, new ways and new means for world mission must be devised." Only by far more vigorous service and more effective ministry will the missionary movement "become recognized as representative of a supranational universal community of believers in which peoples of the East, West, and the Third World unite and point the way to their brethren!" (Glasser 1971b, 153-154)

[18] Glasser appears to suggest in this introduction that the conveners of GL '71 desired delegates to be exposed to writers from different backgrounds, and these five books were chosen. Winter is noted as the Director of WCL, who arranged for the reprint of these five out-of-print books.

[19] April 27, 1971 letter from Donald McGavran to the Mission Faculty, 1. Copy of this two page letter and an attached two-page "assignment" sheet listing each topic and writer is in Winter's E-17 writing file.

...the constant friction between the educated leaders of the Africansian denominations and the missionaries and the missions. The work of many missions is frustrated. Time is spent in working out mutual adjustments not in multiplying churches. Constitutions are written and rewritten. A few missionaries are sent home because they 'cannot work with the nationals.' Other missionaries stand around on one foot and then another thinking that the main task of the missionary in 1971 is to keep out of the way of the national.[20]

McGavran continues, including a quote from Norman Cummings, who was helping organize GL 71, as saying, "I fear a panic about church-mission relationships. 'GL 71' may degenerate into a discussion of mechanical arrangements between church and mission which entirely by-pass the task that both Church and mission exist to do – disciple the nations."[21] McGavran was reminding his faculty that there are an "unimaginable number of men who know nothing of Jesus Christ" and who have no relationship to existing churches.[22] That article led the issue, and was called: *Will Green Lake Betray the Two Billion?*[23] (McGavran, 1977, 149-157)

---

[20] April 27, 1971 letter from Donald McGavran to the Mission Faculty, 1. McGavran liked to put together the continents, and is probably better known for, Latafriasia.

[21] April 27, 1971 letter from Donald McGavran to the Mission Faculty, 1. Apparently this was an indirect quote from Cummings.

[22] This was from an outline of articles to be written, which was attached to the April 27, 1971 letter from Donald McGavran to the Mission Faculty, 1. Articles written by others at the Fuller SWM were:

1. "Since We Are All Growing Older, Let's Grow Bolder!" by Arthur Glasser. Glasser included a summary of the "multibook" Crossroads in Missions, and challenged the mission leaders attending GL 71 to be bold in new mission work as they lead their organizations into the future. (Glasser, 1971a, 153-155)

2. "An Anthropologist Looks at Mission-Church Transition" by Alan Tippett, who argues for effective inter-relationships between the national church and the missionary, and how that can increase the effectiveness of both. (Tippett, 1971a, 155-157)

3. "Younger Churches – Missionaries and Indigeneity" by Charles Kraft, who argued that a church can be self governing but still not indigenous. Our goal is that they think of the Lord as their own, not a god shaped by outsiders. (Kraft, 1971, 159-161)

4. "Occupy Till I Come" by Edward Murphy, who closes the entire issue with a focus on the need to recognize that the Bible and Christ himself commands us to go. Certainly, in that going, we must avoid paternalistic attitudes and work effectively with the nationals. (Murphy, 1971, 161-162)

[23] *Church Growth Bulletin*, July 1971, 6:6, 1. In 1977, this was also published in the Second Consolidated Volume of the *Church Growth Bulletin*.

The article by Winter was: "Churches Instead of Missions?" (Winter, 1971a) In it, he echoes some of the arguments of McGavran and Glasser regarding the need of the unevangelized and he points out the potential over-emphasis on the national church being independent from the missionaries or mission organizations.

To counter an overemphasis on organizations during that period, he points out two errors. First, he observed in his own work in Guatemala that as the established national church grows and takes leadership of the ministry they tend to forget the mission agency without which they would not have come into being. "The first error puts so much emphasis upon the wonder and joy and rightful selfhood of the new national church that it seems to argue for the demise of the mission agency that was instrumental in its creation." Winter called this the "unbiblical syndrome of 'focusing on the one sheep that is found rather than on the ninety-nine that are still lost.'" There are, in fact, some two billion untouched people he notes. Every church, western or not, needs help and can offer help.[24] (Winter, 1971a)

The second error is "far more subtle than the existence of the two billion non-Christians." Since we can easily see the need for on-going outreach, arguing for helping one another in that worldwide task seemed obvious. But, "The first error wars against the Western-based missionary society and says it isn't needed. The second error is the strange assumption that not even younger churches need missionary societies. Illogically it is assumed that once an overseas national church is well planted, it will just naturally grow and reach out and finish the job." This, he notes, even happens within the faith mission tradition as well as the denominations "back home [that] may have grown cold." (Winter, 1971a)

For older denominational missions, the situation is different. The churches they established were eventually encouraged to establish their own denominational boards of both home and "foreign missions." Winter notes, "This seems to be the logical thing, but in most cases it has been too late and too little." Winter questioned some of the apparent assumptions of these groups, whose practice seemed to imply that a centralized structure was the only way to accomplish the task of missions. He argues, "the fullest expression of Christian faith and obedience in the lands of the younger

---

[24] Quoting R. Pierce Beaver, Winter adds, "Effective mission throughout the world in the future demands the giving up of false pride and the baseless assertion of full sufficiency. There is no church large or small, ancient or very young, in any country today which appears thoroughly adequate to its responsibilities in evangelism and ministry." (Winter, 1970b) Winter does not footnote this quote. Its source is not known and not verified.

churches will require the development of semi-autonomous national mission societies, not just national churches nor even national churches with centralized mission boards." Winter concluded with the summary, "For twenty-five years we learned that missions cannot take the place of churches. Now we must understand that the opposite is also true."[25] (Winter, 1971a, 159)

The Planting of Younger Missions - 1972

Finally, in the fall of 1971, 400 "carefully selected mission and church leaders" connected with the U.S. mission associations (IFMA and EFMA) gathered for the Green Lake event.[26] In a follow-up event, a handful of mission leaders and scholars met to further discuss issues raised during GL 71. Winter presented a paper at this event called "The Planting of Younger Missions". (Winter, 1972e, 133 italics his) which addressed an issue that was not raised at the conference. He wrote:

[As] GL '71 unfolded, we all began to realize that what has carelessly been termed "church/mission relations" really refers, it turns out, to mission/church relations: the relations between an American *mission* and an overseas national *church* (which is probably the product of the U.S. mission's work over the years). To these mission/church relations, GL '71 added church/mission relations, namely, the relation of the *churches* back home to the *missions* they support. (Winter, 1972e, 133 italics his)

---

[25] The Evangelical Missions Information Service planning group for GL 71 also recommended Winter's book, *The Twenty-Five Unbelievable Years* (Winter and Latourette, 1970), which sought to update Latourette's work on the expansion of Christianity covering the years 1945 to 1970. (Gerber, 1971, 23)

[26] Referred to as GL 71.

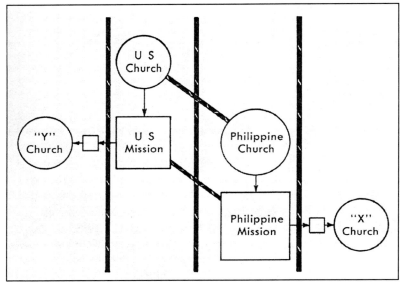

Figure 14 – Third-Generation Church Planting[27]

Winter believed he saw a glaring error in the GL 71 discussion related to mission outreach. He used the Conservative Baptist Association in the Philippines as an example:

> ...there is no question about the clarity of purpose in church-planting. The goal is an autonomous, nationally run Conservative Baptist Association in the Philippines or perhaps an even larger association including other Baptists. 'Some day' this Philippine association may sprout its own home mission society or foreign mission society. But when? How will it go about it? Why not now? Why is not a nationally run mission as clearly and definitely a goal as is church-planting? That is, why do the various goals prominent in everyone's mind not include both *church*-planting and *mission*-planting? And why do we talk so little about such things? Or, to take another tack, why is it that only the foreign missionary (no doubt not by plan but by default) has

---

[27] Winter's description for Figure 14 is: "Both national church and national mission are now autonomous. The national mission establishes relations as an equal with the United States mission, and both it and the United States mission (elsewhere) plant churches across new cultural barriers. This is 'third-generation church planting' for the United States mission and 'second-generation church-planting' for the Philippine mission." (Winter, 1972e,135)

the right, the duty or the opportunity to 'go here or to go
there and plant a church'? (Winter, 1972e, 130-131 italics his)
Missions failed to see their *own* structure as a part of the kind of what
should be established as new churches were started globally. Winter
envisioned a younger church would establish a younger mission, which, in
turn, would reach out and start new churches, as shown in Figure 14.

The Two Structures of God's Redemptive Mission - 1973

Winter presented further refinements of these ideas in the paper "The
Two Structures of God's Redemptive Mission," first presented on
September 1, 1973, at the All-Asia Mission Consultation in Seoul,
Korea.[28] The event drew together mission leaders from around Asia to
further collaboration and effectiveness. It drew 26 Asian mission leaders
from thirteen countries, plus some from the U.S. These mission leaders
gathered around the purpose to: (1) promote cooperation for Asian mission
activities among Asian countries; (2) seek cooperation between the East
and West; (3) form an organization to coordinate efforts among Asian
countries. (Chun, 1975, 8)

One of the main outcomes of this event was to bring the awareness of
non-Western missionaries into sharper focus, especially in Asia.[29]

Motivation for talking about the idea of specifically establishing
mission structures was fueled by recent events in missions in Asia. A report
on the event noted that 100 agencies had been established in Asia over the
previous twenty years, but "there had been no conference during the
previous two decades which was specifically geared to Asian missions and
missionaries at home and on the field."[30] (Chun, 1975, 7)

In his presentation, Winter made the case that New Testament
patterns followed Old Testament culture and customs. The first structure
"so fondly called 'the New Testament Church' is basically a Christian
synagogue." It "was essentially built along Jewish synagogue lines and it

---

[28] This was edited slightly and first printed in the journal *Missiology* in 1974. (Winter,
1974b)

[29] The event was reported in an article in *EMQ* called, "Overseas Churches Starting to
Send Missionaries" by Clyde W. Taylor. (1974, 62-63) Taylor was the General Director of
the National Association of Evangelicals at the time.

[30] The All Asia Mission Consultation was followed by weeks of intensive training for
64 Asian mission candidates. Winter and the others invited assisted the Asian leaders of
this training by leading segments of it.

contained the community of the faithful in its entirety in any given place." Of course, it grew in such a way that allowed Greeks to be part of it. It did not require them to take on "the ritual provisions of the Mosaic Law." (1)[31]

The second "structure" also had background in Jewish history. This was a group that banded together in missionary endeavors to expand the work of God. The Pharisees had a small group from their membership who could be called Jewish evangelists, who "travel land and sea to win a single convert."[32] The details are not clear beyond this one reference in the NT, neither are the details of how the church was to form, "the absence of any such definition implies the pre-existence of an understood pattern of relationship, whether in the case of the church or the missionizing team which Paul formed." Paul's team, "can be considered a prototype of all subsequent missionary endeavors, organized out of committed, experienced workers who affiliated themselves <u>as a second decision beyond that of becoming a Christian</u> and joining a fellowship of Christians." (1-2)

Winter emphasized that both were borrowed patterns.

> The profound implication is that the New Testament is trying to show us <u>how to borrow effective patterns</u>: it is trying to free all future missionaries from the need to follow the precise <u>forms</u> of the Jewish synagogue and missionary band, and to choose comparable indigenous structures in the countless new situations across history and around the world, which will correspond faithfully to the <u>function</u> of the patterns Paul employed, not their <u>form</u>! (2-3)

The bulk of Winter's presentation was a recounting of how these structures impacted the expansion of Christianity through the centuries.[33]

---

[31] From a copy of the typewriter written paper, "The Two Structures of God's Redemptive Mission." This was probably the version of the paper presented by Winter at the event in Asia. This was in his writing files, #E004, 1. While a later version appears in the book *Perspectives on the World Christian Movement* (Winter and Hawthorne, 2009) page references that immediately follow are from this typewritten paper unless noted otherwise.

[32] Matthew 23:15. This was a negative illustration of Jesus pointing out the way the Pharisees corrupted others. They were trying to extend their understandings about God. Winter used it often to point out the history of the "missionary" work of the Pharisees before the NT period.

[33] He compared the diocesan structure with the monastic structure during the first one thousand years of church history, demonstrating "the fact that it would be hard to imagine the vital continuity of the Christian tradition across the centuries apart from this [sodality] structure." (4) He argued similarly from the history of the Medieval period, noting that as the Roman Empire in the West began to decline, so did the church or diocesan pattern. "The monastic, or sodality, pattern turned out to be much more durable and as a result gained greater importance in the early medieval period than it might have otherwise." (5)

Winter saw the fact that Protestants were reluctant to embrace sodalities as a key factor delaying outreach and expansion. The attempt to do without the sodality was "the greatest error of the Reformation and the greatest weakness of the resulting Protestant tradition. Had it not been for the Pietist movement, the Protestants would have been totally devoid of any organized renewing structures within their tradition." (7-8) It was almost three hundred years until William Carey wrote his booklet on the "use of means," which Winter linked specifically to the need for a sodality. An increasing number of societies were formed in the late 1700s and early 1800s.[34]

Winter hoped this presentation would "promote better understanding and harmony between these two structures." Relating to his Asian audience, he wondered when the younger churches in the "mission territories of the non-Western world" would realize "there need to be sodality structures, such as William Carey's 'use of means,' in order for church people to reach out in vital initiatives in mission, especially cross-cultural mission." (10-11) He also wondered if, as they go out in mission, they will go beyond simply planting churches to include establishing sodalities. The tendency was that as churches grow, they "characteristically overlook the emphasis of this paper."[35] (11)

By the end of the period, both the diocese and monastery were able to function without debilitating conflict, which "is perhaps the most significant single characteristic of this phase of the world Christian movement and continues to be Rome's greatest organizational advantage to this day." (6) Winter illustrated the impact of the sodalities with the fact that it was "Hildebrand or Gregory VII who brought the ideals and commitments and discipline of the monastic movement straight into the Vatican as had happened many times before and would happen many times again." (6)

[34] Since they were an association of ministries connected to a denomination, (but not involved in the day-to-day life of the "diocese") the audience appears to have been very friendly toward the idea.
The Nineteenth Century moved the Protestants into active engagement in mission while conversely Catholic mission energy was at particularly low ebb. Winter wrote: "In this one century Protestants, building on unprecedented world expansion of the West, caught up with the eighteen centuries of earlier mission efforts. There is simply no question that what was done in this century moved the Protestant stream from a self-contained impotent European backwater into a world force in Christianity. Looking back from where we stand today it is hard to believe how recently the Protestant movement has become prominent." (8)

[35] Another concern expressed in this presentation was the issue of control. "The same structural danger of secularization exists today whenever the special concerns of a mission sodality fall under the complete domination of an ecclesiastical government, representing as the latter inevitably does the much broader and no doubt mainly inward concerns of a large body of all kinds of Christians." (Winter, 1974b, 129-130)

Winter wrote and spoke about this topic in other venues and the motivation behind his thinking became clearer. On April 19, 1980, he presented "The Modality – Sodality Concept" to the meeting of the Affiliation of Lutheran Movements Theological Conference.[36] (Winter, 1980)

He connected the tensions between sodalities and modalities to issues within denominational circles to express recurring themes of tension:

> I'm a Presbyterian, not a Lutheran, but we've got the same basic problem you do. We have beautiful organizational structures, but somehow there is not an exact coordination of the power of the Holy Spirit with those structures. There is not a one-to-one equivalency between our human organizational structures—what we ordinarily call the *Church*, a misnomer I believe—and the evidence and power of the Holy Spirit working among us and in our hearts. It is not possible for there to be a one-to-one correspondence, and as a result there is very obviously a potential conflict between the spirit and the structure. (Winter, 1980, 2)

The "movements" within the church structures were often "the result of the Spirit of God leading some individual or group of individuals to do something that was not on the agenda of an existing structure." (Winter, 1980, 5) Winter saw the split between Paul and Barnabas in Acts 15 as positive in that it resulted in the formation of two different movements. He mentioned that church historian Kenneth Scott Latourette "raised eyebrows when he said that a proliferation of movements is the sure sign of the vitality of the Christian tradition at any point in history."[37] (Winter, 1980, 6)

Illustrating from his own Presbyterian connections, by this time Winter had started four different "movements" under Chapter 28 provisions in the Presbyterian constitution as mentioned. These fit the picture of sodality he was proposing: they were apparently started as a way to accomplish a specific vision and were recognized within the denomination but were not directly under the denomination's organizational control. For example, the Presbyterian Frontier Fellowship focused on mobilizing Presbyterian evangelicals for the purpose of reaching cultures without the gospel.

Winter noted that there was "nothing necessarily holy about a sodality in itself. I do believe, however, that when the sense of the holy invades our

---

[36] This document was in Winter's file E136.

[37] Winter did not footnote this comment, nor say it was a direct quote.

own lives, we will find voluntary initiatives that the lumbering democratic structures of our churches can't ever keep up with." (Winter, 1980, 12)

Ghana: Preparation for Marriage Experience - 1978

Winter used the analogy of a marriage to describe the merger of the World Council of Churches (WCC) and the International Missionary Council (IMC).[38] The "engagement" period began in 1948, when both organizations expressed a desire to be "in association with" each other. The actual "marriage" occurred when they merged, which took place in Delhi in 1961. The marriage ceremony was followed by a "honeymoon" phase, which was reflected in the relationships Winter observed when he attended the 1963 Mexico meeting of the WCC, as conference staff. Finally, reflected in meetings such as those called by Billy Graham in Berlin in 1966 and Lausanne in 1974, Winter saw the children or perhaps step-children of the marriage of the WCC and IMC. In the article where Winter describes his marriage analogy, he argues that there should be an ongoing distinction between church and mission agencies. He reflected on recent historical events that followed as consequences of the much-disputed merger of the WCC and the IMC and finds justification for separate structures.

However, rather than merely taking a negative perspective on what many considered the "absorption" of the IMC into the WCC, Winter begins by giving a succinct biblical argument for two structures:

> When Paul and Barnabas departed from Antioch, their move and their new organizational relationship to each other were not regarded as a breakdown of unity in the body of Christ, but did clearly constitute a separation of functions. The new missionary team that was formed carried all the authority of a travelling church, and in this sense foreshadowed the Roman Catholic missionary strategy involving the appointment of apostolic bishops (apostolic vicars). But both organizational forms, the team and the church, were "church;" both the stationary Christian synagogue that remained in Antioch and the travelling missionary team (which, note well, no longer took its orders from the Antioch church) were essential elements in the body

---

[38] The IMC became the new Commission on World Mission and Evangelism within the WCC in 1961.

of Christ, the people of God of the New Covenant, and were
equally the church. (Winter, 1978, 339)

As he had done in other situations, Winter draws generously from
others whose points of view help bolster his argument. In this case he
draws on Lesslie Newbigin and his comments to the General Assembly of
the United Presbyterian Church in the USA. Winter believed Newbigin
was well qualified to understand missions as he was the director of the
IMC from 1958-1963. He quoted Newbigin, and then three distinct tasks:

> We have to begin making some verbal distinctions if we
> are going to have our thinking clear. The first is between
> *mission* and *missions*. When we speak of the *mission of the
> Church* we mean everything that the Church is sent into the
> world to do—preaching the Gospel, healing the sick, caring
> for the poor, teaching the children, improving international
> and interracial relations, attacking injustice—all of this and
> more can rightly be included in the phrase *the Mission of the
> Church*.
>
> But within this totality there is a narrower concern which
> we usually speak of as *missions*. Let us, without being too
> refined, describe this narrower concern by saying: it is the
> concern that in the places where there are no Christians there
> should be Christians. And let us narrow the concern down
> still further and say that within the concept of *missions* there is
> the still narrower concern which we can call—or used to
> call—*Foreign Missions*—which is the concern that Jesus
> should be acknowledged as Lord by the whole earth.[39]
> (Newbigin 1960, 23)

Winter identified these three tasks as (1) the work of the church, (2)
evangelism, and (3) frontier evangelism. "But" Winter pointed out that in
the transition of the WCC and IMC into a single organization, "there
would come a time when neither the prominence of this specific mission
structure nor the specific task of evangelism could be easily discerned."
(Winter, 1978, 342) In other words, two of the three tasks became
obscured in the further development of the ministry of the WCC. Winter
suggested that there were a number of small decisions leading up to and
during the meetings of the WCC in Ghana which inevitably resulted in
this loss.

Protestant mission societies began to proliferate in the twentieth
century and were growing in size. Many of these were connected with

---

[39] Italics added by Winter in his article. (Winter, 1978, 340)

specific home churches or denominations and were focused on establishing local churches in other countries, along with other ministries. But rarely did these other ministries include the establishment of indigenous missions organizations. Rather, as those indigenous churches were established and grew, they took over the work of the missionaries and formed relationships with other churches. Over time church councils and national councils of churches developed. And since these were to reflect the indigenous churches, expatriate missionaries were not included in the decisions of these councils. Winter recognized this pattern well, since he had experienced it first hand in Guatemala.

While Winter saw the value of the new Christians in a nation taking leadership for the indigenous church, he argued strongly for the need for missions to continue to press into new areas and cultures, where, as Newbigin noted, there were not Christians. He wrote:

> At Ghana, then, there was an irreversible element which the delegates had no power to change. It is true that there had been no preparation of pro and con document, as Max Warren pointed out. But the overarching *fait accompli*, which was hardly the fault of either the IMC or the WCC leadership, and indeed was due to mission field successes, was the "great new fact of our time"[40] …the rise of the younger churches. Yet the very existence of those precious churches crowded out the concept of representation for indigenous mission agencies in the receiving countries, even though it proved the power of the gospel and the workability and legitimacy of the missionary enterprise. The cultivation of these tender plants became the major focus of Western mission energies (less and less the penetration of new frontiers). … This is all very understandable since conventional mission perspectives did not include the concept of the very indigenous mission societies that could have possibly formed missionary councils parallel to the missionary councils of the Western countries. (Winter, 1978, 344)

The probable options of the faltering missions movement among these new churches were:[41]

---

[40] Winter specifically referenced this phrase to William Temple's comments at a Madras WCC meeting. He does not give the source document.

[41] Winter noted that he read the entire, verbatim transcript of the Ghana meeting as found in the WCC files in Geneva. He found only one presenter, John V. Taylor, who talked about the ideas of the mission fields establishing their own mission agencies.

1) only Westerners could be missionaries, or that 2) only Westerners could learn how to run missionary societies, or that 3) non-Western churches should discreetly wait 250 years before starting missionary societies like the Western (Protestant) churches did, or that 4) missionary societies ought not to exist, or most likely, 5) that the new churches would somehow automatically carry forward missionary theory and practice without being instructed, or 6) something else. (Winter, 1978, 344-345)

Those who were calling for a moratorium on missionaries after Ghana (such as John Gatu from Kenya) made sense to Winter, *if* one understood the local situation. He suggested Gatu's plea as well as Emerito Nacpil's "Mission but not Missionaries" was an "eminently reasonable proposal that missionaries, however useful they may be in reaching non-Christian populations, are not always a benefit to well-established younger churches." (Winter, 1978, 346) It was reasonable because the Philippines, where Nacpil was from was 97% "Christian." Kenya also had high Christian populations. "Not being involved in mission structures of their own, the non-Western churchmen could not easily have been expected to understand the unique purposes of mission societies, Western or otherwise." (Winter, 1978, 348)

Thus the IMC was not seen as a necessary but separate arm. It understood itself as representing mission structures or councils of missions around the world and so it was unable to maintain that distinctive when it was integrated into the WCC.

Winter wanted mission structures to be recognized as crucial for frontier work.[42] He sought to argue his point without offending WCC leadership, which he had done before. He expressed his hope for the future of the WCC:

The Ghana decision may have failed to convert the WCC into a mission organization but it has succeeded in taking mission into the very heart of the WCC. The WCC has always carried forward the first of Newbigin's three tasks—*the mission of the church*. Nairobi stressed his second—the concern for evangelism. We hope that Melbourne, 1980

---

[42] Especially where the church was not yet present.

will stress the third—the remaining frontiers. (Winter, 1978, 352)[43]

Protestant Mission Societies: The American Experience - 1979[44]

In 1973 Winter began working on an article of this title for inclusion in a book that was to be published. Ross P. Scherer of the department of Sociology at Loyola University of Chicago was editing the work.[45] The book, *American Denominational Organization*, (Scherer, 1980) included perspectives from a range of church backgrounds, including Roman Catholic, main line Protestant denominations and evangelicals.[46] As a result of delays, Winter was able to edit and add to the paper over a relatively long period of time. Much of the material formed the basis for a talk Winter gave in 1976, with the text of the talk appearing in the journal *Missiology* in the April 1979 issue.[47]

---

[43] Winter saw the meetings in Berlin in 1966 and in Lausanne in 1974 each as a "second child" of the Ghana marriage of the WCC and the IMC, as natural consequences of their union.

[44] An alternate title is: "Protestant Mission Societies and The 'Other Protestant Schism'" a chapter in the book, *American Denominational Organization* by Ross P. Scherer. (1980)

[45] A number of letters between Scherer and Winter exist from between May 1973 and July 1977. The article first appeared in *Missiology*, April 1979 (7:2:137-178). The book appeared in 1980. In Winter's computer database listing of his writing, he wrote in a field in his computer database:

"The second name [the section title above] actually came first. It constituted the (outgoing) Presidential Address of the American Society of Missiology on the occasion of the first and only joint meeting of the American Society of Missiology and the International Association for Mission Studies, at Maryknoll, NY, in June of 1976. I had written it up for the book, *American Denominational Organization*, by Ross Scherer, but when that was delayed I used the material, with considerable revision in a few places, for the Presidential Address, which actually came out first, in *Missiology*."

The version from *Missiology* is the one referred to in this section. It has an additional section at the end called, "Hardening the Breach," as well as a conclusion.

[46] The book was delayed in production and at least one publisher backed out of the project because of the length of the final work.

[47] William Carey Library eventually published the book in 1980. Winter told this author, when working on non-profit organization issues with the U.S. government's Internal Revenue Service, that WCL published the book in order to have a book in print that gives evidence that argued for the validity of Protestant religious missionary orders, similar to the Catholic orders. Winter's article in the book is the Protestant complement to the chapter that preceded his, which was: "Catholic Religious Orders in Sociological Perspective" by Thomas M. Gannon, S.J.

While Winter had left Fuller SWM and full-time teaching by that time, his thinking on this issue continued to develop. His research files for the article are quite extensive and include careful statistical work on select Protestant missionary organizations as well as data from the member missions of the EFMA and IFMA.

Winter begins his *Missiology* article by pointing out the "disturbing thought" that he had when, as a Presbyterian seminary student, he discovered from a "*Baptist* writer" (Kenneth Scott Latourette) that, "for all intents and purposes, the early band of highly evangelistic *Methodist* circuit riders adhered to characteristically *Roman Catholic* vows of poverty, chastity, and obedience." (Winter, 1979b, 139 emphasis original) As Winter discovered through his own study and pilgrimage, "the emergence of the Protestant mission society as a parallel to the Roman Catholic order despite the fact that within the Protestant stream of history it is still viewed as a major yet somehow 'foreign' structure." (Winter, 1979b, 139 emphasis original)

Similar to the patterns seen in Catholic order history, Protestant structures sometimes lost their vitality and thus required renewal. In other situations, entirely new societies came into being in order to meet specific needs. "Protestantism as a movement has to a considerable extent survived both *in spite of* and curiously *because of* the constant *emergence* and re-emergence of *new groups*..." (1979b, 140-141)

Winter concludes his introduction by expressing one of his theses for the article: "The writer is convinced that the *Roman Catholic* tradition, in its much longer experience with the phenomenon of the 'order,' embodies *a superior structural approach to both renewal and mission*." Winter felt it reasonable to attribute the survival of the Roman Catholic Church "into the high medieval period as being to a considerable extent the result of the sheer durability and spiritual and Biblical vitality of the earlier monastic tradition." While he recognizes the excesses of both groups noting, "on balance I am irretrievably convinced that the inherent *decentralization, mobility and eliteness* of the Roman religious communities *must urgently be recovered by the Protestants.*" (1979b, 140-141, emphasis original)

Winter used this 39-page journal article to present his case to Protestant church and mission leaders. He emphasized the need for both the sodality and the modality, suggesting that the commonly used term "para-church" for the sodality "may even be questioned if neither structure is any more normative, and more *church*, than the other. (Why not call churches *para-missions!*)" And, "...to make either of the two structures central and the other secondary, as the term *para-church* seems to imply, is

probably unwise. The two are indeed interdependent and the evi
history do not allow us to understand either as complete wit
other." (1979b, 143-144 emphasis original)

His first example from history is drawn from William Carey and his
book *An Enquiry into the Obligation of Christians to Use Means for the
Conversion of the Heathens*. (1891) He expressed the expectation that
Carey's "tightly reasoned essay" may some day be seen as "the most
influential single piece of literature in the worldwide expansion of
Protestantism since the Reformers." (1979b, 145) In a footnote to that
statement, Winter recognizes that Carey was not original in his work or his
essay. There were already mission societies in the U.S. The Moravians had
preceded Carey by many decades and Justinian Welz had sought similar
influence in his work in the Lutheran sphere more than a hundred years
earlier. "If Carey's *Enquiry* was immensely influential, it is to his honor, not
so much to his credit. It was well done, but so was what Welz did. Carey's
material simply played an infinitely greater role. *The Protestant missionary
movement is in some ways as important as Protestantism itself.*" (1979b,
176n2)

That footnote statement clearly showed what Winter held of high
value: the mission societies that "burst" on the scene after Carey. While
church structures (modalities) have an important role to play, the "average"
local church does not have the ability to make a lasting impact on
something as complex and yet essential as Bible translation, for example.[48]

Winter details the outline of Carey's "remarkable" approach, tracing
the impact of it on the Protestant tradition and its outreach. "Protestants
suddenly discovered how to sprout the same kind of organizational arms
and legs that were not only to carry them around the *world* in the extension
of their faith but also potentially to rebuild and renew their home
traditions from *within*." (1979b, 145) Winter presented the case for the
wide-ranging impact of sodalities throughout Protestant church history,
which eventually touched not only the so-called "faith" missions, such as
Hudson Taylor's China Inland Mission, but also the National and World
Council of Churches.

Winter believed that the original Protestant "revolt" was largely a
cultural decentralization, one in which the Northern European, non-
Romanized groups became decoupled from the culture that was originally

---

[48] Winter often used this particular area as an illustration of the nature of sodalities who
focus on one area and become experts in that skill or task.

focused in the Mediterranean, Romanized populations of Southern Europe. (1979b, 149)[49]

Much of the rest of the article uses examples of the different types of relationships between field mission work and the denominational organizations from which they started. He listed four ways denominational missions relate to their parent organization, as in Figure 15.

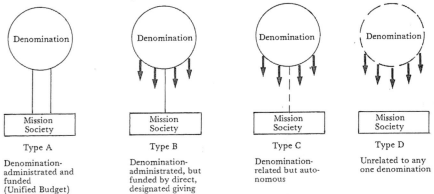

Figure 15 – *Relationship Between Church and Para-Church Organizations (Winter, 1979b, 150)*

Winter portrayed the trend "*away from* the nearly universal use of voluntary societies as a means of active service *toward* the use of denominational boards, and then a more recent *reversal* of that trend." (1979b, 151) See Figure 16.

The result of this historical process was that North American agencies fell into one of two categories: "Type A: denominationally connected" or "Type D: completely unrelated denominationally." At the same time, European missions and Roman Catholic were of the "Type C nature: Denominationally related but autonomous." Winter mentions only one North American mission structure of which he was aware which had

---

[49] In a paper Winter returned again to this theme, writing that the Reformation was really when, "our faith went from Latin Christianity to German Christianity." (2003b, 80) Winter saw this as the second Reformation. The first was what Winter called the shift from Jewish clothing to Greek and Latin clothing during the time of the NT. The document he wrote was originally called "Eleven Frontiers of Perspective." (Winter, 2003b, part one) and (Winter, 2003c, part two) Later he added another and changed the title to "Twelve Frontiers of Perspective." (Winter, 2008) It describes twelve major shifts in his own thinking over his life up to that point.

denominational connections, but was autonomous: Conservative Baptist
Foreign Mission Society.[50]

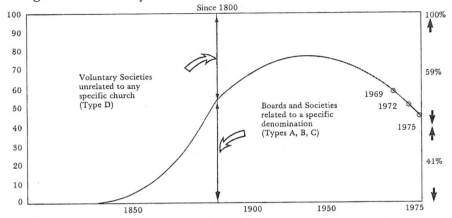

*Figure 16 – Proportion of American Missionaries Under Voluntary Societies and
Under Denominational Boards (Winter, 1979b, 151)*

Winter then detailed the impact and growth of the "faith missions."
He covered the overall increase in the number of organizations and also
selected a few fast-growing, large groups which were either new or whose
parent denomination was relatively new. He added two additional figures,
with the same scale, to demonstrate (1) the growth of different types of
mission societies (Figure 17) and, (2) the overall size of church-related
versus independent societies (Figure 18).

---

[50] The CBFMS has changed its name to World Venture. Winter's denominational
background shaped his thinking in this area, and the leaders of the CBFMS seemed to
appreciate Winter's thinking and activism. The head of the mission often participated in
activities in which Winter was also involved, such as the International Society of Frontier
Missiology.

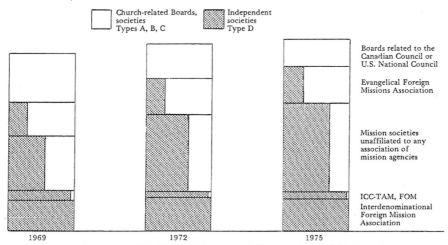

Figure 17 – Growth of Different Types and Categories of Mission Societies
(Winter, 1979b, 153)

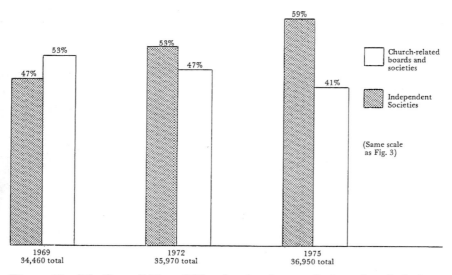

Figure 18 – The Overall Size of Church-related versus Independent Societies
(Winter, 1979b, 153)

There were a multitude of factors that brought about this major shift. They included: 1) denominational splits over various factors such as doctrinal purity; 2) the success of church growth creating more confidence about the future of Christianity and, thus, the creation of competition between denominations; and, 3) the rise of cross-denominational organizations, even while denominations split or were reducing traditional mission work. (1979b, 154-157)

Winter used five questions to help him bring order to the tremendous variety within Protestant mission structures. He associated 19 response categories with the five questions, as detailed below. In his writing Winter used specific agencies as examples, illustrating how they or their work could be characterized by the responses to these questions embodied by their agencies: (1979b, 157-161)

A. How closely is an agency related to the organized church?

1. Church-related/independent (ABC vs. D)
2. Denominational/interdenominational (ABC vs. D)
3. Intradenominational/interdenominational (C vs. D)

B. How is the agency related to churches that exist in the field of its mission efforts?

4. Church planting agencies/service agencies
5. International church/national church

C. How is the agency related to other agencies?

6. Affiliated/unaffiliated

D. How is the agency structured internally?

7. Board-governed/member-governed/donor-governed
8. Centralized/decentralized administration
9. Polynational/mononational
10. "Home office" in one country/"homes offices" in many countries.
11. Formal/non-formal

E. For what function is the agency designed?

12. Home missions/foreign missions
13. Sending/non-sending
14. Church planting/service (same as above)
15. Evangelistic/Christian presence
16. Institutional/non-institutional
17. Cross-cultural/mono-cultural
18. E-1/E-2/E-3
19. First stage Missions/Second stage Missions/Consolidation Missions

Winter discusses points seventeen and eighteen in more detail, in part because they needed more explanation. Point seventeen was crucial in his argument, because this was what was declining in many denominational circles, while their work was increasingly in political or social areas.[51] In 1974, Winter had presented the "E-Scale," which he briefly explained here.[52]

Winter calls point nineteen "a most important distinction." At this point in his life, he was focused on challenging mission societies to reach out to totally non-Christian groups. He notes here that "...well over ninety percent of all American missionary effort is now concentrated on churches established yesterday rather than upon the penetration of totally non-Christian groups where there is not yet any well-established, truly indigenous church."[53] (1979b, 160)

The similarities between Roman Catholic and Protestant societies were mentioned. Other than the concept of celibacy, many characteristics that are common to both mission structures are listed. He explains the Protestant equivalent of the Catholic vow of poverty, in the pay structure, or what Winter calls "parity" of support: people are paid based on need and not on position, education, or tenure. For Protestants, it is not seen as a spiritual virtue, as the Catholics would, so much as a pragmatic, "making the money go further" issue. (1979b, 164) He describes the discipline of the people in these organizations as well as the durability of the organization in some detail.

The article closes with a list of suggested lessons that denominational and non-denominational structures could learn from each other, as well as from Catholic circles, stressing the importance of each group learning to understand the others and building closer relations across churches in mission outreach.[54]

---

[51] Winter's points here, and at other places in the article, reflected the perspective of Fuller's SWM at the time. McGavran said similar things, at times alternately pointing out the danger and the value of "social" work.

[52] As noted earlier, see the full E-Scale description in Appendix O. Here he summarized: "E-1 means evangelism where the only barrier is the 'stained glass barrier' – the special culture of the church. E-2 means there is an additional, serious culture barrier, but at least some significant common denominator. E-3 means the work is being done in a totally different culture. For example, reaching Navajo tribal people in the U.S. may be for Anglo-Americans far more difficult than working among Spanish-speaking people in the U.S. (or Argentina) since Spanish is a sister language and Navajo is not. Thus, to an Anglo-American, the Navajos (and Zulus and Chinese) are at an E-3 distance – that is, totally different." (Winter, 1979b, 160)

[53] This subject was the focus of Winter's work after leaving the SWM. It will be discussed more fully in the next two chapters.

[54] Winter seems to be addressing his comments specifically to those of his own denominational background when he concluded the long, detailed article by stating:

Select Issues in the Sodalities and Modalities Debate

The discussion of these issue reflected events and relationships within the global church during the period of the 1960s and 1970s. Central to the discussion was the definition of *church* and *mission*. Some focused on the importance of unity if the church was to accomplish missions while others feared for the loss of a mission emphasis if the concept of church unity consumed all of what God was seen to be doing on earth. Others feared a loss of outreach through the church, if volunteerism were primarily channeled through missions organizations.

Biblical Debate

At issue was who is responsible for mission, the church (however defined) or mission organizations (whatever their mission). Like many debates over the interpretation of passages, there were people on different sides of the debate, which only informs the arguments to a point.

Bruce Camp[55] wrote a DMiss thesis in 1992 entitled *Scripturally Considered: The Local Church has Primary Responsibility for World Evangelization.* (Camp, 1992) As the title suggests, his perspective was that the local church should take the lead in missions. His study sought to cover the theological history of church as both local and universal in its outreach, and included several Biblical concepts. He believes and argues that the concept of "modalities and sodalities" originally proposed by Winter in 1973 is one that can be justified historically but not Biblically.

Camp argued against Winter's interpretation of Acts 13 and the sending out of Barnabas and Paul, and suggests that it is unwise to read theological patterns into or derive doctrine from Acts in the same way we would from didactic literature. He argues that both church *and* agency are to nurture and do outreach, and he agrees with Winter that agencies are exclusive or selective (meaning they can say "no" to people who want to join), while churches usually are not. Camp's main argument against the

---

"Rightly or wrongly, in the near future it would appear that structures not governed by denominations will have an increasingly larger role unless the older denominations can allow their mission-minded minorities to express themselves more fully than at present. Even so it is not clear whether there will be a major recovery of interest in frontiers, but there are many hopeful signs." (Winter, 1979b, 175)

[55] Camp worked as a local church mission pastor with an Evangelical Free Church and later as a consultant to local churches in missions.

concept of modalities and sodalities grows out of the New Testament metaphor of the body of Christ. Camp notes that Paul's missionary band did not have all the necessary characteristics to be a church.[56] He provides references for and discusses a number of other writers who take various sides of this issue, both in his dissertation and in a journal article that later followed.

While Winter and Camp agreed on the need to see the gospel extend to new cultures, they disagreed as to who held primary responsibility for this. Winter argued that the agency (the "mission") was responsible, while Camp believed the church was. Yet just as Camp claims Winter argued from historical pattern and not theologically, Camp's arguments are based on a historical interpretation of the church and seem, at times, more culturally based than Biblical or theological. Camp takes a modern Western view of church, as did the commentaries he referenced, thus seeing the church as an institution or structure.[57] When interpreting Acts 13, Camp did not seriously discuss the culture and background of the Biblical setting at the time of Acts and Paul. He also disagrees with Winter's point that people such as Barnabas and Paul, seeking to further God's name to new areas, are by nature and gifting different from those called to a particular local church.[58]

One of the key theologians in the west who was considering how to define "church" from a Biblical and practical perspective was Howard Snyder.[59] Snyder viewed denominational structures themselves as parachurch in nature. According to Winter, Snyder also included seminaries, Christian colleges, publishers, etc. all as "parachurch." (Winter, 1995a)[60]

---

[56] Others have argued that Paul's missionary band was also "church." Ralph Winter did not agree, instead seeing a clear difference in function between the church and the "apostolic band."

[57] There is certainly room for all kinds of "church" structure, but many of Camp's references seem to argue from what the church has become rather than from what it was in the first century, and more importantly, how the Bible portrays the concept (often as smaller groups or home fellowships).

[58] I do not deal with Camp's book in the chapter on Sodalities and Modalities.

[59] Snyder was Dean of the Free Methodist Theological Seminary in Sao Paulo, Brazil. He presented a paper at the 1974 Lausanne Congress on "The Church as God's Agent in Evangelism." He also wrote several books on issues related to church mission relations. Probably the best known and used was *Community of the King* (1977).

[60] From an addendum to his writing #E 875.6 on page 4, Comments on a paper by Professor Darrell Guder. Privately, Snyder told Winter that all structures need to be considered parachurch since the church is the people of God and the way God's people organize themselves.

Snyder clearly stressed the need for flexibility and Winter wrote a note that said that Snyder believed, "There are no Biblical structures but it is Biblical to have structures and in fact there are structures in the Bible."[61]

Winter included his view of the Biblical perspective on structures: "The Pauline task force is clearly in the Bible. It was so natural, so well known – as was the synagogue – that the pages of the N.T. do not take the time to explain exactly how it worked. (We would follow it exactly if it had!) But it was there." [62]

Definition of Church and Mission

Recognizing that some questioned the validity of independent mission agencies, Winter wrote in 1971:

> Thus one reason for the apparent neglect of the subject is the strong feeling on the part of many that the *church* is the central and basic structure, whereas the *mission* is somehow secondary or perhaps merely a temporary aid in establishing churches: the scaffolding must come down when the building is done. But is this an adequate analogy? (Winter, 1971b, 194)

There was a lot of discussion about the nature of mission at Fuller's SWM. A quote from McGavran from that time sheds light on how he as a faculty member at the SWM understood the redefinition of mission:

> Then, too, the word *mission* has been redefined. It used to mean "the proclamation of the good news to the non-Christian world," but now *mission* is held to be any activity of the church which God desires. Theologians say the mission is God's, not the church's, hence anything God wants done, anything God is doing, is part of His mission and therefore part of the mission of the church. This is a very wide mandate. The church-in-mission becomes the church-in-motion. American Christians sending their sons and daughters off to summer camp, winning their neighbors to

---

[61] Winter wrote this note in a set of hand-written notes related to his presentation at the Congress at Lausanne in 1974. This note was probably written in 1973, in part because the issue of mission structures was raised by Winter's pre-Congress paper and the main topic he was assigned: Cross-Cultural Evangelism. The packet of papers was called INGREDIENTS and this comment was on page 8.

[62] INGREDIENTS hand-written note packet from Winter's Lausanne '74 folder E-67, 11.

Christ over a cup of coffee, or conducting a sit-in in favor of school integration are said to be "in mission." (McGavran, 1972a, 189)

While Winter did not attempt to succinctly define church or mission, he did draw on historical concepts of both church and mission, in order to cause readers to ponder their own perspective on these issues and to raise new issues within the broader discussion. But he took that a step further:

We can say, for example, that churches start churches, churches start missions, and that missions start churches, but do missions start missions? Churches, they say, *are* missions, yet missions *are not* churches. The church has *a* mission, churches have missions and missions have churches. Churches are part of the church; are missions part of the church? Can we say that, as a seed gives up its life to a new plant, the mission must die when the church is born? At this point we must try to get at some underlying distinctions, even if we end up with two new terms. (Winter, 1971b, 195)

W. Harold Fuller was a missionary in Africa and leader in the Serving in Mission.[63] He sought to maintain a balance between two aspects of the church/mission discussion: the value of missionaries on the one hand, and the "issues" that come with them on the other hand; such as control and Western approaches to ministry. Fuller's response to the question: "Which is central in God's cosmic plan for this age–'the church' or 'the mission'?" is that the church/mission distinction should not be an issue. God uses both churches and missions. Rather it is the failures of people on both sides of the issue that give rise to problems. (Fuller, 1980, 71-72)

R. Pierce Beaver summarized his perspective, noting a mission could turn into churches helping churches around the world, or what he called *interchurch aid*:

... The crisis is the product of an abysmal decline in faith and concern. ... In the realm of theory one may suspect that the crisis is in part a consequence of the merger of the International Missionary Council into the World Council of Churches, as was foreseen by such persons as Max Warren and Helen Kim. They feared that local concerns, ecclesiastical bureaucrats, confessional politicking, professional evangelists in the secularized West, and the growing parochialism would conspire together drastically to reduce commitment to witness

---

[63] Earlier called the Sudan Interior Mission (SIM), a non-denominational mission that started a denomination in Nigeria.

"to the ends of the earth" and to the discipling of the nations. Ecumenical studies and discussion have come up with the slogan "Witness on Six Continents" and with a definition of mission as the church's witness to the world in the situation of each local congregation and community of Christians. The "sending" dimension of the total mission has been written off as an anachronism, and it is being phased out in a diminishing system of interchurch aid. (Beaver, 1971, 345-346)

Issues in Modalities and Sodalities[64]

Rodger C. Bassham[65] recognized that as the church became "a worldwide phenomenon," opinions about what is mission and who is responsible increased.[66] With respect to church/mission issues he pointed out the problems of various evangelical groups, who became involved in all kinds of activities around the world, some of which did not seem to

---

[64] Kenyan John Mbiti, an Anglican who authored several books related to church and mission work in Africa and African culture, wrote with regard to both the need to be engaged in the missionary task and to have unity, something he considered a major issue retarding missionary effort: "Any Christianity which does not carry out its missionary task is like a big clock which has no hands.... True mission-mindedness is one where the church is making an aggressive expansion.... From the very beginning of its history the church was mission-oriented, and if any branch of the church loses that orientation it also risks the extinction of its own life."

He continued: "Division retards growth.... Church divisions are against the proper execution of mission in our continent, and until we wipe them out or greatly reduce them we shall be fighting a losing battle.... Church division is a relic of imported Christendom and this import is costing us a high rate of customs duty.... Ecumenism is the central force in mission, for until we reach Christian unity our plans and execution of mission will be half-hearted." (Mbiti, 1971, 4-5)

[65] Bassham is from Australia and for five years was a circuit minister before obtaining his PhD at Southern Methodist University. He and his family lived in Papua New Guinea where he was lecturer in theology at the Rarongo Theological College of the United Church of PNG and the Solomon Islands.

[66] He writes: "...never has there been such intense debate and radical difference of opinion within the Church over the nature of her mission. Some argue her task is to concentrate on the work of planting churches in those areas and among those peoples where none now exist. Others contend that the central task is to do what is needed to make Christians far more authentic than they now are. They should be the serving and reconciling presence of Jesus Christ in the midst of the world's acute material and social need. Still others contend that the church should be in the vanguard of all movements struggling for justice, for human rights and for the equitable redistribution of the world's resources." (Bassham, 1979, xiii)

contribute to missions and others, which contributed negatively.[67] (Bassham, 1979, xiii)

I will address select issues of concern from these broader concepts below.

Fear of Losing "Mission" in Church Structures

The fear that mission would be lost if it were subsumed into church structures was particularly given impetus because of the merger of the International Missionary Council into the WCC. Glasser and McGavran described their perspective on how this issue became a defining one for evangelicals, one proven through history from their perspective.

> Mission societies were seen as no longer needed. Enthusiasts coined a new slogan: "The Church is mission!" And they ecstatically exclaimed, "All future growth will issue from the witnessing congregation and from an anonymous *laos*!"[68] This dismissal of parachurch agencies as irrelevant reflected abysmal indifference to two thousand years of church history with its long record of the fruitful organized labors of specific missionary vocations. (Glasser and McGavran, 1983, 95)

One student wrote an MA thesis under Glasser on the church/mission issue, which echoed concerns about the IMC/WCC merger.[69] A voice from Latin America, Orlando Costas, also reflected this concern. He wrote, "One wonders whether the WCC has not been guilty at times of quenching the energies of sodalities and thus concentrating so much on preserving the unity of its member churches (which in some cases

---

[67] He wrote, "Many evangelical mission groups function as service agencies involving literature, radio, aviation, and the like, and therefore do not directly contribute to building churches. Other independent bodies form individual congregations which do not easily relate to other churches—the problems created by this situation in Latin America, for example, have been quite undesirable, as many evangelicals testify."

[68] Laos is a transliteration of the Greek word meaning "people." It is from this word that the word laymen (lay person) or laity is derived.

[69] In his opinion, "the disastrous absorption of the International Missionary Council by the World Council of Churches in 1961 resulted in almost immediate redefinition of 'mission'. The church became mission!" (Mottinger, 1986, 2) He also quoted from the Glasser/McGavran book, perhaps reflecting the discussions at the SWM at that time, "…the missionary involvement of churches within the conciliar movement went almost immediately into sharp decline, and today their total commitment in career missionaries numbers less than one-tenth of all Protestant missionaries." (Glasser and McGavran, 1983, 95)

simply means keeping happy the ecclesiastical 'hierarchy') than in fulfilling the Great Commission." (Costas, 1974, 173) Further, he agreed with Winter in the general area of the need for mission sodalities:

> Winter is right in pointing out the unique and essential role of horizontal structures in the history of the missionary movement from the West. If it had not been for these "shock troops" the gospel would not have reached as far as it has. The Holy Spirit has used "mission sodalities" to advance the gospel as a mighty wind. Voluntary societies have provided the necessary outlet for the energies of millions of Christians. They have helped preserve "the wholesome diversity" of the body of Christ. (Costas, 1974, 168)

But Costas also expressed the concern that Winter had "established a universal generalization out of a historical particularity." He wondered if missionary societies represented God's judgment upon the church and felt they were something within God's permissive rather than his perfect will. He felt there was no NT basis for "the concept of mission apart from the church, just as there is no concept of the church apart from mission." (Costas, 1974 168, 169) He felt there was no room for sodalities and modalities working separately; they must work together as one. His "biblical-theological model of the church does not allow for a missionary structure apart from the church" because it would lead the church to lose its missionary responsibility. (Costas, 1974, 169)

Winter saw modalities and sodalities not in competition, but as complementary and fitting within their God-given functions. While Costas believed that it was unwise to "make a theological principle out of a missiological failure," (Costas, 1974, 171) Winter was not describing these issues in terms of the "universal church," as Costas and others with closer WCC connection framed the discussion. Instead Winter used examples of those who stepped out in faith against opposition within their own denominations, such as William Carey. Within his own denomination he was more likely to promote new structures within the denomination rather than looking to an external structure to meet an unmet mission need.

Each mission leader or thinker involved in the debate approached it from his or her own perspective and expanded on different aspects of the discussion. Some focused on the role(s) of churches and/or mission agencies, while others focused on the need to continue to do mission work. As the church grew around the world, it was natural to see an increase in the need to care for the church and, as some felt, to see a corresponding decrease in new mission outreach. This concern was expressed in both

WCC and evangelical circles. SWM faculty member C. Peter Wagner recognized this tension among evangelical missions as well as IMC/WCC groups. He observed that "...(this) does not mean that evangelical missions are immune to this problem, either. For different reasons, both ecumenical and evangelical missions have fallen victim to what an increasing number of missiologists are calling, 'the syndrome of church development.'" (Wagner, 1972, 1)

Wagner also pointed out that if you look through history, both recent and distant, most missions started with a focus to reach the world beyond existing mission efforts, "...whether you are ecumenical or evangelical you will, almost without exception, find that your mission started with a passion burning in the hearts of some dedicated Christian leaders to reach the fourth world."[70] (Wagner, 1972, 3) Wagner realized that evangelicals could be faulted for a similar lack of original pioneering mission work. Missionary efforts engaged around the world where there are Christians can easily lose their original missionary vision to take the gospel where there are no Christians or churches:

> ...this must be done by missionaries who will encourage in <u>deed</u> as well as <u>word</u>. Nothing avoids the syndrome of church development more than a missionary out there in the fourth world setting the example of winning men and women to Jesus Christ, planting churches, turning the churches over to the national denomination, and getting back to the fourth world as quickly as possible. (Wagner, 1972, 6)

Like Wagner, Winter also recognized that the issue of church functions overshadowing mission functions was a potential problem for both groups.

Winter strongly argued for flexibility within existing structures. He finished the *International Review of Mission* article by stating:

> The mandate for the modern church is therefore not so much to keep ahead of its constituency by trying to please everyone from a central office, but to provide the proper climate for the development of maximum creativity and participation of its membership in the many missions of the Christian mission, that is, in the necessarily many responsible mission orders of the World Church. The line between domination and encouragement will always be hard to draw, but at least the distinction between the two must be clearly understood. Only in this way will the many new missions of

---

[70] The "fourth world" is beyond the "third world" to where there was no church, no believer in that culture, no Christian resources reaching out to the people.

today and tomorrow share fully in the mission of the Church. (Winter, 1971c, 100)

Decline in Mainline Missionaries

The IMC was not established to be operational in nature. It "was to be a centre of information and consultation, a place of thought and study, organizing from time to time assemblies and conferences in which the results of years of thought and study could be pooled." (Neill, 1959, 106) These activities were performed well, according to Stephen Neill. But during WWII the IMC was forced to become operational. Many missions and missionaries were separated from their home administrative offices, and thus from financial support. The IMC developed the 'Orphaned Mission' project to transfer and raise funds. "Large sums of money were raised and most scrupulously administered; the missions were kept in being." (Neill, 1959, 107)

Neill notes that the WCC's history was parallel. Neither was it founded to be operational, but rather was to be a "meeting-point of thought, study, and prayer. But during the war the practical genius of its General Secretary was other possibilities of service" including prisoners of war and later an "immense programme of reconstruction and service to refugees in the ravaged countries." (Neill, 1959, 107) After the war, the IMC returned to its founding purposes and the Orphaned Missions project gradually was closed. But the WCC continued to develop programs on a broad scale, working in areas that no single denomination could do well alone. Some of these areas, such as the Inter-Church Aid projects, overlapped with what had been traditionally mission society work. This, it seems, became part of the impetus for the merger of the IMC into the WCC.

The difference in perspective for those aligned with the WCC and those aligned with the evangelical perspective became clearer. Some from WCC circles saw what they considered problems related to the shift in the WCC. The Right Rev. John R. Reid, Bishop of the Church of England, Diocese of Sydney wrote:

> Many evangelical Anglicans in Australia were apprehensive about the merger of the International Missionary Council and the World Council of Churches. ... The absorption of missionary work into the general ministry of the church has obscured the priority of evangelistic missionary work. By and large, missionaries from mainline denominations have decreased in numbers (up to 31% in six

years in some places) while the number of missionaries sent by voluntary agencies has greatly increased. In the USA Division of Mission (NCC), 1959-1979, the number decreased from 8279 to 4817 (-42%) while EFMA + IFMA + parachurches have increased their numbers from 25,011 to 48,677 (+95%). The latter ten times more numerous! (Reid, 1981, 276)

Reid also highlighted the problems as seen from the WCC and denominational perspective: they felt voluntary mission societies were ignoring the local church in the places where they worked. Not only had there been a great increase in agencies and churches planted around the world, but there was also a growing number of voluntary agencies and denominational agencies outside of the west in places like Africa, Asia and Latin America. Reid noted that at the Lausanne Congress in 1974 it was pointed out that there were several hundred non-Western agencies "and they will probably discover the need to care for their own missionaries who are in a different cultural context." (Reid, 1981, 279)

Fear of Losing 'Church' in Voluntary Missions Organizations

In a chapter called Church and Mission, Stephen Neill outlined events leading up to the WCC Ghana Missionary Assembly of 1958. He had summarized results from a report three years earlier on the All-African Lutheran Conference at Marangu in Tanganyika (now Tanzania). He wrote:

> In the course of my review, I expressed the opinion, derived from reading the Marangu report, that the Lutheran Churches and societies were still thinking too much in terms of 'missions', and had not yet adequately realized that we have moved forward into the period of the Church. In order to make my point with some emphasis, I ended that paragraph of my review with the words, 'Down with missions!'
>
> There is a great deal of talk today about the 'theology of mission'. This may be a good thing; but I apprehend certain dangers in both of two contrary directions. The first is that we may cast our net too wide and so make the enquiry almost meaningless. If everything is mission, nothing is mission. If everything that the Church does is to be classed as 'mission', we shall have to find another term for the Church's particular responsibility for 'the heathen', those who have never yet

heard the Name of Christ; and that, in 1959, means half the people now living on the earth.[71] (Neill, 1959, 81-82)

Neill goes on to express his perspective that modern mission societies are "in no sense a necessary part of the existence of the Church; they are simply temporary expedients for the performance of certain functions that could be performed in entirely different ways." (Neill, 1959, 82) Neill focuses on a correct theology of the Church, which "would include everything that we now regard as the special and separate problems of 'missions'..." (Neill, 1959, 82) He described how 'foreign missions' were seen as divorced from the church, and 'missionaries' regarded as a special office of the church.

Neill defines "church" within the framework of denominational structures. He details the relationship of the early missionaries of the Church Mission Society (1799) as having "no direct connection with the Church of England; their point of reference was the headquarters of the missionary society in London, and the General Secretary of the Society was their final authority." (Neill, 1959, 84) And it was "even worse on the continent of Europe" where missionary societies began to ordain their own missionaries. (Neill, 1959, 84) This, in Neill's mind, led to his negative view of missionary societies. Yet, he could see when this had gone too far, such as when a missionary had been trained in very similar ways to minister, but was not ordained by the Church, and thus could not preach in a church while on leave.[72] (Neill, 1959, 85) This, he noted, is changing, but still leaves many confused and inadvertently communicates the wrong message to the newly established churches.

Winter also discussed the subject of losing Church in mission outreach in the article "The New Missions and the Mission of the Church in 1971." (Winter, 1971c) There, he detailed the decline of the NCC mission efforts and the rise of IFMA/EFMA organizations over the period of 25 years from 1945 to 1969. The one characteristic of the nearly 150 new agencies was "the fact that almost without exception they are not part of the official government of any church denomination. Thus not only their number but their structure leads us to ask about the relation between these new "missions" and the "mission of the Church." (Winter, 1971c, 90)

Winter referred to the Roman Catholic tradition when arguing for "orders" *within* existing structures and denominations. "It is still true (and has always been the case) that almost all mission work in the Catholic

---

[71] Neill noted that he did not like the word 'heathen' realizing that, while a good word and necessary to make this point, it had taken on pejorative connotations.

[72] "Church" here means denominational structure back in the home country.

church has been based upon the *mission-order* structure. If we think of Gregory the Great sending Augustine to England, we gain a very false impression. The initiative has rarely been with the Pope." (Winter, 1971c, 94)

Historically, the larger the organization, the harder it was to gain consensus and maintain vision. In a September 1970 meeting of the NCC General Board in Phoenix, Arizona, the question arose of "what to do when there is less than full consensus for some project or some proposal for meeting a certain need. Now under study is a new policy that will quite deliberately discard the goal of full consensus where necessary." Is this good for the large denominations, Winter wondered? (Winter, 1971c, 92) Winter felt that one of the lessons in the emergence movement of new missions, "is the observation that the vision of the individuals is inevitably more specific than the total vision of any aggregate of individuals."[73] (Winter, 1971c, 97)

Winter believed that democracy did not foster new mission efforts. As denominations grow older, there was increased diversity within them and, at the same time, fewer and fewer differences between them. "The social differences between the Methodists, the Presbyterians, and the Episcopalians becomes daily more trivial." (Winter, 1971c, 96)[74]

Summary and Analysis

The central issues distinguishing church and mission could be summarized as:

1. Churches include all who will come, whole families or individuals, without expecting anything more than a basic commitment to what that church believes.

---

[73] He often used the illustration of William Carey or J. Hudson Taylor needing to start their own organization because the existing church or mission efforts were ignoring what they believed needed to be done. This is outlined in his article "Four Men Three Eras" found in each of the editions of the book: *Perspectives on the World Christian Movement.* (Winter and Hawthorne, 2009) But more often in his earlier writing, Winter pointed out his own Presbyterian involvement and its Chapter 28 organizational structure option. This allowed room for a "spontaneous emergence of other organizations which organize first and ask approval later," (Winter, 1971c, 97) noting that only six such small organizations had fallen into that category in the past few years.

[74] The desire to see creativity and advance of Christian mission was one of the reasons for Winter leaving Fuller and establishing a mission that would focus on advancing the gospel where it had not yet gone. This will be discussed in the next chapter.

2. Missions include those who make a second commitment, normally bringing in individuals who submit to a more refined and clarified purpose and "mission." Winter called this a "second" commitment, beyond that of a commitment to Christ and a church. Of course, some missions have limitations of gender, such as the Roman Catholic orders.

3. Churches serve the needs of members and work on the basis of consensus. They are normally led by pastors and elders and are focused on *shepherding the flock* and helping it to grow, but historically not being "prophetic" beyond their area of influence.

4. Missions are often begun, at least, specifically to meet a perceived need related to something that is not being done. They often start with a prophetic figure, who believes he/she has a burden or call of God to meet that need. The need is not within the mission but is their external focus.

5. Local churches cover a geographic area and, if they expand, they overlap with other churches.

6. Missions, at least at the pioneering "missional" stage, are working where no others are working. They leave when their mission is accomplished.

7. In many ways, the missionary band is able to function like a church. Paul and his team did, even as they established local churches in many cities.

Winter framed the discussion on church/mission relationships by shaping the ideas in the terms sodalities and modalities. He sought to express his deep concern about the loss of mission to both the evangelical and the WCC circles.

In his last substantial work on the subject of sodalities and modalities, "Protestant Mission Societies: The American Experience," a number of themes are revealed from his background and experience. Winter's development of the subject of the relationship between modalities and sodalities is a classic example of his approach.

Those who are familiar with Winter's life see an interest in the subject of mission "structures" beginning with his first studies while preparing for the mission field until the time of his death. Perhaps this was because he saw his own denomination declining every year from the height it had reached in 1965, when the Winters left Guatemala.[75] He was not disturbed at the trend to hand over the work to nationals, and the associated change for expatriates from being "missionaries" to being "fraternal workers," but was deeply concerned that new mission structures were not being formed.

In other Latin American countries where he traveled, much work was being done and new work was necessary beyond the existing missionary efforts. The limited resources of the local national believers would not permit them to do all they needed to, without partnering with others. The idea that the church in one location can work with the church in another in mission outreach was discussed. McGavran reflected this in his comments of concern about the then upcoming GL 71 meeting, when he talked about missionaries working with growing churches and wondering what their role should be, often waiting for permission, filling out paperwork and otherwise sidelined from the real task of helping the church grow. Winter paraphrased this idea as a modern day interpretation of the Great Commission (Matthew 28:19-20) to read: "go ye into all the world and meddle with the national churches."[76] His growing interest in pioneering missions was becoming more prominent in his writing and speaking towards the end of his time at the SWM.

Throughout his life Winter was impacted by a number of denominational churches. As a child, his first church was part of the Presbyterian denomination. Later, when that church created a youth program with the intent of replacing the role of Christian Endeavor, the Winter family reluctantly moved to Lake Avenue Congregational Church. LACC was also connected with a denomination, though a much smaller one called the Conservative Congregational Christian Conference or the "4 Cs." LACC's sister church, Park Street Church in Boston, was also a member. At the same time, LACC maintained ties with non-denominational groups as well. It maintained a close relationship with Christian Endeavor and had a number of different speakers from Christian Endeavor present during evening and special services. This denominational and non- or inter-denominational exposure allowed Winter to see the potential impact of churches working together, rather than one church here or there trying to accomplish everything by itself.

---

[75] As of 2009, the total membership of the PC(USA) is 2,077,138, which reflects a roughly 3% decrease, or 63,027 members, from the previous year. According to the office of the general assembly: http://oga.pcusa.org/newsstories/stats2009.htm accessed on July 26, 2010, it has declined every year since 1965 and is now one-half of its size at the highest point.

[76] He meant that missionary work was becoming inter-church assistance rather than the pioneering work that characterized what Winter considered the true missionary task.

In Guatemala, Winter worked with a Presbyterian denomination that had been in the country for more than 70 years, some of his co-workers for 30 years. He also met workers from non-denominational agencies with a long history (Central American Mission) and some workers with specific, unique skills (SIL), similar to his own educational background in linguistics.

During his ten years at the SWM, Winter was exposed to even more agencies and denominations. During the 1968-69 school year there were 45 students at the SWM who worked in or were from 28 different countries. Twelve were from non-denominational mission societies. The remainder were from more than 20 different denominations, Church of Christ and Presbyterians being the largest number.[77]

The breadth of the student body increased Winter's exposure to different parts of the world and different kinds of agencies at work there. The SWM "associates" were evenly spread out, coming from or working in countries in Asia, Africa and Latin America, but with only one student from a country in Europe.

Winter also traveled to a number of other countries. While still serving in Guatemala and more so while teaching at the SWM, he had had the opportunity to travel to a number of Latin American countries with regional TEE efforts. As mentioned previously, Winter traveled with Ralph Covell to present seminars on TEE in August of 1971, and was under the sponsorship of both the IFMA (non-denominational) and the EFMA (mainly denominational at the time).[78] This gave him more exposure to mission leaders globally and opportunities to share what he learned with North American leaders. Covell had served with the Conservative Baptist Foreign Mission Society, which Winter used as his illustration earlier in this chapter to demonstrate an agency that worked with both denominational and non-denominational local churches in mission. Because this trip took them to Islamabad Pakistan, Bangkok Thailand, Hong Kong, Manila and Cebu in the Philippines, and Tokyo, Japan, the trip gave him a broader experience with both the denominational work of the Presbyterians in Pakistan, Christian & Missionary Alliance in Indonesia, Overseas Crusades work in Taiwan and the Oriental Missionary Society in Hong Kong.

Winter's increasing global perspective was reflected in his writing and presentations. He respected mission workers, yet critiquing them was part

---

[77] Fuller Theological Seminary Archives, SWM Box 1-2, page 8 from the office of Public Affairs is a list of students names, field served and sending board.

[78] This was under CAMEO, the Committee to Assist Missionary Education Overseas.

of the learning process and missiological training—both for them and for Winter. They helped him identify weaknesses in the "missions" system, some of which he could see at work in his own denomination, resulting in decline. The challenges to his ideas at Fuller, through people such as Costas (related to church growth) and Hayward (related to Winter's historical view of HUP), helped him to refine his thinking, and help us understand him more clearly.

All of this growing knowledge and experience related to new mission organizations, patterned after the Roman Catholic orders, was leading Winter to believe that such structures continue to be needed to expand existing church capacity in new areas. Historically, local churches and national church denominations filled different roles. Organizations were needed which would focus on specific tasks outside of a local church's breadth of ministry, such as linguistics, translation, church planting, or establishment and development. Without this kind of specialization in mission, some missionary tasks would not get done.

And, Winter applied that to mission field churches as well. This is why Winter asked the question, "Why is not a nationally run mission as clearly and definitely a goal as is church-planting?" (Winter, 1972e, 131) Missions that sent specialized people needed to recognize the imperative of establishing missions where they had been establishing churches. The newer churches of the world needed newer missions to accomplish what they believed God was leading them to do beyond the normal role of local churches or denominations structures.

Assessment and Contribution

Naturally, the debate concerning the structure, role and purpose of sodalities and modalities in God's plan will not be settled by this thesis.[79] Winter's study, teaching and writing on church history drew particular attention to sodalities and their strengths. His efforts prodded evangelicals to begin to reflect on this issue more deeply. Winter's conviction was that sodalities should focus their efforts on establishing new missions, especially those that pioneer. They should work with churches but not be directed by them.

As the evangelical faith mission's discussion of sodalities and modalities took place, there were disagreements as to the role and

---

[79] That debate centers on how the church and its mission are defined and who fills what role.

responsibilities of each. But generally, few faith missions disagreed with Winter's basic idea: that sodalities are needed.[80] These organizations were sodalities already, yet they did not always grasp all that meant and rarely fueled the establishment of new sodalities on the mission field, what Winter called "younger missions."

The primary sources of arguments against the distinct work of independent mission structures came from denominational circles, perhaps because of a fear of the problems these organizations can cause and/or because of a desire to control their activities. So Winter sought to carefully promote his perspective regarding sodalities within the WCC world. Sodalities are a structure that denominations should be glad to employ to accomplish their purposes because it will be a boost to their ability to reach their organizational purposes and goals.[81]

Winter did not directly interact with Bishop Stephen Neill nor mention his work in what he wrote. Through Neill's experiences in India and with the WCC he could see the valuable role that the combined IMC and WCC filled during WWII. As a historian, Neill wrote about the previous century of success and a needed transition, which he believed came at the Edinburgh meeting in 1910. The church in the west needed to recognize and make room for, if not get out of the way of, the increasing role of the very churches they had established in the previous century. While he was aware of the needs to reach those without the gospel, much of his writing concerning church and mission issues focuses on the relationship of the missions and missionaries with the sending and receiving churches. His experiences gave him a desire to clearly speak into the church/mission world, trying to give a voice to the younger churches and improve unity and effectiveness of all existing churches.[82]

Winter was focused on the role of the sodality as pioneering structures.[83] As I noted, one unique contribution was his challenge for younger churches on the mission fields to establish their own mission sodalities. This was a call to missions everywhere, and especially to Asian

---

[80] One example was Bruce Camp's thesis, which while arguing that the church has ultimate responsibility in mission, did not oppose sodalities as a concept. (Camp, 1992)

[81] An example of this is his work within his own denomination, to gain recognition for, but not control, of sodalities within the PCUSA.

[82] Neill's ideas included, for example, that when a missionary lands on their field "overseas" that they cease being a missionary and are now a part of the church in that country. That "church" worker, in say Africa, becomes a "missionary" when he goes back home. (Neill, 1959, 92)

[83] This burden grows deeper while Winter is at Fuller, and its full expression is detailed in the next chapter.

church leaders, encouraging them to pioneer in new ways. It was a call to church leaders to leverage the sodalities' agility and ability to focus.[84]

In regard to how "home" churches should relate to "mission field" churches where they exist, I believe Bishop Neill was correct and Winter would have agreed with him. But Winter was deeply concerned about the implications for mission work, especially pioneering missions, if a modality hierarchy like the WCC or NCC were the controlling body over sodalities' efforts.[85]

Neill wrote his comments in 1959. Winter's first article on sodalities was written five years after his return from Guatemala in late 1969. In it he quotes from Bishop Lesslie Newbigin's 1960 article outlining three distinct tasks (mission, missions and where there are no churches). Newbigin's distinctions between these roles opened the door to Winter's argument for the value and necessity of sodalities, especially as it related to Newbigin's category of the places where there are no churches.[86] Once sodalities establish new churches on a new mission field, missionary concerns and outreach are gradually lost in the strong pull of the church to nurture. All too often, the local churches that resulted were not involved in the task of new mission outreach.

Costas was a prophetic voice to the church regarding her role and the need to integrate mission within it.[87] His argument, which came still later, in 1974, was based on the idea that the effectiveness of mission could best be seen when it was an integral part of the church's character. The role and nature of the church was lost in mission work that was independent from

---

[84] The most widely known of Winter's presentations (outlined earlier in this chapter) was given in Asia to Asian church leaders. Another was given to mission leaders in one denomination and the bulk of the rest were presented or written for mission leaders and missionaries. Winter sought to encourage national churches to also set up their own mission structures.

[85] He had seen the strengths of the Catholic Orders and the weaknesses of the central control in Rome, which the orders sought to avoid or ignore at times. He had also seen the downside of the WCC and its relationship to the IMC, which he believed had great potential prior to their merger. The post-WWII mainline missions decline was also a part of that concern. The fact that the new non-denominational or faith-mission sodalities were growing rapidly fueled that debate. During this interaction, as before with TEE, Winter drew in experts, in this case R. Pierce Beaver, who, as a University of Chicago Professor, could say things about the WCC that only a respected "inside" scholar could say. Winter was 45 years old when they worked together on this project. Beaver was 64.

[86] Newbigin was in leadership with the WCC, helping oversee the integration of the IMC into the WCC.

[87] Including poverty and injustice.

churches. In principle, he could not separate the two. (Costas, 1974, 8, 157)

Winter, believed that a sodality was not intended to compete with the church but to provide a prophetic voice on issues the church did not effectively address. Costas' ideal did not match the reality; in general, churches were not doing mission. The track record of the WCC and its decline was a concern to both Winter and Costas. Winter saw the potential impact of churches working with the sodalities, each within their distinct calling. Both sides agreed that both structures needed to work together.[88]

Costas' concern about the dangers of the northern and western influences in the south and east were certainly valid and need to be evaluated in any ministry. When an outsider injects himself into another culture, those outside influences change the culture, for good or for ill, in small and large ways. Working closely with national leadership helped Winter, Emery and Kinsler to keep the ministry from some of those influences.[89] It also exposed those local leaders to helpful influences. From my studies and exposure to Winter and others at the time, there was a strong value of working closely with local leaders to minimize unhelpful influences and obtain "buy-in."[90]

Since Costas' perspective on sodalities was that they were based more on sociology than theology, there was also a need for more detailed biblical and theological foundation. As noted earlier, some at Fuller wrote about this in thesis or journal articles, but these were not circulated widely. Winter wrote more about the historical record and the Catholic patterns, at times including biblical references or illustrations. A more detailed biblical foundation would have helped his argument.[91]

Agreeing upon what *church* is and what *mission* means is crucial to this debate. That is part of the reason this issue will never be completely resolved and the discussion will continue. Neither sodalities nor modalities are complete without the other. Sodalities tend to be in the lead in the area of their narrow focus, but no one in favor of them was arguing that their work should be done in isolation from the church.

---

[88] Winter would often use Bible translation as an illustration, noting that no church (denomination or local fellowship) could take that task on alone.

[89] I recognize that the mere presence of westerners, usually with funding behind them, colors all relationships and alters the situation in many ways.

[90] Still, when his vision for something was strong, he would move forward without the need for others to agree.

[91] He held to the idea that a sodality should be independent, using Acts 13 seeing Paul and Barnabas as a missionary band, reporting back to the church in Antioch, but not getting direction from it.

A Growing Concern

In the process of discovering and developing these ideas, Winter was also preparing himself for what would become the next chapter in his life.[92]

Winter's experiences with McGavran fed into Winter's next steps. McGavran often repeated quotes such as "[the] unimaginable number of men who know nothing of Jesus Christ"[93] or wrote articles with similar themes, such as "Will Green Lake Betray the Two Billion?"[94] referring to the two billion people without a gospel witness.

As noted above, after leaving the SWM in 1976, Winter wrote the following in 1979, "...well over ninety percent of all American missionary effort is now concentrated on churches established yesterday rather than upon the penetration of totally non-Christian groups where there is not yet any well-established, truly indigenous church." (1979b, 160)

Central to Winter's thinking in this area were two concepts: (1) there need to be sodality structures to accomplish work that the church tends not to do, especially to send workers into areas unreached by the gospel, and (2) as missions establish churches among new people groups, those new fellowships should establish their own sodalities to do what God is calling them to do, because vast populations around the world are untouched by gospel ministry.

In Winter's mind, with the growing attention to missions studies and activities during his life to this point, there were huge populations in the world that remained in need. Something had to change.

---

[92] As noted above, the last paragraph of *Warp and Woof* contrasted church-to-church relationships with mission work to the "vast ethnic groups in whose midst there is not yet any adequate national church..." (Winter and Beaver 1970, 61-62)

[93] This was from an outline of articles to be written, which was attached to the April 27, 1971 letter from Donald McGavran to the Mission Faculty, 1.

[94] *Church Growth Bulletin*, July 1971, 6:6, 1.

Chapter 7

Lausanne 1974 Congress and Cross-Cultural Evangelism

Background in Winter's Writing

Following the pattern he had used in the past, before his presentation at Lausanne, Winter began to process his thinking about the frontier missionary task to several forums. Increasingly his attention turned toward those settings where there were no Christians and no missionaries. Up until 1971, Winter had primarily been voicing his views on church history, church growth, sodalities, and modalities. He now began to think more about areas where the church was not present. Others were also contributing to the discussion. One example was McGavran's article in the July 1971 *CGB*, "Will Green Lake Betray the Two Billion?"[1]

Winter seemed to be working through related issues as he tracked the historical and statistical factors in the growth of the church. In January 1972, he published one-page in the *CGB* called "The Quantitative Case for Continuing Missions Today." (Winter, 1972f, 202) In it, he argued for the value of the church and the need for believers to be reconciled to both God and man. "Yet, it is uniquely true that there is no more potent ingredient in bringing about ethical relationships than the multiplication throughout any given population of churches of Jesus Christ—units of God's peace and righteousness." (Winter, 1972f, 202) Winter included a chart that gave a breakdown of the number of Christians around the world and the large number of non-Christians in Asia (see Figure 19[2]). Winter's focus was the fact that (1) there are Christians around the world that need to grow and

---

[1] In it McGavran said: "By 'the two billion' I mean those multitudes of men and women who do not know Jesus Christ as Lord and Saviour. They are found in all six continents, but by far the largest numbers are in Asia, Africa and Latin America. In these lands, blocks of humanity are found (numbering tens of thousands and sometimes millions in each block) in the midst of which can be found no church, no Bible and no Christian. In the whole world, only about one billion call themselves 'Christians.' Two billion have never heard His name effectively." (McGavran, 1971, 150)

[2] The highlighted or shaded descriptions in Figure 19 were added for clarity and are not original.

reach out to their neighbors and, (2) that there are massive regions where billions need to be reached. He noted, "The most urgent task in the world today must continue to be the proclamation of the gospel in these areas and the bringing of their peoples to faith in and obedience to Jesus Christ." (Winter, 1972f, 202)

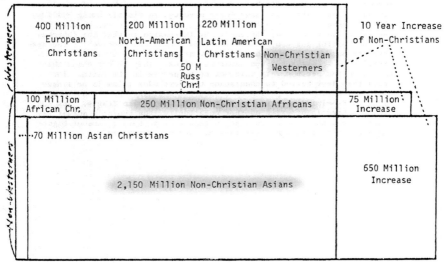

Figure 19 – Christian Populations Needing Mobilization (1972, 202)

In a follow up article in March of 1972, Winter made clear that he was not arguing that U.S. missionaries should be the only or even the main missionaries to reach all these non-Christians. He also continued to argue for the need for sodalities to be raised up from Christian populations worldwide to deal with various parts of this task.

> ...not even the Indian Christians can do this job unless (1) they understand it to be a task of full-blown <u>missionary</u> complexity, and (2) they set up the proper <u>mission</u> machinery to do the job. That is to say, what is most needed in India today is the development of liberating fellowships of Christian faith among the hundreds of millions of Indian people who live in the hundreds of unreached subcultures. But the point is that these essential, crucial new fellowships in the unreached subcultures will not be planted by existing <u>churches</u> as much as by <u>mission</u> structures that can effectively express the true Christian obedience of the existing churches.

> ...It is impressively clear that the two thousand million non-Christian Asians will not be reached unless it can

become fashionable for the younger churches to establish younger missions. (Winter, 1972c, 212)

Key 73

Early in 1973, five of the SWM faculty wrote articles for *Christianity Today*. The theme of this issue was "Key 73." Key 73 was a focused program on making the gospel available to everyone in America. *CT* editor Harold Lindsell[3] wrote announcing, "The next issue of *Christianity Today* will feature Key 73, whose evangelistic thrust we hope will result in the conversion of many unbelievers this year." (Lindsell, 1973, 3) *CT* had pushed for the idea in editorials for several years.

The *CT* editorial staff expected that some of the ideas coming out of Fuller's missions school might help churches in the U.S. reach out to those around them. It raised the issue of the need to reach out more effectively to subcultures within the country. McGavran, Tippett, Kraft, Glasser and Winter each contributed articles. William Carey Library published a 96-page workbook to help churches think through the issues related to outreach written by Virgil Gerber.[4] (Gerber, 1973)

Winter focused his writing on the need to plant new churches, rather than the usual expectation that churches are "ends" rather than "means." His article "Existing Churches: Ends or Means?" (1973a, 10) suggested that in order for the leaders of the program to attract churches and denominations, they had described the goals in ways that would encourage these to expect that the consequence of a successful Key 73 was that they would grow bigger. Winter pointed out, however, that it was *new* churches that were multiplying and growing globally, not necessarily existing churches.[5]

---

[3] Lindsell taught at Northern Baptist Theological Seminary, then came to Pasadena, California, where he was a founding faculty member at Fuller Seminary in 1946. He was the editor at *CT* from 1968-1978

[4] Gerber was a Conservative Baptist missionary to four countries in Latin America from 1949-1965. He was the Missions Secretary of the Conservative Baptist Home Mission Society and then the Executive Director of the Evangelical Missions Information Service, which produced the journal *EMQ*.

[5] For summaries of the other SWM faculty articles and more of Winter's comments, see Appendix P.

CT reported on the nationwide program several times during 1973.[6] A report in the editorial noted, "In thousands of churches across North America this year, there have been unprecedented efforts in evangelism. It is fairly safe to say that never before have so many Scriptures been distributed, so many Christian tracts presented, and so many doors knocked upon for the sake of the Gospel."[7] (Editorial, 1973, 38)

The Broader Evangelical Scene in the 1960s

The desire to expand Christ's church globally was fueled by regional and global gatherings. Beginning in the latter half of the nineteenth century, national and regional missionary conferences were convened in Asia, South and North America, and Mexico. (Stott, 1997, xi) There was also the international level World Missionary Conferences (WMC):

> ...which were self-consciously international in their membership, [and] were held in Liverpool (1860), London (1888) and New York (1900). These three were highly significant events, providing guidelines for the church's global task, but they were also stepping-stones to the much more influential WMC held in Edinburgh in 1910, whose Continuation Committee became the International Missionary Council (IMC), which in its turn was one of the streams which flowed into the World Council of Churches. (Stott, 1997, xi)

In his review of this history, John Stott traces the impact of Edinburgh 1910 by noting the thorough global study that preceded the event as well as the "note of euphoria, even triumphalism" on which it ended. (Stott, 1997, xii) But with the onset of war four years later, the church's perception of missions became more diffuse, culminating eventually in the absorption of the IMC into the WCC, as mentioned earlier. However, the social revolutions in the west and the aggressive expansion of the

---

[6] For example, in the June 8, 1973 issue of *CT* they mentioned that 150 denominations and organizations were part of Key 73. In the November 9, 1973 issue they discussed continuing Key 73 into 1974.

[7] At least one reader who was impacted by that *CT* issue on Key 73 in particular was well-known California Pastor, Rick Warren. Warren was in Japan on a short term and found the issue in the home of a missionary. He "devoured it, cover-to-cover" and said, "I had never seen anything like it. It changed my mind, it shifted my paradigm." This is a quote from a video produced on the life of Ralph Winter produced in 2008. Warren repeated this to me when I gave him an extra copy of Key-73 from Winter's files. Warren had not seen it since then, because the copy he read in Japan was not his.

Communist ideologies in the east during the 1960's were evidence to some that neither the secular worldviews of east or west were meeting the needs of the peoples in their spheres of influence and that a new thrust of world missions was imperative.

Growing out of the Berlin World Congress on Evangelism in 1966, Billy Graham called the evangelical constituency together to reach the world. According to Stott, Graham:

> ...knew that, although the gospel is unchanged and unchanging, it cannot be preached in a vacuum. He was convinced that the historic, crucified, resurrected and reigning Christ is himself good news for the world, and that he speaks to alienated young, the drug subculture, racial conflict, the breakdown of moral values, the cult of violence, the search for freedom and the longing for love. (Stott, 1997, xiii)

The theme in Berlin was *One Race, One Gospel, One Task*.[8] Graham wanted to see a larger event in the 1970s, focused on strategies for world evangelization. He consulted with over 200 evangelical leaders around the world, "asking if they considered such a congress to be needed." Hearing from them a primarily positive response, Graham moved forward with the planning.

Warwick Olson of Australia was the Director of Communications for the International Congress and wrote an article before the event in *EMQ* describing the meeting's intent to focus on world evangelization, challenging men and women with the gospel.[9] He ended his article with the following:

> What happens in Lausanne next July may well change the course of the church's involvement in world evangelization. This Congress could be the means of providing the church worldwide with an up-to-date awareness of opportunities for evangelism: practical information, guidelines, and tools to help get the job done. It should also provide a clearly enunciated biblical foundation for world

---

[8] The proceedings of the event are recorded in a book by the same name. (Henry and Mooneyham, 1967) Several regional conferences on evangelism were held in subsequent years.

[9] He wrote: "The purpose of the Congress is to arouse the churches of the world to a new thrust in world evangelization. The planners of this Congress believe that never before have the opportunities been so great to proclaim the gospel, and that men and women are more open to consider spiritual realities. They believe that the church stands on the threshold of a new era, and that new doors are opening which present Christians in our generation with a greater challenge than at any time in history." (Olson, 1974, 174)

evangelization declared not by East or West, but a cross-section of evangelical Christians. And, finally, it should pioneer a new sense of cooperation in planning to meet the opportunities and challenges facing the church at this time. (Olson, 1974, 176)

Plans for the Congress had begun.

Winter's Focus in 1973

In summer 1973, after Winter presented the "Two Structures of God's Redemptive Mission" (Winter, 1974b) at the All-Asia Mission Consultation, there was a question and answer session with speakers, and Winter touched on the issue of the unfinished task and its connection with sodalities:

> ...there are at least 2,150 million non-Christians in the world (400 million Hindus, 500 Muslims, 800 Million Chinese) as compared to 100 million Western Christians and 70 million Asian Christians. In order to reach these millions, we need to mobilize missionary forces which are not from the usual church-oriented modality type of missionary outreach. (Chun, 1975, 80)

The writer continued his description of the discussion. "Dr. Winter finally spoke to the confusion of 'mission' and 'evangelism.' He explained that mission involved cross-cultural, cross-linguistic, and cross-racial evangelizing while evangelism refers to taking the Gospel to one's own people whether inside or outside the homeland." (Chun, 1975, 80)

His writing about sodalities included the idea that younger missions needed to be established, not only to multiply involvement in mission beyond westerners, but because those indigenous missions would likely do a better job for two reasons. First, they would be more effective than missionaries in reaching their own people, which would free up western missionaries to focus on new frontier areas. Second, they would also be more effective in reaching certain unreached groups for which their culture was uniquely equipped in some way.

By fall of 1973, Winter and McGavran had been contacted by the Lausanne leadership to present a paper at the meeting the next summer. Winter circulated drafts of his thinking toward the end of 1973 and beginning of 1974.[10] One group that saw it was the board of Fuller Seminary.[11] At that meeting of the board, each of the SWM faculty presented. Winter's was listed first called "Is the Task Too Big to Grasp?" He said the "ultimate focus of our [whole] school…is not less than the salvation of all mankind, [and] the renovation of the whole earth." (1)[12] Winter expressed concern that, while there were 1,000 mission societies and some 100,000 missionaries, there was no "significant research *on the overall picture*.…It is as though the world missionary enterprise has no research department to draw on." (2) Winter then summarized a small booklet that the board had for reference. It included global level statistics comparing Christians and non-Christians in major regions of the world. After explaining statistics from the remaining task, Winter pointed out "a very disturbing new fact" which was that "ninety-five percent of the missionaries working in the non-Christian world were working among those whom we have lumped together in the category called 'other', and that the vast majority of the non-Christians—that is, the Hindus, Muslims, and Chinese—are receiving very little attention proportionately." (2)

Seeing the Task Graphically

Increasingly, Winter's writing directly connected with what he would present at Lausanne. In late October 1973, after he had submitted drafts of his pre-Lausanne Congress presentation, he wrote an article for the tenth anniversary of the *Evangelical Mission Quarterly* (*EMQ*) called "The

---

[10] Winter's E-File includes two large folders. The one numbered E-67 is the main Lausanne paper including correspondence and various drafts. The file labeled E-68 includes the *EMQ* article mentioned below. It is probable that he wrote the *EMQ* article after submitting his initial draft to Lausanne. Since Winter determined the E-File number based solely on the order in which he started the project, this would mean his first work was on the Lausanne pre-Congress paper. But, naturally, because he worked on it for most of a year, much of what is in the file was produced or placed into the file after the *EMQ* paper was submitted.

[11] According to documentation of this in Winter's writing file E-73, the Board of Trustees of Fuller Seminary (February 4, 1974 meeting) was one of the groups who heard this material. It appears that the papers were printed for the board in a packet, with a listing of each paper and presenter attached. The numbers to specific quotes are from this packet. The board also received a copy of the paper "Seeing the Task Graphically," which is summarized in Appendix R.

[12] This is from page one of the documents mentioned in the above footnote, as are other page references in this paragraph.

Decade Past and the Decade to Come: Seeing the Task Graphically."
(Winter, 1974a)

The lengthy lead article included global statistics and interpretation.
Winter addressed the mission leaders and professors who subscribed to
EMQ to argue for the huge need among cultures without gospel witness.
For a detailed summary, see Appendix R.

Pre-Lausanne Congress Preparations

A survey was sent around the world to mission leaders to seek to list
the groups of people or cultures that were not being impacted by the
gospel. This led to World Vision starting the Missions Advanced Research
and Communications Center (MARC). Edward R. Dayton was the
director. They identified 600 groups of people around the world who were
less than twenty percent Christian. Once the meeting at Lausanne was
planned, another more detailed study was produced for the 1974 meeting
and in conjunction with the SWM at Fuller. A booklet was produced from
the latter study called, *Unreached Peoples*.[13] (Missions Advanced Research
and Communication Center, 1974) For the first time with the help of
computers, they were able to sort the list by language, country, religion,
population, and other fields. Their question was, "Will anyone put this vast
amount of information to work?" (Dayton, 1974, 7-8) According to the
Bulletin of FTS, SWM Dean Arthur Glasser had prepared a fairly
substantial 'Unreached People Survey.' "This data, gathered from
missionaries and national church leaders, will be the basis for much of the
discussion at Lausanne."[14] Winter wrote the main article in this booklet
called "God has Always Sent the Gospel to Peoples" which discusses the

---

[13] This phrase, and "unreached people groups" is the phrase that was finally agreed
upon. Winter never preferred it because people would use it to talk about their unsaved
friends or anyone without the gospel, even if they are culturally near. In the early 1980s he
coined the phrase "hidden peoples" to signify these cultures being "hidden" from our sight
(not because they were hiding from us). Winter, along with a number of mission leaders
and MARC representatives, met in 1980 and agreed to use the "unreached people group"
phrase with the specific definition that included the idea that it was a whole people (not
individuals) and that the factor that qualified a group was the presence or absence of a viable
church able to see the gospel spread within the group.

[14] This is from undated and unnumbered pages in a FTS promotional newsletter. This
was the first publication in MARC's (Mission Advanced Research Center) *Unreached
Peoples* book series, which continued for several years.

concept of a people group and the divisions between groups as it relates to the spread of the gospel.[15]

Major Presentations During the Lausanne Congress

The International Congress on World Evangelization was held from July 16 through 25, 1974. There were 2,430 participants with 570 observers from 150 countries. The Congress theme was *Let the Earth Hear His Voice*, which is also the name of the 1,471 page book (Douglas, 1975) detailing every major presentation and response before and during the event.

Billy Graham opened the event with a wide-ranging message about the need for evangelism today.[16] In it, he described the purposes and presuppositions of the event. In addition to being in the tradition of evangelicalism, and seeking to bring that body together, Graham emphasized the basic beliefs of evangelicalism and the desire to consider the issues of the unevangelized world and the resources of the church to finish that task.[17] Those issues in turn gave rise to a number of items for the agenda of the congress, and the congress was structured around these. John Stott wrote about the event and the movement that grew out of it in his book *Making Christ Known: Historic Mission Documents from the Lausanne Movement, 1974-1989*. In that book, Stott outlined the main issues from Graham's presentation. The organizers hoped:

> ...that the Congress would (1) 'frame a biblical declaration on evangelism', (2) challenge the church 'to compete the task of world evangelization', (3) 'state what the relationship is between evangelism and social responsibility',

---

[15] In his keynote address in Lausanne, Billy Graham mentioned the SWM and MARC for its work in "assembling hard facts on unreached populations" which helped inform the Congress. (Douglas, 1975, 32-33) Focused as the event was on missions and evangelization, it made sense to draw on the resources at Fuller's SWM. A number of the faculty were asked to present on various subjects. Both McGavran and Winter gave major plenary presentations. The entire SWM faculty attended the Congress, as well as FTS President Alan Hubbard and a number of alumni and SWM Associates. Alan Tippett gave an extensive Evangelistic Strategy Summary Report called "Evangelization Among Animists." (Tippett, 1975) Some of the plenary papers were circulated prior to the Congress to allow for feedback from the delegates and to help them prepare for the event.

[16] His presentation was called "Why Lausanne?" (Graham, 1975b)

[17] John Stott summarized Graham's five points under "basic beliefs": a commitment to the authority of Scripture, the lostness of men and women apart from Christ, salvation in Christ alone, the need to witness in both word and actions, and the necessity of evangelism for salvation. (Stott, 1997, xiv)

and (4) help to develop 'a new "koinonia" or fellowship among
evangelicals of all persuasions' ... (Stott, 1997, xiv)
Graham himself also hoped that the congress would be undergirded by "a
tremendous emphasis on prayer" and that everyone would leave the event
"filled with the power of the Holy Spirit." (Stott, 1997, xiv)

Bishop A. Jack Dain[18] stressed as a "vital truth...the personal
responsibility of each member of the Body for the growth of the Body" in
the opening sessions. (Douglas, 1975, 11-12) Select other plenary
presentations are briefly summarized in Appendix Q.

A closing communion service included Billy Graham and John Stott
explaining the Lausanne Covenant and challenging participants to sign it.
The messages and other details of the Congress were recorded, transcribed,
and compiled into a compendium called *Let the Earth Hear His Voice.*
(Douglas, 1975) Eleven plenary papers were written and circulated in
advance to official responders to conference delegates. "At the congress
itself those who gave these papers responded to these comments in their
presentations. This was a significant step toward participant involvement
and toward identifying the crucial points of each subject." (Reapsome,
1974, 261)

In their verbal presentations at Lausanne, which had been prepared in
manuscript form, both Winter and McGavran mention the feedback they
received. Samuel Escobar, another plenary presenter, said that he received
700 responses to his paper.[19] Thus, participant feedback fed into the
presentation at the Congress itself, helping the presenters to be clearer or
to adjust their actual presentation. Winter and McGavran also had official
respondents assigned by the conference leadership to reply onstage at the
Congress.[20] All of this input before the event led Winter to clarify his
Congress presentation.

In addition to the plenary presentations there were small-group
programs focused on four major areas:
1. A discussion by national strategy groups of the central issues
   confronting evangelism in their region[21]

---

[18] Assistant Bishop of the Anglican Diocese of Sydney

[19] Email correspondence from Samuel Escobar to the author dated: January 15, 2011,
1.

[20] In the compendium, the official responders' papers follow both the pre-Congress
version and the transcription of the on-stage verbal presentations. These rejoinders were
available to Winter at the congress.

[21] Such as East Africa and the debate on moratorium and Eastern Europe on the
difficulties of living behind the "iron curtain" at that time.

2. Demonstrations of various evangelistic methods with cultural adaptations
3. Specialized evangelistic strategy groups on a range of topics and discussion
4. Theology of evangelization study groups dealing with issues such as Charismatic renewal, contextualization and regional issues in theology (Reapsome, 1974, 261, 287-289, 292-299)

Winter's Pre-Congress paper "The Highest Priority: Cross-Cultural Evangelism"[22]

While introducing his paper by noting with thankfulness the heroic service of missionaries of the past, and recognizing the great progress of the gospel towards the ends of the earth, Winter contradicted those who would suggest that the job was nearly done. "Many Christian organizations, ranging widely from the World Council of Churches to many U.S. denominations, even some evangelical groups, have rushed to the conclusion that we may now abandon traditional missionary strategy and count on local Christians everywhere to finish the job." (Winter, 1975, 213)

Perhaps with a nod to the Billy Graham focus on evangelism, Winter then mentions the fact that evangelism is a unifying factor in evangelicalism.[23] He then turns to why local believers need help:

> Most conversions[24] must inevitably take place as the result of some Christian witnessing to a near neighbor, and that is evangelism. The awesome problem is that the additional truth that most non-Christians in the world today are not culturally near neighbors of any Christians, and that it will take a special kind of "cross-cultural" evangelism to reach them. (Winter, 1975, 213)

---

[22] This is the title of Winter's paper circulated prior to the event. His actual plenary presentation and a paper that merged points from both was called an Issue Strategy Paper, listed as the eighth plenary and given on Saturday, July 20, 1974.

[23] Winter often said that he was forced to use "evangelism" rather than "missions" in his materials, which, he noted, was because the Billy Graham Evangelistic Association was backing the Congress.

[24] This is another word Winter used differently from how it is broadly understood today. In his use, conversion meant simply turning (repentance) from sin to belief or faith in Christ. To my knowledge, he never used it to mean a change of religion, or when he did, it was only to "put down" the idea as unnecessary in order to trust in Christ. In other words, one does not have to change their religion to become a believer and follower of Christ.

Winter illustrates this with the nation of Pakistan. There were many Christians in Pakistan at the time. One denomination was the Church of Pakistan and another the Presbyterian Church of Pakistan. These are national churches in that they are in the country, but "they can hardly be called national churches if this phrase implies that they are culturally related to the vast bloc of people who constitute the other 97 per cent of the country, namely the Muslims. Thus although the Muslims are geographically near neighbors of these Christians, normal evangelism will not do the job." (Winter, 1975, 214)

He also illustrated from India, where the Christians, who are mostly in the south, cannot easily relate to "95 other social classes, which make up the vast bulk of the population."[25] (Winter, 1975, 214)

Winter used these illustrations to introduce the E-Scale, discussed earlier.[26] He then illustrated the application of the scale using several countries or people groups including the Naga, Taiwan, the Japanese, and his own mission work with the Mayan Mam. When in Guatemala, he noted, "When I spoke of Christ to a Peace Corpsman in English, I was doing E-1 evangelism. When I spoke to a Guatemalan in Spanish, it was E-2 evangelism. When I spoke to an Indian in the Mayan language, it was the much more difficult E-3 evangelism." (Winter, 1975, 215-216)

Naturally, a Spanish speaker to another Spanish speaker or a Mam to another Mam would be E-1 for them. The problem was: what do you do when there is no one able to do E-1 evangelism? When the E-scale distance is more than E-1, the problem was not only a language issue.

First, Winter turned to discuss the Biblical mandate for cross-cultural evangelism. He argued that in Act 1:8, Jesus does not merely include the whole world (he does that in other places) but includes both geographic and cultural distance, as illustrated by Samaria. He further argued that Paul had barriers to cross to reach the Greeks. Winter then makes a distinction between prejudice and cultural distance: "There may have been high *walls of prejudice* involved where Jews encountered Samaritans, but it is obvious that the Greeks, who did not even worship the same God, were at a far greater *cultural distance* from the Jews than were the Samaritans, who were close cousins by comparison." (Winter, 1975, 217)

---

[25] He also illustrated from the Batak church in Northern Sumatra and its problem in relating to other language groups in Indonesia, and the Nagaland church in Northeast India, which, after seeing great growth within similar cultures, was actually in the process of planning to reach out around the world, but needed to use a different kind of evangelism than it had at home.

[26] See Appendix O.

The insights gained through the E-Scale argued for a focus on missionary work. Missionaries should not be doing E-3 work if there are local Christians doing effective E-1 outreach. He generalized that, naturally E-1 evangelism would be "more powerful than E-2 or E-3," but that did not mean that E-3 was unnecessary or out-of-date.

> ...the truth about the superior power of E-1 evangelism must not obscure the obvious fact that E-1 evangelism is literally *impossible* where there are no witnesses within a given language or cultural group. ... This kind of initial, multiplying work is the primary task of the missionary when he rightly understands his job. He must decrease and the national leader must increase. (Winter, 1975, 220)

Winter saw the need to first have E-2 and E-3 efforts made to cross cultural barriers, then E-1 would carry the work forward by the newly established church within the culture.

This led to discussion of the size of the task remaining. As mentioned previously, Christians were being led to believe that because there were believers in every country, the mission task was done. Having Christians or churches in every nation was not the same as having churches in every culture or people group. Because he saw how widespread this kind of thinking was, he gave it the name "people blindness" or "blindness to the existence of separate *peoples* within *countries*."[27] (Winter, 1975, 221)

Winter used statistics similar to those in the *EMQ* article "Seeing the Task Graphically" noting the 1,993 million in Africa and Asia who are virtually without a witness. But the immensity of this task is not its "bigness," rather the complexity of the cultures to be reached by existing Christians. As important as it is, merely retranslating the Great Commission (Matthew 28:19-20) to reflect the people group idea present in the Greek word *ethné* was not enough. (Winter, 1975, 223)

Winter then poignantly illustrated from the American situation, focusing on the fruit of evangelistic crusades in particular:

> Are we in America, for example, prepared for the fact that most non-Christians yet to be won to Christ (even in our country) will not fit readily into the kinds of churches we now have? The bulk of American churches in the North are middle-class, and the blue-collar worker won't go near them. Evangelistic crusades may attract thousands to big

---

[27] For the international delegates who were reading this, he added, that people blindness seemed, "more prevalent in the U.S. and among U.S. missionaries than anywhere else."

auditoriums and win people in their homes through television, but a large proportion of the newly converted, unless already familiar with the church, may drift away simply because there is no church where they will feel at home. Present-day American Christians can wait forever in their cozy, middle-class pews for the world to come to Christ and join them. But unless they adopt E-2 methods and both *go out after these people and help them found their own churches,* evangelism in America will face, and is already facing, steadily diminishing returns. (Winter, 1975, 221-222)

Winter illustrated the idea of the new cultures coming to Christ from the world and the New Testament. He closed this pre-congress version noting, "Nothing must blind us to the immensely important fact that at least *four-fifths* of the non-Christians in the world today will never have any straightforward opportunity to become Christians unless the Christians themselves go more than halfway in the specialized task of cross-cultural evangelism. Here is our highest priority." (Winter, 1975, 225)

General Questions/Responses from Delegates prior to the Congress

The size of Winter's file on Lausanne 74 clearly shows he worked on this paper as much if not more than any other during his life.[28] Apparently in reply to some of the feedback, in a handwritten note, Winter wrote: "I was asked to talk about cross-cultural <u>evangelism</u> not cross-cultural nurture and edification. I understand evangelism to be those early stages of <u>repentance and faith</u>."[29]

Donald E. Hoke, Congress Director, wrote a memo regarding Winter's pre-Congress draft paper.[30] Hoke said that the paper was "highly

---

[28] There are several drafts of both his pre-congress version and the presentation version, notes on comments from the hundreds of responses, and other people's writing on the paper. There is a post-congress version that combined the two editions. Comments from hundreds of the delegates are not in this file. I believe these were required to be returned to the Lausanne leadership.

[29] From E-67 in Winter's writing files. Document title: INGREDIENTS, 9. This appears to be in response to questions Winter received in reply to the pre-congress paper.

[30] The memo is dated February 20, 1974 and is addressed to: Paul Little, Leighton Ford, Samuel Escobar and Ralph Winter. Paul Little was the Program Director for the Congress and Leighton Ford was the Chair of the Program Committee. Samuel Escobar was also on the Program Committee and gave a plenary address.

stimulating, innovative and helpful." He suggested four areas where it could be "sharpened up for maximum impact." First, he felt Winter may have gone too far when he talked about a foreign missionary being "one who merely crosses a geographic boundary" and may have neglected the emphasis on geography. Hoke wanted "those for whom the geographic barriers are deterrent to [be] taken seriously…"

Second, he felt Winter's main point was stated too far back in the paper. The paragraph Hoke referred to read:

> This is why the easiest, more obvious surge forward in evangelism in the world today will come if Christian believers in every part of the world are moved to reach outside their churches and win their cultural near neighbors to Christ. They are better able to do that than any foreign missionary. It is a tragic perversion of Jesus' strategy if we continue to send missionaries to do the job that local Christians can do better. There is no excuse for a missionary in the pulpit when a national can do the job better. There is no excuse for a missionary to be doing evangelism on an E-3 basis, at an E-3 distance from people, when there are local Christians who are effectively winning the same people as part of their E-1 sphere. (Winter, 1975, 219-220)

Hoke wanted that point up front and repeated. He also felt, third, that Winter covered the same E-Scale material that McGavran had covered.[31] Lastly, Hoke thought Winter should expand his conclusion and make it easier to understand, restating and illustrating the material covered.

Others, such as Glasser and McGavran, gave feedback to an even earlier version of the paper as well. Glasser's feedback contained some corrections and minor clarifications. McGavran wanted to see Winter do a "good deal more" polishing and, like Hoke, clarifying, "so that readers are not mislead by words which are correct enough but not <u>clear</u> enough."[32] McGavran made extensive wording suggestions and two comments on content in the margins, which Winter incorporated to some degree.

Another set of notes includes both Ralph's and Roberta's handwriting.[33] Her notations cover questions and points made in reference

---

[31] McGavran's paper preceded Winter's in the Congress program.

[32] One page Letter from Donald A McGavran to Ralph Winter, February 18, 1974.

[33] It is in a stapled set of lined, hole-punched notebook paper, 24-pages long.

to the pre-Congress version of Winter's paper.[34] Some of the questions or comments Roberta recorded were:

1. Where E-2 people are treated like E-1 they come in the front door [of a church] and out the back.

2. It would be terrible if I had to label everyone E-1, E-2, E-3 before I won them to Christ.

3. Many Palestinian Christians know, understand and witness to Muslims. Do they win them and keep them won?

4. Where did you get the idea that four of five non-Christians are beyond reach of E-1 evangelism?

5. What are the cultural obstacles?

6. The trouble with churches is that they don't reach out to strange people. And the trouble with missions is that they don't understand church planting well enough. That is to say E-1 people don't believe in E-2 and E-3, and E-3 people don't believe in E-1.

7. This paper offers some exciting possibilities for evangelization if we who call ourselves Christians could shake off our cultural biases and love people for Jesus' sake. What is an E-3 gifted person like?

Winter made a note on one page in the packet of handwritten notes that said, "Christianity is now politically 'world-wide' but it is not ethnically or culturally world-wide." He also wrote a list called: "Urgent Points Left Out":

1. Cross-Cultural Evangelism can be done by Third World people.

2. E-3 workers are sometimes more acceptable than E-1.

3. [Unreadable names] objections to missions as such – churches in general will not want autonomous orders [to] do this work.[35]

4. Cross-Cultural Evangelism is the acid test and is rarely promoted by Christians.

---

[34] These are probably the notes Ralph and Roberta wrote based on the questions or comments made by Delegates in reply to Winter's pre-congress paper. But it could have been ideas generated in working through the responses with Roberta and others. Where it is clear, I have interpreted abbreviations in my transcriptions of these papers, and expanded words such as "ch" to church or "Xians" to Christians.

[35] It seems to be referring to someone ("Bohalele's" could be the name). Likely this person was not one who merely wrote a response, but was someone who objected to Winter's thinking, which came back to Winter at this point.

5. "Let's not win people who cannot fit into <u>our</u> churches."[36]

On an early draft of Winter's presentation paper are a few handwritten comments that did not make it into the final version. In response to question one, he wrote "I have not anywhere in my paper suggested that the E-2 and E-3 cross cultural evangelists need to be white Westerners." In response to another, he wrote "I am <u>not</u> saying that four out of five non-Christians in the world have to be won by E2 and E3 methods. I am saying that four out of five non-Christians in the world live in groups where evangelistic work has to begin on an E2 or E3 level in order for E-1 work to follow."[37] Winter sought to deal with these and other objections or potential objections in his presentation at the Congress.

Both Ralph and Roberta wrote many pages of notes on these and other topics related to Ralph's presentation.[38] Many of the pages are only partial, containing just the heading of a subject or a few lines. Presumably these are topics they thought of adding or discussing, but never got to or decided were not important. Some of these additional topics were understanding issues of gifting for E-3 workers, underestimating the difficulty of E-3, and recognizing that the E-1 approach in an E-2 or E-3 situation was cultural imperialism.

Lastly, Winter noted a few points that he wanted to be sure were clear he was *not* saying:

1. E-1 is <u>always</u> close to home.
2. E-2 & E-3 are always foreigners, much less Westerners.
3. E-3 (not E-2) is cross-cultural evangelism.

---

[36] Winter would often use "tongue and cheek" illustrations or wording to emphasize what he was not saying yet what he felt might be in the minds of some listeners at the Congress.

[37] Handwritten notes by Ralph D. Winter on a draft of his presentation paper at the Congress in Winter E-67 file. It is not known when these were written. The page for both quotes is 5.

[38] There were challenges from some of the written responses to the title of his paper: "The Highest Priority: Cross-Cultural Evangelism." In a packet of twenty-three hand-written pages called "INGREDIENTS" Winter wrote about those challenges, "Why highest Priority? I did not realize I would have to defend my title." He noted that it is the biggest job left, the hardest of all mission work and, it was necessary for pioneers to cross cultures to do this work first, before E-1 could happen. There is how he used the phrase, "The Task of Highest Priority." Winter had applied McGavran's HUP concept to the people of the world who had not yet been impacted by the gospel. If the group is unreached, then it is the highest priority to get there with the gospel and communicate in a way they can understand. That was foundational to Winter's later desire to highlight groups that had yet to be reached or penetrated with the gospel.

Responses to Winter's Pre-Congress Paper

Because of the feedback Winter received, his approach shifted and he used more stories and examples to make these points.[39] When Winter presented his ideas on the platform at Lausanne, he first thanked those who read and responded to his pre-Congress paper.[40] At the beginning of Winter's plenary presentation at Lausanne, he specifically addresses some of the concerns raised by these official responses. His reply to these responders will be discussed in conjunction with his presentation.

"Response to Dr. Ralph Winter's Paper" by Philip Hogan

Philip Hogan[41] first thanks Winter and mentions areas of agreement and clarity which Winter's paper gave. Hogan reflects on what might happen related to Christian unity, should there be "a very great proliferation further within the Body of Jesus Christ" created by E-2 evangelism. "Must we forever remain divided on the basis of culture, language, and color? Is it not possible to believe that newly-won Christians can be so obsessed with the object of their new love that the expulsive power of this new affection will overcome human dividing lines?" (Hogan, 1975, 243)

Hogan goes on to mention what he considers his main contribution: "…simply an appeal to all of us to recognize the sovereignty of the Holy Spirit and to emphasize once again the truth of Acts 5:32, 'And we are his witnesses of these things and so is also the Holy Ghost whom God has

---

[39] Handwritten notes by Ralph D. Winter on a draft of his presentation paper at the Congress in Winter "E-67" file. It is not known when these were written. Additionally, other questions and comments raised issues dealing with how various kinds of evangelism work in different, specific situations. Illustrations were apparently cited where things had gone well, and where they had not. Winter answered some of these directly, some indirectly and left some because of time. In those same handwritten notes, perhaps in response to a question about the idea of including the phrase "The Highest Priority" in the title of his paper, Winter wrote the following, but did not include it in the final paper in this form:
"One of the confusing things to some of you was the fact that while my paper admits that the E-1 method is the best where it is possible that nevertheless E-1 is never possible except where E-2 or E-3 efforts have preceded it. This is where I get the idea of cross cultural evangelism being 'prior' to E-1 evangelism, and therefore of higher priority."

[40] Because the responders were reacting to the earlier version of his paper before he presented his revised paper at the Congress, I include a summary of their responses to his pre-congress paper first, in the order in the compendium.

[41] Hogan served as the Executive Director for Foreign Missions of the General Council of the Assemblies of God.

given to them that obey Him.'" (Hogan, 1975, 243) He noted that he was not "pleading for a kind of 'sitting where they sit and letting God happen' kind of attitude." Rather:

> ...at the end of every human endeavor there must be a simple dependence upon the Holy Spirit who, beyond the shadow of any doubt, is at work in his world in an unprecedented way and if we sow in faith, believing in the magic power of the seed, we must, as well, believe that there will be receptive soil, sometimes suddenly and beyond the power of any human reasoning. (Hogan, 1975, 244-245)

"Response to Dr. Ralph D. Winter's Paper" by Jacob Loewen

Jacob Loewen[42] started by summarizing Winter's paper skillfully, assuming that, while delegates may have read it, they may not remember it. His concerns were mainly focused on the aspect of E-3 evangelism. Loewen did not share Winter's view that 87% of all non-Christians have no near Christian neighbors. Because of his extensive experience in different cultures, he was convinced that:

> For E-3 evangelism to be effective, the recipient culture must be able to separate the true message content from the cultural wrapper in which it comes and then be aware of congenial models for the new life in Christ that will permit healthy spiritual development. Otherwise, it may fall back on syncretistic models of its own old life, or more likely it will try to pattern itself according to the cultural models of the E-3 evangelist's culture. (Loewen, 1975, 248)

Loewen then gave his reactions to the concept of E-3 evangelism under three categories: Biblical concerns, anthropological concerns, and practical considerations. Under Biblical concerns, Loewen did not have a problem seeing E-1 in the Jewish culture or E-2 between Jews and Samaritans, but he did not necessarily see E-3 in Acts 1:8 in the idea of the "uttermost parts of the world." Since the known world was Greco-Roman, he argued, the writers could not have thought of E-3.[43] Further, Paul later

---

[42] Loewen was a translation consultant for the Bible Society who had served in South America and Africa.

[43] This grows out of Loewen's view of Scripture, as noted in his book, *The Bible In Cross-Cultural Perspective.* (2000) In it, as above, Loewen reflects the view that the human authors of Scripture could not have meant something that was beyond their own cultural context or the sphere of general human knowledge at the time. His view seems to reflect a

wrote of Christ tearing down the dividing wall between Jew and Gentile in Ephesians 2:13-16, making both groups one. Instead, Loewen saw the Biblical model of E-1 and E-2 throughout the book of Acts, which he outlined with several examples including Phillip in Samaria and with the Ethiopian eunuch, as well as Cornelius in Acts 10. (Loewen, 1975, 248-249)

Under anthropological concerns, Loewen agreed with Winter's perspective that there is "great cultural distance" which "spells even greater communication problems. The reason is that effective cross-cultural communication can happen only when the new recipient can separate the message content from its cultural form..."[44] (Loewen, 1975, 249) Loewen believed that the gospel would not be spread effectively by an outsider communicating the message. He cited examples along the lines of cultural change from his work among Native American populations in North America and Canada and from tribe to tribe in Africa.[45]

Under practical considerations, Loewen pointed out that despite their dedication and sacrifice, there was, in his opinion, almost a universal failure of E-3 missionaries as described in James Scherer's book, *Missionary Go Home.* (1964) He connected this idea with his idea of the message of the gospel getting "wrapped up" in the culture of the missionary. This led to the evangelized people becoming "imitation Europeans rather than spiritually reborn nationals." (Loewen, 1975, 250)

Under the category of personal concerns, Loewen took issue with Winter about the concept of near-neighbors. He felt that the migration of workers from Christian nations to non-Christian nations mitigated against

---

perspective that God did not reveal many, if any, details to the writers of the Bible, or that God did not intend to communicate a meaning that the human authors would not have understood at the time.

[44] Loewen knew that the message of the gospel can easily get confused when communication crosses cultural boundaries. He continued: "...when the meaning of a message is separated from its cultural wrapper. In the E-1 situation both the message and the wrapper are understood and are meaningful to both the evangelist and the convert. At the E-2 level the two different people in contact usually have an awareness of the cultural differences that separate them, and so the alien wrapper of the message is easily distinguished from its true content. ... Frequently at the E-3 level, the wrapper, no matter how incongruous, has been accepted as part of the message. Often this wrapper effectively choked the real life out of the message." (Loewen, 1975, 249-250)

[45] Loewen used illustrations of how change in both Native American cultures and African tribal cultures happened fairly rapidly across whole regions. In the case of Native cultures in North America, he used the example of peyote as a religious experience, where it spread from Northern Mexico into the U.S. and Canada. In Africa, he referred to an anti-witch medicine used in Central Mozambique originally, but that spread as far north as Tanzania and Kenya. (Loewen, 1975, 250)

this idea, and thus these are examples of new relationships that became near-neighbors. He used the illustration of non-Christian Chinese working alongside Christians in Tanzania and Zambia who were building a new railroad. Loewen wondered if God had placed the Chinese there so they could hear the gospel. (Loewen, 1975, 249-251)

"Response to Ralph Winter and Jacob Loewen" by David J. Cho

Congress organizers pursued voices from around the world, so the last two responders were from non-Western contexts. David J. Cho[46] argued several overlapping ideas, generally agreeing with Winter and disagreeing with Loewen. He saw Loewen as negative on the need for effectiveness in cross-cultural evangelism. While there is a need to critique the failures of the west in missions, he felt critiques should focus on correcting past mistakes rather than being used to deny the legitimacy of cross-cultural evangelism. (Cho, 1975, 253)

Cho felt that the order of the points E-Scale should be renumbered and that E-3 should be labeled E-1, demonstrating priority by the numbering.[47] He felt the geographical distinction in evangelism was not the primary issue, as Winter had said. The use of terms like "home" mission or "foreign" mission were misleading and unhelpful. To Cho, the failure of Euro-American missions was not communication but lifestyle, meaning that the missionary needed to work at learning the culture and language of the people group to whom he was reaching out. He included an illustration of two different missionary westerners in Korea: one who understood the language and culture and one who did not. The latter was ineffective whereas the former was respected and effective.[48]

At the same time, Cho felt western missions were entering a mature stage and the "divine imperative and mandate" must be continued or the church would end up like the now dead ancient Tunisian Church in North

---

[46] Cho is a well known Christian and mission leader in Korea. He brought Billy Graham to South Korea and held a meeting of over 1 million people to hear Graham speak. He is the one who invited Winter to South Korea for the All-Asia Missions Consultation in 1973, where he delivered his paper, *The Two Structures of God's Redemptive Mission* outlined in the previous chapter.

[47] Meaning making it "number one" on our list of missions tasks.

[48] Cho assumes the listener will know this, by stating: "As for the success and effectiveness of the two kinds of missionaries, you do not have to ask me to answer further." (Cho, 1975, 253-254)

Africa and the New Testament churches of Asia-Minor.[49] Lastly, he urged the body of Christ to engage, like the secular world does, in research and investment, but to do so "in cross-cultural enterprises," or "there will come a crisis for mission and evangelism." (Cho, 1975, 254)

"Response to Dr. Ralph Winter's Paper" by Pablo M. Pérez

Pérez[50] agreed for the most part and underscored several of Winter's basic points, including the recognition of cultural distance and the massiveness of the task. At the same time he felt Winter would agree that the E-Scale was an oversimplification of our complex world. (Pérez, 1975, 255)

Pérez pointed out cultural and sub-cultural distinctions that complicate issues of evangelism and create obstacles, which become common across cultures or regions, such as the disdain of youth for their elders. "These and many more have produced appealing arguments and somewhat predictable reactions [on the part of non-Christians] which are not completely controlled by the culture of a particular locality."[51] (Pérez, 1975, 256) Pérez further argues that while there is a need to evangelize peoples who have not been evangelized, he questioned if that also meant that they needed to be formed into new churches with others from their culture. "This may be pragmatically defensible, and even temporarily tolerated, but it will also tend to perpetuate adverse existing conditions and prejudices simply because they can be labeled as culturally determined." (Pérez, 1975, 256) This, he felt, was not what the Bible intended.

Pérez illustrated his point using NT examples and raised the Ephesians 2:14ff passage, as did Loewen, emphasizing the idea that new believers from a new culture are no longer aliens, but fellow-citizens. He felt this has special bearing "in the Third World where social stratification is much more visible than in North America ... this very feature has to be recognized and even used initially for the communication of the gospel, but should never be allowed to remain as a permanent distinctive of the church of Jesus Christ in any place in the world." (Pérez, 1975, 256-257) He

---

[49] He notes that this was due in part to "the loss of missionary vision." (Cho, 1975, 254)

[50] Pérez had been a student of the SWM finishing his DMiss thesis in 1973 on the missiological implications of liberation theology. (1973) He was a visiting professor at Dallas Theological Seminary from Mexico City at the time he wrote his response to Winter's paper.

[51] He is referring to broad, sometimes regional or global cultural patterns, often now attributed to globalization.

expressed concern that in the attempt to take the gospel to new cultures, Christians should not go too far and expect the church to take on unbiblical values and expressions of that culture. He recognized Latourette, as Winter had, when he added, "True, as Latourette constantly points out in his works, the world to which Christianity comes affects the church powerfully, but at the same time the church by its very presence, if nothing else, must definitely affect the world which surrounds it."[52] (Pérez, 1975, 257) He strongly believed that the Holy Spirit should be the determining factor, not culture. "It is he who compels both believer and unbeliever to obey the Word of God and to act upon its claims by meeting them where they are culturally, but imposing his guidelines within God's ultimate plan for man." (Pérez, 1975, 257)

Winter's Paper as Delivered at the Congress

Response to the Responders

After Winter thanked those who responded to his paper beforehand, he noted that "In almost no case am I in any disagreement with their emphases." He thanked Pérez and Hogan for their emphasis on spiritual forces, which "in many cases override all others in importance."

He continued, "there is no conflict, rightly understood, between the guidance of the Holy Spirit and the need for careful, patient, analytical thinking."[53] (Winter, 1975, 226)

Winter answered a number of the objections noted in the response papers by saying:[54]

It is evident that we must not fail to distinguish between what we may expect *God* to do and what God may legitimately expect *us* to do. For example, I feel sure that God,

---

[52] As noted earlier and as Winter often mentioned, Latourette did include both the impact of the expansion of Christianity on the world and the world's impact on Christianity.

[53] Winter noted that the headquarters of the Assembly of God, where Hogan was the CEO, was one of the first to make extensive use of computer facilities and operated the largest print establishment in the state of Missouri at the time. Those activities, Winter argued, required a lot of "active intellectual analysis." A note similar to this was also written in the margin of the paper copy of Hogan's paper in Winter's files.

[54] Winter made handwritten notes on the printout of Hogan's official response paper near the section where Hogan asked about cultural differences and the unity of the church. Winter wrote, "The outpouring of the H.S. did not sweep Greeks into the Jewish church, but produces a Greek church." (Winter, 1975, 226)

if he wished to, would be able by his Holy Spirit to eliminate language differences[55] and merge everyone into a single congregation. But we must respect the fact that the outpouring of the Holy Spirit in the New Testament did not eliminate the Greek language, nor the Greek culture, but in fact allowed an additional Greek-speaking church tradition where there was only a Jewish church before. There may have been many Jewish Christians who fervently wished[56] the Greeks would follow their form of worship, but God apparently had other plans. (Winter, 1975, 226)

Winter gently turned around Pérez's argument about changing culture. He agreed that the gospel changes cultures and does not merely yield to it, but, "…if Dr. Pérez were to go to a foreign country to a new situation, he would then be in a different situation, and would have to be very respectful of the culture and not fight against it as he knows how to do within his own culture." Further, he noted from his own experience that he, "had to learn to respect and not to fight much of the aboriginal culture lest I myself confuse *my* culture with the Gospel." (Winter, 1975, 226)

Loewen and Winter must have discussed their differences before Winter presented at the Congress.[57] Winter mentions in the transcription that Loewen thought that the phrase "near-neighbor evangelism" was intended to refer only to the E-1 arena. Winter said he would have agreed with Loewen, if that was the meaning. But expanding the meaning of "near-neighbor evangelism" to E-2 and E-3 would make the idea that "four out of five non-Christians are beyond the reach of near-neighbor evangelism" meaningless. (Winter, 1975, 226) In the second half of his presentation, Winter spends more time explaining the concept.

Winter mentioned Loewen's pessimism about the difficulty of the E-3 task and both agreed that it is complex and extensive, but that no matter the difficulty, it "must be attempted at all costs where there is no reasonable possibility of effective E-1 or E-2 evangelism." (Winter, 1975, 227) He then gave a number of examples of places where E-3 had been successful, where it was currently being attempted and where it needed to

---

[55] According to the audiotape in the Lausanne archives at Wheaton College, Winter actually said, "to produce a single world fellowship with one language and a single congregation."

[56] According to the audiotape, Winter added here, "as Americans today do, that everyone else would follow their form of worship."

[57] According to a memo in Winter's file on the Congress, Loewen and he discussed his pre-conference paper on the phone while Loewen was in Lusaka, Zambia in East Central Africa.

be pursued.[58] Winter also argued that God might desire to use E-3 situations to accomplish what René Padilla called "cross-fertilization."

> God has not meant for his world family to persist in cultural ghettos. He has not intended, on the one hand, to merge the whole family into a single culture. On the other hand, he does not want ghettos. The body of Christ can be healthy only if there are separate organs, *and* the separate organs serve each other. The two-way flow of E-3 personnel is a most important phenomenon which must increase not decrease in the life of the world Christian family. (Winter, 1975, 227)

Before turning to the main presentation, Winter thanked his listeners for the "many hundreds of responses" from other congress participants in addition to those of the invited discussants. According to Winter, those responses "either concerned the statistical *scope* of the task or the theological *nature* of the task." (Winter, 1975, 227) This was his outline for the remainder of his presentation.

Questions About the Statistical Scope of the Task

Winter includes seven figures in his presentation.[59] First, he describes the basic statistic of the global situation demonstrating the number (in millions) of people in the world, categorized, first, by whether they call themselves Christians[60] or not.[61] (Figure 20)

---

[58] He referred to David Cho and others in Asia who were planning on sending 100 Asian missionaries to Kalimantan.

[59] This was a pattern for him, during this period, and the next few years. I first heard Winter speak in Oct. 1976, one month before the U.S. Center for World Mission was founded. He used acetate overhead transparencies with charts depicting the statistics detailed here.

[60] The number in the far right of the upper portion of the list: 1179 million.

[61] The number in the far right, above grand total: 2723 million.

CHRISTIANS	Western	Africa	Asia	TOTAL	
Nurture	120	40	40	200	
E-0 Renewal	845	76	58	979	
	965	116	98	1179	
NON-CHRISTIANS					
E-1 Ord. Ev.	180	82	74	336	------13%
E-2,E-3, CC Ev.	147	200	2040	2387	------87%
	327	282	2114	2723	
GRAND TOTAL	1292	398	2212	3902	

Figure 20 – Scope of the Task - Christians and Non-Christians

Winter referred to the physical "population clock" which was visible in the Congress entryway. It was counting up the growth of the population of the world during the congress.[62] It was a visual demonstration of the fact that the numbers are constantly changing. As in other settings, Winter used a visual reminder, in this case the population clock, to illustrate the importance of growth rates. He noted that if they had another clock counting the number of new Christians each day, it would show that, "from the opening of this Congress until now, four days later, the number of Christians in the world has grown more than a quarter of a million." Then he added a comment about growth rates: "If we had a really sophisticated clock, we could even record the fact that each day in practically every country of the world, the percentage of Christians is also increasing." (Winter, 1975, 228)

---

[62] The clock counted 1,852,837 people in the world added to the world population during the Congress. A film was produced reporting about Lausanne called "Let the Earth Hear His Voice." Over a picture of the clock in the film were the words: "WORLD POPULATION CLOCK to remind Congress delegates of continual increase in world population, and responsibility to proclaim the Gospel."

Figure 21 – World Population Clock at Lausanne 74

He goes on to say that he directs these comments in particular to those brethren who might feel the task is hopeless. "Dear brothers and sisters, we are being successful right now, and we surely have no statistical reason not to make definite plans here at this Congress to move ahead with Jesus Christ, Lord of History, to finish the task of world evangelization." (Winter, 1975, 228)

Winter then described the core of his presentation: the E-Scale and the concepts behind it. He categorized those who can be reached by near-neighbor evangelism and those who would require cross-cultural evangelism.

Figure 22 below shows "the quantities and distinctions mentioned" (summarized in Figure 20), with the additional difference that the representative areas in it were drawn to scale. The figures on the right side of Figure 22 were the same as those in the right column (outside the box) of Figure 20. The top portion of the chart, called the "Western World," represents Christians who either need nurture or renewal. Below the dark line are those who are also in the Western World, but would not self-identify as Christians. Those 336 million can be reached by "ordinary evangelism." But the 2387 million designated by E-2 and E-3 are "people who require cross-cultural evangelism."

At this point, Winter made two key points. First, "that according to these estimates, 87 per cent of the non-Christians are in the cross-cultural category." He highlighted this in order to alert Christians to the importance and magnitude of the remaining task of evangelism. Second, since most of the people needing cross-cultural evangelism were in Asia, it "helps to account for the instinctive difference between the way most Western Christians think about evangelism and the way people involved in cross-cultural evangelism think about evangelism." (Winter, 1975, 230) In other words, Christians without exposure to Asian non-Christians and their cultures do not have the natural inclination to think about how evangelism might be done in that context.

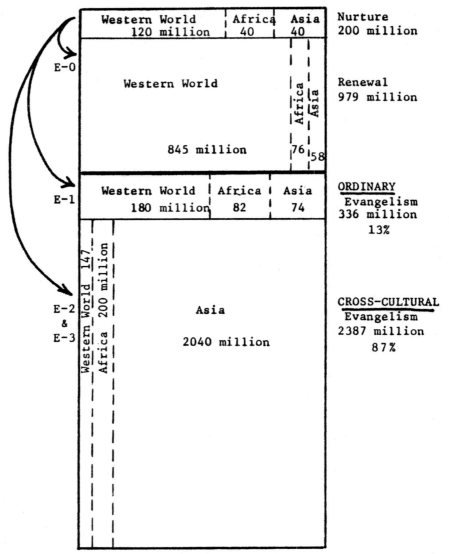

Figure 22 – The World

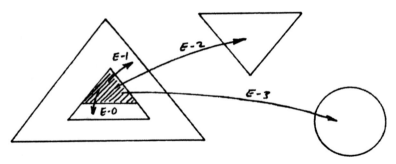

Figure 23 – E-Scale Illustration

His depiction of the E-Scale (Figure 23) shows Christians in the darkened area just above the label E-0. The first arrow pointed to the E-0 sector, those people who share the same cultural context as Christians. These are the nominal Christians, who are "Christian" in name but need to be drawn to personal faith and commitment. The second arrow goes from the church into a culture where the church is at home, or what has been called "the stained glass barrier" which is between the church and the world within its culture and language. Many Christians from existing churches feel comfortable doing E-0 evangelism because they understand the culture and can relate to it naturally.

The next two arrows extend beyond any Christian's local setting. The E-2 arrow reaches outside situations where the church is "at home" to cultures that share some commonalities (the shape is still a triangle), but "nevertheless sufficiently different to make the founding of separate congregations desirable to act as a base for effective outreach to others in that same culture." The E-3 arrow "involves similar church-planting implications, but reaches out to a totally strange culture (the circle)." (Winter, 1975, 230-231)

Winter wanted to be sure that this did not confuse anyone, so he suggested that people could take these ideas and apply them to a town or region or country, which he did in the next diagram (Figure 24).[63]

---

[63] At this point, he did not make a distinction between E-2 and E-3 because they were both cross-cultural and thus involved founding new churches.

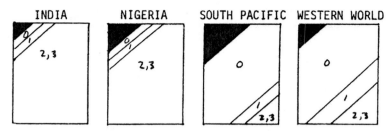

Figure 24 – E-Scale in Different Societies

He noted that he included India and Nigeria because they represented much of the way the non-Western world was at the time, with far more E-2 and E-3 work to be done.

Figures 25 and 26 were positioned and discussed together. Winter took the numbers of Christians/non-Christians and added both the number and general location of evangelical protestant missionaries reaching out to them. His estimates indicated that only five percent of the 10,000 missionaries working in the Western world were working with non-Christians (Figure 25). That, he noted, "is not surprising, because the majority of Westerners are nominal Christians." (Winter, 1975, 233)

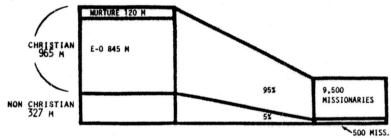

Figure 25 – Western World

In the non-Western world, (Figure 26) 95 percent of the Protestant missionary force worked either with Christians, nominal Christians, or with 403 million non-Christians in Asia. In this case, also, Winter estimated that five percent of workers who serve in the non-Western world were working with the 1933 million Chinese, Muslims, and Hindus. He called these "virtually untouched blocs of humanity." He mentioned that it was "only a guess, but it is safe to say that 95 per cent of all missionaries deployed in the non-Western world are focusing their efforts either on communities that claim to be Christian or upon non-Christian peoples in the immediate environment of the Christians..." (Winter, 1975, 230-233)

Most cross-cultural workers were focused on E-0 within the Christian community.

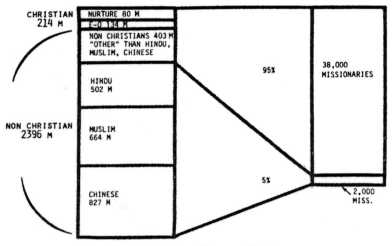

Figure 26 – Non-Western World

Winter used another illustration. Earlier, he mentioned that there were roughly one million non-Christians in the world for every delegate at the Congress.

> If our Congress participants consisted of people whose gifts and calling were focused proportionately on all non-Christians in the world, would we not have to have here one participant for each million in each of these groups? This means we would have to have 502 people here specializing on reaching the 502 million non-Christian Hindus. These would have to be cross-cultural specialists, on the whole. We would also have to have 664 people here specializing on reaching the 664 million Muslims... (Winter, 1975, 233)

While he had just attempted to convince the audience that the task is "doable," here he called this a "grim picture... precisely where the cross-cultural task is the largest, the cross-cultural workers are the fewest. ... *The danger is that we may easily deceive ourselves concerning the proportionate weight of personnel that is going to the evangelism of non-Christians.*" (Winter, 1975, 233-234)

Because of the importance of these points to Winter's presentation, he went on to illustrate them with concrete examples. He had used Pakistan earlier, so he returns to Pakistan (Figure 27).

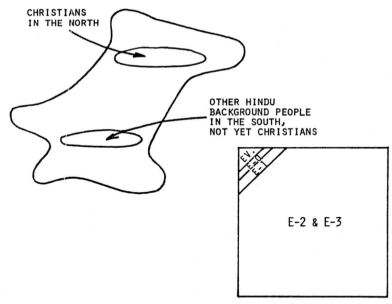

CHRISTIANS
IN THE NORTH

OTHER HINDU
BACKGROUND PEOPLE
IN THE SOUTH,
NOT YET CHRISTIANS

E-2 & E-3

Figure 27 – Pakistan

Why, he asks, would Pakistan with 500,000 Christians have such a small number of people where near-neighbor evangelism (E-1) might be effective? Winter gives details in the attempt to present a clear picture and help those who may not realize crucial details. For example, he talks about the fact that both the Christians and Muslims speak Urdu. While many of the Christians and the major movements to Christ in the country are in the North, there are many Christians in the South as well.[64] So why was it so difficult to reach the Muslims who spoke Urdu? "The answer is that 99 per cent of the Christians have a Hindu (not Muslim) cultural background, whereas 97 per cent of the non-Christians in Pakistan are Muslim." (Winter, 1975, 235)

He seemed to understand that the Christians in Pakistan were under considerable pressures and struggled to deal with many issues of life, education, and economics. There was little free energy left over for them to "readily stretch to radically new ways of evangelizing the Muslims –

---

[64] Winter adds a significant, sensitive issue to the presentation at this point: the lack of production of a New Testament using "the religious language of the Urdu-speaking Muslims, even though there are more than 30 million Urdu-speaking Muslims alone." (Winter, 1975, 235) The NT translation used words that made perfect sense to Hindu-background Christians, but were offensive to Muslims.

especially not to ways that will allow the Muslims the kind of liberty in Christ which the Gospel guarantees them." (Winter, 1975, 235)

Questions About the Theological Nature of the Task

The transcription of Winter's presentation included as much text on the theological nature of the task as he had up to this point. Most of the questions he received before the Congress were on the topics of syncretism and the unity of the church.

Syncretism

Winter summarized these concerns under the question: "Will not the allowance of indigenous life ways lead us into syncretism?" (Winter, 1975, 236) Winter mentions how the church in the West where he grew up, included things such as Easter which came from "a Teutonic spring goddess of fertility called *Eostre*" and Christmas, with December 25 having been chosen by the Romans.[65] He refers to another presenter named Michael Green,[66] who had given a major address at the Congress before Winter called "Methods and Strategy in the Evangelism of the Early Church." (Green, 1975) Winter refers to Green's presentation as "already answering this for us in his excellent discussion of flexibility without syncretism." (Winter, 1975, 236)

Green argued that evangelism should be much higher on the list of priorities than it is for many churches.[67] Later in his presentation Green discusses how the early church's evangelism to the Gentiles was different. While the example in Acts was Christ-centered, there was flexibility in

---

[65] Now, with the re-secularization of the Christmas holiday, we are all fighting to "maintain Christ in Christmas." (Winter, 1975, 236)

[66] Green was a respected college principal from St. John's College in Nottingham England. He had written several books, and was fairly known in the U.S. as well.

[67] In his introduction, he contrasted the early church with the modern church and emphasized the early church's following the lead of the Holy Spirit in "every evangelistic advance recorded in Acts." (Green 1975, 160) He discussed a number of contrasts, and mentions syncretism among them: "The early church was very flexible in its preaching of the Good News, but utterly opposed to syncretism (mixing other elements with the Gospel) of any sort. Many parts of the modern church tend to be rigid in their evangelistic categories, but are inclined to play a great deal with syncretism, as Lesslie Newbigin has forcefully pointed out in *The Finality of Christ*." (Green, 1975, 159)

how it was presented.[68] Green continues to give illustration of his point, noting "while the early Christians would use any pathway to Christ, it was to Christ that these pathways unambiguously led. There was no hint of compromise, of syncretism." (Green, 1975, 165)

While Winter clearly mentioned additional issues of syncretism throughout the remainder of his presentation, he quickly moves on to the question of unity in Christ.

Church Unity

His summary question for this issue was, "Will not our unity in Christ be destroyed if we follow a concept of cross-cultural evangelization which is willing to set up separate churches for different cultural groups within the same geographical area?" (Winter, 1975, 236) Winter shared how his thinking on this issue had changed. Integrating people in America into white churches was practically assumed to mean that everyone would speak English and those from different sub-cultures would eventually come to the white Anglo-Saxon way for church and life. Well-meaning churches did not intentionally exclude anyone by pursuing this path, but that was the practical consequence.

Missionaries who followed this line of thinking had "assumed that there ought to be just one national church in a country – even if this means none at all for certain sub-groups." In contrast, groups like the Southern Baptists expanded across the Northern U.S. and established Arab, Japanese, Portuguese, Greek and Polish churches, while "Anglo churches, with all their evangelistic zeal, simply did not have the insight to do this kind of E-2 and E-3 evangelism." (Winter, 1975, 236)

As he wrestled with this question, he was "no less concerned than before about the unity and fellowship of the Christian movement across all ethnic and cultural lines" and wrote, "but I realize now that Christian unity cannot be healthy if it infringes upon Christian liberty." (Winter, 1975, 237) Healthy diversity in human society and in the world church should be the norm. He illustrated this from Pakistan again, arguing that what might be needed was a church that externally exhibited many of the forms of the local Muslim culture. By filling familiar forms with new content, the church could avoid false stereotypes that were barriers to the gospel and, as

---

[68] For example, in the Gentile context the evangelists did not quote extensively from the Old Testament. In contrast, Paul referred to an altar to an unknown God as an illustration.

a result, would be able to make the gospel clearer to those they sought to evangelize.

> I see the world church as the gathering together of a great symphony orchestra where we don't make every new person coming in play a violin in order to fit in with the rest. We invite the people to come in to play the same score – the Word of God[69] – but to play their own instruments, and in this way there will issue forth a heavenly sound that will grow in the splendor and glory of God as each new instrument is added. (Winter, 1975, 237)

He then turned to the kinds of churches Paul established. Was there an example of Paul establishing different churches for slaves and masters? What is our view of church and the situation Paul found himself in with the churches at Rome? Paul probably did not establish different churches for different social groupings such as slaves and masters. "We cannot believe he ever separated people. However, we do know that he was willing to adopt in different places a radically different approach, as he put it, 'for those under the law and for those not under the law.'" (Winter, 1975, 237) Winter argued that the church in Galatians provides an example of a church with different lifestyle choices, referring to the confrontation between Paul and Peter over Peter's change of behavior when Jewish believers arrived.

In Winter's file is a copy of Rene Padilla's presentation paper called "Evangelization and the World."[70] (Padilla, 1975) It was the fourth paper given at the Congress, just after McGavran.[71] On it, Winter wrote, "We must forever destroy the idea that missionary work is a geographical move. [Such as] Koreans sending missionaries after their own [people] in Germany."[72]

To Winter, traveling to another country to share the gospel does not make a person a missionary.[73] He did not consider it a part of true,

---

[69] At this point in the audiotape of Winter's presentation, the audience clapped, and Winter said, "Don't clap too soon, because this is a really nitty-gritty question."

[70] This is the title on the paper in the files. However, the title in the book is "Evangelism and the World."

[71] A summary of McGavran's paper can be found in Appendix S.

[72] He wrote this below what is the first line of the text on page 144 in the compendium. By "their own" Winter was referring to the practice of Koreans reaching Koreans in Germany, or some other country. To Winter, this was not missions work. It was certainly not E-2 or E-3.

[73] While he did not specifically comment on Koreans sending missionaries to Koreans in other nations at the Congress, he did in other situations.

missionary outreach if Christians merely send people to other countries to work in the same cultural situation they had back home.[74]

On the back page of Padilla's pre-congress paper, as he prepared for his presentation, Winter wrote similar ideas in the following bullet points:

- The E-1 evangelist and all people whose ministry is among people of their own kind find culture to be an obstacle to the gospel, and are constantly fighting against it.
- People who preach that the gospel must be adapted to each particular culture immediately seem to threaten the anti-cultural efforts of the Christians already working within that culture.
- However, the cross-cultural evangelist finds almost the reverse problem – he is tempted to carry his own culture over with his gospel.
- Thus you find an automatic conflict between these two types of people.

And at the bottom of the page he added: "Requiring a cultural shift in order to be a Christian confuses the nature of repentance without which conversion is spurious. The E-3 missionary's worst problem is to make clear what repentance and faith is in the indigenous culture."[75]

Next, Winter turned to Paul's treatment of certain foods, suggesting that in some situations people abide by the sensibilities of the majority. Yet modern parallels are difficult to deal with. The New Testament situation is hard to apply, for example, with Brahmins in India, where Brahmins do not eat meat but Christians do.

The New Testament situation would compare more easily to modern India today were it the case that only Christians in India were Brahmins (and other members of the middle castes) with their highly restrictive diet. Then we would envision Brahmin Christians finding it hard to allow the less restrictive meat-eating groups to become Christian; but the actual situation is very nearly the reverse. In India today it is those who eat meat who are Christians, and the problem is how to apply Paul's missionary strategy to this situation. In regard to food restriction, it is as though the Brahmins are "under the law," not the present Christians. (Winter, 1975, 238)

---

[74] This characterized much of the Korean early missions movement.

[75] Hand written notes by Winter on the back of René Padilla's presentation paper.

Winter would come back to this specific issue toward the end of his presentation. Here, he wondered if Paul would say, "If meat makes my brother offended, I will eat no meat"?[76] But no matter what Paul might have said in the modern world, there is never "a policy of segregation, nor any kind of ranking of Christians in first- and second-class categories. It rather guarantees equal acceptability of different traditions. It is a clear-cut apostolic policy against forcing Christians of one life-style to be proselytized to the cultural patterns of another." It was not a side issue in the New Testament, nor is it today.

In his files on the Congress, Winter handwrote a note, that expressed the situation with the Brahmins a slightly different way:

> If we try to encourage a Brahmin family to begin worship services in their home, we do not need to require them to invite to the very first service outcasts from across town. By becoming Christians they are knowingly joining a world family that includes all people, including outcastes. By allowing Brahmin congregations we are not proposing Brahmin segregation from the world church.[77]

Winter argued that the issue of how other cultural patterns are handled is central to the spread of the gospel. He warns that this was the cause of Paul's martyrdom at the hands of Asian Jews, possibly believing Jews, "who pointed him out in the temple." (Winter, 1975, 239) Anyone who seeks to move from one culture to another in order to work as a cross-cultural evangelist must realize that it will not be without struggle.[78]

We seem to have no problem with missionaries establishing churches in Japan that speak Japanese or churches in Hong Kong that speak Chinese, but somehow if these same believers live in Los Angeles, we expect them to worship together with English worshipers.

---

[76] From I Corinthians 8:13. Winter is commenting on the issue within India because Christians there eat meat, and often required new Christians to eat meat as proof they had left Hinduism. That was something with which Winter completely disagreed.

[77] In hand-written notes in a "packet" called "INGREDIENTS," 5.

[78] Apparently some had asked what Winter meant by the suggestion that youth churches be established. He made clear that he was not suggesting that the youth be segregated. "Youth churches are not ends, but means. We are not abandoning the thought that young people and older people should often be in the same service together. We are merely insisting, with what I pray is apostolic intuition, that young people have the freedom in Christ to meet together by themselves if they choose to and especially if this allows them to attract other young people who would likely not come to Christ in an age-integrated service." (Winter, 1975, 240)

If you talk with different people, you will get different answers. In my opinion, this question about evangelistic strategy in the forming of separate congregations must be considered an area of Christian liberty, and if so be decided purely on the basis of whether or not it allows the Gospel to be presented effectively to more people – that is, whether it is evangelistically strategic. Some go as far as granting separate *language* congregations, but hesitate when the differences between people are social and non-linguistic. Somehow they feel that people may be excused for meeting separately if their language is different, but that the Gospel urges us to ignore all other cultural differences. (Winter, 1975, 241)

Winter proposed that we seek to foster oneness and fellowship between congregations, rather than teaching them all to worship according to the same pattern. He knew this was a difficult subject to communicate and he mentions that he regrets that fact that he brought it up. But he believed raising the issue was crucial for the continued advance of the gospel. He closes his talk, bringing together the statistical reality and the cultural complexity, challenging Christians to seriously consider not only the task remaining but how they might need to change to accomplish that task.

Jesus *died* for these people around the world. He did not die to preserve our Western way of life. He did not die to make Muslims stop praying five times a day. He did not die to make Brahmins eat meat. Can't you hear Paul the Evangelist saying we must go to these people within the systems in which they operate? True, this is the cry of a cross-cultural evangelist, not a pastor. We can't make every local church fit the pattern of every other local church. But we must have radically new efforts of cross-cultural evangelism in order to effectively witness to 2387 million people, and we cannot believe that we can continue virtually to ignore this highest priority. (Winter, 1975, 241)

Reactions to Winter's Congress Presentation

In Winter's files were a few handwritten notes.[79] One was from Robertson McQuilkin:[80]

> *Ralph,*
>
> *A masterful job. I stand amazed. I also continue to thank God for you – you strengthen us all. Thank You!*
>
> *Robertson*

Another note, said:

> *Dear Ralph,*
>
> *What a brilliant piece of work!*
>
> *I really think you sold the concept – comments where I was sitting were all affirmative. I am so proud to call you friend –*
>
> *Bruce*
>
> *[p.s.] Most exciting was to see some 3rd World folks who were "anti" suddenly discovering that you were on their side – joyously admitting it!*[81]

Both Ralph and Roberta commented that they were not sure if Ralph's message was really heard. Winter said that since his talk was given on a Saturday, the auditorium was half full. The fall 1974 issue of Fuller Seminary's quarterly, *Theology, News and Notes*, included two-pages of brief reports from Fuller alumni and faculty who attended the Lausanne Congress. Winter wrote (in full):

> Reading the many reports you see everywhere on what happened at Lausanne, I am convinced that I failed my own assignment there. I was asked to use one of the plenary sessions to describe the extent to which non-Christians are beyond the reach of the kind of *local evangelism* people usually talk about in evangelism conferences. I was supposed to explain the dimensions of the need for special *cross-cultural evangelism*. I did my best, but day after day the emphasis was

---

[79] In addition to various versions of the presentation, Winter's E-67 file for Lausanne 74 contains various handwritten calculations for the statistics and charts, notes to and from the publisher and notes to Winter from others.

[80] The note does not include his last name or the date. It is on stationary from Hotel Mirabeau Lausanne. I assume this is from Robertson McQuilkin, who had been a missionary in Japan, and then served as the President of Columbia Bible College from 1968–1990, when he retired early to care for his ailing wife. The school is now called Columbia International University.

[81] The note does not include his last name. It is not clear who this is. It was written on a torn-off half-sheet of lined paper.

upon strategy within nations along lines of local evangelism. Briefly, I showed that about 87% of the non-Christians in the world today (numbering 2.7 billion people) are sufficiently different in linguistic, social or economic culture so that ordinary personal or church-based evangelism is very unlikely to reach them. This calls for massive new efforts at cross-cultural evangelism, with all its requirements in special training and structures. But, as I say, this effort of mine was either too new, too technical or too unbelievable for report of the congress to take note! (Winter, 1974c, 13)

It may have taken some time, but many did pick up on various aspects of what both Winter and McGavran presented. Edward Dayton, director of World Vision's Mission Advanced Research and Communications Center (MARC) wrote about it in the fall of 1974. They had previously agreed with the core ideas, having directed the efforts to produce the *Unreached Peoples* (Missions Advanced Research and Communication Center, 1974) report for the Congress with the SWM faculty. Certainly, over the next ten years, Dayton's leading of the MARC work in the direction of the unreached people group concepts contributed to people's awareness. He wrote a three-page article on the Lausanne Congress for *World Vision* magazine called "A New Way to See the World." The article mentioned the work of the MARC, and Fuller's SWM in preparation of the event. It also emphasized the ongoing production of materials from the data they had and new data they were hoping to gather. Dayton quoted Winter on the subject of people blindness, which Winter had written about in the article that explained the concept of "people groups" for the *Unreached Peoples* report.[82] (Dayton, 1974,9)

Tim Stafford, now Senior Writer for *Christianity Today*, wrote an article on Winter 10-years later in 1984. He said it this way:

> ...McGavran's observation [was] that Christianity does not usually spread out indiscriminately, like ink in water, but along the lines of cultures and languages. To "jump" from one culture to another is unusual; we should expect "church growth" usually to occur within the boundaries of a particular culture.

> ...Winter simply flipped that idea on its head. If churches normally grow within the boundaries of culture,

---

[82] "People blindness" is the tendency to ignore people from different backgrounds or to consider them strange for some reason we do not understand.

then a culture that has no church may never be reached by normal church growth. (Stafford, 1984, 17)

For many, the impact of Winter's presentation took time to be fully understood. Twenty years after the event, Winter wrote what he felt was central to Lausanne.

>...the most important achievement of the conference was the great emphasis on looking at the world as peoples rather than as countries. Strategically, Lausanne also changed one key word from Berlin: the World Congress on Evangelism of 1966 became the International Congress on World Evangelization in 1974–the word evangelism being a never-ending activity, and evangelization being intended to be a project to be completed. Here, in embryo, was the concept of closure. (Winter, 1995b, 28-29)

Some 35 years later, at the third Lausanne Congress in Cape Town in October 2010, three major points were emphasized from the platform as the core impact of Lausanne '74:

1. The Lausanne Covenant.

2. The clear recognition and need for evangelicals to focus on social issues.[83]

3. The massive need to take the gospel to unreached people groups, as presented by Winter and illustrated by McGavran.

John Stott reflected back on the Congress and made note of information from Winter's presentation:

>...the startling figure that 2,700 million people remained unevangelized, but that nevertheless they could be reached if we were to break down the world's population into 'people groups,' distinguish between E1, E2 and E3 evangelism, and remember the 'great new resources for world evangelization' constituted by the younger churches. (Stott, 1997, xv)

In 2009, the Lausanne web site included the following as part of their tribute to Ralph Winter after his death:

>Many of the accomplishments of Ralph Winter's long career as a missionary, mission professor and "mission engineer" stemmed from his conviction that Christian organizations accomplish more when they cooperate in

---

[83] This is reflected in Section 5 of the Lausanne Covenant, found in Appendix T, and in the presentation by René Padilla, "Evangelism and the World" and Samuel Escobar, "Evangelism and Man's Search for Freedom, Justice and Fulfillment."

strategic ways. It was at the 1974 Lausanne International Congress on World Evangelization that Winter shared the concept of "unreached people groups" that significantly influenced evangelical mission energies ever since.[84]

The *L.A. Times* included this detail in their obituary for Winter: "Winter stepped onto the world stage in 1974 at the International Congress on World Evangelization in Lausanne, Switzerland. There he issued a call for other Protestant evangelists to proselytize[85] to the world's 'unreached people,' those who had not been exposed to Christianity."[86]

Some Reactions and Outcomes from Lausanne '74

Beyond the select responses and evaluation related to Winter's presentation above, the general reactions to Lausanne revealed several perspectives growing out of the event.

Arthur Johnston,[87] in his book *The Battle for World Evangelism*, wrote:
The magnitude and significance of the Lausanne...overwhelms the careful student of the history of Christianity. Its theological depth was not only apparent in the plenary paper, but also evident throughout the Congress and, especially, in the Lausanne Covenant.[88] (Johnston, 1978, 291)

In its 2011 obituary for John Stott, *TIME* magazine said, "The Englishman headed the drafting of the 1974 Lausanne Covenant, which led 2,300 leaders from 150 nations to affirm their dedication to global

---

[84] Accessed on January 17, 2011: http://www.lausanne.org/lausanne-connecting-point/remembering-dr-ralph-winter.html

[85] L.A. Times, May 24, 2009. Accessed on January 17, 2011: http://www.latimes.com/news/obituaries/la-me-ralph-winter24-2009may24,0,6876811.story

It should be noted that Winter almost never used the word "proselytize" except to distance himself from it. As should be clear in this section, he was not interested in turning people into "Christians" from some other religious/cultural background. He did not believe that faith in Christ required religious change (external), but change of the heart (internal).

[86] Winter would not be interested in exposing anyone to "Christianity" per se, but to Christ and the Bible.

[87] When he wrote, Johnston was the Chair of the Division of World Missions and Evangelism at Trinity Evangelical Divinity School. He had served more than twenty years with The Evangelical Alliance Mission in France and had a PhD from the University of Strasbourg.

[88] He continued: "The ethnic and national diversity ... revealed evangelicalism as a significant unifying element in Christendom." (Johnston, 1978, 291)

evangelism, cementing his status as an ambassador and supporting the faith in the developing world."[89] (TIME, 2011, 24)

The *Evangelical Missions Quarterly* (*EMQ*) produced an entire issue on Lausanne '74. In it, editor James Reapsome, who attended the Congress, addressed the question many people had asked beforehand, namely, that since previous missions congresses (such as Berlin '66) had been dominated by the WCC, would Lausanne '74 turn out to be similar. He concluded:

> ...participants seemed more concerned about what they could learn at the congress that would help them get on with the job of evangelism in their own countries, and how national churches could indeed be instruments in the hand of God for world evangelization, working together with missionaries from the traditional "sending" countries. (Reapsome, 1974, 260)

Reapsome noted that the issue of unity was not ignored, but was "explored more fully. Some of the debates centered on crucial issues indeed: social action and the struggle for justice among the oppressed; church growth technology; full self-hood among the younger churches; and the message of the gospel itself in terms of theological, cultural and political considerations." (Reapsome, 1974, 261)

The event became a launching pad in several ways. The Lausanne movement itself grew out of the meeting. It was not planned, but the location of the meeting in Lausanne, Switzerland, became the name of a movement. First, there was the Lausanne Covenant.[90] Looking back now, the document may have been more widely used by various organizations in the evangelical movement than any other. (Douglas, 1975, 5)

Participants at the Congress were offered the opportunity to sign the Lausanne Covenant. It was described as a "'commitment that leads to action.' It thoroughly commits signers to the 'urgency of the evangelistic task' as well as to 'Christian social responsibility.' It will possibly become a major statement of evangelical convictions in the history of the church and

---

[89] *TIME* continued: "Indeed, his focus on earthly concerns such as poverty and social justice served as a counterpoint to more-boisterous Evangelical leaders who set their sights firmly on the afterlife."

[90] The word Covenant was used for the commitment document produced at the event. The idea was more along the lines of a contract or binding agreement, rather than a biblical covenant.

missions." (Reapsome, 1974, 262) By the time the Congress was adjourned, about 2,200 had signed it.[91]

When presented with the idea of a group that would continue to grapple with these issues, "Over 90 percent voted for a continuing communication link, and 72 percent for a Lausanne Continuation Committee." (Douglas, 1975, xvi) A number of other outcomes from the Lausanne Congress can be found identified and evaluated in the PhD thesis by Klas Ingvar Lundström, *Gospel and Culture in the World Council of Churches and the Lausanne Movement* with particular focus on the period 1973-1996. (Lundström, 2006)

Lundström concluded:

> Lausanne movement was organized primarily through its continuation committee, the *Lausanne Committee for World Evangelization* (LCWE) which started its work in 1975. In 1976 the continuation committee organized four working groups, of which the *Theology Working Group* (TWG) and the *Strategy Working Group* (SWG) became the most influential. There has however been some tension between these two groups as they represent two different approaches to mission.[92]

There were six consultations from 1977 to 1982 instigated by the Theology and Education Group and the Strategy Working Group. One of those was on the Homogeneous Unit Principle, discussed earlier.[93]

There were certainly those who left Lausanne with concerns or frustrations. The same article noted that the Lausanne Covenant itself "might take more seriously the enormous and varied E-2 and E-3 evangelistic needs..." (Works, 1974, 426) A later article, also in the *Church Growth Bulletin*, was called "Congress Covenant Falls Short". (Montgomery, 1974) Montgomery recognized that the task of world evangelism would be furthered by Christians getting more serious about living out their faith. But he wanted to see more suggestions about specific

---

[91] John Stott described the seven major emphases to look for when reading the Lausanne Covenant: "the authority of Scripture, the nature of evangelism, the grounds of Christian social responsibility, the costliness and urgency of world mission, the problems of culture and the reality of spiritual warfare." (Stott, 1997, xv)

[92] Lundström later gives example of these debates, such as the Homogeneous Unit Principle consultation previously mentioned.

[93] Other consultations included topics such as: the Willowbank meeting in Bermuda on Gospel and Culture; a consultation on Muslim evangelization; a consultation on Simple Lifestyle; a large consultation in Pattaya Thailand following up the Lausanne '74 theme of "Let the Earth Hear His Voice" with the theme: "How Shall They Hear?"

Ralph D. Winter: Early Life and Core Missiology

strategies. "...many thoroughly evangelical churches with mature Christians in them have become sealed off from the great harvests about them. What is needed is for these churches to break out of their ghettos and make hard, bold plans to give a dynamic testimony to the world." (Montgomery, 1974, 463) He also believed that the Covenant needed two statements added, one on "Goals for World Evangelization" and "A Strategy for World Evangelization." This basic strategy was to be developed from the Scriptures as applied to the present conditions in the world.

Ralph Covell, mission professor from the U.S., felt there was a "willingness to listen to the Third World voices on a variety of issues." Those third world leaders may "pick and choose" from the strategies presented, "They like the broad concepts, but do not want the whole package." He felt the congress did not deal with cross-cultural evangelism enough, and "only seriously grappled with 'missions'" here and there. He also expressed concern over the "amazing lack of emphasis on China, one-fourth of the world's population."[94] (Reapsome, 1974, 302)

Christianity Today continued to report on Lausanne 74. Many of those reports were more general, mentioning major issues and personalities such as Billy Graham or Jack Dain or John Stott. A few mentioned one or two of the plenary presentations, usually the ones related to the social issues by Escobar and Padilla.[95]

One year later, *CT* produced most of an issue on Lausanne 74. Billy Graham wrote the cover article. His only reference to Winter or McGavran was, "We must pray for and be prepared for evangelism in parts of the world whose doors are seemingly closed; some are already opening, and others may soon open." (Graham, 1975a, 4)

Peter Wagner, professor at the SWM, wrote one of the *CT* articles, pointing out three elements that had the potential to derail the Congress or "torpedoes," and three that are a great help to world evangelization or "boons." First, the potential "torpedoes":
1. An attempt to confuse evangelism with social action.
2. An attempt to confuse evangelism with Christian cooperation.
3. An attempt to confuse evangelism with church nurture. (Wagner, 1975, 7-8)

His three "boons" or points of information, which the Congress raised, were:

---

[94] Covell was mentioned earlier in relation to his trip with Winter for TEE in the early 70s. James Reapsome, editor of *EMQ*, apparently interviewed Covell.
[95] See for example, "The View from Lausanne" (Plowman, 1974).

328

1. New awareness of the amazing progress of world evangelization (particularly shown the broad global participation in the Congress).
2. New awareness of the challenge ahead, noted by McGavran in 2.7 billion to be reached (the status quo could not remain).
3. New awareness of the complexity of the task, as Winter had pointed out in "Seeing the Task Graphically." (Wagner, 1975, 8-9)

Wagner, co-worker of Winter at the SWM, was not the only person to reference Winter's input with regard to his presentation at Lausanne. While most of the general reports do not include much about the unique missionary task, the *CT* editorial team wrote: "At Lausanne congress missionary theoretician Ralph Winter delivered a paper on this subject that may well become a standard treatise of the needs of this age."[96] (Editorial, 1974, 40)

Certainly, other concerns were voiced. Johnston noted that (1) some felt there was a weakness related to the view of inspiration of Scripture. More conservative groups wanted a stronger statement. (2) While the issue of evangelism versus social concerns was dealt with in a significant way, people on both extremes of the issue may not have felt the answers were clear enough. (3) Others felt the issue of the role of church and mission society was not clearly handled. And connected with that ideas, that (4) the "institutionalized ecclesiology" characterized the Lausanne Covenant. (Johnston, 1978, 324-329)

Summary and Analysis

Winter was 49 years old when he stepped onto the platform in Lausanne Switzerland in 1974. The event was both a literal and figurative platform where he sought to communicate what he had identified to be the most significant problems in missions. He had served ten years as a missionary in Guatemala and eight years as a faculty member at Fuller's School of World Mission. His ability to generate new ideas and identify problems had been honed by exposure to missionaries, mission, and church leaders at the local, regional, national and international levels. Now, instead of brainstorming with only a few friends and colleagues, such as Jim Emery or Ross Kinsler, he was interacting with all of Fuller's faculty

---

[96] The editorial writer had just made a reference to Winter's point that it "may be easier for Latin American Christians to reach Muslims in India than it would be for nearby Hindus who become Christians to do so." (Editorial, 1974, 40)

and associates. This rich context provided the fertile soil for the growth and cultivation of the ideas for his Lausanne presentation.

For Winter, one set of needs and solutions naturally led to his next focus area. He is best remembered for his ministry in Guatemala revolving around solving the problem of providing training for rural pastors. TEE was the result. That TEE involvement led him to SWM. While training mission leaders at the SWM, he found himself focusing on the unique role of sodalities. This growing interest in sodalities came, in part, from his teaching on the historical expansion of Christianity globally. His historical and engineering perspective led him to apply the same tools – statistics – to the current state of missions. As he contemplated both historical and current data he gained new insights into the challenges of reaching those requiring cross-cultural evangelism.

While Winter remained a creative thinker and prolific writer throughout his life, at the SWM his focus gradually shifted from teaching and writing about TEE to other topics. McGavran brought Winter to the SWM because of his creative thinking about missions, missionaries and TEE. This was reflected in the Gimmickitis article. The relationship between Winter and Dan Fuller must have helped, too, since Dan was a part of the leadership at Fuller when Winter joined the faculty.

Working with McGavran continued to shape and expand Winter's knowledge and understanding. Undoubtedly no other Christian at that time had a greater depth of exposure to the world and the global missions scene than McGavran.[97] His long and rich experiences in India provided both a context and a passion for his life and work. Beyond that, his travels in Africa and many other countries and his interest in learning more from associates garnered authority in mission circles – not to mention deep respect from Winter.[98] McGavran significantly influenced Winter's focus

---

[97] I am not aware of anyone Winter ever knew well who had broader global experience.

[98] McGavran biographer, Vern Middleton, wrote, "each year after 1954 he traveled extensively. In 1954 he hitchhiked across Africa from Mombasa to Lagos. He visited all the countries of Eastern Asia except North Korea and Mongolia. He visited and studied countries in SE Asia. I was with him on trips to Dacca Bangladesh. He did extensive studies in the Caribbean and Latin America. He visited Canada on several speaking engagements. I am certain he visited most of the countries in Central America. He visited New Zealand and Australia. What is significant is not the number of countries visited but the number of countries he studied the missionary histories and was aware of the factors causing growth and impeding growth. Many books were published both by McGavran and his students that would easily cover more than 70 countries." Email from Vern Middleton to the author, Feb. 21, 2011, 1.

as he prepared for Lausanne '74 and continued to influence his thinking for the rest of his life.

Naturally, there were differences between Winter and McGavran. McGavran had a "laser like" focus on church growth.[99] While McGavran had other interests and there are many nuances within church growth, his writing and speaking focused on this issue. Winter certainly gave unwavering energy to whatever he was working on, sometimes for months or years. But his breadth of interests led him naturally from one idea to another. The three significant contributions this thesis includes – TEE, Sodalities and the Lausanne focus on unreached people groups – are examples of this kind of progression.[100]

Winter's on-going study and teaching of history fed other areas of interest and study. While never "trained" in history, as with any other subject he set his mind to, he learned quickly and continually. He and Roberta absorbed all they could from any source possible.[101] When he traveled and worked with associates from other nations, he observed their culture and often referred to illustrations from those cultures in his presentations.

The SWM faculty articles for Key 73 published in *Christianity Today* provided an opportunity for the Fuller missiology and strategies to be highlighted. Key 73 sought to mobilize outreach and challenge the evangelistic approaches of American Christians within the borders of the U.S. The SWM input contributed a perspective on reaching the growing ethnic diversity in the country. In his article, Winter indirectly raised the sodality/modality role distinction. Many pastors and churches needed to realize that new believers from non-Christian backgrounds would not likely be comfortable at their churches, at least at first. While churches would not necessarily start sodalities for this kind of work in the U.S., some might. But for many individual churches, the idea of starting a new

---

[99] In a verbal conversation on February 18, 2011, Vern Middleton agreed that this was true. He also recounted the story of when McGavran was on the mission field in the 1930s. Because of the Great Depression, the mission had to cut back to 25% of the budget they had two years before. McGavran interviewed all of the missionaries to see how much time they were spending in evangelism. When it turned out that it was very little if any, he helped institute a requirement that at least 8 hours a week be spent in such work.

[100] Future study of Winter's life should no doubt reveal continual progression of thought.

[101] In addition to the books purchased regularly by Winter, he subscribed to many magazines and journals as well. He agreed with those who noted that often the best thinking is first expressed in journals, not in books.

church in the U.S. was a pioneering idea requiring sodality-like giftings and skills.

By 1973, the distinction in roles between church nurture and mission pioneering had become an integral part of Winter's solution to the problem of two-billion people needing cross-cultural evangelism. New and existing agencies were a crucial part of the solution. But this new vision developed gradually, as Winter worked through a series of interactions as he taught, wrote, spoke, edited and revised his understanding of the problem at hand, which he later called "the task remaining." As was his habit, he sought to explain the concept in such a way that others would get engaged in helping to solve it. But he also suggested first steps toward solutions to the problem. This is similar to his attempts to increase interest in Guatemala by people back in the U.S. or to mobilize business investments in the region.

In addition to the influence of associates and mentors, many other skills, interests, and experiences contributed to his thinking. Earlier, in Guatemala he worked with numbers for business and local mission accounting. At the SWM, growth rates for churches and regional or global statistics became common. Statistics raised awareness of where in the world the church was growing and where it did not exist. That led to the consideration of questions like, "how are we doing in the missionary task?" in his writing in the 1970s.

Winter's work combined raw global statistics with regional population and growth rates and missionary deployment. At the time, basic, global level statistics were available to mission leaders. It would not have been surprising to the mission world that 2.3 billion people were non-Christians.[102] However, Winter gently but firmly pointed out that: 1) These unreached groups were concentrated in the Hindu, Muslim and Chinese (later Buddhist) cultures, 2) No matter how much the church was growing in one culture it would not impact the millions of people in thousands of other cultural groups because these unreached groups were beyond the reach of existing Christian efforts of any kind.

Winter concluded then, that, 3) the national church could not do the job alone. In fact, at times, they were a stumbling block to the process.[103] The support for this conclusion was both statistical and logical. First of all,

---

[102] For example, in 1959 Stephen Neill talked about "those who have never yet heard the Name of Christ; and that, in 1959, means half the people now living on the earth." (1959, 82, quoted earlier)

[103] Something Winter indirectly pointed out in his comments at Lausanne referring to some Indian Christians who expect Hindus to eat meat when they become Christians.

statistics demonstrated that they were not reaching these populations. Beyond that, there were cultural reasons (the groups to be reached were very different from the nearby Christians) and logistical reasons (the sheer size of the task) that militated against the national churches succeeding. Thus, Winter noted that 4) a special kind of missionary work was needed, which he called cross-cultural (E-3) evangelism.[104] It did not matter what culture or country the missionary was coming from, it would still be E-3, because the missionary would be crossing cultural borders.[105]

Only if missions, missionaries, and churches took E-3 cross-cultural evangelism seriously, could the cultural distance between Christian and non-Christian people groups be bridged and the door open for the spread of the gospel within the culture (as E-1). Winter suggested that in order for missionaries to do cross-cultural evangelism, not only was learning the new language and non-Christian culture necessary, but 1) Christians would have to "unlearn" some of their own cultural distinctives and learn to distinguish between how Christians live out their faith in one culture versus another. Winter's references toward the end of his Lausanne presentation suggested that he believed a part of the process would be to 2) seriously consider what the Bible actually says and means, not what our cultural Christianity has led us to believe about a given issue. The E-3 missionary, no matter what culture s/he is from, must learn to discern what is merely cultural and what would not necessarily be a part of how new believers would practice faith.[106]

Winter argued that the distance between the Christian and non-Christian in E-3 evangelism was so huge that it would require a new level

---

[104] Early USCWM staff member D. Bruce Graham first pointed out the idea of a new, special kind of missionary in my hearing. I do not remember the date.

[105] As he writes about Winter's central idea, Alan Johnson writes that "implicit within our two thousand years of mission theologizing are also understandings about *where* mission should take place.... This is the genius so to speak boiled out of all that frontier missions and unreached people thinking brings to us; without answering 'among whom' and thus 'where' mission is to be done in light of the witness of Scripture and God's intent for the world, we do not yet have a full blown missiology." (Johnson, 2009, 5) Johnson was not talking about geography. Instead he was adding a forth point based upon David Bosch's three basic questions: (1) why mission, (2) how mission and, (3) what is mission? (Bosch, 1993, 179)

[106] Later, Winter would argue even more strongly for the necessity of missionaries to "unlearn" their own culture and many Christian practices in order for the gospel to be effectively communicated. This was called "Dewesternization" and was discussed at length in the magazine *Mission Frontiers* (of which Winter was the editor until months before his death) and the journal *International Journal for Frontier Missions*, (to which Winter contributed and, for various periods, served as editor).

of understanding and commitment on the part of Christians and missionaries. Historically, many of the breakthroughs of the gospel were not achieved with the kinds of approach that would be necessary for these remaining cultures and for which Winter was calling. Where churches had been established, many followed patterns of the missionary's church culture back home, often without either the missionary or the nationals realizing it.[107]

A central idea then was that a whole new approach would be needed to penetrate these cultures that did not have the gospel.[108] Usual and accepted missionary approaches to cross-cultural evangelism including language and culture learning were not enough. A new, serious level of cultural engagement would need to be applied, which would be difficult even for a committed Christian focused on world mission to comprehend. By addressing this issue at Lausanne, Winter shed light on a gap in Christian perception.

At Lausanne Winter challenged others but he and Roberta also felt personally challenged concerning peoples where there was no church or effective gospel witness. The huge need for the gospel to take root among groups within the Muslim, Hindu and Chinese blocs, where existing missions efforts were not addressing the issue and attempts to reach these unreached required a new level of sensitivity to cultural differences for those efforts to be successful.

Winter began discussing with top leaders the idea of having an "implementation annex" at FTS. The idea was to engage mission agency collaboration and focus attention on the remaining task. However, Fuller turned down the idea. Additionally, on a global level there were many places and some missions for whom Fuller's ability to help had become limited. Winter's involvement with associates from a wide range of mission organizations and his exposure to leaders from around the world (such as David Cho from Korea) may have contributed to his growing sense that the "Fuller platform," which originally drew him away from Guatemala, was becoming too limited for him.

---

[107] Often resulting in a church that is not considered indigenous to the culture.

[108] Winter had been exposed to many in history who did seek to do this kind of outreach. Even during his lifetime, he met missionary to Muslims Samuel Zwemer and heard him talk about the value of Muslims hearing Christians pray.

Assessment and Contribution

Winter's core ideas developed as he interacted with various experiences. For example, his ideas surrounding TEE were the product of his Guatemala experiences and his emphasis on unreached peoples grew out of his time at Fuller's SWM. Being around people like Jim Emery, Donald McGavran and others, helped Winter develop and hone his ideas. At Fuller, Winter became increasingly focused on the remaining missionary task.[109] Today, many people trace their involvement in reaching unreached cultures to Winter's presentation at Lausanne, even if their personal exposure to him or his presentation is only indirect.

Some of Winter's contribution to evangelical missiology leading up to the Lausanne plenary and the impact of the presentation is summarized below. Not all of these thoughts were original with Winter, yet he combined them into a uniquely coherent and compelling framework for understanding the overall unfinished mission task.

His contribution:

1. was a correction to the "missionary go home" mentality from the 1960s, which was misinterpreted to mean that because foreign missionaries were not needed or wanted in some places in the developing world, that they were not needed or wanted anywhere.

2. highlighted large portions of the world's population that were unreached but which were being overlooked by the global church. Though the remaining task was large, he emphasized that it should not seem overwhelming.

3. hinted at the idea that sodalities could be created to reach people who were beyond existing church or mission efforts. Asians in particular were challenged in this way.

4. occurred at a time that was ripe for change, when social upheaval and unrest in the west left a new generation of young people eager for something worth giving their lives. Many embraced the vision that Winter articulated and it shaped their lives and vocation to a significant degree.

5. was a challenge to see the unreached world in a new way through a cross-cultural perspective and to think about whole new ways to effectively present the gospel so that it could more readily cross cultural borders.

---

[109] From the perspective at that time by evangelicals interested in global mission outreach.

6. raised the issue of cultural distance between the missionary and the least reached people and pointed out that cultural distance can be large despite Christian and non-Christian people groups living within close geographical proximity.

7. emphasized Christian liberty within cultures new to the gospel over unity of Christians across cultures with respect to initial evangelism strategies.

8. was a challenge not merely to send more missionaries, but to consider more carefully *where* they were sent, and to set that vision high so as to meet the large needs that existed.

9. became a rallying point for the newly available computer data and information systems and those who used them. It helped provide new categories that increased the awareness and understanding of the unreached and helped in guiding prayer and outreach for them.

10. highlighted the strong need for new expressions of church through cross-cultural evangelism. These churches would need to be appropriate for believers from cultures newly reached with the gospel.

11. sought to recognize the need for plans and cultural learning on the part of the missionary, done in the power and work of the Holy Spirit.

12. helped to focus more attention on missionaries being sent from non-Western cultures.

13. recognized that syncretism is a problem in both new and established churches. Christians should look very carefully at their own practices and what they expect new believers in another culture to embrace, based on Scripture.

14. distinguished between "going overseas" to do church or evangelism ministry with your own culture in another country with working cross-culturally wherever an unreached culture happens to be located.

15. was a part of what helped to impel the Lausanne Movement and further global networking and cooperation among Christians.[110]

---

[110] This point is not intended to ignore the long and significant history of what is now called the World Evangelical Alliance, (http://www.worldevangelicals.org) whose purpose is broader than the Lausanne Movement. (www.lausanne.org)

16. helped launch new agencies focused on frontier in mission, including the U.S. Center for World Mission, and many other mission agencies or departments within existing missions.

17. raised the issue of how existing Christians in established churches as "stronger" brothers and sisters are to treat "weaker" brothers and sisters in the body of Christ.[111] This raised, and continues to raise, additional issues related to how Muslims, Hindus and Buddhists are viewed and approached by Christians, and how they might express faith in Christ in their context.

There were also issues where significant critiques were voiced:

1. It was too obscure or technical for the average Christian and could easily be ignored, misunderstood or be seen as overcomplicating the task.

2. The focus on specific people groups could become an oversimplification of what needed to be done. Cultures and how they differ is highly nuanced.

3. For some, unity is always more important than evangelism strategies. Or said less strongly, the unity of the body of Christ should always be taken seriously as strategies are developed and implemented. Those who believe unity is a higher value, do not hold this as a matter of preference, but as a mandate.

4. Some, especially from South Asia, see an emphasis on culturally specific mission work among unreached people groups or castes as having the potential to become a form of racism.[112]

5. Many, especially in areas with strong Christian populations, have struggled to understand what Winter meant when he talked about using different approaches in reaching out to Muslims, Hindus and Buddhists.

6. Many mission leaders got the message and through them over time the missionaries they serve, but there are many churches and missionaries who have not heard or understood the task remaining as outlined by Winter.

7. For some, Lausanne did not go far enough in response to Winter and others' calls for taking seriously these untouched

---

[111] This is related to passages in the Bible by the apostle Paul, especially in Romans 14 and 1 Corinthians 8 and 9.

[112] I believe this ignores a number of arguments Winter, McGavran and others made, as noted earlier in this thesis.

cultures. Many tended to confuse evangelism and cross-cultural evangelism with Christian cooperation or church nurture.[113]

8. Some people responded to the unreached focus by becoming defensive and felt the need to defend the legitimacy of their work. Usually, these were missionaries who were working where there already was a church.[114]

9. It would be easy to forget the need for regular evangelism among "Christianized" people groups in places like Western Europe.

10. Finally, many cultures have been reached or now have either believers in Christ or missionaries on site. But much of the Muslim, Hindu and Buddhist blocs are largely unaffected by evangelical Christianity.[115]

Even today, within evangelicalism, debates on these issues continue, especially over: 1) how much of one's culture or society a new follower of Christ can retain and what must be rejected, 2) the balance between unity and liberty, and 3) the complexity and changing nature of the task remaining in a globalized world. There is no clear approach that is applicable in every situation, which certainly fuels the debate.

No matter what others thought, Ralph and Roberta felt compelled to act on where they sensed God was leading them.

Next Step: A Mission Sodality for Frontier Mission– 1976

Winter was not one to plan or set goals far ahead.[116] By his own admission, he simply followed where the available information led him. As

---

[113] As C. Peter Wagner pointed out. (Wagner, 1975, 7-8)

[114] Winter made a point not to push for the "redeployment" of missionaries in "reached" fields as some had. They were arguing that we should put all our mission resources into the unreached groups, even if that meant moving people from one country or language group to another. Winter argued that a missionary working among an already reached group, or a group that has a solid church, was in the best position to mobilize that church to begin work among unreached groups. While it cannot be attributed to Winter or any one person, there are now more than 12,000 missionaries from Latin America serving around the world. Such was not the case in 1974.

[115] And thus, by evangelical definitions, remain unreached or least reached.

[116] He wrote: "Plans over purpose need to succeed. A 'plan' can become a replacement for success. Trust the plan and you will miss the purpose." From Winter monthly schedule/planner: Dec. 10, 2002.

stated earlier, he was continually learning and identifying problems that needed to be solved. I have sought to demonstrate that the core missiological ideas and strategic actions of Winter's life each successively built on the previous and led to the next. Lessons in Guatemala led to observations about pastoral training needs, which led to TEE. TEE helped open doors at Fuller. His teaching at Fuller and studies of history and the Catholic orders over many years led him to his interest in sodalities. He realized that sodalities are core structures that God has used throughout history to identify gaps that the modalities are not suited to fill and plug them. But the study of them also demonstrated to Winter that there were areas of missions where neither sodalities nor modalities were at work and where modalities would likely be ineffective.

Winter thought that once others understood the data he was presenting, they would respond positively and help take on this new focus on cross-cultural evangelism to groups without the gospel. Given his way of looking at information and statistics, if someone did not "get it" or agree with him, it meant that he simply needed to communicate it differently or perhaps use a more transparent illustration. He could not comprehend that there were those who understood his point but argued against the core ideas.[117]

When highlighting the need for workers among the unreached peoples, Winter talked about 1,000 missionaries in his classrooms at the SWM. None had come from unreached cultures.[118] His illustration seems to have had its greatest impact on him and Roberta. They began to think that perhaps the time had come to create an organization, a sodality that would focus on these unreached peoples, that continued to confront them so unrelentingly. They began to consider the prospect of leaving Fuller in order to start such an organization.

Most friends felt leaving the Fuller platform was a bad idea. Fuller President Hubbard pointed out to Winter that tenured faculty do not usually leave unless there is a moral or ethical problem. Hubbard knew that if Winter left, he would be asked why. But as we have seen in other situations, Winter could separate himself from the opinions of others, and without qualms, make decisions contrary to prevailing opinions.

---

[117] He often argued the reverse of this. As a leader who was required to listen to the ideas of younger leaders, if he did not do what they suggested on a given issue, they would complain that he must not have heard them. Yet he felt he did hear and understand, but was merely doing what he felt he should, given his position and responsibility.

[118] As noted previously, these students were either westerners working around the world or international students coming from their own nations.

Other than his immediate family, only one person encouraged Winter. While standing on a balcony in 1976 near the offices of the SWM, Winter asked McGavran if he should leave Fuller and attempt to start an organization that would focus on the needs of unreached peoples. McGavran said, "Ralph, you have bigger fish to fry."[119] McGavran did not grasp all of the implications of Winter's impending decision, but he understood that Winter's vision had developed to the point where he needed a broader platform from which to contribute to the cause of missions worldwide, much as his transition from missionary to Fuller faculty member had accomplished ten years earlier.[120]

So, in the fall of 1976, Winter took a sabbatical from Fuller. He and Roberta felt compelled to act. At the same time, a modest college campus was available three miles north of Fuller. It would involve raising some $8 million.[121] They had virtually no money and no mailing list to approach for support.[122]

It is not my purpose, nor will space allow telling more of the story of the U.S. Center for World Mission.[123] Roberta wrote a book detailing the story of the early founding years called *Once More Around Jericho*. (Winter, 1979c) When Roberta revised it in 1987, she referred to a verse in Isaiah 43:19 and called it *I Will Do A New Thing*.[124] (Winter, 1987)

Some of the ministries that Winter started reflect directly his three key contributions detailed in this thesis. With Roberta, Winter also founded the William Carey International University in 1977 as a distance

---

[119] This is from an undated comment Winter mentioned several times in my hearing. Kraft mentioned that he believed that McGavran was "enamored" with Winter and his creative approach to all kinds of issues and ministry.

[120] According to Winter, McGavran did not quite understand all of what Winter was doing until several years later. This was especially true when Winter founded the William Carey International University in February of 1977, just three miles from Fuller. However, to Winter, the approach of the University had almost no overlap with Fuller. Later, McGavran joined the board of WCIU and Winter seemed pleased that McGavran appeared to understand what Winter was trying to accomplish.

[121] The entire campus purchase, which ultimately included about 85 homes on 17 acres as well as a 17-acre campus was priced at 11.5 million or just under £7.1 million.

[122] The Winters were on salary in Guatemala and at Fuller.

[123] Winter preferred the name "Center for World Mission" but others felt that would look like he was claiming to be THE center for world mission, something Winter did not intend.

[124] This was later revised to tell the whole story of the campus purchase years, including the "Last $1000 Campaign" which raised the final $8 million for the property (about £4.9 million) in 1987. After Roberta's death and before Ralph's, additional material was added. The latest edition is dated 2011 and is available from www.missionbooks.org

institution focused on international development, as Winter uniquely defined it before it became a popular term, offering the MA and PhD degrees.[125] The MA World Christian Foundations degree course was and is designed on the TEE core value of keeping men and women in ministry while they get further equipping. Students are not required to be residential, but are mentored face-to-face on a weekly basis.[126] The POWE is another example of a sodality that Winter founded. There were many other organizations that he helped to start together with others, such as the PUMA and the ASM.[127]

His efforts, from the end of his tenure at Fuller through the founding of the USCWM, were focused on reaching the unreached with the gospel through cross-cultural evangelism, as defined above. But during that same period and until Winter's death, he continued to be interested in a broad and continually growing range of issues or problems to be solved. These might seem disconnected to the issue of unreached cultures, but not to Winter. Winter pointed out that evangelism that stopped with merely "enlisting new Christians" and the planting of churches was incomplete. What are these new believers supposed to *do*, other than enlist more new believers? What should these believers be doing to demonstrate God's will or Kingdom on earth? For Winter, this raised the issue of eradicating disease later in his life, he considered it a battle with Satan to restore God's reputation, empower believers' evangelism, and demonstrate what God's will on earth should look like.[128]

---

[125] Winter had a very broad perspective on this phrase, which included much more than international aid, or development projects in needy regions. While these ideas would have been included, Winter would not have limited WCIU related studies to that kind of international development. His broad definition would include anything that helps develop a society. WCIU has had plans to offer a Bachelor of Arts degree as well.

[126] The WCF and the Perspectives course also use an adapted form of study which Winter learned at Prairie Bible Institute as detailed in Chapter 1, 70-71.

[127] Although these may not be technically "sodalities" in the pattern of the Roman Catholic orders, they were established to meet a need not usually met by a modality structure.

[128] Email from Beth Snodderly to the author on March 11, 2011, 1. Beth worked closely with Winter during the last years of his life, and especially on helping to shape the Roberta Winter Institute (RWI), which has the vision of a world in which believers establish eradication initiatives to demonstrate God's character and empower our witness. They seek to champion the cause of disease eradication for the glory of God. An early version of the RWI web site said: "We believe that God is sovereign over all things—including evil and suffering. Yet we also believe that He does not approve of evil or desire that people (or creation) suffer. What then do we make of the pervasive violence in nature? What do we make of the cleverly adapted parasite that ravages its host?" http://www.robertawinterinstitute.org/?page_id=2 Accessed on March 14, 2011.

He compiled a list of some of the problems he had been thinking about in a document initially called "24 Problems to Be Solved."[129] The document includes a brief summary as well as a full description of each problem.[130] During his last year of life Winter often said that correctly identifying the problem to solve is more important than working on the problem yourself. Winter was not willing to accept any obstacle in the way of what he felt needed to be done to help peoples from all cultures more clearly see God. At the time of the Lausanne '74 presentation, his problem list would have been centered around cross-cultural evangelism, but by the time of his death he had come to believe that evangelicals were blinded to certain realities which were, humanly speaking, keeping those without the gospel in darkness, by making God seen unconcerned, distant, or evil.[131]

While we will not all agree with Winter's selection of problems to be solved or his approach to solutions, it is my hope that others will study his later life to help us all understand better the crucial problems that we face now and in the future.

---

[129] See Appendix U for an expanded list of the 24 problems. Winter was considering what to do about some of these problems as far back as his time at Princeton.

[130] This was done, in part, to explain what he meant to those who would not understand why he would work on some of these seemingly unrelated problems as well as to be sure that those who wanted to help solve them would know specifically what Winter thought the problem was.

[131] He wrote: "In all my life I have never ever come across as large a realization of wrong. In the case of Unreached Peoples there was a huge course-correction that needed to be made. Now, in regard to corruption in nature, especially the micro-world, this is a much graver crisis and far more difficult to exposit." Winter Seven Star planner, January 18, 2003.

Chapter 8

Findings and Conclusion

Findings

Ralph D. Winter was a creative, counter-cultural, diligent entrepreneur who set out to identify and solve significant problems wherever he encountered them. I have sought to detail enough of his life and core missiological contributions to demonstrate the significance of his work and to address the central research issue: to explain how the influences in Ralph Winter's life came together to produce a missiologist whose endeavors helped shaped a global movement. To the degree I have succeeded, this study should be foundational to understanding the development of his life and his interaction with others.

I have sought to address the central research questions as listed below.

1. *How did historical events, trends, and key individuals shape Winter's development?*

I have demonstrated how his upbringing and the historical situation in America in the early 1900s shaped his life and direction. Central experiences which made an impact on Winter included:

1. His family upbringing and church experiences
2. North American fundamentalism and evangelicalism
3. World War Two and its social impact on the United States
4. The opportunities afforded by post-war Southern California
5. Life and study in seven different sub-cultural settings in the U.S. and Canada
6. Living and working in Guatemala
7. Training mission leaders at Fuller Seminary.[1]

Ralph's tendency to be introverted may have contributed to his countercultural approach and his willingness to engage and confront problems and people without letting the possible ramifications of his opinions sway his resolve. On the one hand these traits can be beneficial

---

[1] Many other "side" ideas, interests and activities were noted in this thesis during the Guatemala and Fuller years.

for a visionary leader like Winter. On the other hand, when possible consequences are not fully thought through, people and relationships may be impacted negatively.

Ralph was influenced by his father in many ways, as well as by his older brother's direction into engineering as a field of study.[2] Paul joining the Navy and the influence of the Navigators encouraged Ralph in that direction. As he began making decisions as a young adult, his desire to make a positive impact for the gospel and influence society grew. The fact that his undergraduate studies were accelerated because of the war helped focus his attention. The end of the war brought new options and Ralph took advantage of those in his choices for graduate schools. From the earliest information available, his family and those around him recognized in him one who thought and acted differently from most people. As a consequence, some people really liked to be around him, such as Dan Fuller, while others found interacting with him a difficult challenge.

The entrepreneurial spirit present in California during Ralph's formative years may have also contributed to his counter-cultural mentality, yet it is not clear whether it was this, his engineering approach or other factors that were more determinative. He approached his linguistic studies with the perspective of an engineer and thus approached learning and teaching Greek and Hebrew in a way that seemed to him to be more straightforward than conventional methods.[3]

His educational experiences contributed to:

1. His becoming a life-long learner
2. His way of teaching through an inductive approach with questions based in the text added to direct the studies[4]
3. Exposure to a range of subjects and mentors including:
   o Bible memory with Loren Sanny and the Navigators
   o Youth leadership with Christian Endeavor
   o Engineering with professors like Linus Pauling
   o Military pilot training
   o Inductive Bible study with Kuist
   o Studied the teaching of English
   o Linguistics, Statistics

---

[2] These include Hugo's committed church involvement and Ralph's choice of Caltech because of his father's background as an engineer and Paul's decision to go there before him.

[3] Whether others agreed with him mattered not.

[4] Used in curriculum that he wrote, edited or influenced like the Perspectives course or the World Christian Foundations.

- o Theology
- o History, with Latourette

Further, through interaction with these he also learned:

1. Discipline in life and faith, including how Christians are discipled and trained
2. Science, its interaction with Christian faith, and its impact upon the world
3. Linguistics, language learning and analysis, including both ancient Biblical and current languages
4. The use of maths and statistics
5. How to connect people with similar interests or professions

2. What are some key insights Winter embraced and promoted, and how did these insights lead him to take action?

I have noted many of his ideas. While Winter changed his opinions on some issues, many of his convictions were values which he continued to develop over his life. A few of those mentioned include:

1. Financial frugality with a purpose
2. Remaining unmarried so as to serve God undistracted
3. Efficient methods for language learning
4. Motivating others and enlisting their involvement in projects
5. The importance of businesses or "tent-making" roles for pastors[5]
6. The importance of publishing ministries[6]
7. The importance of scholarly journals[7]
8. Learning from history and teaching its lessons

Winter looked for opportunities to test his ideas. His life pattern reflected the pattern he learned from Dawson Trotman: why he was doing what he was doing the way he was doing it. His relationship with Roberta grew out of his respect for her willingness to counter peer pressure and church culture and be different.

I have sought to demonstrate three core areas of Winter's missiology efforts where he recognized problems that needed solving and then advanced solutions. With TEE he recognized the practical needs of rural poor pastors and leaders to be equipped in the context of their everyday lives and ministry. He, with others, developed what was originally a local

---

[5] While in Guatemala.

[6] While at Fuller.

[7] One of which became *Missiology*.

tool into something that could serve the church worldwide.[8] In fact, some TEE programs remain and thousands of students continue to receive training. A few of the critiques to TEE were noted and include:

1. The cultural bias of the expatriate missionaries whose leadership guides much of what is taught
2. The dependency on outside input and resource production, at least initially to maintain programs
3. The tendency of some programs or students to focus on recognition (a certificate) rather than learning and growing
4. Teachers had not been trained in appropriate teaching methods
5. The extra effort required for instructors to travel to effectively mentor students
6. Increased volume of students per teacher and the resulting decrease in the ability of the teacher to effectively manage mentoring relationships

The idea of the sodality, and its role in the modern evangelical movement, was an application of Winter's study of church history and field experience tied with the practical mission problems which appear at any given time period. While Winter included Biblical arguments, notably from Acts 13, his particular contribution was to demonstrate the role of sodalities as distinct from modalities, especially in identifying and focusing on problems that need to be solved and thus advancing the gospel in new ways through appropriate structures focused on the specific task.

His Lausanne '74 presentation highlighted the massive need for evangelism among half the world's population. Christians were not reaching out to large blocs of people groups in cultures where there were no existing churches. But his most significant insight was that it would take a new level of cross-cultural understanding, adjustment and evangelism, to do this type of mission among people groups without a church within their culture.

After his presentation at Lausanne in 1974, in 1976, Ralph and Roberta took the implications of his statements to their natural conclusions, starting a sodality focused on this problem. That sodality (the U.S. Center for World Mission) was a direct application of the principles he presented at Lausanne in 1974 but also a reflection of other shaping events in Winter's development. From the 1977 founding of William Carey International University, Ralph and Roberta envisioned it as a

---

[8] Especially where traveling long distances to obtain training was expensive and disruptive.

distance learning institution providing workers high quality training in their own ministry and work context.

In most of the examples given in this study, I also sought to demonstrate how Winter tried to draw others into projects he was working on at various levels. He repeatedly worked at leveraging recognized leadership and experience to draw others toward involvement.[9]

3. What are the primary endeavors undertaken by Winter, what was he able to accomplish through them, and how did the success or failure of these endeavors influence him?

As Winter acted upon what he was seeing and learning, new initiatives were spawned. I have demonstrated how one area of work and thought influenced another and how each major area of work fed into the next. I showed that some of his core insights continue today in the form of organizations, while others had their time and ended, and some remained at the idea stage.[10]

The major endeavors researched (TEE, Sodalities, Lausanne '74) were platforms of increasing learning, influence and opportunity. In Guatemala, it involved learning about the cultural situation and the needs as he served pastors, leaders, missionaries, regional officials, and business owners. That work resulted in TEE. At Fuller, it involved learning about missionary situations globally and learning from and influencing missionaries, other professors, and Christian leaders.[11] What he learned there fed into his work on sodalities as well as his Lausanne presentation. At Lausanne he was engaged with global evangelical leaders involved in evangelism, church work and mission from a multitude of cultural situations.

I have given several examples of those who disagreed with Winter's ideas or practice. These included:

1. A relational struggle with a missionary colleague[12]
2. Several who differed from Winter on TEE or who saw the long term impact of weaknesses within the movement
3. A number who resisted independent sodalities and saw them, at a minimum, as less than ideal or as a competition to denominational or other church structures

---

[9] Two examples were Hopewell and Ward with TEE.

[10] I have personally observed Winter initiate projects, ministries or ideas, seek to motivate someone to involvement in a project, lose interest and move on to other ideas and, at times, come back to the idea later.

[11] Most of the Fuller SWM missionary students or associates were already leaders with increasing influence.

[12] In Guatemala.

4. Many who struggled with the possibility of either syncretism or disunity in the global church when reaching out in cross-cultural evangelism.

Still, Winter saw the potential of:

1. Getting leaders the equipping they needed (resulting in TEE)
2. Reaching out in a new way to the unreached (from Lausanne '74)
3. Leaders establishing their own sodalities to solve the problems that confront them

4. *Where do Winter's ideas and endeavors intersect the mission movement and the broader evangelical movement, in relation to both theory and practice?*

Winter's involvement had an impact on the rural leaders in Guatemala and with missionaries. Minor and major examples include:

1. Ruben Dias and others Winter mentored
2. A SIL missionary linguist who was helped by Winter in his translation
3. Missionaries with several other agencies or denominations who were part of the elementary education completion program in Guatemala
4. The 159 agencies and denominations who had adopted TEE as a tool for training by 1973[13]
5. The hundreds of missionary associates as well as faculty at the School of World Mission who were impacted by Ralph[14]
6. Expanding the vision of other mission leaders to see the distinct potential of sodalities and modalities in accomplishing tasks
7. The need for a serious engagement in cross-cultural evangelism to people groups without the gospel was recognized by mission leaders

In addition to these areas of direct influence, there are many others who interacted with him or his ideas, resulting in even larger circles of influence.[15]

---

[13] As noted earlier, see Appendix H.

[14] This included those who appreciated his teaching and those who struggled with his seemingly disorganized approach. Roberta worked alongside him in this, as noted in the thesis.

[15] He recruited some, like myself, into a life of service focused on these three core ideas. Of course, Winter wrote extensively, far beyond what has been referenced here. I hope to continue studying his writings after 1976.

Conclusion

This study has not included a quantitative measure for the impact of Ralph D. Winter's life. The evidence I have presented makes clear that his life and core missiological reflections have significantly influenced evangelical missiology and practice and he continues to be cited in the current missiological literature.[16] Ralph Winter shaped global evangelical mission engagement with the least reached. Winter was a visionary innovator who applied the skills, talent and education he had in three core areas leading up to his founding the USCWM in 1976: TEE, sodalities and the reaching of unreached people groups. I have previously outlined the majority views of the dissenting voices.

1. TEE was an idea birthed in the context of immediate need and not as carefully designed as necessary, at least for a western audience. Yet it remains a viable training option that extends additional training opportunities in certain situations, especially where the church is strong enough to develop their own materials.

2. Highlighting the sodality/modality distinction grew from his observations throughout Christian history. The concept can be applied to many different contexts, not only missions-focused structures. Disagreement continues regarding how sodalities relate to modalities and with regard to undue cultural influence from the north and west. Yet few question the potential value of "second decision" organizations that seek to do things that a local church is not normally equipped to accomplish.

3. The vision for the least reached was a strategic insight that helped capture the hearts and minds of thousands of missionaries, giving direction to their ministry. While few debated this global need within evangelicalism, most did not grasp his call for a new kind of cross-cultural evangelism. The issues of the unity of the body of Christ and the danger of syncretism, in both the church itself and in distinct cultures, continue to be issues of debate.

---

[16] By "generally available" I mean in the writings and responses of others about issues that Winter started or reenergized the debate. The fact that Winter is still written about in these three main areas as well as others, gives tribute to the impact of his life.

TEE was a "delivery method" to extend training (in this case theological or pastoral) to as many people as possible. Sodalities are a "structural form" which enable a specific mission to be accomplished. The core ideas Winter presented at Lausanne were a "strategic insight" that he hoped would be multiplied by means of sodalities and thus mobilize as many people as possible toward deeper involvement.

Throughout his life, Ralph Winter sought to apply what he considered a calling to the: "studied application of modest ingenuity to the Christian cause..."[17] Both regret and that sense of calling can be seen in Winter, as a 34-year old, reflecting on "the cycles of unrest and confusion through which my life went, and the degree to which they were disturbances in the life of the church... I only seek to know and do His will."[18] Those "disturbances" and the "modest ingenuity" continued to impact those around him. Some reacted to Winter and his ideas and argued against them. Others were spurred on to follow him closely or at a distance, seeing his vision and ideas as a stimulant to their own sense of calling and inspiration. Still others could not relate to his restless desire to identify problems and seek new solutions. Ruth Wardell is an example of someone who continued in her own approach to life and ministry, unaltered by her interaction with Winter.

There seems to be a general pattern that Winter followed, though not in a methodical way. Observation of a problem (equipping rural pastors) led him to a solution (deliver the training where the pastors were). The solution implemented (TEE) became something toward which he began to mobilize others. Establishing a new sodality was a useful pattern in order to harness energy for a clear focus (Lausanne '74 and the USCWM).[19]

Over the years, I have talked to hundreds of leaders who, while they may not agree with many of Winter's ideas, none-the-less would say that they were challenged and motivated toward serious involvement in the cause of global mission by him. Much of that grew out of Winter's highlighting the remaining task of world mission at Lausanne. His insight 35 years ago, regarding the need to successfully cross not merely geographic but cultural boundaries with the gospel, remains a crucial issue in missions today. It is my hope that in the long run, believers will more deeply understand his observation that without concerted new efforts, we will continue to fail at true cross-cultural evangelism to the least reached.

---

[17] Undated letter (fall of 1957) from Ralph D. Winter to Hugo and Hazel Winter, 1. He was 32 at the time.

[18] August 8, 1959 letter from Ralph D. Winter to his pastor Dr. and Mrs. Hutchins, 1.

[19] Winter did not propose or establish a sodality specifically for TEE.

Appendices

Appendix A

Sample Lesson Example of Winter's Ideas for Learning Languages

This is an example of how Winter sought to use the known language (in this case English) as a basis from which a new language (in this case Greek) could be learned.

Module 2A: Greek Lesson 1

Θεός (the-oss') — (a) god

ὁ Θεός (ho the-oss') — (the) god or God

θ, theta, is pronounced like the th in 'with'. The capital is Θ.

ε, epsilon, is pronounced like the e in 'let'. The capital is E.

o, omicron, may be pronounced like the o in 'soft'. The capital is O. (Actually, we do not know how it was pronounced in Koine Greek; some people prefer to pronounce it like the o in 'obey' or the o in 'hot'. You may, if you like, simply pronounce it the way you would an English o.)

ς, sigma, is pronounced like the s in 'dress'. It is written this way only at the end of a word; elsewhere in a word, it is written σ. The capital is Σ.

In the beginning ὁ Θεὸς made the heven and the earθ. But the earθ was unσightly and unfurnished, and the Σpirit of ὁ Θεὸς moved over the water. And ὁ Θεὸς σed, Let ther be light, and ther was light. And ὁ Θεὸς σaw the light that it was good, and ὁ Θεὸς divided between the light and the darkneς. And ὁ Θεὸς called the light Day, and the darkneς he called Night, and ther was evening and ther was morning, the fiρσt day.

And ὁ Θεὸς σed, Let ther be a firmament in the midσt of the water, and let it be a division between water and water, and it was σo. And ὁ Θεὸς made the firmament, and ὁ Θεὸς divided between the water which was under the firmament and the water which was above the firmament. And ὁ Θεὸς called the firmament Heven, and ὁ Θεὸς σaw that it was good, and ther was evening and ther was morning, the σecond day.

And ὁ Θεὸς σed, Let the water which is under the heven be collected into one plaς, and let the dry land appear, and it was σo. And the water which was under the heven was collected into its plaσes, and the dry land appeared. And ὁ Θεὸς called the dry land Earθ, and the gatherings of the waters he called Σeas, and ὁ Θεὸς σaw that it was good. And ὁ Θεὸς σed, Let the earθ bring forθ the herb of graς bering σeed according to itς kind and according to itς likeneς, and the fruit-tree bering fruit whose σeed is in it, according to itς kind on the earθ, and it was σo. And the earθ brot forθ the herb of graς bering σeed according to itς kind and according to itς likeneς, and the fruit tree bering fruit whose σeed is in it, according to itς kind on the earθ, and Θεὸς σaw that it was good. And ther was evening and ther was morning, the θird day.

Γένεσις (Genesis) 1:1-13, LXX (Septuagint)

Say aloud and copy: ὁ Θεός _____

Copy these words, but use as many Greek letters as possible to replace English *sounds*.

said _____ breath _____ stress _____ Esther _____ Seth _____

this _____ strength _____ thought _____ bath _____ so ____

In the beginning ὁ Θεὸς made the heven and the earθ.   Γένεσις 1:1, LXX

Appendix B

Sample Lesson Patterns

This example is referred to on pages 62 and 70. The first sample is from the *World Christian Foundations* course study guide. Page two follows.

Lesson 73 Winter	Module 2: *Classical World* (400 BC - AD 200)
The Spread of Christianity	
Objectives: To be able to...	Personal Response, Intellectual Journal, Notes

Objectives: To be able to...

a. Describe how Christianity spread during the second century.
b. Describe the various factors in the second century Christian experience that limited active public evangelism.
c. Describe why and how Christianity expanded in the east during the second century.

Assignments:

Introduction
Winter, ed: *Global Civilization, Classical World: Lesson Overviews*
298-299   Lesson 73 Introduction

General
Barraclough, ed: *Hammond Concise Atlas of World History, 5th ed.*
26-27   The World Religions, c. 500 BC–AD 500
38-39   Christianity and Judaism, c. 600–1500

Moffett: *A History of Christianity in Asia*
1-80   The First 200 Years
Read 50 pages from this selection

Stark: *The Rise of Christianity*
49-71   The Mission to the Jews: Why It Probably Succeeded

Winter, ed: *Global Civilization, Classical World: Reader*
417–424   Moffett: The Spread of Christianity in Asia

Winter, ed: *Global Civilization, Classical World: Lesson Overviews*
299-300   Lesson 73 Review

Optional
Johnstone: *Operation World*
334   India: Tamil Nadu

Language
Greek Lessons
Greek 73

Hebrew Lessons
Hebrew Final Test

Module 2: *Classical World* (400 BC - AD 200)	Winter	Lesson 73

The Spread of Christianity

Reflection Questions	Notes

1. List some of the mechanisms of expansion for Christianity during the second century.

2. What forces were at work preventing the spread of the gospel, and how did these factors end up affecting the spread of the gospel?

3. What were the major factors which caused Christianity to spread eastward during the second century?

Appendix C

Field Relational Issue Details

Before the Winters moved to the Mam Center, Winter was able to visit, see the Pecks, and meet Ruth Wardell. He noticed the relational struggle between Ruth and the Pecks:

> These Pecks are really some people. Indefatigable, pile drivers, at their age tremendously vigorous and surprisingly open-minded. A lot more so than Ruth Wardell. ... She makes no attempt to be polite to the Pecks and is near to a nervous breakdown due to reacting negatively to absolutely everything in the Center. Imagine however, that the basic problem is that her leadership and creative powers have no very great outlet.[1]

Ralph wrote a letter explaining how difficult this relationship was, stating directly his perspective on Ruth's way of working and its impact not only on the Mam, but on work in the whole area. He noted "that we have about decided that there is no bright future for the Mam Center or for any significant experimental work in the Indian problem of the Americas in this place with her actively engaged in the work."[2] Winter explained that he sought to set up a neutral ground for Ruth, which he felt was a "favorable situation in which she could meet us when and how she liked. Even so the relationship did not even remotely approach what could be considered a workable one."

The Winters believed, "the fact that no one we know of in the mission has expressed the opinion that any one else in the mission could work effectively with her." He did not feel that her problems had anything to do with the Winter family or others on the field. The Winters realized that they could not stay working in the situation as it was, but they sought to make it clear that they [the Winters] were in no way looking to resign. They did want to express a, "willingness to make a new beginning in a similar work rather than mark time here," partly because "Ruth is not able to participate in nor desist from critically opposing the kind of work that needs to be done here."[3]

---

[1] Undated letter (fall of 1957) from Ralph D. Winter to Hugo and Hazel Winter, 1.

[2] November 4, 1959 letter from Ralph D. Winter to Don Fletcher, 1.

[3] November 4, 1959 letter from Ralph D. Winter to Don Fletcher, 1-2. Winter often chose his words very carefully, so as to leave the interpretation clear yet without

In a letter two months later, Winter outlined that he did not feel it would be good financial stewardship to stay at the Mam Center. He considered the $6,000 the mission paid him to be a "moral debt."[4] Later in that same letter he wrote, "This year, then, must be one in which Ruth decides that she cannot work under our ideas for a program or that she can, or we decide finally that we can or cannot work in cooperation with her."[5]

The leadership of the mission got more involved in the situation. A leader in the New York office wrote to a doctor working with mission leadership in relationships with many of the missionaries, noting, "Mr. and Mrs. Peck seem to have an impregnable barrier and permanent prejudice against Miss Wardell which stems from their earliest associations. The Pecks are apparently satisfied with the Winters and either do not see, or discount, the Winters inadequacies."[6] The Pecks wrote to the Winters mentioning that it might be possible for them to restructure the work at the Mam clinic and have Ruth's work come under the jurisdiction of a hospital in the city.[7]

Part of the conflict between Ruth and the Winters stemmed from Ruth's belief that medically trained missionaries needed to decide what the medical work should include. In contrast Winter believed missionaries needed to understand how anthropology and culture might inform decisions about medical or any other kind of work. While Winter wanted to see an effective connection between medical work and church growth, he was not trying "to say that medical work has no value except as it acts as bait to get people to hear the gospel."[8]

Ruth did not like the idea of connecting evangelical work with her medical work, although she shared excitedly when someone converted because of her work.[9] In part to prove his perspective on the value of the connection between church work and medical work, Winter invited Ira

---

engendering ill feelings. In this situation it was very clear what they felt, which may demonstrate how long and deep the relational strain was.

[4] US$6,000 in 1960 is worth approximately US$45,800 or UK£ 28,480 in 2011.

[5] January 9, 1960 letter from Ralph D. Winter to Don Fletcher, 1-2. This letter suggests that the Winters would be happy to work at a nearby language school fifteen miles away in Quezaltenango teaching English to strategic Spanish leaders there.

[6] February 2, 1961 letter from Robert C. Thorp to Nathaniel Bercovitz, M.D., 2. Bercovitz may have been working with the Winters while on furlough in 1961 or may have been anticipating such work.

[7] October 8, 1961 letter from Dudley and Dorothy Peck to Ralph and Roberta Winter, 1.

[8] October 11, 1958 letter from Ralph D. Winter to Don Fletcher, 2.

[9] January 25, 1963 letter from Ruth E Wardell to John Sinclair.

Wallstrom, a medical doctor serving with the Presbyterian Board in Iran, to help research the relationship of medical work and traditional church work or outreach in the region. Winter was also trying to recruit Wallstrom to come to Guatemala, since it seemed that the Wallstroms were not likely to return to Iran.[10]

Winter and Wallstrom responded to a report done on the MCC[11] by proposing a broader study of effective work among other Maya peoples, noting:

> Among the Highland Maya (of which the Mam are a part), the most outstanding break-through of the Christian mission would seem to be the work in the Reformed Church of America territory (Amado Nervo, Chiapas) in Mexico among the Chol people. This work was accomplished from the very beginning by an intimate relationship between medical and preaching functions of the mission approach, aided, reportedly, by a $5,000 grant that came through Douglas Forman for the training of Indians in an intermediate medical work.[12]

Winter and Wallstrom also noted what might have been part of the tension between the Pecks and Wardell:

> The early work of the Pecks, even before the establishment of the Mam Christian Center, but also after, up until the arrival of a missionary specifically for medical work, was one in which these two functions were closely related. It was this early work which seems to have been much more effective than the work during the last decade when the arrival of a "specialist" in the healing art has made the medical work largely independent of the Center and the Church. ... We feel sure that it is tremendously important to discover how medical work can be decentralized in rural areas and integrated into the existing church at its growing edge. [13]

---

[10] Winter met Wallstrom while on furlough in California.

[11] Based on a report commissioned by the mission called, *Report on the Work and Personnel of the Mam Christian Center*, by F.G. Scovell and Wm. L. Wonderly, Ostuncalco, Guatemala, July 16 to 27, 1960.

[12] February 14, 1961 joint statement from Ralph D. Winter and Ira C. Wallstrom, M.D. to John H. Sinclair, 1. The statement was Winter/Wallstrom's "proposal for implementing the Chiapas study recommended by the Scovell-Wonderly Report on the Mam Christian Center."

[13] February 14, 1961 joint statement from Ralph D. Winter and Ira C. Wallstrom, M.D. to John H. Sinclair, 1.

Winter was so convinced of this connection between medical work and church growth that before he met Wallstrom, he had considered going to medical school to gain the credentials to effectively argue his point and then to return to further Native American work throughout the region. He wrote about this when he shared his ideas about the connection between these two kinds of work with Wallstrom:

> ...he not only said he could firmly back the ideas, as a missionary doctor, he even went on to say that this was exactly the kind of thing he was struggling to visualize while working in Iran. ... Even now I cannot forget the amazement I had when he said that he, as a medical doctor, was seriously considering getting a B.D. and being ordained in order to do the job he felt should be done. I, meanwhile, as an ordained man, was secretly considering in agony the possible necessity of getting an M.D. in order to accomplish the task I felt had to be done.[14]

Winter believed that the approach about which he and Wallstrom had brainstormed was crucial to the furtherance of the mission work:

> ... until a national doctor-anthropologist-minister is ready to step into that work, the cooperation of Wallstrom and myself in pioneering an experiment in a medical work decentralized and integrated with the leadership of the church could easily be the most strategic thing at this time, both for the Mam work and also as an experiment our organization can be proud of in this day of new insights into overseas medical programs.[15]

Winter could not remember (at the time or later when interviewed) being angry or bitter toward Wardell. The differences with her were never heated, nor were harsh words exchanged. His drive and extensive communications grew from his feeling that the work through the MCC had been "pretty stagnant for about ten years."[16] It was noted of Winter that "Dr. Winter is considerate of others and would prefer a transfer to another field rather than staying on there if that meant being influential in the nurse being removed from that work to which she came earlier than he."[17]

---

[14] February 25, 1961 letter from Ralph D. Winter to John Sinclair, 3.

[15] February 11, 1961 letter from Ralph D. Winter to John Sinclair, 4.

[16] January 12, 1960 letter from Ralph D. Winter to Stanley Rycroft, 1.

[17] February 2, 1961 letter from Robert C. Thorp to Nathaniel Bercovitz, M.D., 2.

Due to Ruth's seniority, mission leadership suggested the Winters return to a different location after their first furlough. The mission board based that proposed relocation on some issues in Roberta's health. From Ralph's perspective, Roberta's health was being "overblown" in order to place the Winters somewhere else because of the conflict with Ruth. According to one letter from the supervisors of the Guatemala work, Winter offered to go to the language school in Costa Rica to assist in the language-learning program.[18] The Winters would have been happy to move, and it would have probably made the schooling of their daughters much easier.[19] Jim Emery also suggested other field assignments in places such as Pakistan or Venezuela that might be a good fit for Ralph to use his PhD and engineering background.[20]

About this time, the mission placed Jim Emery back in a position to work with Ruth since they were from the same home church in the U.S. Right after Ruth returned from furlough, Jim noted to Ralph that she was just as hard as ever to work with.[21] In the end, others realized that Ruth was difficult for everyone to work with and the Winters were back near the Mam center for the rest of their field service.

But the situation did not change at all. After the Winters returned from that furlough, Ralph wrote to Sinclair about a number of issues. He seemed to feel he must write, even if (as the last page notes) it was something the MCC should have decided rather than the supervisors of the work in Guatemala City or New York. In that ten-page letter, Winter wrote the following about Ruth;

> Toward us she is alternately courteous and friendly, and then bitterly resentful and critical, and the fountainhead of a flow of gossip that is truly virulent. In her soul must rage a terrible struggle between her deeply conscientious nature (which tells her she ought to be cooperative) and her profoundly rooted suspicions of us and all whose existence in any sense impinges upon her autonomy. I really think that to demand that she cooperate closely with anyone is to ask an eagle to live in a bird cage.[22]

---

[18] Winter did not remember making this suggestion.

[19] Interview with Ralph Winter by the author on August 14, 2006, 8.

[20] Eventually, Roberta began to take thyroid medication, and it was a great help to her throughout her life.

[21] Interview with Ralph Winter by the author on July 26, 2006, 18.

[22] February 28, and March 13-14, 1962 letter from Ralph D. Winter to John Sinclair, 5.

The board knew that Winter was opposed to seeing her removed, and the Winters also realized that the locals would not understand why anyone would drive away their only "doctor" and would not understand what they were trying to accomplish in removing her to free up the ministry possibilities. Finally, Winter continued:

> Surely if after ten years a U.S. nurse cannot bring herself to train more than one or two Indians in any way (and neither of these in any diagnostic processes), then it is time (not to throw her out but) to add to her work something in the realm of the kind of training program that will produce a rural self-supporting medical service. This, you see, does not depend on the validity of the idea Wonderly has opposed. But, should the idea be sound, the program will automatically benefit from it.[23]

There was a contentious meeting of the staff of the MCC, where proposals for future work integration were discussed. This meeting had been delayed for months, ostensibly because of Ruth. When they did meet, Winter recorded the following, as he described it to Sinclair:

> It came up about what Roberta should do when Ruth is absent (for a week or weekend). [Ruth] said that inasmuch as she is the director of medical work, when she goes the clinic is closed. 'And if someone comes to Roberta while you are gone, with an emergency case?' The answer, 'There are always hospitals in Quezaltenango they can go to.' Roberta then said that this would make her to appear either ill-trained or heartless in the eyes of the people. Ruth said under her breath, but distinctly, 'One of the two of us will have to leave.' She then said something about Roberta coming to replace Dorothy Peck. Dr Wallis broke in and challenged this strenuously: 'The field request was for an ordained man trained in linguistics, and the wife to be a registered nurse. Dorothy was not a registered nurse and was not expected to do medical work.' ... [Ruth] stood up and left with these words: 'You now have a new director for the clinic, and you have my resignation--this is very official.' Everyone felt very bad. No further discussion with her was possible.[24]

---

[23] February 28, and March 13-14, 1962 letter from Ralph D. Winter to John Sinclair, 6 (parenthesis in the original letter).

[24] February 28, and March 13-14, 1962 letter from Ralph D. Winter to John Sinclair, 7-8.

She did not end up leaving, but reported the work of the clinic to the hospital in the city, as Dudley Peck had suggested.

Appendix D

Winter's Work Responsibilities and Side Projects

Here is the detail in one of Winter's *Shoptalk* newsletters.[25]

Under the New York Office

> General survey of Mam-Center-type Indian projects in all of Latin America
>
> Assemble a picture story of Presbyterian work in Guatemala
>
> Maintain relations with you folks back home

Under the Guatemala Mission

> Learn the Mam Indian tongue, making technical studies in preparation for translation work
>
> Be chairman of the Audio-Visual Committee (for whole country)
>
> Produce the Annual Picture Calendar of the Mission
>
> Be a member of the Conference Grounds Governing Board
>
> Make a special study of the use of vehicles in the mission

Under the Quezaltenango Station (i.e. Western half of the country)

> Be chairman of the Station. (This is more of a nuisance than a heavy load. I'm in charge of visitors coming into Western Guatemala, responsible for the weekly Station Prayer Meeting locations and leaders, for buying birthday presents on behalf of the Station, etc. also to preside at meetings.)

Under the Governing Board of the Mam Christian Center

> Be treasurer of the Center
>
> Produce a special study of all operations for the October Board meeting
>
> Assigned to Department of Extension (we just got back from a two-week program up in the 10,000' mountains)
>
> Assigned to teach in the Institute

Under the Administrative Council of the Mam Christian Center

> Give talks in Clinic services
>
> Teach class in Accounting
>
> Supervise vocational classes and projects
>
> Supervise recreation hour of the institute
>
> Install telephone system and class bell system
>
> Make a surveyor's map of the Center land

---

[25] *Shoptalk* newsletter, August 8, 1959, 1. It is not clear which assignments were roles that Winter took on of his own volition.

Under the Synod of the Guatemalan National Church
> Edit the department on Indians in the Guatemala "Presb Life"
>
> Manage distribution of this magazine for the Western Presbytery

Under the Interdenominational Sponsorship
> Be Secretary for '59 and '60 of the Translators' Conference of Guatemala–all missions

More specifically, by 1960, just before the Winters' first furlough, Ralph was involved in many other activities, including being the director of a "Farm and Work" program. It was described as a "catch all" department that included maintaining the Mam Center, operating the ten acres of property (which was under a farm/coop program at the time), keeping the purebred bull available for the community for breeding, maintaining a three-ton compost heap for the farm and the bull, and providing other services to the community. In that context, Winter developed a "cost-accounting" system to better understand and track the profit/loss from these efforts, and he sought to introduce manufacturing on a small scale.[26]

There were also those who wondered why the Winters were involved in so many different ministries and activities. In the middle of their ten years of service in Guatemala, Winter wrote of the "avalanche of responsibilities" that had descended upon them:

> He was made the director of the Institute program at the MCC, emphasizing Bible, history, science, accounting, farming, etc. and seeking to begin to "include outright business training and guidance in the actual establishment of light manufacturing industries (including florescent lamps, radio assembly, woven furniture, Indian textiles, etc.) and also rural service industries (such as credit unions, simple medicines, and dentistry of an elementary variety)." This also included running the first private school of 44 students, first through sixth grade, the first to be accredited. Thus this program is not merely to help the students earn their way through school, but more important, to enable them to support themselves after they graduate, and to do so in some wholesome "good work" that is itself economically strategic to the community. But perhaps most basic: it is to permit our students to prove themselves faithful stewards on a level of

---

[26] *A Report on the Work and Personnel of the Mam Christian Center*, by F.G. Scovell and Wm. L. Wonderly, Ostuncalco, Guatemala, July 16 to 27, 1960, 14-15.

concrete love before being given more extensive responsibilities of a purely Spiritual nature.

Advisor to the Mam Center Treasurer.

Secretary of the Board of the Seminary.

Member of the Mission Audio-Visual Committee and the Rest House Committee.

Superintendent of the Local Sunday School.

Vice President of the Middle America Conference for Indian Work (formerly Translators' Conference).

Member of the Council of the new Bilingual Annex of Colegio La Patria.

Winter also made note of other activities since returning from furlough, including "intensive Christmas and Easter meetings, the Central American Pastor and Missionary Retreat, Evangelism-in-Depth Conference, Rural Economics Retreat, Presbyterian Men's Spiritual Retreats, Preliminary Synod Meetings, Indian-Work Conference, and the InterMission Conference."[27]

Even before this, Winter had written about a number of projects that were unfinished when they left, not knowing if they would be back. These included preparing the annual financial report on the Mam Center, dealing with the farm harvest that year, studying the nearby town of San Juan Ostuncalco's water system with the local mayor (including presenting technical information on a new pump he had discovered while in the U.S.), supervising a new electrical installation at the Mam Center, serving in a job with the bi-annual Translators' Conference for Latin American languages, overseeing a group from an engineering firm where he had worked over the summers in New Jersey while at Princeton, and studying the Mam language.

He also wrote for permission to finish a project on furlough that he had started at Princeton. He described it as "Hebrew and Greek scholarly aids, which were well along before we came under the Commission." [28] This letter from Winter has a two-page attachment detailing the work on various study tools and lexical handbooks for both biblical languages. Earlier, Winter wrote about his first work on this kind of resource in a newsletter to friends and churches back in the U.S. He mentioned that he wrote a preface to a preliminary edition of a new book, *Lexical Handbook of the Hebrew Bible*. (Fritsch and Winter, 1957) He continued, "Boy am I glad to see this beginning to appear. I began to work on the basic idea of it

---

[27] Annual Meeting Report by Ralph D. Winter, 1962, 1-3.

[28] October 28, 1960 letter by Ralph D. Winter to Rev. Robert Thorp.

back in 1947. It would not be appearing even now without Dr. Fritsch's alertness to the problem and his contribution of the meaning of the Hebrew words. I merely did the mathematical side, the engineering so to speak, the design." [29]

GENESIS - CHAPTER I

1:1	בְּ	IN. insep. prep. (1:1,1:6,1:11,1:12, 1:14)	88-A2	52	1 6		*
	רֵאשִׁית	BEGINNING. n.cf.ראֹשׁ HEAD.(1:1,10:10, 49:3)	912-A3		1 2 3	51	*
	בָּרָא	CREATE. v. always of divine creative activity.(1:1,1:21,1:27³)	135-A5	69	1 6 10	50	*
	אֱלֹהִים	GOD. n. pl. in form, s. in meaning. Common Semitic rt. for God.(1:1,1:2, 1:3,1:4²)	43-A5	29	1 6 202	2445	*
	אֶת־	sign of direct, definite obj.(1:1², 1:4,1:7,1:16)	84-B2	47	1² 6		*
	הַ	THE. art. (prefixed)(1:1²,1:2²,1:4)	206-A9	93	1² 6		*
	שָּׁמַיִם	HEAVEN(S). n.(1:1,1:8,1:9,1:14,1:15)	1029-B4	370	1 6 40	405	*
	וְ	AND. conj.(prefixed)(1:1,1:2⁴)	251-A8	107	1 6		*
1:2	אֶרֶץ	EARTH, LAND. n.f.(1:1,1:2,1:10,1:11²)	75-B9	43	1 6 287	2375	*
	וְ	AND. conj.(prefixed) (1:1)	251-A8	107	3⁴ 6		*
	הַ	THE. art.(prefixed) (1:1)	206-A9	93	3⁴ 6		*
	אֶרֶץ	EARTH, LAND. n.f. (1:1)	75-B9	43	2 6 287	2375	*
	הָיְתָה	BE. v.(1:2,1:3²,1:5²)	224-A1	97	1 6 316	3563	*
	תֹהוּ	FORMLESSNESS, UNREALITY, DESERT. n. (1:2)	1062-B2		1 1 1	20	
	בֹהוּ	EMPTINESS, VOID. n. (1:2)	96-A4		1 1 1	3	
	חֹשֶׁךְ	DARKNESS. n. (1:2,1:4,1:5,1:18)	365-A1		1 4 4	78	*
	עַל־	UPON. prep.(1:2²,1:7,1:11,1:15)	752-B1	267	1² 6 310	5460	*
	פְּנֵי	FACE. n. pl. in form, s. in meaning. With עַל "in front of, before". (1:2,1:20,1:29,2:6,3:8)	815-B6	290	1 6 130	1976	*
	תְהוֹם	THE DEEP. n.f and m. cf.Akk. "Ti'amat", tho primeval salt-water ocean. (1:2, 7:11,8:2,49:25)	1062-B8		1 3 4	35	
	רוּחַ	WIND, SPIRIT. n.f.(1:2,3:8,6:3,6:17, 7:15)	924-B2	325	1 6 11	362	*
	אֱלֹהִים	GOD. n. (1:1)	43-A5	29	2 6 202	2445	*
	מְרַחֶפֶת	HOVER. v. like a bird. cf. Dt.32:11 (1:2)	934-A8		1 1 1	3	
1:3	מָיִם	WATER(S). n. pausal form.(1:2,1:6³,1:7)	565-A5	204	1 6 50	557	*
	יֹּאמֶר	SAY. v.(1:3,1:6,1:9,1:11,1:14)	55-B4	34	1 6 668	5140	*
	אֱלֹהִים	GOD. n.(1:1)	43-A5	29	3 6 202	2445	*
	יְהִי	BE. v.(1:2)	224-A1	97	2³ 6 316	3563	*
	אוֹר	LIGHT. n.(1:3,1:4,1:5,1:18)	21-B2		1 4 4	116	*

Winter wanted to produce these tools available for "the use of beginning students for the Biblical languages, especially for pastors beyond initial studies, but also for scholars, and for Bible translators, whether of the 'older' or 'younger' churches." In his 1960 letter suggesting this study

[29] Princeton professor Charles T. Fritsch provided the Hebrew word definitions. Winter wrote to him (and his wife Julian) and suggested additional changes and improvements for future printings of the book, which never occurred. That letter is dated: January 28, 1958. The quote is from the Winters' personal newsletter, *Shoptalk* #8, dated January 20, 1958, 2.

during his time in the U.S., he continued, "The unique feature of these materials is that they are based on statistical and engineering handling of the quantities involved in vocabulary."[30] A portion of a page is seen above. Winter was applying his doctoral work to show that if you focus your learning of a language on the words that are used more often, you will see much faster progress. In the listing of the words in each verse of Genesis 1 through 20, once a word had appeared five times, it was not repeated again, assuming the student now was familiar with the word and its basic meaning:

> ...to smooth out the rough places for seminary students of Hebrew.... I pray that through a study of Hebrew...ministerial students will more often be challenged and intrigued both by the Biblical message that is bound up in the very different Hebrew culture of the Old Testament, and also by the sheer linguistic novelty of the first language they've ever studied that is shockingly different from English. French, German, Spanish, even Russian, are all close cousins to English compared to Hebrew or the American Indian languages, Swahili, Thai, Hindi, Chinese, or in fact almost all of the languages missionaries have to deal with.[31]

---

[30] October 28, 1960 letter by Ralph D. Winter to Rev. Robert Thorp, attachment, 1.

[31] *Shoptalk* #8, January 20, 1958, 3.

Appendix E

2006 Guatemala Update

After thirty-nine years, Winter returned to Guatemala in 2006. Much of that time, Ralph and Roberta could not communicate with friends or national leaders on the field because of repercussions with guerilla warfare. After a trip with Barbara,[32] all four daughters and others from the family, they wrote a newsletter to friends described the situation in the region,

> Jan. 12-22 Guatemala, visited Ralph and Roberta's work there after 39 years of absence. Three churches are now 35, young men are now grandfathers. Scarcity of land is so serious that the only thing preventing starvation is splitting up of families whereby father and older sons work in the USA (as illegals) and send money back: a serious problem as young children get into drugs and gangs. It was a wonderful time of reunion with folks who thought they would never see Ralph or the girls again (all four daughters, one son-in-law, 9 grandchildren accompanied us). No communication has been possible in most of the intervening years due to endangering the Mam Indians' lives. Barb also renewed friendships established by the David Scotchmer family and was warmly welcomed.[33]

While it could not be proved, Winter's attempt to get a US AID grant to attract businesses to the region might have helped to keep men productive in the society, rather than forcing them to work a long way from home.

---

[32] As noted in the body of the thesis, Barb Winter is Ralph Winter's second wife. Roberta died in 2001 of multiple myeloma.

[33] From the Winters' Newsletter, 2006.

Appendix F

Select Pre-TEE on Mission Fields in the 1900s

In Guatemala in the late 1930s, a Presbyterian missionary from Nicaragua was concerned about current training models not serving those in ministry away from the city. He observed two general methods of training at that time. One was the more traditional approach of seminaries and Bible schools. He wrote that even though the existing training in Guatemala was trying to be creative by feeding students into the system, there were two problems:

> With a seminary teaching staff made up entirely of missionaries this approach ought to lead to the preparation of men capable of serving in churches in the chief cities and towns of the country. But the method leaves untouched the many pastors who are already at work in their fields, although lacking academic and theological training. (Peters, 1940, 371)

The second method of training was, "that of training the men now in active service who for economic and family reasons cannot be drafted into years of formal study in the classes of a seminary or Bible School." (Peters, 1940, 371)

As a result, they were working with a modified correspondence course, which included general courses in science, history and Spanish composition, to give background to the leaders. By starting an "annual institute for training pastors and evangelistic students", they sought "to provide the stimulus to study, and the opportunity for class work, fellowship and the exchange of ideas that comes naturally with the institutional type of education..." (Peters, 1940, 372) Much of that helped those near Guatemala City, but still did not do much to serve rural pastors.

Since 1921 the International Missionary Council (IMC) had been involved with missionaries. In 1957 the IMC carried out a series of surveys on "the training of the ministry" in various denominations in Madagascar. Their analysis turned up flaws in the training program, questioned their ability to sustain some of the existing programs, and expressed concern regarding those who were not able to obtain much needed training.

The focus of a booklet produced the year after the surveys were completed in 1957 was on training for pastors, and they noted:

> ... a great number of men are at present in the service of the Church and carrying on a pastoral ministry though they have received neither the theological training of pastoral

schools nor official ordination to this ministry. These are catechists, who after being trained in Bible schools, sometimes sketchily and sometimes more thoroughly, are given pastoral care in local congregations and in country villages under the spiritual oversight of an evangelist or a district chairman (i.e. a pastor in charge of a wide area). (Ranson et al., 1957, 15, italics original)

Pre-TEE Evaluation of Mission Field Theological Education

The International Missionary Council research and report, later published as *Survey of the training of the ministry in Madagascar: report of a survey of theological education in Madagascar undertaken in September to November, 1956* (Ranson et al., 1957), noted the importance of these *catechists* in the work and ministry of the church. It sought to raise the issue of what role this kind of part-time leader could play. They realized the value of people in ministry, but could not see how training could be extended to them. They actually looked forward to the day when these would be replaced by a "better-trained body of pastors, helped by a growing number of voluntary lay assistants, capable of taking over a share of pastoral responsibility in the many little local communities, and receiving adequate training for this purpose." (Ranson et al., 1957, 16) Many of the current "pastors" were not ordained. Yet in a comment to calm possible concerns of the readers over the issue of ordination and what it meant, "We are justified then in reminding our readers that the same terms do not always cover the same realities and that there are different categories of pastoral ministries." (Ranson et al., 1957, 16) Still, there was a desire to see these pastors do well and keep their focus on "urgent, daily evangelization" and "real care for souls in a complex and critical time." (Ranson et al., 1957, 16-17)

They sensed a tension between "high" and "low" requirements for the ministry. If a training program attempts to set too high a standard, many men and women cannot reach it, and certain distant areas of the country will not be served by the training provided. If a low standard is attempted, then people in the ministry may lose respect, which may cause some to go into other areas of work. The authors argued for increasing the level, rather than lowering it further.

One of the schools surveyed (connected with the London Missionary Society) had a standard training program at a Bible school, but only held classes four months a year. Students were encouraged to continue their studies at home during the rest of the year. (Ranson et al., 1957, 25-26)

The authors mentioned the need to train the candidates "in close contact with the setting in which they will later on be working" (Ranson et al., 1957, 43) but there is no hint of getting training out to pastors on the job. The overall suggestion of the study and the booklet is to condense the schools to two (one at each end of the country), to consolidate the resources and improve the quality. Because of the link between the IMC and the WCC, this information may have been available to Hopewell, and perhaps a part of his reasoning for combining seminaries or seminary resources.

More Recent Extension Education Background

Getting education "to the masses" was seen as a tool to raise up the oppressed. One of the most respected theorists in education was Paulo Freire. His books, *Pedagogy of the Oppressed* (1970) and *Education for Critical Consciousness* (1973), emphasize furthering education as the "practice of freedom." To Freire, "extending" education to someone in need was the way of liberating them from oppression: "the role of extension agents is to extend, not their hands, but their knowledge and their technical capacities." (Freire, 1973, 94) He saw extension as something "between human beings and the world in order for human beings to be better equipped to change the world." (Freire, 1973)

While it is clear that Winter and Emery knew they were not the "inventors" of TEE and they also knew of others involved in such programs, it is not clear which programs they were aware of, except, as Winter wrote:

> Extension methods have been on the increase in the United States in the last twenty years, to the point where many universities have more extension students than they have resident students. These students are often of far higher caliber, for example, then the usual high school graduate. The University of North Carolina has enrolled at this present time more than 100,000 students in forty-five extension centers. You can readily realize that these students are on the very front line of the problems that society faces. (Winter, 1969d, 140)

There were other programs in both secular and religious settings. After World War II, the Southern Baptist Convention (SBC) realized that only one-third of their pastors in the U.S. had attended both college and seminary; another third had college only; and another third had no formal training past high school. As early as June, 1951, the SBC began the first

Christian extension program. They started a correspondence course that year, and six extension centers were established. By 1960, 3,000 students were enrolled. This enrollment was limited mainly to U.S. SBC circles, but it did expand quickly. Early on, their training also included training of different ethnic groups such as Black and Latino.[34] It also led to a college diploma with various emphases.[35] Since correspondence courses were a central part of the SBC's pattern, it was a very different model than the TEE "Guatemala Experiment."

Winter was aware of articles regarding external studies at both the University of London and the beginning of the Open University.[36] The existence of similar activities at universities fostered an environment of acceptability for TEE merely by association:

> In the secular world, where educators have realized that their institutions will not be able to sustain growth rates equal to those of the population explosion, methods which have been found helpful in the extension seminary are being applied. In January 1971 "The Open University" in England will begin courses leading to a B.A. degree. (Covell and Wagner, 1971, 2)

The concept embraced by the Open University in the UK was seen as a powerful one, in the west and especially in Africa. The Open University web sites describe it as the world's first successful distance teaching university:

> Born in the 1960s, the 'White Heat of Technology' era, the Open University was founded on the belief that communications technology could bring high-quality degree-level learning to people who had not had the opportunity to attend campus universities.[37]

With the first student enrolled in 1970, by 1980, OU had 80,000 students and by its 25th anniversary, 200,000 graduates. As of 2007, OU has approximately 150,000 undergraduates and 30,000 graduate students. It has 50,000 students who are sponsored by their employers.[38]

---

[34] http://www.seminaryextension.org/history.asp Retrieved on January 7, 2010.

[35] Email communication, September 19, 2001, from Leonard Hill to Vivian Buttrey for an upcoming book tentatively called: *Seminary Extension's First Fifty Years: 1951-2001.*

[36] There was a reference to OU in Winter's files related to his work on the TEE book he edited in1969.

[37] http://www.open.ac.uk/about/ou/p3.shtml Retrieved on July 16, 2007.

[38] http://www.open.ac.uk/about/ou/ Retrieved on July 16, 2007. The article in the *Expository Times* on the Open University said that "A Prospectus has been published and courses are to start in January 1971." (Mitton, 1970, 223)

OU's operation was noted in Christian sources as well. *The Expository Times* reported on The Open University's decision to begin operations in 1970. The student OU sought to serve was one who had not been able to "avail themselves of the more traditional type of university, either because they lack the necessary academic qualifications or because their present circumstances make it quite impossible for them to give up everything else and become internal students at a university for three consecutive years." (Mitton, 1970)

Asian evangelical mission theologian Bong Rin Ro noted that:

This will prove a real godsend to older men and women who feel equipped to proceed to degree work, but cannot absent themselves from the duties which provide their livelihood, or to women who cannot discard the responsibilities of home and family. (Ro, 1970, 224)

At least one other model predated OU and probably all the rest: the University of South Africa. A had a vision for correspondence education in the 1940s. In 1946, UNISA explored "the possibility of devising a system of postal or correspondence tuition for non-residential students. On 15 February 1946, the Division of External Studies was established. This transformed UNISA into a teaching university that became the pioneer of tertiary distance education in the Western world."[39]

Field missionaries like Winter and Emery saw similar issues in training leaders "on the ground" as those that the OU and UNISA were seeking to address. In Winter's case, it was the pastors of a growing church around the world. And others who got involved with TEE saw the huge population centers of Asia and Africa in need of a model of training that would shy away from residential schools with the attenuating building, travel, and tuition costs.

---

[39] http://www.unisa.ac.za/default.asp?Cmd=ViewContent&ContentID=20555 Retrieved on May 21, 2008.

Appendix G

Extension Newsletter Example

THE MONTHLY AIR MAIL

NEWSLETTER

135 North Oakland Avenue   Pasadena, California 91101

DECEMBER 1972   VOL. I NO. 2

A Programming Techniques Workshop will be held in Wheaton, Illinois on March 19-24, 1973. Cost is $50.00 plus food, plus travel. Applications, accompanied by the $10.00 registration fee (included in the $50.00), must be sent before January 31 to:
R. B. Buker, CAMEO Coordinator
2210 Park Place
Boca Raton, Florida 33432

WEF Programming News of October 1972 features an article by Peter Savage entitled Preparing to Write. Among other useful suggestions it proposes the following steps that the potential writer will take:
1) Defining the TOPIC AREA
2) Defining the TARGET POPULATION
3) Stating the EDUCATIONAL GOALS
4) Analysis of TARGET POPULATION
5) Build a Pyramid of Objectives and Sub-Objectives
6) Establish Strategy

TAP-Asia is producing the report of nine Programmed Instruction workshops held in Asia last summer. Those who want these reports as well as other detailed TEE information from that area should send $10.00 for TAP-Asia membership to:
Dr. Bong Ro, S.E. Asia Coordinator
TAP-Asia
33A Chancery Lane
Singapore 11

Theological Education by Extension edited by Ralph Winter, which relates the history of the movement in Latin America, will be updated for a second edition soon.

Extension in Haiti was stimulated by a workshop in June conducted by Harold Alexander and James Sauder. TEE students in June numbered 250. A second workshop in August was attended by 30 professors from 5 organizations. Student enrollment has risen to 650. Coordination of TEE in Haiti is by
Centre d'Information et de Statistique Evangelique (CISE)
B.P. 458
Port-au-Prince, Haiti

Inquiries concerning TEE in the Near East and North Africa should be directed to:
Bob Meloy
P.O. Box 126
Tripoli, Lebanon

Evangel Publishing House of Kisumu, Kenya has agreed with AEBICAM to publish all of the TEE materials to be used in Africa. The first text, Talking with God, is also available in Swahili under the title Kuzungumza na Mungu. Prices are $1.50 and $1.00 respectively, with discounts for quantity orders. Bringing People to Christ, an evangelism text, will be in print in January. This book written by Jonah Moyo and Grace Holland in Zambia will also be translated into Swahili. Eight more texts are being validated for production at present and plans call for printing of these materials in French as well as in English and Swahili. For more information write:
Evangel Publishing House
P.O. Box 969
Kisumu, Kenya

Appendix H

Mission Agencies and Denominations Sponsoring or Involved in TEE from *The World Directory of Theological Education by Extension* by Wayne C. Weld, 1973

No attempt has been made to update organizational names. This list does not include the names of seminaries that sponsored programs. Several organizations are listed in more than one program and in more than one country, but are listed here only once. The portion of the directory that includes these programs is listed from pages 164–318 and A1–A8 in the Directory. There are 159 groups listed below.

African Evangelical Fellowship
African Reformed Church
Alianca Bíblica do Brasil
American Baptist Mission
American Lutheran Church
American Lutheran Mission
Anglican Church
Assemblies of God
Associate Reformed Presbyterian Church
Association of Baptists for World Evangelism
Association of Evangelical Church of Magdalena
Association of Interamerican Churches in Ecuador
Baptist Convention of Piaui-Maranhao
Baptist Convention of Venezuela
Baptist Conventions of Argentina, Chile, Uruguay, Paraguay
Baptist Mid-Missions
Baptist Union of South Africa
BEA Churches
Berean Mission and Gospel Missionary Union
Bethany Home
Bethesda Church
Bihar Mennonite Church

Board of World Missions, Presbyterian Church, U.S.
Brethren Church
Brethren in Christ Church
Brethren Mission
Bumila Fellowship of Baptist Churches, Inc.
California Yearly Meeting of Friends
Central African Presbyterian Church
Central American Yearly Meeting of Friends
Centre d'Information et de Estatistique Evangelique
Chinese Baptist Convention
Christian Advent Churches in the Philippines
Christian and Missionary Alliance
Christian and Missionary Alliance National Church
Christians in Action
Church of Christ in Thailand
Church of England, Diocese of Armidale
Church of God in East Africa
Church of God World Missions
Church of Pakistan (Anglican, Methodist and Scotch Presbyterian)
Church of South India
Church of Sweden Mission

Church of the Brethren
Church of the Nazarene Mission
Churches of God in Guatemala
Conservative Baptist
Conservative Baptist Foreign
  Mission Board
Conservative Baptist Mission of
  Brazil
Cumberland Presbyterian Church
Danish Pathan Mission
Division of Overseas Ministries New
  York
Eritrea Evangelical Church
European Baptist Mission
Evangelical Baptist Mission of South
  Haiti
Evangelical Christian Union
Evangelical Church (African)
Evangelical Church Mekane Yesus
Evangelical Church of Iran
Evangelical Churches of West Africa
Evangelical Covenant Church of
  America
Evangelical Covenant Church of
  Ecuador
Evangelical Covenant Mission
Evangelical Lutheran Church
Evangelical Lutheran Mission
Evangelical Mennonite Church
Evangelical Mennonite Church of
  Honduras
Evangelical Mennonite Mission
Evangelical Union of South America
Federation of Independent
  Evangelical Churches of Spain
Finnish Lutheran Mission
Finnish Missionary Society
Foreign Mission Board of the
  Southern Baptist Convention
Foursquare Gospel Church
Free Methodist Church of Brazil.
Free Methodist Mission
Free Methodist Mission of Brazil
Free Will Baptist
Full Gospel Church

General Conference Baptist
General Conference Mennonite
  Church
General Conference Mennonite
  Mission
German Hermansburg Mission
Gospel Mission for South America
Gospel Missionary Union
Igrejas de Cristo do Brasil
Independent Pentecostal Church of
  Northern Sumatra
India Baptist Mission
Interamerican Missionary Society
  (OMS)
International Christian Fellowship
International Fellowship of
  Evangelical Students-Pakistan
International Missions, Inc.
Korea Evangelistic Inter-missions
  Alliance
Kyodan (United Church of Japan)
La Federacion de Iglesias Evangelicas
  Luteranas en Bolivia
La Iglesia Evangelical Luterana
  Boliviana
Lahore Church Council
Latin American Mission
Lutheran Church
Lutheran Church in America
Lutheran Church Missouri Synod
Luzon Baptist Convention
Marburger Mission
Mennonite Brethren Church
Mennonite Brethren Mission
Mennonite Church
Mennonite Church of Paraguay
Mexican Evangelistic Mission
Mindanao Baptist Convention
Mission Aviation Fellowship
Missionary Board of the Church of
  God Anderson Indiana
Missionary Church Mission
Moravian Church
National Baptist Convention of
  Mexico

National Presbyterian Church
Norwegian Lutheran Mission
Open Bible Standard Churches of
  Trinidad
Open Bible Standard Missions
Oriental Missionary Society
  International
Overseas Crusades
Pakistan Christian Fellowship
  Church
Panamerican Mission
Pentecostal Church of God
Philippine Baptist Mission
Philippine Gospel Church
Poona and Indian Village Mission
Presbyterian Church of Brazil
Presbyterian Church of Colombia
Presbyterian Church of Guatemala
Presbyterian Church of the U.S.
Presbyterian Mission for Northern
  Chile
Presbytery of Cuiaba of the
  Presbyterian Church of Brazil
Primitive Methodist Church of
  Guatemala
Regions Beyond Missionary Union
Roman Catholic Church (Jesuits)
Salvation Army
South American Missionary Society
Southern Baptist in the USA
Sudan Interior Mission
Swedish Lutheran Mission
Thailand Baptist Mission
The Evangelical Alliance Mission
The Missionary Church
Unevangelized Fields Mission
União Batista Evangelica
United Andes Indian Mission
United Brethren in Christ
United Evangelical Church of
  Ecuador
United Missionary Church of Africa
United Missionary Society
United Presbyterian Church of
  Pakistan

Wesleyan Church
Wesleyan Mission
West African Methodist
West Indies Mission
World Evangelization Crusade
World Gospel Mission
World Mission Prayer League
World Missionary Prayer Leagu

Appendix I

"What Happened to TEE?" By Ted W. Ward[1]

What went wrong?[2] *Theological Education by Extension* seemed like a good idea. Increasing the number of pastors; providing improved basic pastoral education at lower cost; allowing leaders to stay "on the job" while engaged in studies—any possibility to achieve these outcomes would surely be greeted with enthusiasm. Yes, it might require a bit of change, but no one would object. Theological Education by Extension (TEE) would also resolve the economic problem that slows the growth of the church: requiring the most promising of the emerging leaders to undergo the social and economic hardships of taking two or more years to prepare to serve the church. These hardships are especially burdensome in the typical "third world" situations where the support of family and local churches is especially limited, and where the personal stresses are burdensome and unfamiliar within the culture. Long periods away from family and community often result.

TEE seemed to promise an alternative to formal schooling as typically required for ministerial preparation and academic qualification. The necessity of relocating to an institution at distance and taking on unmanageable expense would be eliminated.

The idea seemed so *exciting,* so *promising,* so *simple,* and so *cheap.* Perhaps the answer lies in the series of hopes just mentioned.

EXCITING? Yes, to the believers it was great fun to speculate what TEE would mean for educational reform, effective ministry, and church growth. But to the majority of educators, especially the power-managers of schooling, it sounded very much like one more episode in the ancient story of boom-and-bust educational innovations. This newest educational gimmick brought along an additional handicap. It is especially

---

[1] Professor Emeritus of International Studies and Education, Michigan State University and Trinity International University. This was in response to a request from this author, that Ward answer the question: What do you believe to be the reason TEE declined in the West? (Ward, 2011)

[2] I have not edited this text and I have used his formatting for this Appendix to retain his emphasis.

hard to support new strategies, especially when they suggest *no more school buildings* and worse, *learning without teachers*. Looking more closely, and with a bit of stretched imagination, the promoters assumed that while seeking new employment, the best of the present-day supply of teachers would happily become the designers and writers of these much-needed new miracle study-books.

The caricature above is somewhat exaggerated to help the reader begin to understand why the excitement rapidly gave way to suspicious disdain.

PROMISING? The hopes were very optimistic. Here is "the innovation of the century" with its prospect for ushering in a whole new mode of theological education that could transform the field as surely as Abraham Flexner's work had led to the functional effectiveness of medical education at the turn of the twentieth century. But Flexner's efforts were research-based, not simply speculation.

TEE was pioneered by engineers, preachers, and a handful of administrators. Most of the authors of the movement had little scientific experience beyond rudimentary demography. They lacked the major requisites of effective change agents, such as an understanding of social change and the necessary conditions for it to occur. Innovation was expected to happen; no one knew how to instigate it.

Distrust and suspicion were very real. Resistance grew rapidly. Even the "early adopters" became aware of the obstacles. The few who had made investments with such great hopes became disillusioned. The sleeping giant, formal schooling, yawned once or twice and nodded off. Why? What went wrong?

Many of the promoters of TEE were particularly keen about developing a new specie and a whole body of instructional literature, programmed instruction (PI). Very few knew much about PI or how it was designed, but was all of that really important? The promises seemed enough to assure success. Not only did it sound too good to be true, it indeed proved to be a fading vision.

The miracle stuff turned out to be extraordinarily difficult to develop. The few trial programs seemed to be limited to "Sunday School" levels of trite information-memory. The hope for curriculum that would prepare seriously attentive and responsive pastors seemed to be out of reach.

Experienced teachers turned out to be vigorously disinterested in putting themselves out of business. Thus the very idea of teaching without teachers was seen, early on, as an ill-conceived goal. Similarly, the level of linguistic facility demanded for the design and writing of programmed instruction was well beyond the majority of missionary-volunteers. Whatever was assumed about TEE, the coupling with programmed instruction was ill-conceived. It proved to be an Achilles heel.

The dominant promoters of TEE were evangelizers and experienced flag-wavers. One of the most disturbing problems was the disinterest in utilizing the educational community itself to guide the search for a better way. It is readily acknowledged that institutional people tend to be defensive, resistant to change, and somewhat stubborn about their own *status quo*. In retrospect, a successful introduction of the innovative features could have resulted from a more careful, orderly, and less vigorously promoted attack on the time-honored traditions of the academy. Successful change agents know the hazards that can be avoided: misjudging the capacity, motivation, and competency of the "old guard," for example. When the campaigns toward TEE began, there was little attention given to the innovative leaders with proven insights about the ways and means of working toward change. In fact, the efforts were invested too narrowly in the mistaken belief that change could be made rapidly and with a minimum of preparation.

The failure to recruit persons with research experience in educational management and innovation was evident very early. Instead, much time and effort was wasted by exalting a handful of willing disciples; few of these had any actual experience with even the most relevant forms of nonformal education-- literacy campaigns, rural development, community development, and collaborative promotion of industrial and agricultural innovation. At the heart of the issue was the evident narrowness of missionary competencies. In sum, the TEE failure has proved to be a major stimulus for broadening the scope of missionary recruitment.

SIMPLE? Theological Education by Extension was heralded as a valid solution to the major gap in the evangelization-to-church growth enterprise. Development of leadership for the church is a major concern. Christian converts need to be introduced to the Bible if they are to grow spiritually. At the heart of Christian growth is prayer partnership. The Christian life is not solitary; discipleship is a shared task. Churches are strong when the community of faith grows together. The leader must develop the capacities for listening attentively and interacting wisely, informed by the truth of Scripture. Thus the pastor is a community leader, and the wisdom required demands an education rich in experience and nurtured in respectful sharing of understanding.

Surely a more effective approach to leadership education is still needed. Seminaries seem handicapped by a rapturous infatuation with an accumulated mass of erudite information. Pastors seem to be dissatisfied with the way they have been trained: too much information, too little attention to applications to real human needs, inadequate emphasis on the formation of understanding and the nurture of spirituality.

CHEAP? Although education hardly seems "cheap" from any perspective, the sad fact is that what is tolerated as competent education in the "keeping school" mode is already carried out at nearly minimal costs. Short of inventing an intellectual funnel to fill human brains on a wholesale basis, lowering costs and increasing intellectual competencies are rarely compatible. That proposition makes for difficult propaganda. Education, responsibly defined, is a complex matter, hardly given to short-cuts and clever schemes. Schooling itself may be part of the problem.

Far too often, teaching is practiced as if all it involves is memory. The focus is on information. The proverbial ancient professor who teaches from his threadbare notes exemplifies this mode. Even each "joke" is scripted, to be recited at its own particularly dull moment. Yes, this sort of "teaching" does occur in crowded lecture halls and can be packaged and sold (or given away *cheap*) in a PI textbook. But does this sort of teaching and learning meet the standards for a competent theological education?

TIME TO START OVER? The pace of technological progress is increasing. A new start for TEE, as it was imagined in the past, is unthinkable. Programmed instruction has had its day on the scene. Some good came of it, but, very early on, PI was by-passed by a wide variety of educational uses of the computer. Already we, live in a very different age.

TEE had been touted as a way to vastly increase the number of students that could be educated, especially in hard-to-reach places. There really was no practical limit; just keep printing the PI booklets. And, of course, mass production suggests greater cost-effectiveness. For the more experienced and sensitive educator, this image was quite repulsive. For those who committed themselves to a relationship-grounded form of education, the quantitative argument for TEE fell on deaf ears. Or worse.

Certain things still hold true. (The defunct professor described earlier still can be found tiresomely at work in his lecture hall—but his newest problems are keeping the dullards he faces from thumb-texting each other or flipping over to the more compelling internet to escape his drone.) Of more significance are the emerging reminders that learning must be understood as two different mental processes: 1. Learning is what happens when information is committed to *memory*. 2. Learning is reflected by what we simply call *understanding*. Two rudimentary ideas, but two very different modes of mental function, these two different ways to conceptualize learning represent a virtual watershed that differentiates competent teaching from incompetent teaching. The first of these concepts is represented by rote-learning, drill-and-practice, repetitions, and usually "out loud" reciting and mechanical repeating of word sequences and their sound patterns. As you stroll toward an elementary school in many primitive societies, especially in much of Asia and in various Islamic regions, the dull buzz slowly becomes meaningful as a rhythmic pattern— always a sort of accented monotone. And there it is: what much of the world has long accepted as the sound of "busy learners"!

By contrast, the heavy lifting of human learning is the discussion between two or more persons, interacting as they bring their thoughts together as they explore *what an idea means*. This represents the other meaning of learning: **developing understanding**. In conclusion, the issue is not selecting methodologies on the basis of their cleverness or technological possibilities, but rather to consider what sort of teaching and learning will meet the standards for a competent theological education?

PORTIONS MAY BE QUOTED WITH PERMISSION OF THE AUTHOR[3]
FEBRUARY 12, 2011   TED W. WARD   twward@comcast.net

---

[3] Permission to print this was received in an email dated February 26, 2011 from Ted W Ward to this author.

Appendix J

HUP Consultation, Pasadena, California 1977

From May 21-June 2, 1977, Fuller Theological Seminary hosted the Consultation on the Homogeneous Unit Principle, sponsored by the Lausanne Theology and Education Group. John R. W. Stott was the moderator. The list of presenters follows:

Topic	*Presenter*
The Genesis and Strategy of the Homogeneous Unit Principle	Donald McGavran
Discussant	Harvey M. Conn
Anthropological Perspectives on the Homogeneous Unit Principle	Charles H. Kraft
Discussant	Robert L. Ramseyer
The Homogeneous Unit Principle in Historical Perspective	Ralph D. Winter
Discussant	Victor E.W. Hayward
How Biblical Is the Homogeneous Unit Principle?	Arthur F. Glasser
Discussant	C. Rene Padilla
How Ethical Is the Homogeneous Unit Principle?	C. Peter Wagner
Discussant	John H. Yoder

The full version of the presentations and responses can be found at the Fuller Theological Seminary Library. The Pasadena HUP Consultation Statement, produced as a result of this event, became the first of 65 Lausanne Occasional Papers.[4]

---

[4] As of January 28, 2011. The written results and positions can be found at:
http://www.lausanne.org/all-documents/lop-1.html All Lausanne Occasional Papers are listed at:
http://www.lausanne.org/lausanne-occasional-papers-lops.html

Appendix K

Select Early Faculty for the School of World Mission, Fuller Theological Seminary Fall 1965-1968

Donald A. McGavran	Fulltime
Alan R. Tippett	Fulltime
Warren Webster	Visiting Lecturer from Conservative Baptist Foreign Missionary Society, Taught first quarter course: "Theology of Mission to Resistant Peoples"
William Read	Visiting Lecturer from United Presbyterian Church and Church Growth Research–Latin America. Taught course, first quarter: "The Church in Latin America"
Ralph D. Winter	Fulltime
J. Edwin Orr	Part-time Professor of History of Awakenings and Dynamics of Missions
Winfield C. Arn	Adjunct Professor, Director of the Institute for American Church Growth, American Church Growth Seminars
Frederic L. Holland	Adjunct Professor, Executive Secretary of the Association of Evangelical Institutes and Colleges of Africa and Madagascar, Theological Education by Extension

Appendix L

Select Course Descriptions Taught by Ralph D. Winter at Fuller Theological Seminary School of World Mission 1966-1976[5]

The Historical Development of the Christian Movement

An analysis of the growth dynamics of the Christian movement from Pentecost to the present with particular attention to the early evangelization of Europe, the geographical, cultural, and structural factors beyond the Reformation, the delayed emergence of Protestantism as a missionary force, and the contemporary theological indigenization of world Christianity.[6]

And Later:

The Historical Development of the Christian Movement

An analysis of the growth dynamics of the Christian movement, from its roots in the Abrahamic covenant to its fruits in the age of Billy Graham and its prospects by the year 2000. Emphasis on the period beginning with World War I, the indigenization of world Christianity, the new mission agencies and new rules for old ones, the structure and function of missions today. 2 hours.[7]

Training the Ministry — Lay and Ordained

Training lay and ordained ministers to obtain development of the Church and extension of the faith. Theological, historical, cultural, and practical factors in designing right kinds of training for radically different contexts, particularly extension programs. 2 hours.[8]

The Emergence of the Western Christian Tradition

A geographical, cultural and structural analysis of the expansion of Christianity prior to the Reformation, emphasizing the Western, Roman tradition, and the peoples involved: the Jews, the Greeks, the Romans, the Celts, the

---

[5] This is not a complete listing. Since there was no date on many of these listings, these are not in any specific order.

[6] Undated listing in the SWM archives, Box 1.

[7] Undated typeset listing in the SWM archives, Box 1.

[8] This course had a 9 page Bibliography with 132 books listed, as well as an "additional bibliography" with additional books, magazines, published and unpublished materials.

Goths, the Vikings, the Muslims, the rebel Christians. 2 hours.

On the same page, crossed out, as if it was a proof:

Sources of World Christianity

The Reformation as the political and theological indigenization of the northern peoples, missions and the worldwide expansion of Europe, the delayed emergence of Protestant mission structures, foundations of a world movement, to the World Missionary Conference of 1910. 2 hours.

Appendix M

Student Experiences with Ralph D. Winter as a Teacher

In the fall of 1966, Paul McKaughan was just off from his first four years in Brazil, and was allowed a special exception so that he could study at the SWM. The Winters were not yet full-time faculty. In his introductory comments, Paul also mentions Roberta's involvement with Winter, auditing classes, filling in for Ralph.

> No one really knew who Winter was at that point, except that he was involved with TEE in Guatemala, and that program was truly ground-breaking. Many of the older students were frustrated with Winter's course because it was mostly the Winterian stream of consciousness that we all came to appreciate. There was a textbook, but we didn't really follow it. Contrary to many of my more mature student colleagues, I was totally enthralled, because amid the rambling in each class was at least one scintillating original idea or insight that I had never heard anyone express before those classes.
>
> At that end of the trimester, Ralph said that he would give an A to anyone who could give him an outline of the course. Even he must have realized it was a little disorganized. Since I had kept copious notes and dictated them for my wife to type up each night, I had a lot of what he shared with us. I organized the material and gave it to him. He then gave me an A for the course. That class began a personal relationship that lasted over all these many years. It was largely because of Winter's suggestion that the PCA's Mission to the World made contact with me and eventually I became their mission Coordinator.[9]

In 1969 to 70, Winter mentored Roger Hedlund in his thesis on *The Protestant Movement in Italy*, where he had been serving. Roger would spend the rest of his lifetime of mission work in India. He remembered that Winter's instructions to him about his thesis were "at SWM we're not interested in a thesis, we want a book...." Roger continues:

> Eventually Ralph Winter said that I really ought to be handing in some written chapters, which I did. And so did

---

[9] Email from Paul McKaughan to the author on September 6, 2010, 1.

386

he: writing comments and additional information everywhere in the margins, most of which I incorporated into the text. Years later Ralph claimed that I taught him about "evangelical Catholics" in Italy, but I'm positive it was the other way around: Ralph definitely broadened my understanding of "evangelical." I've had a profound appreciation for St Francis of Assisi ever since—and Mother Theresa is one of my favourite 'saints.'

Eventually the 'book/thesis' was completed, and accepted by the Library as well as by the faculty, then published—by WCL of course—my first book (1970).

Ralph's lectures were always informative...broad, covering various subjects—usually related to the topic at hand.

Then it was time for the FINAL EXAM. The class met in the classroom as assigned. And waited. The Prof did not show. Finally one of us was deputed to go down and across to Ralph's office as a "reminder".... Soon Ralph appeared, out of breath from climbing the back stair, and proceeded to write the Exam Question/s on the board. I'm convinced he made it up on his way up the stairs (but that's my private opinion). In any case I recall the exam [one question total?] as "broad and comprehensive." i.e. covering everything in the course (my interpretation 40 years later).

One day I came to Ralph's office and found him busy clearing off his desk. He explained: "I'm not really supposed to be operating a publishing house out of the back door at Fuller...." He was expecting a visit from the Provost or the President.[10]

Vern Middleton produced a PhD on McGavran's life, referenced earlier. During the period from July 1971 till 1972, he met Winter and took a class from him, noting that:

For the most part I found his teaching to be stimulating. His extensive use of Latourette's 7-volume set laid the foundation for my future teaching of the history of missions. There were times when the history course would break into a lesson on cosmology or a lesson on microbiology. After one such lesson I approached him and politely suggested that I was unable to see the connection between mission history and

---

[10] Email from Roger Hedlund to the author on September 6, 2010, 1. Formatting and spelling is original.

his lecture on microbiology. His response was, "I feel sorry for you."[11]

Like other students who were studying at Fuller's School of Theology, Bob Blincoe was required to take one course in the SWM. Having been a history major at the University of Oregon, he decided to take a history class, and chose Winter's January 1976 course on the Expansion of Christianity:

> In his first lecture he picked up the chalk and drew the cross of Christ in the middle of the blackboard. He said, "Let's not start the history of Christianity in 32 A.D." He walked to the farthest left hand corner of the blackboard, which stretched across the entire wall behind him, and he said, "Let's start with Abraham." And he wrote the year 2000 B.C. on the blackboard. "What is this!" I thought. Then Dr. Winter made the connection between Abraham and Jesus Christ's Great Commission, and then he connected all the history of the Bible and all of the Psalms into one unity of the Bible, "I will bless you and you will be a blessing to all the families of the earth." I had never heard of the Bible as a single story, and never heard anyone suggest a unity based on the Great Commission that began with God's call to Abraham, "blessed to be a blessing." Then Dr. Winter said, "This course is about what God did with the Bible in history."
>
> All through…Dr. Winter lectured on the history of the expansion of Christianity. … his theory [was] that church history is divided into five 400 year epochs. Roberta Winter always came with him to class, helping him to carry his books. He wore a suit with a bow tie, and drove an aging station wagon.
>
> My interest in being a pastor ebbed like an outgoing tide; I began to sense a new ambition to preach the gospel where Christ was not known, and thus to expand "Christianity" to more people in more places.
>
> One off-hand comment he made was that "no one's education is complete until they have spent two years living in another culture." Oh, no! I thought: I've been in school already for 18 years, and now I have to admit that I know nothing about other cultures. The result of this was that I and my bride, Jan…spent two years in Thailand.

---

[11] Email from Vern Middleton to the author on September 13, 2010, 1.

He was first of all a teacher, the best I ever had, and endlessly patient with his students.[12]

After serving in Thailand, he was a pastor in rural California. Then, Winter recruited him to work with him at the U.S. Center for World Mission. Bob did so, on his way to serve in Iraq. He is currently the U.S. Director of a mission agency.

Leiton Chinn was working with international students on a college campus. He also mentioned Roberta Winter's involvement in his class, occasionally teaching the class for Winter. At this point, Winter had left the SWM and had founded the U.S. Center for World Mission, but had been asked to teach his course once more at Fuller.

Leiton's story is directed at how Winter sought to mobilize the students and others around him for various "tasks" that he felt needed to be done:

> Towards the end of the 1979 Spring semester course on the Historical Development of the Christian Movement, which was Dr. Winter's final semester of teaching at Fuller, he told the class of an upcoming global consultation for mission agency executives and leaders that would take place in Edinburgh in 1980.[13] It was to be the 70th anniversary of the Edinburgh 1910 World Missionary Conference and would be fashioned like it, in terms of leaders sent by mission agencies and focusing on the unfinished task of world evangelization. Whereas the 1910 conference focused on taking the gospel to non-Christian lands, the 1980 consultation would focus on unreached people groups...also, 1910 was basically a meeting of Western mission leaders, but 1980 would include a significant delegation of Non-Western mission agency leaders. As Dr. Winter spelled out the features of the 1980 consultation, he also mentioned that there was nobody coordinating it, but that point did not register with me personally.
>
> As I took notes, I jotted down a personal note to inform the president of my mission agency...and encourage him to attend the Edinburgh 1980 meeting. Needing more information to share with my president, I approached Dr. Winter when the class ended, and asked him, "Dr. Winter,

---

[12] Email from Bob Blincoe to the author on August 31, 2010, 1-2.

[13] Winter continued to teach the "history" course at Fuller after he had resigned and founded the U.S. Center for World Mission in 1976.

can you tell me more about the meeting next year." Rather than answer my question, he replied with, "Why don't you coordinate it?" I was shocked by his response, and as I staggered to sit down, I had a rush of thoughts about why I should not accept his proposal. I felt so inadequate, inexperienced, wondered as to why mission leaders would follow a "no name" like me, and questioned my abilities to handle a responsibility of such great magnitude. ... I asked Dr. Winter if I could pray about it. ... [and] I accepted the challenge to be the International Coordinator for Edinburgh '80: World Consultation on Frontier Missions.[14]

---

[14] Email from Leiton Chinn to the author on August 31, 2010, 1.

Appendix N

William Carey Library Publishers Book Titles in Chronological Order — 1969-1976

Title[15]	Author
Church Growth through Evangelism in Depth	Malcolm Bradshaw
Theological Education by Extension	Ralph D. Winter, Editor
Church Growth Bulletin Volumes I - V	Donald A. McGavran, Editor
The Emergence of a Mexican Church	James Mitchell
New Patterns for Discipling Hindus: The Next Step in Andhra Pradesh, India	
	B.V. Subbamma
God's Miracles: Indonesian Church Growth	Ebbie C.Smith
Approaching the Nuer of Africa Through The Old Testament	Ernest A. McFall
The Protestant Movement in Bolivia	C. Peter Wagner
Challenge for Evangelical Missions to Europe, The: a Scandinavian case study	
	Hilkka Mäläskä
Church of the United Brethren in Christ in Sierra Leone, The	Emmett D. Cox
Friends in Central America	Paul Enyart
History of the Lutheran Church in Guyana, A	Paul B. Beatty, Jr.
Peoples of Southwest Ethiopia	Alan R. Tippett
Profile for Victory: New Proposals for Missions in Zambia	Max Ward Randall
Protestant Movement in Italy, The: Its Progress, Problems and Prospects	
	Roger E. Hedlund
Revolutionary Masses and Christ's Will, The	Donald McGavran
Tonga Christianity	Stan Shewmaker
Warp and the Woof, The: Organizing for Mission	Ralph D. Winter,
	R. Pierce Beaver
25 Unbelievable Years, The: 1945-1969	Ralph D. Winter
Bibliography For Cross-Cultural Workers	Alan R. Tippett
Evangelical Missions Quarterly: Volumes 1-3	James W. Reapsome, Editor
Evangelical Missions Quarterly: Volumes 4-6	James W. Reapsome, Editor
Extension Seminary Primer	Ralph R. Covell,
	C. Peter Wagner
Missions in Creative Tension: The Green Lake '71 Compendium	Vergil Gerber, ed.
Role of the Faith Mission, The: A Brazilian Case Study	Fred E. Edwards
Bibliography For Cross-Cultural Workers	Alan R. Tippett
Animistic Aymaras and Church Growth	Quentin Nordyke
Industrialization: Brazil's Catalyst for Church Growth, a study of the RIO AREA	
	C. W. Gates
World Directory of Mission-Related Educational Institutions, The	Compiled

---

[15] There are 76 titles in this list. More details on these books and all others published by WCL can be found at: http://isbndb.com/d/publisher/william_carey_library.html

Ralph D. Winter: Early Life and Core Missiology

Raymond B. Buker,
Ted Ward

Message and Mission: The Communication of the Christian Faith Eugene A. Nida

New Englishman's Greek Concordance, The George V. Wigram

American Directory of Schools and Colleges Offering Mission Courses, An
Glenn Schwartz, Editor

Aspects of Pacific Ethnohistory Alan R. Tippett

God's Word In Man's Language Eugene A. Nida

Holdeman People, The: The Church of God in Christ, Mennonite, 1859–1969
Clarence Hiebert

Manual for Evangelism/Church Growth, A Vergil Gerber

Protestants in Modern Spain: The Struggle for Religious Pluralism Dale G. Vought

Verdict Theology in Missionary Theory A. R. Tippett

World Directory of Religious Radio and Television Broadcasting International
Christian Broadcasters

Yankee Reformer in Chile, A: The Life & Works of David Trumbull Irven Paul

Manual of Articulatory Phonetics, Revised Edition William A. Smalley

Baha'i Faith, The: Its History and Teachings William McElwee Miller

Century of Growth, A: The Kachin Baptist Church of Burma Herman G. Tegenfeldt

Church Growth in Japan: A Study in the Development of Eight Denominations 1859–1939 Tetsunao Yamamori

Everything You Need to Grow a Messianic Synagogue Phillip E. Goble

Means of World Evangelization, The: Missiological Education at Fuller School of World Mission Alvin Martin, Editor

Principles of Church Growth, second edition Wayne Weld,
Donald A. McGavran

Reaching the Unreached Edward C. Pentecost

Readings in Missionary Anthropology William A. Smalley, Editor

Religious Dimension in Hispanic Los Angeles, The Clifton L. Holland

Understanding Latin Americans Eugene A. Nida

Christopaganism or Indigenous Christianity? Tetsunao Yamamori,
Charles R. Taber

Circle of Harmony: A Case Study in Popular Japanese Buddhism with Implications for Christian Mission Kenneth J. Dale,
Susumu Akahoshi

Culture and Human Values: Christian Intervention in Anthropological Perspective
Jacob A. Loewen

Customs and Cultures: Anthropology for Christian Missions Eugene A. Nida

Defeat of the Bird God C. Peter Wagner

Education of Missionaries' Children: The Neglected Dimension of World Mission
D. Bruce Lockerbie

New Day in Madras, A: A Study of Protestant Churches in Madras
Amirtharaj Nelson

People Movements in the Punjab Frederick and Margaret Stock

Writing for Theological Education by Extension   Lois McKinney
New Macedonia, The: A Revolutionary New Era in Mission Begins Ralph D. Winter
Becoming Bilingual: A Guide to Language Learning   Donald N. Larson,
William A. Smalley
Birth of Missions in America, The   Charles L. Chaney
Church Planting in Uganda: A Comparative Study   Gailyn Van Rheenen
Committed Communities: Fresh Streams for World Missions   Charles J. Mellis
Crucial Dimensions in World Evangelization   Arthur F. Glasser,
Paul G. Hiebert,
C. Peter Wagner,
Ralph D. Winter
Crucial Issues in Bangladesh   Peter McNee
Here's How: Health Education by Extension   Ronald S. Seaton &
Edith B. Seaton
How and Why of Third World Missions, The: An Asian Case Study Marlin L. Nelson
Manual for Church Growth Surveys, A   Ebbie C. Smith
Protestantism in Latin America: A Bibliographical Guide   John H. Sinclair, ed.
Readings in Third World Missions   Marlin L. Nelson, ed.
Treasure Island: Church Growth Among Taiwan's Urban Minnan Chinese
Robert J. Bolton
World Handbook for the World Christian   Patrick J. st. G. Johnstone
Church and Cultures, The: An Applied Anthropology for the Religious Worker
Louis J. Luzbetak
Church Growth and Christian Mission   Donald A. McGavran, ed.

Appendix O

E-Scale

In the Appendix of Winter's paper: "The Homogeneous Unit Principle in Historical Perspective"[16] he wrote:

> The briefest possible review of what is meant by the E-0, E-1, E-2, and E-3 symbols may be in order. For missiological purposes, all mankind can be divided into four categories:
>
> 1. Committed Christians, who are spiritually able to do evangelism. I estimate there will be 222 million people in this category by mid-1977.
>
> 2. Nominal Christians, who are culturally within the church but are not decisively reborn. These require the work of evangelistic renewal, or E-0 evangelism. I estimate there to be 1,023 million of these E-0 people.
>
> 3. Culturally near-neighbor non-Christians, who do not profess to be Christians, and who would suffer some culture shock in crossing the "stained glass barrier," but who in other respects will readily "fit" in some existing church that may or may not reach out [to] them. I estimate there to be only 467 million of these people reachable by E-1 evangelism (the "one" referring to the one stained-glass barrier).
>
> 4. Culturally distant non-Christians, who for missiological purposes are defined simply as those who are culturally just far enough away from existing congregations so that special cross-cultural techniques for planting new congregations need to be employed in order to reach effectively into their whole homogeneous unit. I estimate there to be 2,411 million such people. Some are just far enough away to need separate congregations, but yet possessed of a considerable cultural common denominator with existing Christians. These are E-2 peoples.
>
> Others have no significant cultural common denominator with existing Christian congregations. We may label them E-3 since it takes especially gifted missionaries to reach them.

This was more recently summarized in the 2009 edition of *Perspectives on the World Christian Movement* (Winter and Hawthorne, 2009) as:

---

[16] (Winter, 1977) All figures are for 1977.

The E-Scale compares the cultural distances that Christians need to move in order to communicate the gospel. E0 refers to evangelism of church-going Christians. E1 is reaching one's own culture across the barrier of "church culture." E2 is cross-cultural evangelism into a similar, but different culture. E3 evangelism is taking the gospel to cultures very different from that of the messenger. (Winter and Koch, 2009)

Appendix P

Christianity Today and Key 73

Several of the Fuller SWM faculty wrote for the special issue of *Christianity Today* on Key 73, a nationwide program to bring a gospel message to everyone. Donald McGavran wrote "The Dividends We Seek" focused on the idea that church growth was "paying off around the world" and so, he argued, it could be applied with benefit to the American scene as well. (McGavran 1973, 4)

Charles Kraft's article was titled "North America's Challenge" and highlighted the myth of "infinite assimilability of foreign people into a single homogeneous 'American Way.'" He suggested that a "fitting goal for Key 73 might be: that every group may hear and respond to the gospel message in a culturally appropriate way." (Kraft 1973, 7)

Alan Tippett wrote "A Not-So-Secular City" in which he sought to destroy the myth that cities are somehow of "non-faith" and secular in nature, and thus resistant to the gospel. Instead, discerning why a particular group of people are rejecting the gospel can help one determine how to share the gospel in a way more appropriate for the intended audience. (Tippett 1973, 8)

In his article, "What Key 73 Is All About" Art Glasser quoted the resources book for the event, "That Key 73 carries the vision of every unchurched family in North America being visited by someone who comes with loving concern to share his faith in Christ." He used his page and a half to argue for the importance of the Scriptures and the importance of believers acting on the truths in them. He sought to set aside the call for unity among denominations, instead suggesting that when Jesus prayed for unity in John 17:20-21, the focus of his prayer was not on the unity itself but on the result: that the world might believe. "That," Glasser wrote, "is what Key 73 is all about." (Glasser 1973, 13)

Winter introduced his article by noting that the Key 73 goals of confronting every person in North America "requires something new in American evangelism: *planting new congregations in subcultures strange to those who are doing the evangelizing.*" The Key 73 plans were, in his opinion, "drastically inadequate: they assume that existing congregations are ends and not means." (10)

Winter then pointed out several "Axioms" that related to this point. The first one was "*evangelism is truly effective only where those who are won become incorporated into ongoing Christian fellowship.*" On that, everyone seemed to agree. "Axiom 2 says that *people do not readily join Christian fellowships that clash with their own cultural backgrounds.*" (10) This, Winter felt, was overlooked in Key 73 materials, as Kraft's article suggested also. Axiom 3 discussed the need to penetrate the sub-groups within American culture, and noted that "*churches as churches are unlikely to punch through successfully into pockets of people that are significantly different from themselves.*" (10-11) Then Winter mentioned the E-Scale to describe the cultural differences and distance between the evangelist and the non-Christian culture. As examples of groups that displayed E-3 cultural distance to the dominant U.S. culture he cited the Navaho culture, new arrivals to America from Hong Kong and Jewish people.

Winter suggested that those who had served as foreign missionaries had gained valuable experience that could be helpful in learning to bridge cultural distance in the U.S.

> The great difference between the missionary and the ordinary Christian witnesser is that the missionary is working with people whose resulting Christianity will very likely be different from that of his home church. The missionary may more easily come to this approach overseas, but the approach is not less necessary in the United States. (11-12)

He described missions that had worked in the U.S., some with more success than others, in working through these cross-cultural issues. The missionaries, he noted, "on many fields have faced the toughest test of their careers in seeing the power of the Gospel burst forth in ways they had not expected. But new wine needs new wineskins! And churches that seek merely to save their own lives will lose them." (12)

Winter closed his article arguing for the need of churches to better understand and support the "para-church structures" that reach out to unreached subcultures.[17]

---

[17] As noted previously, while he never liked the terminology "para-church," he realized that the general Christian audience represented by *CT* would not readily understand alternate terms like sodality/modality.

Appendix Q

Lausanne 1974 Select Plenary Summaries[18]

The importance of being faithful to the Bible, the importance of being open to hear other perspectives of the Bible, and the Bible's use in evangelism (by John Stott and Susumu Uda)

"The Dimensions of World Evangelization," the billions to be reached, the need for cross-cultural evangelism (including the E-Scale), and the interface of social issues with the gospel[19] (Donald McGavran)

The shift of culture that is occurring around the church (Harold Lindsell and Malcolm Muggeridge)

The need to give voice to the church outside of North America with a gospel that is theologically sound and relevant to a world suffering from injustice (René Padilla and Samuel Escobar)

The need for our evangelism to avoid triumphalism, remain true to the NT and demonstrate social concern for the issues of our day (Michael Green)

The evaluation and discussion of various evangelism strategies and methods (George Peters, and at smaller sessions)

The work of the Holy Spirit and various views of it (Gottfried Osei-Mensah)

The current "Kingdom of Grace," the future "Kingdom of Glory," and the end times (Peter Beyerhaus)

The need for the renewal of the roles of the church, denominations, and missions, or the need for their replacements with new structures (Howard Snyder)

The way to touch the current generation with clear doctrine, honest answers, true spirituality, and community life among Christians (Francis Schaeffer)

Biblical unity with allowance for differences that do not destroy unity (Henri Blocher)

A closing message pulling together many threads from the week (E.V. Hill)

---

[18] All presentations were transcribed and are in the book, *Let the Earth Hear His Voice* (Douglas, 1975).

[19] See Appendix S for a longer summary of McGavran's presentation.

Appendix R

The Decade Past and the Decade to Come: Seeing the Task Graphically

Using an outline with the points: How are we doing? Who is to be won? How 'far away' are they? What we must do? How can we do it? Winter began his article by comparing global statistics starting with 1900 and including data up to 1965, with estimates for 1975, 1985 and the year 2000. Similar to his presentation to the Fuller Board, his opening statement clarified his perspective on the SWM at Fuller:

> Without apology, we see the entire world as the legitimate target of Christian expansion. This does not mean we envision forcing anyone to be a Christian, nor forcing anyone to change his language or his culture in order to become a Christian. This is not an institutional "triumphalism." We simply believe everyone has an equal right to knowledge of, and faith in, Jesus Christ. But if this is our goal, how are we doing? (Winter, 1974a, 11)

How are we doing?

Following that brief introduction, he launched directly into the first section called "How are we doing?" Winter detailed what most Christians might consider depressing information about the growth of the non-Christian populations in Africa and Asia during this eighty year period. He included a series of graphs.[20] The first displayed the overall population summary (Figure 28).

---

[20] All but one of these charts were grouped together with one or two others for comparison and clarity.

399

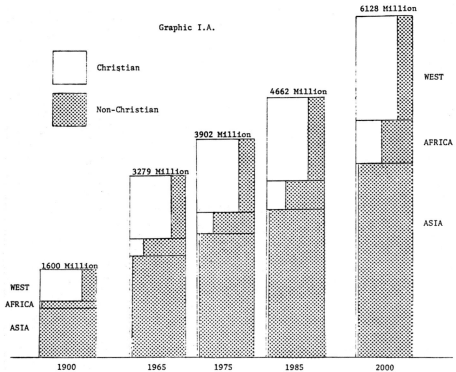

Figure 28 – World Population Growth During the "Christian Century"

The next figure demonstrated that the most important factor to Winter was not the total number of Christians or non-Christians, nor was it that there were more non-Christians and they were growing in number. To him, the crucial piece of information was the rate of growth, which he illustrated by noting, "...while non-Christians in Africa and Asia have more than doubled since 1900 and will more than triple by the year 2000, the number of Christians in Africa and Asia is today *thirteen* times what it was in 1900, and by 2000 it will be 34 times as large. The crucial factor is the difference in *rates* of growth." (Winter, 1974a,13)

This graphic answered the question: for every 100 people in the population, how many more will there be in one year? He observed, with regard to Figure 29, "For every 100 non-Christians in Africa there were 1.2 more at the end of the year, while for every 100 Christians, there were 4.6

more!"[21] In Asia, it was 1.0 more non-Christians and 2.8 Christians, and so on. (Winter, 1974a, 13)

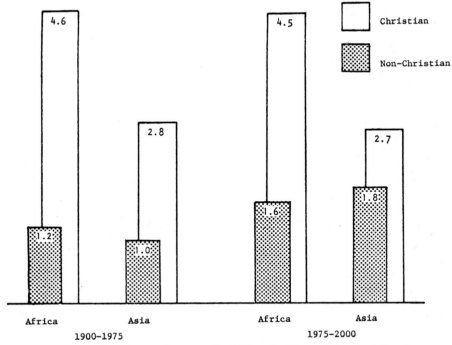

Figure 29 – Population Increase Each Year for Every Hundred People

Figure 30, the third in Winter's explanation of this first point, portrayed the significance of growth rates, showing remarkable progress over the last hundred years. In the year 2000, there would be only 17 non-Christians for every Christian in Asia.

---

[21] This was for the period from 1900-1975. Other details of the calculation are in the article and its footnotes.

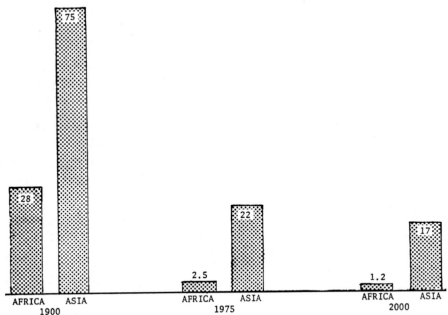

Figure 30 – The Number of Non-Christians Per Christian

Who is to be Won?

However, the growth in Asia, while remarkable where it occurred, was not all that was necessary. Amazing progress had been made, however his question heading the next section allowed him to turn to the focus of his thinking at the time: "Who is to be won?"[22] First, he recognized the ongoing situation in places where the world has seen Christian growth, namely in the Western world of Europe and America.

> [The West], where most people consider themselves Christians, is not a problem to be ignored. Every new generation has to be reevangelized, and hollow, nominal Christianity is a massive, urgent problem, even in the so-called mission lands, where unevangelized second and third generation Christians are as nominal as the average citizen of the Western world. (Winter, 1974a, 14)

But, he added, "Big as this problem is, the task of winning non-Christians, Asians and Africans is both far different and far larger." These

---

[22] This section includes overlapping content with the paper he submitted to Lausanne for the July Congress.

groups of people are broken down "into cultural rather than geographic categories." The ones that loom the largest are the Muslims, Hindus, and Chinese (Figure 31). (Winter, 1974a, 14-15)

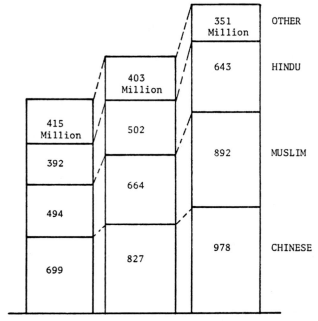

Figure 31 – Growth of Non-Christians in Africa and Asia

But the broad statistics of these religious and ethnic blocs would be merely huge numbers, something difficult for the average reader to graph. So his second graph in this pair showed where missionaries were working in relation to the Hindu, Muslim, and Chinese spheres. Figure 32 graphs the disparity. The 1993 million people living in these major non-Christian religious blocs were the "object of the attention of only five percent of the missionary force." (Winter, 1974a, 16)

Winter pointed out that he was not implying that it was unreasonable to have 47,500 Protestant missionaries from all countries serving the 403 million people who were not Chinese, Hindu or Muslim. Assuming the same ratio of personnel investment, the logical assumption was that it would take an additional 235,000 missionaries to reach those remaining major blocs.

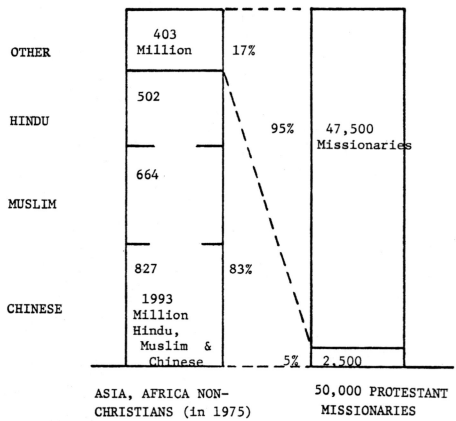

Figure 32 – Disparity of Missionaries Serving to Major Non-Christian Religions

How 'Far Away' are They?

This section of the paper demonstrated the disparity in the cultural distance between the existing Christians and the major unevangelized blocs. These Christians could actually be within or near a particular unreached culture, though separated from them by a large cultural gulf. He illustrated with two examples, one from a typical village in India and one from the New Testament period.

There might be thousands of villages with churches in India at that time, (Figure 33) but there were:

...still over 500,000 villages without any worshipping Christian group! Worse still, even where there is a church–

note the cross–it is in most cases located in the ghetto of former "untouchables," in Telegu called *Palem*.[23] The distance from this ghetto to the center of the village may be only half-a-mile *geographically*, but it is like 25,000 miles *culturally*. In this same sense, at least *80 percent of the non-Christians in the world today are beyond the reach of existing churches!* (Winter, 1974a, 17)

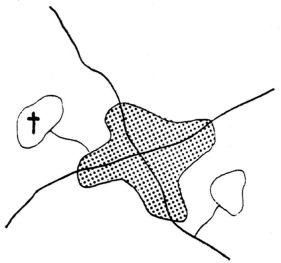

Figure 33 – Cultural Distinction Illustrations

Winter used the relationships between different groups in the NT times to illustrate the E-Scale (Figure 34) First, Jesus' words in Acts 1:8 ("Judea, Samaria, and the ends of the earth") were not primarily geographic references. Evangelizing your own people is E-1. But reaching the small community "on the doorstep of the Judeans, called Samaritans, with whom the Jews were not on speaking terms…" presented an example of cultural and ethnic relationships where significant enough differences existed for these to be considered an additional barrier to evangelism. This was E-2 evangelism. The last phrase in Acts 1:8, "ends of the earth" described "where you don't expect any linguistic head start at all, no cultural affinity whatsoever. This is E-3 evangelism and is, humanly speaking, the hardest kind." (Winter, 1974a, 17-18)

---

[23] Today, these are known as Dalits.

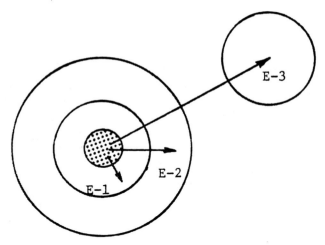

Figure 34 – Cultural Distance from Evangelist to the Culture

What We Must Do?

Winter combined ideas underlying church growth and cross-cultural evangelism/church planting. He emphasized that all four of these kinds of growth "must take place" as (Figure 35). (Winter, 1974a, 19)

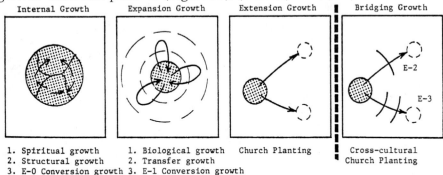

Figure 35 – Types of Growth

How Can We Do It?

The answer he gave was drawn from his research and writing about mission structures. Here he uses the phrase "para-church," arguing that:

There is powerful evidence that while Paul *began* at Antioch, he did not simply work out of Antioch. He apparently employed a "missionary band" structure or an "apostolic team" structure borrowed from the Pharisaic proselytizing movement, just as he borrowed the Jewish synagogue structure for his local churches. Thus then and now we see both church and mission—two separate, very different structures which must both be considered normal. (Winter, 1974a, 21)

He felt it was crucial for people to understand the different kinds of mission organizations and how they relate. "We must become much better acquainted with the subject, however, because successful world evangelization depends almost totally on the proper relation of the para-church mission structure to the on-going churches in both the sending and receiving countries." (Winter, 1974a, 21)

There are four types of relationships between para-church structures and churches depicted in (Figure 36).[24] The Type A Mission is related to a specific church body that administers and funds mission work. The Type B mission is the same except that the funding is not direct but the mission arm raises its own funding. The Type C Mission has a close relationship to the home churches and denomination, but is separate in its authority, administration, and budget. The Type D Missions have no special relationship to any specific church. While some churches feel a special relationship to the mission, there is no legal connection. It is more like a partnership, where each participant has a role.

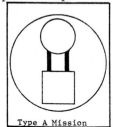 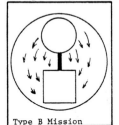  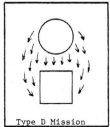

| Type A Mission | Type B Mission | Type C Mission | Type D Mission |

Figure 36 – Types of Mission-Illustration A

Figure 37 illustrates another aspect of church mission relationships, namely the relationship between churches and missions in one culture with those in another. "The two short vertical lines–Church-to-Mission–may be taken to imply any of the four cases." (Winter, 1974a, 21) Winter saw the "mission to church" relationship as temporary, noting that "Once a national church is able and autonomous it may choose to be related to a

---

[24] For a similar chart, see, "Protestant Mission Societies: The American Experience" in *American Denominational Organization* by Ross P. Scherer (1980) in the last chapter.

sister church directly rather than through a mission agency." Church-to-Church is when a "new national church is related directly to a sister church in a foreign land, [and] thus signifies full equality and maturity."

Then, under his description of Mission-to-Mission relationships, Winter emphasized again the need for ongoing mission work.

> The tendency in some quarters is to phase out the older mission apparatus in favor of the church-to-church relationship. This is a profound mistake, since (as we have seen) the non-Christian world is not dwindling. Far better: encourage the national church to sponsor its own E-2 and E-3 outreach by means of its own mission initiative. This then allows the two mission structures to continue on, in relationship with each other, to complete the task of world evangelization. (Winter, 1974a, 21)

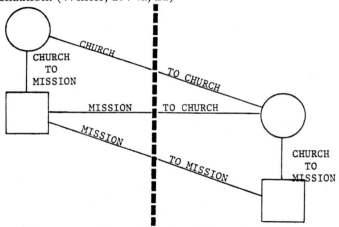

Figure 37 – Types of Mission-Illustration B

Winter ended this section and the entire article, by noting the amazing impact Christian missions had already had:

> A relatively tiny trickle of missionaries from the Western world has, under God, produced over 200 million Christians in the non-Western world. This is a significant achievement. It proves that Christianity, unlike any other religion, is truly universal. It provides an unprecedented base for what must, in the days ahead, be an unprecedentedly strong new push forward. (Winter, 1974a, 21)

Appendix S

McGavran's Paper[25]

McGavran's topic was "The Dimensions of World Evangelization" and it became the third major presentation listed under Plenary Papers and Responses in the Contents of the compendium. (Douglas, 1975, VIII) Referring to the study that Billy Graham mentioned in his opening address, McGavran noted that participants would "receive a definitive account of hundreds of populations of the world unreached or alienated from the Gospel." (McGavran, 1975, 95) At the event itself, McGavran mentioned, "more than a thousand of you sent in responses..." (McGavran, 1975, 108)

In his introduction he noted the "huge numbers of men and women [who] will never be reached by Christian neighbors" and, "the awesome challenge to evangelize three billion living with no knowledge of Jesus." (McGavran, 1975, 108) McGavran mentioned Winter and the E-Scale[26] as part of the methodological dimension, which led into a more detailed description of the kinds of evangelism that are done in different situations.

McGavran then talked about four kinds of evangelism, "one-by-one-against-the-family" and the negative impact of this. Yet he noted that, "God used it to begin the process, but he blesses other modes to better and greater growth." (McGavran, 1975, 105) The second mode of growing the church is "the family movement to Christ" where several in a family accept Christ at the same time. The third is "the people movement to Christ," where, "chains of families, all within the same segment of populations become Christians." (McGavran, 1975, 105) The fourth mode is house churches, which he does not further describe.

At the event, McGavran sought to answer some of the questions that many had asked about: "When has a man or a society been evangelized? When is the job complete?" To McGavran, the answer was clear:

> A man has been evangelized *when becoming a disciple of Jesus Christ becomes a real possibility for him*. Not when he has heard the Gospel once, not when he has been fed or taught, not when he joins a liberation movement, or passes the doors of a church; but when becoming a Christian appears to him as a genuine option. He has then truly "heard" the Gospel. Most

---

[25] This section covers both McGavran's pre-conference paper and his actual presentation at the event.

[26] See Appendix O for a description of the E-Scale.

men will be evangelized when some of the kith and kin become Christian and they hear the Gospel from and see it lived out by *their own kind of people.* (McGavran, 1975, 109)

Another question that McGavran says about ten percent asked was about social action. He replied:

Christians engage in social action. Social structures, when evil, must be changed. Christians have always done this, are doing it and always will. Ethical improvement, both personal and social, are the fruit of salvation. They issue naturally from sound conversion. The Holy Spirit leads Christians into all righteousness – both individual and corporate. Biblically well-instructed Christians are the world's greatest reformers. The most potent forces for social change are Bible-reading, Bible-obeying churches.

But first, my friends, you must have some Christians and some churches!! First you must have reborn men. Evangelism is persuading men to accept Christ and his gift of forgiveness, new power, and new righteousness. Evangelism is not proclaiming the desirability of a liquor-less world and persuading people to vote for prohibition. Evangelism is not proclaiming the desirability of sharing the wealth and persuading people to take political action to achieve it. Christians who judge these and others like them to be good ends will of course, work for them, pray for them and fight for them. And I will enthusiastically back such Christians....

But evangelism is something else. Evangelism is proclaiming Jesus Christ as God and only Savior and persuading men to become his disciples and responsible members of his church. That is the first and basic task. (McGavran, 1975, 109)

Delegates, for the most part, "rejoiced in the thought that 'God accepts world cultures'" but wanted to know more about it. McGavran said that there are good and bad elements in any culture and the bad elements need to be "cleansed or eliminated. But people come to Christ using their language, live and work in the same houses and factories, wear the same cloths." (McGavran, 1975, 110)

The greatest response was related to the new mission agencies (some 200) and missionaries (estimated at 3,400) from Latin American, Africa and Asia. McGavran noted that when all the facts are known, the numbers would be even greater. (McGavran, 1975, 110) When hundreds of people asked about McGavran's strategy methods for evangelism (one-by-one, families, by people groups, in house churches), he suggested they, (1) study church growth materials; (2) translate the materials into their language; (3) teach all four methods to your churches and in the training programs; and, (4) observe and study the methods in your own lands. (McGavran, 1975, 113)

Finally, McGavran's bent toward multiplication was clear. We should be multiplying churches, evangelists (going E-1), and missionaries (going E-2 and E-3). (McGavran, 1975, 114)

Appendix T

Lausanne Covenant Section Five[27]

Christian Social Responsibility

We affirm that God is both the Creator and the Judge of all men. We therefore should share his concern for justice and reconciliation throughout human society and for the liberation of men and women from every kind of oppression. Because men and women are made in the image of God, every person, regardless of race, religion, colour, culture, class, sex or age, has an intrinsic dignity because of which he or she should be respected and served, not exploited. Here too we express penitence both for our neglect and for having sometimes regarded evangelism and social concern as mutually exclusive. Although reconciliation with other people is not reconciliation with God, nor is social action evangelism, nor is political liberation salvation, nevertheless we affirm that evangelism and socio-political involvement are both part of our Christian duty. For both are necessary expressions of our doctrines of God and man, our love for our neighbour and our obedience to Jesus Christ. The message of salvation implies also a message of judgment upon every form of alienation, oppression and discrimination, and we should not be afraid to denounce evil and injustice wherever they exist. When people receive Christ they are born again into his kingdom and must seek not only to exhibit but also to spread its righteousness in the midst of an unrighteous world. The salvation we claim should be transforming us in the totality of our personal and social responsibilities. Faith without works is dead.
(Acts 17:26,31; Gen. 18:25; Isa. 1:17; Psa. 45:7; Gen. 1:26,27; Jas. 3:9; Lev. 19:18; Luke 6:27,35; Jas. 2:14-26; Joh. 3:3,5)

---

[27] This and the full document can be found at: http://www.lausanne.org/covenant and was accessed on April 13, 2011. See also John Stott's commentary on it in *The Lausanne Covenant: An Exposition and Commentary*. (Stott, 1975)

Appendix U

Winter's List of 24 Problems to be Solved

This is a list created by Winter as of 2006 and used with new staff joining the Frontier Mission Fellowship. The list continues on the next page.

The Mission Problems We Have Sought to Solve

Ralph D. Winter • Friday, August 25, 2006

We have often said that "The role of the FMF, the USCWM and the WCIU can be stated in one sentence: to fix and/or improve the effectiveness of mission agencies at work at frontiers of mission." That boils down to detecting problems or "frontiers" which need to be solved or crossed.

To solve a problem, however, does not necessarily mean to *implement the solution*—that might mean sending missionaries to engage, and eventually to reach, unreached people groups. Instead, we have often sought to *create and promote the solution*, and hope that all or most of the existing mission agencies will take it up, as they have,

in fact, in the case of challenge of unreached peoples. Unfortunately, we have to some extent failed to explain to our members the urgency of tackling these problems from "behind the scenes." Or, they have been unable to appreciate the strategy of winning over many agencies in order to resolve those problems. Thus, most staff have left for the far corners of the earth in the *implementation* of that vision.

However, can *promoting solutions* be more exciting if we often remind ourselves of *the problems we have sought to resolve*? In one sense we have been a think-tank focused on agency reengineering. So let's think about it!

Year	Mission Problem (1-13 predate the USCWM)	Solution
1954	The need for an accessible Greek concordance of both the NT and the OT.	*Word Study Concordance, New Light from the Greek Bible* now exist
1961	The need for a system of selection of pastoral leaders superior to the residential training of immature younger people.	The Theological Eduction by Extension movement now exists, WCIU follows
1968	The need for a specifically mission-oriented publishing company.	William Carey Library now exists
1972	The need for a *comparative* Greek New Testament instead of the inaccurate and inherently flawed "eclectic" Nestle text.	WCIU's Swanson project now almost finished
1972	The need for a global level meeting on the subject of mission frontiers.	In 1980, the World Consultation on Frontier Missions. The next is due in 2010 (100 years after 1910)
1972	The need for a scholarly journal of missiology.	*Missiology, an International Review, International Journal of Frontiers in Mission* now exist, the latter since 1983
1972	The need for a society of mission scholars.	ASM 1972, EMS 1982, ISFM 1984
1972	The need for insight into the missional nature of the entire sweep of God's work on earth, from Abraham to the present.	Embedded in Perspectives materials, World Christian Foundations, Insight
1974	The need for a major cooperative mission research center.	USCWM 1976 now exists

Ralph D. Winter: Early Life and Core Missiology

Year	Mission Problem *(1-13 predate the USCWM)*	Solution
1974	The need for a major cooperative mission research center.	USCWM 1976 now exists
1974	The need for an awareness of bypassed subgroups on the mission field.	A need promoted in *Mission Frontiers, Perspectives*, and *Vision for the Nations*, and William Carey Library
1974	The need for specific international orientation for those who promote missions or go as missionaries.	The Perspectives Study Program
1975	The need for a global level association of mission agencies.	The fledgling Global Network of Mission Structures
1975	The need for a secular university adapted to missions.	WCIU now exists
1977	The need for a competent but inexpensive accounting system for mission agencies.	Not effectively pursued, now too late
1979	The need for a pew-level mission periodical.	*Mission Frontiers* now exists
1981	The need for a daily "World Christian" experience.	*Global Prayer Digest* started in 1982
1981	The need for a global network of centers for world mission. There are 50?	Not effectively pursued thus far
1986	The need "to return or reassign" $8 million advanced to us. MPC,	small progress
1990	The need to combat extensive secularization of the liberal arts curriculum.	World Christian Foundations, Insight
1990	The need for a solid liberal arts/seminary curriculum as a basis for all Ph. D. degrees.	World Christian Foundations
1990	The need to integrate and condense the liberal arts/seminary curricula for the benefit of pastors, Christian leaders and lay alike whose social involvement requires them to study part time at a distance.	World Christian Foundations
1995	The need for strategic study of the ethnic realities of the entire globe in order to understand more objectively and statistically where the most crucial needs are.	Joshua Project, Colorado Springs
2001	The need to reintroduce to mission agencies and Evangelicals in general the full implications of the Gospel of the Kingdom.	Roberta Winter Institute, first consultation, October 2006

Correspondence and Reports

Field, Annual and Other Reports

Year	From:	Subject:
1955	Unknown	Field Report Guatemala on the Presbyterian mission
1956	Paul Burges	Annual Meeting Report (entire field)
1956	James Emery	Annual Meeting Report (Mam region)
1959	Dudley H. Peck	Personal Report Annual Meeting
1959	Roberta Winter	Annual Meeting
1960	F.G. Scovell and Wm. L. Wonderly	Report on the Work and Personnel of the Mam Christian Center, Ostuncalco, Guatemala
1961	R.H. Baird	Report the Commission on Ecumenical Mission and Relations
1962	James Emery	Annual Meeting Report (Mam region)
1962	Roberta Winter	Annual Meeting
1962	Ralph Winter	Annual Meeting
1964	Ralph Winter, Ray Strong, et. al.	The Extension-Seminary Plan in Guatemala
1965	Ralph Winter	Personal Report
1970	M/M Scotchmer	Annual Report

Letters

Date	From:	To:	Subject:
11/3/1954	Donald McGavran	Vernon Sly	Outline of a school of church growth
6/23/1954	Robert Thorp	W.S. Rycroft	Cable re: Missionary evacuation from Guatemala
9/5/1956	Donald McGavran	Elfers, Publisher	Church growth questions
7/4/c.1957	Ralph Winter	Hugo and Hazel Winter	Complaint about how Spanish was being taught
8/25/c.1957	Ralph Winter	Hugo and Hazel Winter	Greek Textual Lexicon, the hybrid-test project
c.10/1957	Ralph Winter	Hugo and Hazel Winter	Complaint about how Spanish was being taught
Fall of 1957	Ralph Winter	Hugo and Hazel Winter	Reflections from his first visit to Guatemala
9/16/1957	Ralph Winter	Rev. Stevens	Detailed activities he hopes will help mobilize people back home
9/28/1957	Ralph Winter	Dr. Rycroft	Detailed activities he hopes will help mobilize people back home
10/15/1958	Ralph Winter	Don Fletcher	Details regarding the situation with Ruth Wardell
10/27/1958	Ralph Winter	Don Fletcher	Recommendations for Spanish language program
8/8/1959	Ralph Winter	Dr. and Mrs. Hutchins	Ralph's self-reflection on his youth at LACC
1/3/1960	Ralph Winter	Don Fletcher	Importance of the language school

2/2/1961	Robert C. Thorp	Nathaniel Bercovitz, M.D.	Winter's non-conformist pattern with learning Spanish
2/2/1961	Robert C. Thorp	Nathaniel Bercovitz, M.D.	Opinions about Ralph and his not learning the language.
6/15/1961	Archie Crouch	Ted Romig	Noting Winter was an engaging speaker
7/10/1961	John H. Sinclair	Ralph and Roberta Winter	Encourage focus on Mam language learning
10/8/1961	Dudley and Dorothy Peck	Ralph and Roberta Winter	Request for Ralph's speech they had heard about
1/25/1963	Ruth E Wardell	John Sinclair	Details about her role and reporting
2/4/1963	Ralph Winter	John H. Sinclair	Ordination of Mam leaders.
6/10/1964	Ralph Winter	F. Ross Kinsler	Question about his thoughts on TEE
6/11/1964	Ralph Winter	Jim Emery and Chuck Ainley	The future of the residential seminary
10/6/1964	Ralph Winter	Dick Wallis	Reasons for a school for children from the U.S.
10/20/1964	Ralph Winter	John H. Sinclair	General update and reason for delay in writing
12/17/1964	Daniel P. Fuller	Eugene Nida	The beginning of the SWM
2/22/1965	Daniel P. Fuller	Eugene A. Nida	Input and feedback requested about the SWM
3/15/1965	F. Carlton Booth	Eugene A. Nida	The beginning of the SWM
6/10/1965	F. Ross Kinsler	John H. Sinclair	Resources needed for TEE professors

10/29/1965	Ralph Winter	John H. Sinclair	Showing a masthead with info promoting Guatemala
11/3/1965	F. Ross Kinsler	John H. Sinclair	Meeting for seminary graduation/celebration
11/8/1965	F. Ross Kinsler	John B. Housley	Meeting report on TEE graduation/celebration
12/7/1965	Eugene A. Nida	Donald McGavran	Input on the SWM starting
1/19/1969	Donald McGavran	Ralph Winter	Input on the TEE book
4/27/1971	Donald McGavran	The SWM Faculty	Green Lake 71
12/20/1971	Martin Conway	Ralph Winter	The RISK journal article criticizing TEE
12/21/1971	Ralph Winter	Gerald Anderson	The RISK journal article criticizing TEE
12/28/1971	John H. Sinclair	Ralph Winter	The RISK journal article criticizing TEE
12/29/1971	James H. Emery	James E. Goff	The RISK journal article criticizing TEE
2/11/1972	Rex Davis	Ralph Winter	The RISK journal article criticizing TEE
3/13/1972	F. Ross Kinsler	James E. Goff	The RISK journal article criticizing TEE
9/5/1972	Eugene Nida	Ralph Winter and Alan Tippett	Practical Anthropology becoming Missiology
7/27/1973	Glenn Schwartz	Incoming SWM students/ spouses	A job at WCL
2/18/1974	Donald A	Ralph	Feedback on

	McGavran	Winter	Lausanne paper
2/20/1974	Donald Hoke	Paul Little, Leighton Ford, Samuel Escobar and Ralph Winter	Lausanne 1974 presentations

Emails

Date	From:	To:	Subject:
10/21/05	Wilbur Shenk	Greg H Parsons	Biography as PhD
10/25/05	Mark Noll	Greg H Parsons	Biography as PhD
1/21/09	Sara Parker (Scotchmer)	Greg H Parsons	On learning Mam before Spanish
2/12/09	Ralph Winter	Greg H Parsons	Management of the team in Guatemala
2/12/09	Ralph Winter	Greg H Parsons	Fever seizures in children
4/13/09	Ralph Winter	Greg H Parsons	His role and that of Max Lathrop in the 1st Christian Indian Congress
11/10/09	Vern Middleton	Greg H Parsons	On McGavran
9/2/10	Charles Kraft	Greg H Parsons	Students at the SWM
1/15/11	Samuel Escobar	Greg H Parsons	Responses from Lausanne 74 delegates
2/21/11	Vern Middleton	Greg H Parsons	McGavran's worldwide travel
3/9/11	Paul Emery	Greg H Parsons	Information about Ruth Wardell
3/11/11	Beth Snodderly	Greg H Parsons	Winter's beginning the Roberta Winter Institute

Interviews

Date	Interviewee	Time Length[1]	# of pages[2]	General Subject(s)	Refer-enced[3]
2/10/05	Arthur Glasser	?	22	Fuller, includes Fuller alumni in panel discussion	y
3/7/05	Dan Fuller	1:28	9	Relation to Ralph, LACC, Princeton, CE	y
7/27/05	Paul Winter	?	11	Family, LACC, Navy, Navigators	y
7/26/06	Ralph Winter	1:14	25	Guatemala, Latin and Mam culture	y
7/31/06	Ralph Winter	:68	18	Background, family, early education	y
8/2/06	Ralph Winter	:53	18	Dan Fuller, Navigators, CE, school	y
8/6/06	Ralph Winter	:48	14	SWM continued, WCL beginnings	
8/7/06	Ralph Winter	:56	14	Education, schools, LACC, Afghanistan	y
8/14/06	Ralph Winter	:49	14	SIL, Afghan. Inst. of Tech., Guatemala	y
8/16/06	Ralph Winter	:55	12	TEE	y
8/23/06	Ralph Winter	:40	9	Latourette, historical interests	y
8/30/06	Ralph Winter	:56	16	Fuller SWM	y

---

[1] Times are in minutes and are approximate.

[2] Not all interviews were transcribed.

[3] If I had more space, I would have quoted from almost all of these interviews. While some are not actually quoted in the thesis, almost all of the interviews helped to give overall clarity to specific subject areas or confirm views others expressed. In the future, audio and transcriptions of these will be posted at: www.ralphdwinter.org

9/13/06	Ralph Winter	:39	11	SWM to unreached focus, Lausanne 74	
10/16/06	Ralph Winter	:29	9	Leaving Fuller, Institute of Intl. Studies, USCWM	
10/18/06	Ralph Winter	:44	12	USCWM, Mission Frontiers begins	
10/25/06	Ralph Winter	:35	10	Unreached vision, Institute of Intl. Studies	
11/16/06	Steve Sywulka	:58	9	Guatemala history, personalities	
12/12/06	Paul Hiebert	:53	11	Fuller, ASM, Perspectives, anthropology issues	
12/12/06	Wayne Weld	:34	9	TEE in Latin America and at Fuller SWM	
1/15/07	Ralph Covell	:36	6	TEE in Asia, and Fuller	y
3/6/07	Ross Kinsler	:33		TEE in Guatemala + (tape stopped)	y
3/24/07	Edwin "Jack" Frizen	1:24		IFMA, North American mission background	
7/19/07	Glenn Schwartz	:67	16	Fuller SWM	
8/22/07	Lee Merritt	:14		Fuller	

11/1/07	David Cho	:45	5	Asia/Korean missions, history with Winter	
4/10/08	James Reapsome	:38	6	EFMA, IFMA, *EMQ*, North American Missions	
1/29/09	Robert Ferris	:27	5	TEE	y

Bibliography

Action, United Evangelical 1947 "Afghanistan Seeks American Teachers". *United Evangelical Action,* 5:11, April 15, 1947.

Anderson, Gerald H. 1998 *Biographical Dictionary of Christian Missions,* New York, London, Macmillan Reference Simon & Schuster and Prentice Hall International.

Anderson, Rufus & Beaver, R. Pierce 1967 *To Advance the Gospel : Selections from the Writings of Rufus Anderson,* Grand Rapids, Eerdmans.

Arles, Siga 2006 *Missiological Education : An Indian Exploration,* Bangalore, Centre for Contemporary Christianity.

Barro, Antonio Carlos 1993 *Orlando Enrique Costas : Mission Theologian on the Way and at the Crossroads,* Pasadena, Fuller Theological Seminary, PhD.

Bassham, Rodger C. 1979 *Mission Theology, 1948-1975 : Years of Worldwide Creative Tension--Ecumenical, Evangelical, and Roman Catholic,* Pasadena, William Carey Library.

Beaver, R. Pierce 1968 *The Missionary Between the Times,* Garden City, Doubleday.

_____ 1971 "The Christian Mission, a Look into the Future". *Concordia Theological Monthly,* XLII:6, June 1971, 345-352.

_____ 1973 *The Gospel and Frontier Peoples : A Report of a Consultation, December 1972,* South Pasadena, William Carey Library.

Bebbington, D. W. 2005 *The Dominance of Evangelicalism : The Age of Spurgeon and Moody,* Downers Grove, InterVarsity Press.

Bennett, Charles 1968 *Tinder in Tabasco : A Study of Church Growth in Tropical Mexico,* Grand Rapids, Eerdmans.

Beyerhaus, Peter & Lefever, Henry Charles 1964 *The Responsible Church and the Foreign Mission,* Grand Rapids, Eerdmans.

Blauw, Johannes 1962 *The Missionary Nature of the Church : A Survey of the Biblical Theology of Mission,* London, Lutterworth Press.

Blincoe, Robert Alan 2012 *A New Social Contract Relating Mission Societies to Ecclesiastical Structures,* Pasadena, William Carey International University, PhD.

Bloesch, Donald G. 1988 *The Future of Evangelical Christianity: A Call for Unity Amid Diversity,* Colorado Springs, Helmers & Howard.

Bloomfield, Leonard 1933 *Language,* New York, H. Holt and Company.

Bosch, David J. 1993 Reflections on Biblical Models of Mission, in Coote, R. T. & Phillips, J. M. (Eds.) *Toward the 21st Century in Christian Mission.* Grand Rapids, Eerdmans, 175-192.

Bosch, David Jacobus 1980 *Witness to the World : The Christian Mission in Theological Perspective,* Atlanta, John Knox Press.

_____ 1991 *Transforming Mission : Paradigm Shifts in Theology of Mission,* Maryknoll, Orbis Books.

Brady, Robert L. 2007 Confessions of a Reformed Church Growth Consultant. Self published.

Brainerd, Edwin 1974 "The 'Myth' of Programmed Texts". *Evangelical Missions Quarterly*, 10:3, July 1974, 219-223.

Bready, J. Wesley 1942 *This Freedom - Whence?*, New York, American Tract Society.

Brokaw, Tom 2005 *The Greatest Generation*, New York, Random House.

Bruner, Edward M. (ed.) 1984 *The Opening Up of Anthropology*, Washington, D.C., The American Ethnological Society.

Burgess, Dora 1962 "Integration Accomplished". *Guatemala News*, LIII:3, 1-2.

Burnett, Virginia Garrard 1989 "Protestantism in Rural Guatemala, 1872-1954". *Latin American Research Review*, 24:2, 1989, 127-142.

Cahill, Thomas 1995 *How the Irish Saved Civilization : The Untold Story of Ireland's Heroic Role from the Fall of Rome to the Rise of Medieval Europe*, New York, Doubleday.

Call, Merlin W. 2007 "Reflections on the Journey of Fuller Seminary". *Theology News and Notes*, 54:2, Spring 2007, 4-8.

Camp, Bruce K. 1992 *Scripturally Considered, the Local Church has Primary Responsibility for World Evangelization*, La Mirada, BIOLA, DMiss.

Carey, William 1891 *An Enquiry into the Obligations of Christians to Use Means for the Conversion of the Heathens. In Which the Religious State of the Different Nations of the World, the Success of Former Undertakings and the Practicabilty of Further Undertakings, Are Considered*, London, Hodder and Stoughton.

_____ 1988 *An Enquiry into the Obligations of Christians to Use Means for the Conversion of the Heathens*, Dallas, Criswell Publications.

Carpenter, Joel A. 1997 *Revive Us Again : The Reawakening of American Fundamentalism*, New York, Oxford University Press.

Chen, Stephen Lei 1977 *Church Growth - Textbook for Theological Education by Extension*, Fuller Theological Seminary, ThM.

Cho, David J. 1975 Response to Ralph Winter and Jacob Loewen, in Douglas, J. D. (Ed.) *Let the Earth Hear His Voice*. Minneapolis, World Wide Publications, 253-254.

Chun, Chaeok 1975 *The All-Asia Mission Consultation*, Pasadena, Fuller Theological Seminary, MTh.

Clark, Francis E. 1903 *The Christian Endeavour Movement : With Details Pertaining to the History, Theory, Principles and Practice of the Society*, Chennai 2000 Edition, Christian Literature Society.

Coke, Hugh Milton, Jr. 1978 *An Ethnohistory of Bible Translation Among the Maya*, Pasadena, Fuller Theological Seminary, PhD.

Costas, Orlando E. 1974 *The Church and its Mission : A Shattering Critique from the Third World*, Wheaton, Tyndale House Publishers.

Covell, Ralph R. 1974 "Last Decade a Remarkable One in Publishing of Mission Books". *Evangelical Missions Quarterly*, 10:1, January 1974, 112-117.

Covell, Ralph R. & Wagner, C. Peter 1971 *An Extension Seminary Primer*, South Pasadena, William Carey Library.

Creswell, John W. 1998 *Qualitative Inquiry and Research Design: Choosing Among Five Traditions,* Thousand Oaks, Sage Publications.

Crystal, David 1991 *A Dictionary of Linguistics and Phonetics,* Oxford UK, Cambridge, USA, B. Blackwell.

Dawson, Christopher 1991 *Religion and the Rise of Western Culture,* New York, Doubleday.

Dayton, Edward R. 1974 "A New Way to See the World". *World Vision,* 18:9, October 1974, 7-9.

Denzin, Norman K. 1989 *Interpretive Biography,* Newbury Park, Sage Publications.

Denzin, Norman K. and Lincoln, Yvonna S. 2008 *Collecting and Interpreting Qualitative Materials,* Thousand Oaks, Sage Publications.

Douglas, J. D. 1975 *Let the Earth Hear His Voice,* Minneapolis, World Wide Publications.

Editorial 1967 "CAMEO Assists Education". *Evangelical Missions Quarterly,* 2:1, Winter 1976, 115-116.

_____ 1973 "Key 73: Planning a Sequel". *Christianity Today,* 28:25, September 28, 1973, 38-39.

_____ 1974 "Missions : From All Six to All Six". *Christianity Today,* 29:4, November 27, 1974, 40-41.

Emery, James H. 1963 "The Preparation of Leaders in a Ladino-Indian Church". *Practical Anthropology,* 10:3, 127-134.

Escobar, Samuel 2002 *Changing Tides : Latin America and Mission Today,* Maryknoll, Orbis Books.

_____ 2003 *The New Global Mission,* Madison, InterVarsity Press.

Ferris, Robert W. 1986 The Future of Theological Education, in Youngblood, R. L. (Ed.) *Cyprus: TEE Come of Age.* Exeter, Paternoster on behalf of the World Evangelical Fellowship and the International Council of Accrediting Agencies, 41-64.

Field, Vance R. 1972 *Theological Education by Extension,* Portland, Western Evangelical Seminary.

Fong, Bruce W. 1996 *Racial Equality in the Church : A Critique of the Homogeneous Unit Principle in Light of a Practical Theology Perspective,* Lanham, University Press of America.

Freire, Paulo 1970 *Pedagogy of the Oppressed,* New York, Herder and Herder.

_____ 1973 *Education for Critical Consciousness,* New York, Seabury Press.

Fritsch, Charles T. & Winter, Ralph D. 1957 *Lexical Handbook of the Hebrew Bible : Vol. I, Genesis 1-20,* Princeton, Self.

Frizen Jr., Edwin L. 1991 "Tributes to Donald McGavran". *Evangelical Missions Quarterly,* 27:1, January 1991, 62.

Fuller, Daniel P. 1955 Letter to Alumni Regarding Inductive Bible study, *Theology News and Notes* 2:4, 6-9

_____ 1972 *Give the Winds a Mighty Voice : The Story of Charles E. Fuller,* Waco, Word Books.

Fuller, W. Harold 1980 *Mission-Church Dynamics : How to Change Bicultural Tensions into Dynamic Missionary Outreach,* Pasadena, William Carey Library.

Gair, James W. 2006 *Charles Francis Hockett: Biographical Memoir,* Washington, D.C., National Academy of Sciences.

Gerber, Vergil 1971 *Missions in Creative Tension : The Green Lake '71 Compendium,* South Pasadena, William Carey Library.

_____ 1972 Introduction, in Wagner, C. P. (Ed.) *Church/mission Tensions Today.* Chicago, Moody Press,

_____ 1973 *A Manual for Evangelism/Church Growth,* South Pasadena, William Carey Library.

_____ 1980 *Discipling Through Theological Education by Extension : A Fresh Approach to Theological Education in the 1980s,* Chicago, Moody Press.

Glasser, Arthur F. 1971a "Since We Are All Growing Older, Let's Grow Bolder!". *Church Growth Bulletin,* 7:6, July 1971, 153-155.

_____ 1987 "Church Growth at Fuller". *Missiology,* 14:4, 401-420.

_____ 1991 "My Last Conversation with Donald McGavran". *Evangelical Missions Quarterly,* 27:1, January 1991, 58-62.

Glasser, Arthur F. (Introduction) (Ed.) 1971b *Crossroads in Missions,* South Pasadena, William Carey Library.

Glasser, Arthur F. & McGavran, Donald A. 1983 *Contemporary Theologies of Mission,* Grand Rapids, Baker Book House.

Goff, James E 1971 "The TEE Programme". *RISK,* 7:2, April 1971, 30-36.

Goff, James E. 1970 "A Critical Review: Latin American Church Growth". *Centro Intercultural De Documentacion,* 70:205, January 25, 1970, 9.

Graham, Billy 1975a "Our Mandate from Lausanne '74 : an Address to the Lausanne Continuation Committee". *Christianity Today,* 29:20, July 4, 1975, 3-6.

_____ 1975b Why Lausanne?, in Douglas, J. D. (Ed.) *Let the Earth Hear His Voice.* Minneapolis, World Wide Publications, 22-36.

Green, Michael 1975 Methods and Strategy in the Evangelism of the Early Church, in Douglas, J. D. (Ed.) *Let the Earth Hear His Voice.* Minneapolis, World Wide Publications 159-172.

Grimley, John B. & Robinson, Gordon E. 1966 *Church Growth in Central and Southern Nigeria,* Grand Rapids, Eerdmans.

Hall, Clarence W. 1971 "Must Our Churches Finance Revolution?". *Reader's Digest,* 99:594, Oct 1971, 91-100.

Haynes, Gerald A. 1994 *Meanings of the Term "Unreached People Groups": Consequences for Mission Purpose,* Deerfield, Trinity Evangelical Divinity School, PhD.

Hayward, Victor E. W. 1977 *The Homogeneous Unity Principle: The Record of Worldwide Missionary Expansion,* Pasadena, June 1977.

Henry, Carl Ferdinand Howard 1947 *The Uneasy Conscience of Modern Fundamentalism,* Grand Rapids, Wm. B. Eerdmans publishing company.

Henry, Carl Ferdinand Howard & Mooneyham, W. Stanley 1967 *One race, One Gospel, One task; Official Reference Volumes : Papers and Reports,* Minneapolis, World Wide Publications.

Hill, David Leslie 1973 *Designing a Theological Education by Extension Program,* Fuller Theological Seminary, MA.

_____ 1979 *Theological Education in Missions as a Factor in Baptist Church Growth with Special Emphasis on the Philippines,* Fuller Theological Seminary, School of World Mission, DMiss.

Hoefer, Herbert E. 1991 *Churchless Christianity,* Madras, Asian Programme for Advancement of Training and Studies.

Hogan, Philip 1975 Response to Dr. Ralph Winter's Paper, in Douglas, J. D. (Ed.) *Let the Earth Hear His Voice.* Minneapolis, World Wide Publications, 242-245.

Holland, Fredric L. 1978 *Theological Education in Context and Change: The Influence of Leadership Training and Anthroplogy on Ministry for Church Growth,* Pasadena, Fuller Theological Seminary, DMiss.

Hopewell, James F. 1967a "Guest Editorial". *International Review of Mission,* 56:2, April 1956, 141-144.

_____ 1967b "Mission and Seminary Structure". *International Review of Mission,* 56:2, April 1967, 158-166.

_____ 1969a An Outsider's View, in Winter, R. D. (Ed.) *Theological Education by Extension.* Pasadena, William Carey Library, 101-103.

_____ 1969b Preparing the Candidate for Mission, in Winter, R. D. (Ed.) *Theological Education by Extension.* Pasadena, William Carey Library, 37-53.

Jeynes, William & Robinson, David W. 2012 *International handbook of protestant education,* Dordrecht [etc.], Springer.

Johnson, Alan R. 2009 *Apostolic function in 21st century missions,* Pasadena, CA, William Carey Library.

Johnston, Arthur P. 1978 *The Battle for World Evangelism,* Wheaton, Tyndale House.

Kane, J Herbert 1974 "Changes Observed in Missiological Studies". *Evangelical Missions Quarterly,* 10:1, January 1974, 54-59.

Keikung, L. Anjo 1986 *Development of the Theological Education by Extension in India with Special Reference to Extension Education Ministry of Union Biblical Seminary; Pune,* Deerfield, Trinity Evangelical Divinity School, DMiss.

Kim, Hyungjo 1997 *Missiological Study for Reaching the Unreached People Groups: Special Reference to the Korean Mission,* Pasadena, Fuller Theological Seminary, ThM.

Kinsler, F. Ross 1971 *Inductive Study of the Book of Jeremiah : The Word of the Lord in a Time of Crisis,* South Pasadena, William Carey Library.

_____ 1978 *The Extension Movement in Theological Education : A Call to the Renewal of the Ministry,* South Pasadena, William Carey Library.

_____ 1983 *Ministry by the People: Theological Education by Extension*, Geneva, Maryknoll, WCC Publications & Orbis Books.

_____ 2008 *Diversified Theological Education : Equipping All God's People*, Pasadena, William Carey International University Press.

Kinsler, F. Ross & Emery, James H. 1991 *Opting for Change: A Handbook on Evaluation and Planning for Theological Education by Extension*, Pasadena, William Carey Library & Programme on Theological Education-WCC.

Klein, Mary Anne 1947 "Student Convention Unequaled in 35 Years". *United Evangelical Action*, 5, February 15, 1947.

Kornfield, William J. 1976 "The Challenge to Make Extension Education Culturally Relevant". *Evangelical Missions Quarterly*, 12:1, January 1976, 13-22.

Kraft, Charles H. 1971 "Younger Churches – Missionaries and Indigeneity". *Church Growth Bulletin*, 7:6, July 1971, 159-161.

_____ 2005 *SWM/SIS at Forty : A Participant/Observer's View of Our History*, Pasadena, William Carey Library.

Kuist, H. T. 1947 *These Words Upon Thy Heart : Scripture and the Christian Response*, Richmond, John Knox Press.

Latourette, Kenneth Scott 1937 *A History of the Expansion of Christianity*, New York, London, Harper & Brothers.

_____ 1953 *A History of Christianity*, New York, Harper.

Laubach, Frank Charles 1943 *The Silent Billion Speak*, New York, Friendship press.

_____ 1947 *Teaching the World to Read : A Handbook for Literacy Campaigns*, London, United Society for Christian Literature.

_____ 1951 *Wake Up or Blow Up! America: Lift the World or Lose it!*, New York, Revell.

_____ 1958 *The World is Learning Compassion*, Westwood, F. H. Revell Co.

Lewis, Jonathan 1994 *World Mission : An Analysis of the World Christian Movement*, Pasadena, William Carey Library.

Lindsell, Harold 1973 "Editorial". *Christianity Today*, 27:7, January 5, 1973, 3.

Loewen, Jacob 1975 Response to Dr. Ralph D. Winter's Paper, in Douglas, J. D. (Ed.) *Let the Earth Hear His Voice*. Minneapolis, World Wide Publications, 246-254.

Loewen, Jacob A. 2000 *The Bible in Cross-Cultural Perspective*, Pasadena, William Carey Library.

Lundström, Klas Ingvar 2006 *Gospel and Culture in the World Council of Churches and the Lausanne Movement with Particular Focus on the Period 1973-1996*, Uppsala, Sweden, Uppsala University, PhD.

Mandryk, Jason 2010 *Operation World*, Colorado Springs, Biblica Publishing.

Marsden, George M. 1987 *Reforming Fundamentalism : Fuller Seminary and the New Evangelicalism*, Grand Rapids, W.B. Eerdmans.

_____ 2006 *Fundamentalism and American Culture*, New York, Oxford University Press.

Mbiti, John S. 1971 *The Crisis of Mission in Africa,* Mukono, Uganda Church Press.

McConnell, C. Douglas 2007 "Choosing the Deep Water Instead of the Shallow End". *Theology News and Notes,* 54:2, Spring 2007, 17-19.

McCready, Reyburn R. 1977 *Donald Anderson McGavran: A Register of His Papers* Eugene, Northwest Christian College.

McCune, Rolland 2004 *Promise Unfilfilled : The Failed Strategy of Modern Evangelicalism,* Greenville, Ambassador Group.

McGavran, Donald Anderson 1955 *The Bridges of God : A Study in the Strategy of Missions,* London, World Dominion Press.

_____ 1963 *Church Growth in Mexico,* Grand Rapids, Eerdmans.

_____ 1965a *Church Growth and Christian Mission,* New York, Harper & Row.

_____ 1965b "Social Justice and Evangelism". *World Vision Magazine,* 9:6, June 1965, 7-26.

_____ 1970 *Understanding Church Growth,* Grand Rapids, Eerdmans.

_____ 1971 "Will Green Lake Betray the Two Billion?". *Church Growth Bulletin,* 7:6, July 1971, 149-153.

_____ 1972a Crisis of Identity for Some Missionary Societies, in McGavran, D. A. (Ed.) *Crucial Issues in Missions Tomorrow.* Chicago, Moody Press, 188-201.

_____ 1972b *Crucial Issues in Missions Tomorrow,* Chicago, Moody Press.

_____ (Ed.) 1972c *Eye of the Storm : The Great Debate in Mission,* Waco, Word Books.

_____ 1973 "Five Expectations for the School of World Mission". *Theology News and Notes,* 19:2, June, 6-7.

_____ 1975 The Dimensions of World Evangelization, in Douglas, J. D. (Ed.) *Let the Earth Hear His Voice.* Minneapolis, World Wide Publications, 94-115.

_____ 1977 *Church Growth Bulletin, Volume 2,* South Pasadena, William Carey Library.

_____ 1988 *Effective Evangelism : A Theological Mandate,* Phillipsburg, N.J., Presbyterian and Reformed Pub. Co.

McGavran, Donald Anderson, Editor 1969 *Church Growth Bulletin, Volume 1,* South Pasadena, William Carey Library.

McGavran, Donald Anderson & Hunter, George G. 1980 *Church growth : Strategies that Work,* Nashville, Abingdon.

McIntosh, Gary (Ed.) 2004 *Evaluating the Church Growth Movement : 5 Views,* Grand Rapids, Zondervan.

McKinney, Lois 1986 How Shall We Cooperate Internationally in Theological Education by Extension?, in Youngblood, R. L. (Ed.) *Cyprus: TEE Come of Age.* Exeter, Paternoster, 27-39.

McPhee, Arthur Gene 2001 *Pickett's Fire: the Life, Contribution, Thought, and Legacy of J. Waskom Pickett, Methodist Missionary to India,* Wilmore, KY, Asbury Theological Seminary,

Mead, Walter Russell 2008 "Born Again". *The Atlantic Monthly*, 301:2, March 2008, 21-24.

Middleton, Vernon 2011 *Donald McGavran : His Early Life and Ministry An Apostolic Vision for Reaching the Nations*, Pasadena, William Carey Library.

Middleton, Vernon James 1990 *The Development of a Missiologist: The Life and Thought of Donald Anderson McGavran, 1897-1965*, Pasadena, Fuller Theological Seminary, PhD.

Missions Advanced Research and Communication Center, MARC 1974 *Unreached Peoples Directory*, Monrovia.

Mitton, C.L. 1970 "Men and Affairs". *The Expository Times*, 81:7, April 1970, 223-224.

Moberg, David O. 1972 *The Great Reversal : Evangelism Versus Social Concern*, Philadelphia, Lippincott.

Montgomery, James H. 1974 "Congress Convenant Falls Short". *Church Growth Bulletin*, 11:2, Nov. 1974, 462-465.

Moreau, A. Scott, Netland, Harold A., Engen, Charles Edward van & Burnett, David 2000 *Evangelical Dictionary of World Missions*, Grand Rapids, Baker Books.

Mottinger, William Douglas 1986 *Readings in Church/Mission Structures*, Fuller Theological Seminary, MA.

Mouw, Richard 2007 "Over Someone's Objections: Fuller's Unique Position in the World of Theological Education". *Theology News and Notes*, 54:2, Spring 2007, 29-35.

Mulholland, Kenneth B. 1976 *Adventures in Training the Ministry : A Honduran Case Study in Theological Education by Extension*, Nutley, N.J., Presbyterian and Reformed Pub. Co.

_____ 1986 TEE Come of Age: A Candid Assessment after Two Decades, in Youngblood, R. L. (Ed.) *Cyprus: TEE Come of Age*. Exeter, Paternoster on behalf of the World Evangelical Fellowship and the International Council of Accrediting Agencies, 9-25.

_____ 1991 "Donald McGavran's Legacy to Evangelical Missions". *Evangelical Missions Quarterly*, 27:1, January 1991, 64-70.

Murphy, Edward 1971 "Occupy Till I Come". *Church Growth Bulletin*, 7:6, July 1971, 161-162.

Neill, Stephen 1959 *Creative Tension*, London, Edinburgh House Press.

Newmeyer, Frederick J. 1986 *Linguistic Theory in America*, Orlando, Academic Press.

Noll, Mark A. 2003 *The Rise of Evangelicalism : The Age of Edwards, Whitefield, and the Wesleys*, Downers Grove, InterVarsity Press.

Olson, Warwick 1974 "Lausanne 74 Will Look at Issues and Opportunities". *Evangelical Missions Quarterly*, 10:2, April 1974, 173-176.

Padilla, René 1975 Evangelism and the World, in Douglas, J. D. (Ed.) *Let the Earth Hear His Voice*. Minneapolis, World Wide Publications, 134-146.

Pérez, Pablo M. 1973 *Misión y liberación : Implicaciones Misiológicas del Concepto de Liberación en la America Latina*, Fuller Theological Seminary, DMiss.
_____ 1975 Response to Dr. Ralph D. Winter's Paper, in Douglas, J. D. (Ed.) *Let the Earth Hear His Voice.* Minneapolis, World Wide Publications, 255-258.

Peters, Harry 1940 "Training Pastors in Guatemala". *International Review of Mission,* 29:1940, 370-373.

Pickett, Jarrell Waskom 1933 *Christian Mass Movements in India, a Study with Recommendations,* New York & Cincinnati, The Abingdon Press.

Plowman, Edward E. 1974 "The View from Lausanne". *Christianity Today,* 28:22, August 16, 1974, 35-37.

Ranson, Charles Wesley, Firkeli, F., Michaeli, F. & Rasendrahasina, T. 1957 *Survey of the Training of the Ministry in Madagascar : Report of a Survey of Theological Education in Madagascar Undertaken in September to November, 1956,* London New York, I.M.C.

Read, William R. 1965 *New Patterns of Church Growth in Brazil,* Grand Rapids, Eerdmans.

Read, William R., Monterroso, Victor M. & Johnson, Harmon A. 1969 *Latin American Church Growth,* Grand Rapids, Eerdmans.

Reapsome, James W. 1974 "Editorial: Lausanne 74 – An Overview". *Evangelical Missions Quarterly,* 10:4, October 1974, 259-262.

Reid, John R. 1981 "The Voluntary Missionary Association". *International Review of Mission,* 70:276-279.

Richards, Jack C., Platt, John Talbot & Weber, Heidi 1985 *Longman Dictionary of Applied Linguistics,* Harlow, Essex, Longman.

Richardson, Laurel 2008 Writing: A method of inquiry, Part 1 Qualitative Writing, in Denzin, N. K. & Lincoln, Y. S. (Eds.) *Collecting and Interpreting Qualitative Materials.* Third ed. Thousand Oaks, Sage Publications, 701.

Rifkin, Alan 2003 The New Believers: Jesus with a Genius Grant, *Los Angeles Times Magazine* 22-25, 38-40

Ro, Bong Rin 1970 "Some Thoughts on the Future of Theological Education in Asia". *The Asian Challenge,* 2:1970, 49.

Scherer, James A. 1964 *Missionary, Go Home!,* Englewood Cliffs, Prentice-Hall.

Scherer, Ross P. 1980 *American Denominational Organization : A Sociological View,* Pasadena, William Carey Library.

Shackelford, John 1962 "Integration - Rethinking Our Task". *Guatemala News,* 53:3, Inside Cover, 7.

Shearer, Roy E. 1966 *Wildfire: Church Growth in Korea,* Grand Rapids, Eerdmans.

Sheldon, Charles Monroe 1897 *In His Steps : "What Would Jesus Do?",* Chicago, Advance Publishing Co.
_____ 1902 *The Reformer,* Chicago & London, Advance Publishing Co. & Ward, Lock & Co.

Shenk, Wilbert R. 1973 Church Growth Studies: A Bibliography Review, in
    Shenk, W. R. (Ed.) *The Challenge of Church Growth: A Symposium.*
    Elkhart, Institute of Mennonite Studies,
    _____ 1983 *Henry Venn–Missionary Statesman,* Maryknoll, Orbis Books.
Shenk, Wilbert R. & Hunsberger, George R. 1998 *American Society of Missiology :
    The First Quarter Century,* Decatur, The American Society of Missiology.
Skinner, Betty Lee 1974 *Daws : The Story of Dawson Trotman, Founder of the
    Navigators,* Grand Rapids, Zondervan Pub. House.
Smith, Christian & Emerson, Michael 1998 *American Evangelicalism : Embattled
    and Thriving,* Chicago, University of Chicago Press.
Smith, Gordon Hedderly 1945 *The Missionary and Anthropology : An Introduction
    to the Study of Primitive Man for Missionaries,* Chicago, Moody Press.
Smylie, James H. 1975 "Sheldon's In His Steps: Conscience and Discipleship".
    Theology Today, 32:1, July, 32-45.
Snyder, Howard A. 1977 *The Community of the King,* Downers Grove, Inter-
    Varsity Press.
Stafford, Tim 1984 "Ralph Winter: Looking for the Hidden Peoples". *Christianity
    Today,* 28:12, September 7, 1984, 14-18.
Stanley, Brian 2003 "Where Have Our Mission Structures Come From?"
    Transformation, 20:1, January, 39-46.
Stark, Rodney 1997 *The Rise of Christianity : How the Obscure, Marginal Jesus
    Movement Became the Dominant Religious Force in the Western World in a
    Few Centuries,* San Francisco, Harper San Francisco.
    _____ 2003 *For the Glory of God : How Monotheism Led to Reformations, Science,
    Witch-hunts, and the End of Slavery,* Princeton, Princeton University
    Press.
Stott, John R. W. 1975 *The Lausanne Covenant : An Exposition and Commentary,*
    Minneapolis, World Wide Publications.
    _____ 1997 *Making Christ Known : Historic Mission Documents from the
    Lausanne Movement, 1974-1989,* Grand Rapids, Eerdmans.
Street, T. Watson 1965 *On the Growing Edge of the Church : New Dimensions in
    World Missions,* Richmond, John Knox Press.
Sunquist, Scott & Long, Caroline Becker 2008 *A History of Presbyterian Missions,
    1944-2007,* Louisville, Ky., Geneva Press.
TAFTEE 1981 *Poverty and Development: A Degree Level Course of TAFTEE,
    India,* Banglore, TAFTEE.
Taylor, Clyde W. 1974 "Overseas Churches Starting to Send Missionaries".
    Evangelical Missions Quarterly, 10:1, January 1974, 61-65.
TIME, Staff 2011 "Breifing : Milestones". *TIME,* 178:6, August 15, 2011, 24.
TIME Staff 1954 "Guatemala: Battle of the Backyard (illustration)". *TIME
    Magazine,* June 28, 1954.
Tippett, Alan R. 1968 *Fijian Material Culture : A Study of Cultural Context,
    Function, and Change,* Honolulu, Bishop Museum Press.
    _____ 1971a "An Anthropologist Looks at Mission-Church Transition".
    Church Growth Bulletin, 7:6, July 1971, 155-157.

_____ 1971b *Bibliography for Cross-Cultural Workers*, South Pasadena, William Carey Library.

_____ 1975 Evangelization Among Animists, in Douglas, J. D. (Ed.) *Let the Earth Hear His Voice*. Minneapolis, World Wide Publications, 884-855.

Titon, Jeff Todd 1980 "The Life Story". *Journal of American Folklore*, 93:276, 276-292.

Traina, Robert A. 1952 *Methodical Bible Study : A New Approach to Hermeneutics*, Ridgefield Park & New York, [distributed by] Biblical Seminary in New York.

Van Biema, David and Booth-Thomas, Kathy, et al. 2005 "Evangelicals in America: The 25 Most Influential Evangelicals in America". *TIME*, 165:6, Febuary 7, 2005, 34-45.

Wagner, C Peter 1972 The Babylonian Captivity of the Christian Mission. Pasadena, Fuller Theological Seminary.

_____ 1975 "Lausanne Twelve Months Later". *Christianity Today*, 29:20, July 4, 1975, 709.

Walls, Andrew F. 1996 *The Missionary Movement in Christian History : Studies in the Transmission of Faith*, Maryknoll & Edinburgh, Orbis Books & T&T Clark.

Ward, Daniel T. 1982 *Theological Education by Extension : A Proposal for India's Free Methodist Church*, Fuller Theological Seminary, ThM.

Ward, Ted W. 2011 *What Happened to TEE?*, Febuary 12, 2011, 4.

Ward, Ted W. & Ward, Margaret 1970 *Programmed Instruction for Theological Education by Extension*, East Lansing, Committee to Assist Missionary Education Overseas.

Ward, W. Reginald 2006 *Early Evangelicalism : A Global Intellectual History, 1670-1789*, Cambridge UK & New York, Cambridge University Press.

Weber, Linda J. (Ed.) 2010 *Mission Handbook : U.S. and Canadian Protestant Ministries Overseas 21st Edition*, Wheaton, EMIS.

Weld, Wayne 1972 "Why Another Newsletter?". *Extension*, 1:1, November 1972, 1-2.

_____ 1973 *The World Directory of Theological Education by Extension*, South Pasadena, William Carey Library.

Weld, Wayne & McGavran, Donald Anderson 1974 *Principles of Church Growth*, South Pasadena, William Carey Library.

White, Jerry E. 1983 *The Church and the Parachurch : An Uneasy Marriage*, Portland, Multnomah Press.

Winter, Ralph D. 1958 *Poverty and Christian Mission*, Ostuncalco Guatemala, 3.

_____ 1962 "The First Evangelical Indian Congress". *Practical Anthropology*, 9:2, March April 1962, 85-87.

_____ 1966a "Gimmickitis". *Church Growth Bulletin*, 2:3, January 1966, 127-129.

_____ 1966b "This Seminary Goes to the Student". *World Vision Magazine*, 10:7, July-August 1966, 10-12.

_____ 1967 The Extension Seminary and the Programmed Textbook. Pasadena, Fuller Theological Seminary.

_____ 1969a "The Anatomy of the Christian Mission". *Evangelical Missions Quarterly*, 5:1, Winter 1969, 74-89.

_____ 1969b "The Reluctant Missionary". *World Vision Magazine*, 13:7, July-August 1969, 4-6.

_____ 1969c "The Seminary That Became a Movement". *World Vision Magazine*, 13:10, November 1969, 8-9.

_____ (Ed.) 1969d *Theological Education by Extension*, South Pasadena, William Carey Library.

_____ 1970a *A Plea for Mission Orders*, Pasadena, August 13, 1970, 3.

_____ 1970b "Church Growth Calculations: Facts and Fallacies, No. 1". *Church Growth Bulletin*, 6:4, March 1970, 59.

_____ 1970c "Jesuits Yes, Presbyterians No!". *Church Growth Bulletin*, 6:5, May 1970.

_____ 1970d "The Acorn that Exploded". *World Vision Magazine*, 14:9, October 1970, 15-18.

_____ 1971a "Churches Instead of Missions?". *Church Growth Bulletin*, 7:6, July 1971, 158-159.

_____ 1971b "Churches Need Missions Because Modalities Need Sodalities". *Evangelical Missions Quarterly*, 7:4, Jan. 1971, 193-200.

_____ 1971c "The New Missions and the Mission of the Church". *International Review of Mission*, LX:237, 89-100.

_____ 1972a "Minipublishing : New Hope for Strategic Dialogue ". *Occasional Bulliten from the Missionary Research Library*, 33:3, Febuary 16, 1972, 1-16.

_____ 1972b Quality or Quantity, in McGavran, D. A. (Ed.) *Crucial Issues in Missions Today*. Chicago, Moody Press,

_____ 1972c "The Demographic Imperative". *Church Growth Bulletin*, 8:4, March 1972, 212-213.

_____ 1972d *The Extension Model in Theological Education: What it is and What it Can Do*, Pasadena, December 30, 1972, 4.

_____ 1972e The Planting of Younger Missions, in Wagner, C. P. (Ed.) *Church/Mission Tensions Today*. Chicago, Moody Press,

_____ 1972f "The Quantitative Case for Continuing Missions Today". *Church Growth Bulletin*, 8:3, January 1972, 202.

_____ 1973a "Existing Churches: Ends or Means?". *Christianity Today*, 27:8, January 19, 1973, 10-12.

_____ 1973b *The Evangelical Response to Bangkok*, South Pasadena, CA, William Carey Library.

_____ 1974a "Seeing the Task Graphically : The Decade Past and the Decade to Come". *Evangelical Missions Quarterly*, 10:1, January 1974, 11-24.

_____ 1974b "The two structures of God's redemptive mission". *Missiology*, 2:1, 122-139.

_____ 1974c "What Happened at Lausanne?". *Theology News and Notes,* 20:3, 13.

_____ 1975 The Highest Priority: Cross-Cultural Evangelism, in Douglas, J. D. (Ed.) *Let the earth hear His voice.* Minneapolis, World Wide Publications, 213-241.

_____ 1977 "The Homogeneous Unit Principle in Historical Perspective". *Consultation on the Homogeneous Unit Principle,* June 1977.

_____ 1978 "Ghana: Preparation for Marriage". *International Review of Missions,* 67:265, July 1978, 338-353.

_____ 1979a "Meet the Director". *Mission Frontiers,* 1:1, 8.

_____ 1979b "Protestant mission societies : the American experience". *Missiology,* 7:2, April 1979, 139-178.

_____ 1980 The Modality – Sodality Concept. *Affiliation of Lutheran Movements Theological Conference.* Self - Filed: E#136, April 19.

_____ 1992 "Defining the Frontiers: A Response". *International Journal for Frontier Missions,* 9:1, January 1992, 9-11.

_____ 1995a *The Story of PCMS, PUMA, POWE, and the PFF,* October 25, 1995, 3.

_____ 1995b *Thy Kingdom Come! : the Story of a Movement ; A Church for Every People and the Gospel for Every Person by the Year 2000 : An Analysis of a Vision,* Pasadena, William Carey Library.

_____ 1996 Missiological Education for Lay People, in Woodberry, D. J., Van Engen, C. & Elliston, E. J. (Eds.) *Missiological Education for the 21st Century.* New York, Orbis Books, 169-185.

_____ 2003a *Autobiography,* Pasadena, October 7, 2003, 3, W1248.1242, October 1247.

_____ 2003b "Eleven Frontiers of Perspective (Part 1)". *International Journal for Frontier Missions,* 20:3, Fall 2003, 77-81.

_____ 2003c "Eleven Frontiers of Perspective (Part 2)". *International Journal for Frontier Missions,* 20:4, 135-144.

_____ 2005 *Growing Up with the Bible: Understanding What It Says, Yielding To What It Means,* Pasadena, May 22, 2005, 6, W1345B.1343, May 1322.

_____ 2008 *Frontiers in Mission : Discovering and Surmounting Barriers to the Missio Dei,* Pasadena, William Carey International University Press.

Winter, **Ralph D.** & Beaver, R. Pierce 1970 *The Warp and the Woof : Organizing for Mission,* South Pasadena, William Carey Library.

Winter, **Ralph D.** & Hawthorne, Steven C. 2009 *Perspectives on the World Christian Movement: a Reader,* Pasadena, William Carey Library.

Winter, **Ralph D.** & Koch, Bruce A. 2009 Finishing the Task : The Unreached Peoples Challenge, in Winter, R. D. & Hawthorne, S. C. (Eds.) *Perspectives on the World Christian Movement.* 4th ed. Pasadena, William Carey Library, 531-546.

Winter, **Ralph D.** & Latourette, Kenneth Scott 1970 *The Twenty-Five Unbelievable Years, 1945 to 1969,* South Pasadena, William Carey Library.

Winter, Ralph D. & Winter, Roberta H. 1968 "When School is Half a World Away". *World Vision Magazine*, 12:2, February 1968, 15-17.

Winter, Roberta H. 1979c *Once More Around Jericho : The Story of the U.S. Center for World Mission*, South Pasadena, Calif., William Carey Library.

_____ 1987 *I Will Do a New Thing : the U.S. Center for World Mission-- and Beyond*, Pasadena, William Carey Library.

_____ 2000 *Winter Initiatives*, Pasadena, September 31, 2000, 43.

_____ 2001 *Five Months and a Week,* Pasadena, Ralph and Roberta Winter.

Wodarz, Donald Mattäus 1979 *Church Growth : the Missiology of Donald Anderson McGavran*, Rome, Pontificia Universitas Gregoriana.

Wold, Joseph Conrad 1968 *God's Impatience in Liberia,* Grand Rapids, Eerdmans.

Wonderly, William L. 1959 "Social Anthropology, Christian Missions, and the Indians of Latin America". *Practical Anthropology*, 6:2, 55-64.

Woodberry, John Dudley, Pierson, Paul Everett, Engen, Charles Edward van & Elliston, Edgar J. 1996 *Missiological Education for the Twenty-First Century : the Book, the Circle, and the Sandals : Essays in Honor of Paul E. Pierson*, Maryknoll, N.Y., Orbis Books.

Woodward, Ralph Lee, Jr. 2005 *A Short History of Guatemala,* La Antigua, Editorial Laura Lee.

Works, Herbert 1974 "The International Congress on World Evangelization". *Church Growth Bulletin*, 10:6, July 1974, 423-426.

Yoder, John H. 1973 Church Growth Issues in Theological Perspective, in Shenk, W. R. (Ed.) *The Challenge of Church Growth: A Symposium.* Elkhart, Institute of Mennonite Studies,

Youngblood, Robert L. 1986 *Cyprus : TEE Come of Age,* Exeter, Paternoster on behalf of the World Evangelical Fellowship and the International Council of Accrediting Agencies.

Yunus, Muhammad & Weber, Karl 2007 *Creating a World Without Poverty : Social Business and the Future of Capitalism*, New York, PublicAffairs.